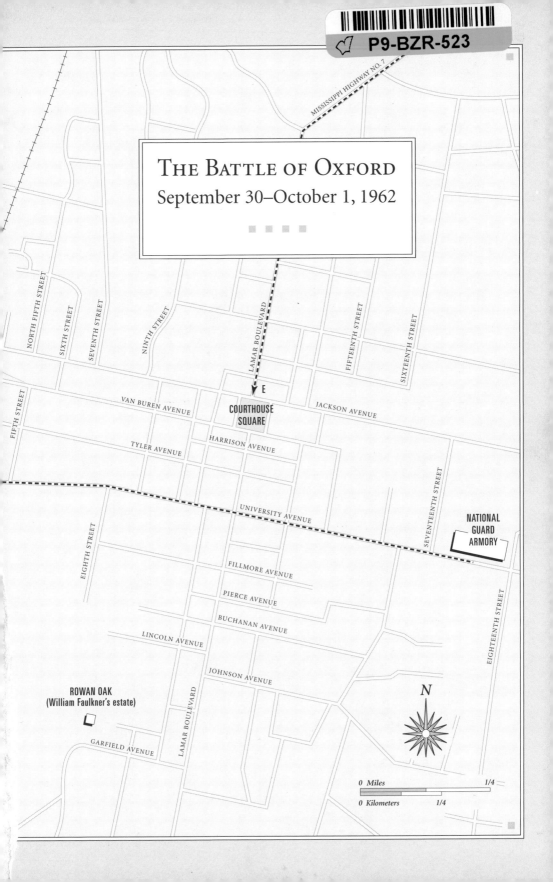

MISSISSIPPI HIGHWAY NO. 7

THE BATTLE OF OXFORD
September 30–October 1, 1962

NORTH FIFTH STREET

SIXTH STREET

SEVENTH STREET

NINTH STREET

LAMAR BOULEVARD

FIFTEENTH STREET

SIXTEENTH STREET

FIFTH STREET

E

VAN BUREN AVENUE

COURTHOUSE SQUARE

JACKSON AVENUE

TYLER AVENUE

HARRISON AVENUE

UNIVERSITY AVENUE

SEVENTEENTH STREET

EIGHTH STREET

NATIONAL GUARD ARMORY

FILLMORE AVENUE

PIERCE AVENUE

EIGHTEENTH STREET

BUCHANAN AVENUE

LINCOLN AVENUE

JOHNSON AVENUE

ROWAN OAK
(William Faulkner's estate)

LAMAR BOULEVARD

N

GARFIELD AVENUE

| 0 Miles | | | 1/4 |
| 0 Kilometers | | | 1/4 |

AN

American

Insurrection

■ ■ ■ ■

AN

American

Insurrection

▪ ▪ ▪ ▪

The Battle
of Oxford, Mississippi,
1962

WILLIAM DOYLE

DOUBLEDAY

New York London Toronto Sydney Auckland

PUBLISHED BY DOUBLEDAY
a division of Random House, Inc.
1540 Broadway, New York, New York 10036

DOUBLEDAY and the portrayal of an anchor with a dolphin
are trademarks of Doubleday, a division of
Random House, Inc.

Book design by Randall Mize

Library of Congress Cataloging-in-Publication Data
Doyle, William, 1957–
An American insurrection : the battle of Oxford,
Mississippi, 1962 / William Doyle.—1st ed.
p.   cm.
Includes bibliographical references (p.) and index.
1. University of Mississippi—History. 2. Meredith, James.
3. College integration—Mississippi—Oxford—History.
4. African Americans—Civil rights.
5. Civil rights—Mississippi—Oxford—History. I. Title.
LD3413 .D69 2001
378.762'83—dc21   2001028580

ISBN 0-385-49969-8

October 2001

FIRST EDITION

10   9   8   7   6   5   4   3   2   1

to Naomi

to my father, William Doyle,
First Sergeant, U.S. Army
813th Military Police Company, 1942–1945
Australia and New Guinea

and to Marilou, Kate, and Joe

Contents

Contents

I was creating images then that were designed for forty years in the future.

—James Meredith

This story in years to come, in generations to come, is going to be really a story that will be impossible to believe.

—Verner Holmes

AN

American

Insurrection

■ ■ ■ ■

The Past Is Never Dead

▣ ▣ ▣ ▣

The past is never dead. It's not even past.

—William Faulkner

MAY 22, 1865, 9:00 A.M.: the Governor's Office, State Capitol, Jackson, Mississippi.

Forty-three days after the surrender of the Army of Northern Virginia at Appomattox, a platoon of black Union troops with fixed bayonets stormed through the ruined streets of Jackson and onto the grounds of the Mississippi State Capitol building. The troops were led by white U.S. Army Brigadier General E. D. Osband. They marched toward the office of Governor Charles Clark.

Two days earlier, the soldiers had invaded the Mississippi state legislature, declared the gathering an illegal assembly, and dissolved it, waving the legislators out of the building at bayonet point. Now Governor Clark heard the measured clap of soldiers marching grow louder in the marble hallway, and presently General Osband appeared in the doorway.

The general saluted the governor, and read to him a proclamation by the president of the United States, dissolving Mississippi's government.

Governor Clark was an elderly, dignified veteran of the Mexican

War whose limbs were shattered at the battle of Shiloh. The old man straightened his battered legs and struggled up onto his crutches.

"General Osband," the governor announced defiantly, "I denounce before high heaven and the civilized world this unparalleled act of tyranny and usurpation. I am the duly and constitutionally elected Governor of the State of Mississippi. I would resist, if it were in my power, to the last extremity the enforcement of your order. I yield obedience because I have no power to resist."

Within moments the federal troops invaded the executive office, seized the governor's office furniture, records, and the Great Seal of the State of Mississippi and escorted the governor out of the building. In that instant the government of Mississippi was decapitated, and the state was under the direct rule of President Andrew Johnson and his military.

They inherited a ruined, ravaged land. Before the Civil War, cotton-rich Mississippi was among the wealthiest members of the Union, but now the state was decimated, with families, fortunes, and entire cities wiped out. It was also home to multitudes of black Americans suddenly living in a strange twilight world where they were no longer slaves but not yet citizens.

After a brief failed experiment with presidential reconstruction by Andrew Johnson, the radical Republican Congress passed the sweeping Reconstruction Acts in 1867 to deliver civil rights to the newly freed black populations of the formerly Confederate states. In 1868 Mississippi adopted a state constitution that promised full political equality to blacks, and in 1870 Congress voted Mississippi back into the Union and federal martial rule ended.

For the next four years, Mississippi enjoyed a fleeting springtime of black political freedom, when black voters outnumbered enfranchised whites and African-Americans held such offices as lieutenant governor, secretary of state, and speaker of the state House of Representatives; they also became sheriffs in a number of counties. The state even sent two black men, Hiram A. Revels and Blanche K. Bruce, to the U.S. Senate.

But a white backlash erupted in 1875, and Democratic-party activists linked up with remnants of the Ku Klux Klan to unleash a wave of riots and terror against blacks and their Republican allies. The mayhem raged up and down the state and killed dozens before culminating in the Democratic capture of the Mississippi state legislature in the fall elections. In 1876 Reconstruction ended as Congress grew fatigued with the problems of the South and President Rutherford B. Hayes withdrew the last federal soldiers from the region.

The ideology of white supremacy in Mississippi was sanctified in 1890 with the adoption of a new state constitution that stripped most blacks of the right to vote, thus denying the most basic right of American citizenship to much of the state's population for the next seventy-five years.

A culture of unrestrained violence against blacks flourished; from 1882 to 1952, recorded lynchings of African-Americans in Mississippi totaled 534, more than in any other state. The sharecropping system held most blacks and many poor whites in economic bondage for decades to come. "Mississippi's official policy of racial discrimination and exploitation prevented over half of its population from becoming productive citizens," wrote University of Mississippi history professor David Sansing. "Industrialization and urbanization were stymied, and economic stagnation produced years of retrenchment." The state did not have a single paved road until the 1930s.

In every aspect of race relations, Mississippi was only an extreme microcosm of the United States at large, a nation often poisoned by racism. None of the state's racial problems were unique, and all were paralleled by white violence, segregation, and oppression against blacks in virtually every corner of the North and South. But as the state with both the highest proportion of black citizens and the most powerful government and police apparatus of white control, Mississippi became the racial heart and soul of the nation.

As the second half of the twentieth century began, the stranglehold of radical white supremacy on Mississippi seemed both absolute and eternal.

It would take nothing less than a miracle to break it.

CHAPTER ONE

Whom Shall I Fear?

■ ■ ■ ■

We could have another Civil War on our hands.

—President Dwight D. Eisenhower, Cabinet meeting,
March 1956

L ITTLE ROCK, ARKANSAS, SEPTEMBER 8, 1957, 8:50 A.M.
A shy fifteen-year-old girl wearing bobby sox, ballet slippers, and a crisp black-and-white cotton dress stepped off a bus and walked toward Central High School, carrying a set of school books.

Elizabeth Eckford and nine other black students hoped to enter the all-white school today as part of a desegregation plan ordered by a federal judge. Because Eckford's family did not have a phone, she had missed the instructions to join the other students this morning, so she was walking toward the school completely alone.

Until today, Arkansas was making slow, peaceful progress toward integration. The state university was quietly desegregated in 1948, the state bus system had been integrated and black patrolmen were on the Little Rock police force. Several school districts were planning to accept black students this semester. In the wake of a lawsuit by the NAACP (National Association for the Advancement of Colored People), the Little Rock school board had approved a plan to gradually desegregate Central High, and ten volunteer students were selected to go in.

Through her sunglasses Eckford could see the school up ahead, and she was amazed at how big it was. She was so nervous, she hadn't slept at all the night before, so to pass the time she had read her Bible. She dwelled on the opening passage of the Twenty-seventh Psalm: "The Lord is my light and my salvation; whom shall I fear? the Lord is the strength of my life; of whom shall I be afraid?"

As she neared the school, the girl became vaguely aware of a crowd of white people swarming around her. Somewhere a voice called out, "Here she comes, get ready!" People started shouting insults. "Then my knees started to shake all of a sudden," Eckford later explained privately to Little Rock NAACP leader Daisy Bates, "and I wondered whether I could make it to the center entrance a block away. It was the longest block I ever walked in my whole life."

Eckford could see uniformed soldiers ringing the entrance and letting white students into the school, and she assumed they were supposed to protect her. But when she approached the entrance, one soldier waved her away. When she tried to move past another soldier, he and his comrades lifted their bayonet-tipped M-1 rifles and surged toward her to block her path.

The soldiers were Arkansas National Guardsmen, and their commander in chief was Democratic governor Orval Eugene Faubus, who had ordered the troops to block the black students at gunpoint. Faubus was a hound dog–faced populist who was born in a plank cabin in a remote Ozark forest near a place called Greasy Creek, and grew up trapping skunks to help his family scrape out a living. Until today, he was considered something of a moderate on racial issues. But Faubus was up for reelection, and sensing a rising white backlash to integration, he decided to become its champion.

When she faced the solid wall of soldiers, Elizabeth Eckford wasn't sure what to do, so she retreated back across the street and into the white mob. Voices called out, "Lynch her! Lynch her!" and "Go home, you burr-head!" She scanned the mob for someone who might help her and spotted an old woman who seemed to have a kind face. The woman spat on her. A voice from the mob announced, "No nigger bitch is going to get in our school. Get out of here!"

The chanting mob swelled toward five hundred. Behind Eckford, someone said, "Push her!" Eckford later explained that she was afraid she would "bust out crying," and she "didn't want to in front of all that crowd." Ahead of her, news photographers snapped photos of a young white student named Hazel Bryan screaming at Eckford behind her back, a searing image that would soon be flashed around the world. "I looked down the block and saw a bench at the bus stop," recalled Eckford. "I thought, 'If only I can get there I will be safe.' I don't know why the bench seemed a safe place to me but I started walking toward it."

Eckford made it to the bus stop and sat down with her head bowed, tightly gripping her books as news cameras whirred and snapped. Someone in the crowd said, "Get a rope and drag her over to this tree." Benjamin Fine, an education reporter from the *New York Times* who had been scribbling notes in his steno pad, sat down next to Eckford, wrapped his arm around her shoulder, and whispered, "Don't let them see you cry."

A furious white woman named Grace Lorch fought her way through the mob, and screamed, "Leave this child alone! Why are you tormenting her? Six months from now, you will hang your heads in shame." Lorch tried to enter a drugstore to call a taxi for Eckford, but the door was slammed in her face.

"She's just a little girl," Lorch declared to the mob as she moved next to Eckford to defend her. "I'm just waiting for one of you to dare touch me! I'm just aching to punch somebody in the nose!"

Eventually a bus came, Mrs. Lorch helped Eckford up the stairs, and the bus pulled away. Eckford got off at the school for the blind, where her mother taught, and ran to her classroom. "Mother was standing at the window with her head bowed," Eckford recalled, "but she must have sensed I was there because she turned around. She looked as if she had been crying, and I wanted to tell her I was all right. But I couldn't speak. She put her arms around me and I cried."

Minutes after Eckford was turned away, her colleagues, who with her would soon become world famous as the "Little Rock Nine," were refused admission as well: Melba Pattillo, Gloria Ray, Carlotta Walls, Minnijean Brown, Thelma Mothershed, Ernest Green, Jefferson Thomas and Terrence Roberts. A tenth black student who was turned back, Jane Hill, chose to return to all-black Horace Mann High School.

Over the next two weeks, frantic negotiations resulted in a summit conference between President Dwight D. Eisenhower and Governor Faubus at Ike's vacation retreat in Newport, Rhode Island, during which the president thought he'd made a deal with Faubus to deploy Arkansas National Guardsmen to protect the black students as they entered Central High. But on September 23, when the Little Rock Nine tried again to enter the school, Faubus ordered the National Guard instead to abandon the premises.

Escorted by Little Rock police, the Nine briefly made it inside the school and started their classes. But outside the building, a furious mob of more than one thousand white civilians was surging against barricades, threatening to overwhelm the police trying to hold them in check. A white woman cried out hysterically to the police, "They've got the doors locked. They won't let the white kids out. My daughter's in there with those niggers. Oh, my God, oh God!" Policemen lashed out with their billy clubs, knocking down two men in the mob. "Come out!" adults yelled to the white students. "Don't stay in there with those niggers!"

A pack of fifty white men peeled off down a side street to chase a tall black journalist named Alex Wilson, civil rights reporter for Defender Publications, a national chain of black newspapers. A voice warned, "Run, nigger, run!" The mob caught up with Wilson and attacked him from behind with their fists. A brick slammed point-blank into the back of his head, and he tumbled to the ground like a mighty tree. Wilson raised himself to a kneeling position, was kicked and punched, but still he rose, grasping his hat in his hand. He brushed off his fedora, recreased it, and resumed walking.

"Strangely, the vision of Elizabeth Eckford flashed before me," Wilson recalled soon after the attack. "I decided not to run. If I were to be beaten, I'd take it walking if I could—not running." He told his wife, Emogene, "They would have had to kill me before I would have run." Another brick scored a direct hit on the back of Wilson's head, but he kept walking. "I looked into the tear-filled eyes of a white woman. Although there was sorrow in her eyes, I knew there would not be any help."

In a frantic effort to take Wilson down again, a crazed-looking, stocky white man in coveralls jumped clear up onto Wilson's back and wrapped his arm around his neck in a choke hold, but the ex-marine Wilson shook him off. "Don't kill him," a voice in the crowd cautioned the mob. Finally Wilson reached his car and escaped.

In front of Central High, a white policeman named Thomas Dunaway suddenly flung his billy club to the street, threw down his badge, and walked away from the barricade. The crowd cheered him, and a young man yelled, "He's the only white man on the force!" A hat was passed around the crowd, and it soon filled up with two hundred dollars in donations for the officer.

Inside Central High School, police and school officials gathered the nine black students. Word was relayed from the mob that they would not storm the building if one black pupil was turned over to them, presumably to be torn to pieces or hung from a tree. Instead, the Little Rock police chief evacuated the Nine out a side door into police cars that blasted away from the school.

At 12:14 P.M., police lieutenant Carl Jackson faced the mob and announced through a loudspeaker, "The Negroes have been withdrawn from the school." Someone in the crowd replied, "That's just a pack of lies!" Then another shouted, "We don't believe you!" A Mrs. Allen Thevenet stepped out from the mob and offered to verify the claim. After a full tour of the building, Mrs. Thevenet marched to the loudspeaker, and proclaimed, "We went through every room in the school and there was no niggers there."

White supremacists across the South rejoiced. Integration at Central High had been defeated in barely half a day.

The next day, September 24, President Eisenhower was back at the White House, and he was furious. He was supposed to still be on vacation. Instead, the old general was sitting at his desk in the Oval Office, dripping with rage over the treachery of Orval Faubus. "He double-crossed me," fumed the president.

On the wall of the elliptical presidential office were two small paintings, one of Union general and U.S. president Ulysses S. Grant, the other of Confederate general and Southern demigod Robert E. Lee. They captured the paradox at the heart of the America Eisenhower led. Nearly a century after the Civil War, as the nation asserted global moral leadership and reached out to explore the heavens, millions of black Americans were effectively not citizens of the country in which they were born.

That morning, the mayor of Little Rock had sent a desperate telegram to the president, who had been still savoring his relaxing vacation in Newport, Rhode Island. "The immediate need for federal troops is urgent," the mayor pleaded. "Situation is out of control and police cannot disperse the mob." Ike now feared a full-blown insurrection in the city.

The battle Eisenhower never wanted was hurtling toward him, and he was afraid it could tear the country apart. As his officials debated civil rights at a March 1956 Cabinet meeting, Eisenhower confessed, "I'm at sea on all this." He added, "Not enough people know how deep this emotion is in the South. Unless you've lived there you can't know. . . . We could have another Civil War on our hands."

On May 17, 1954, in its decision on *Brown v. the Board of Education of Topeka, Kansas,* the United States Supreme Court outlawed government-imposed segregation in public schools, but a year later the Court ruled that the order should be implemented not immediately, but "with all deliberate speed." This ambiguous phrase gave federal judges leeway to impose integration on varying timetables in different school districts, which delayed progress in some places well into the next decade.

Privately, Eisenhower disagreed with the *Brown* decision, and believed it could only be implemented slowly. "When emotions are deeply stirred," he wrote in July 1957 to his childhood friend Swede Hazlett, "logic and reason must operate gradually and with consideration for human feelings or we will have a resultant disaster rather than human advancement."

"School segregation itself," Ike pointed out, "was, according to the Supreme Court decision of 1896 [the *Plessy v. Ferguson* case], completely Constitutional until the reversal of that decision was accomplished in 1954. The decision of 1896 gave a cloak of legality to segregation in all its forms." People couldn't change overnight, Ike believed.

Dwight Eisenhower was a creature of forty years in the hermetically segregated U.S. military, and he personally had no quarrel with separation of the races. Although as president he quietly completed Harry S. Truman's 1948 order desegregating the armed forces and ordered the integration of public facilities in the nation's capital, not once in eight years in office did Ike publicly endorse the concept of integration. In that time he met with civil rights leaders on a grand total of one occasion—in a meeting that took less than an hour.

On the rare occasions he met with other black audiences, Eisenhower would sternly say, "Now, you people have to be patient." His attitude toward the black White House servants was "definitely not friendly" in the words of one of them, "the President hardly knew we were there." In private, he traded "nigger jokes" with his tycoon cronies.

Eisenhower appointed only one black person to his staff, and

E. Frederic Morrow's experience as the first black White House official in history was pathetic. Promised a job during the 1952 campaign, Morrow showed up in Washington only to find the offer was withdrawn because White House employees threatened to boycott their jobs if he entered the building. The White House wouldn't return his calls.

Seventeen months later, an unemployed Morrow was offered temporary work in the Commerce Department. After he was finally moved to the White House two years later to work on miscellaneous "special projects," he was ignored by Eisenhower and humiliated by most everybody else. He couldn't find anyone to be his secretary. Women entered his office only in pairs to avoid talk of sexual misconduct. Morrow was not formally appointed and sworn in until 1959, and he spent much of his time feeling heartsick and ridiculous as he traveled the country defending Ike's indifferent civil rights stand to black audiences.

At the final White House Christmas party, Eisenhower pulled Morrow aside to say he had called all his friends but no one would hire a Negro. "Literally, out on my ear," Morrow reported. "I was the only member of the staff for whom the president could not find a job." It took him three years to find one.

In the days after the *Brown* decision, the man who defeated Hitler was too timid to lift a finger as black Americans and federal courts launched probing assaults on segregation, and white supremacists counterattacked with speed, imagination, brutality, and a strategy of "massive resistance" to integration.

In 1955, when fourteen-year-old black Chicago boy Emmett Till was tortured and executed by a gang of Mississippi whites for allegedly whistling at a white woman, Ike ignored his mother's telegrams pleading for justice.

During the epic bus boycott triggered in 1955 by Rosa Parks to protest segregation in public transportation in Montgomery, Alabama, Eisenhower stubbornly sat on his hands. He even refused to oppose the state's plan to arrest the Reverend Martin Luther King, Jr., for leading the peaceful, entirely legal campaign. In February 1956 Eisenhower did nothing when white mobs went on a rampage at the University of Alabama and chased black applicant Autherine Lucy out of town.

On March 12, 1956, nearly one hundred senators and congressmen introduced a "Southern Manifesto," which rejected *Brown* and pledged "to use all lawful means to bring about a reversal of this decision which is contrary to the Constitution and to prevent the use of force in its implementation." Eisenhower had virtually no comment. Later that year, Texas governor Allan Shivers deployed Texas Rangers to block the federal court–ordered integration of Mansfield High School and Texarkana Junior College. Again Ike did nothing. The armies of white "massive resistance" grew stronger.

Even Dwight Eisenhower had his limits, though. He supported blacks' right to vote and was disgusted by Southern Democratic attempts to block it. On September 9, 1957, he signed the Civil Rights Act of 1957, the first federal civil rights legislation since Reconstruction.

The law empowered the federal government to enforce voting rights, but congressional Democrats, including Lyndon Johnson, John F. Kennedy, and the Southern bloc gutted the act by requiring that voting-rights offenses be prosecuted before jury trials, which guaranteed acquittals in the South. Eisenhower issued a rare public statement on civil rights, saying that the jury-trial requirement of the Civil Rights Act would be "bitterly disappointing" to many millions of Americans who "will continue to be disenfranchised."

Eisenhower also took his constitutional obligations to uphold the laws very seriously, and the mob violence in Little Rock was giving them their first battlefield test.

On the flight from Newport back to Washington, he scribbled angrily on a notepad, "Troops—not to enforce integration but to prevent opposition by violence to orders of a court." Whatever his feelings on *Brown,* he felt, "there must be respect for the Constitution—which means the Supreme Court's interpretation of the Constitution—or we shall have chaos."

Now, at the White House, at 12:15 P.M. on September 24, Eisenhower called the Pentagon and ordered U.S. Army paratroopers of the 101st Airborne Division "Screaming Eagles" to seize Little Rock. "If you have to use force," Ike believed, "use overwhelming force and save lives thereby." Within hours, fifty-two planeloads of airborne infantry troops were racing westward from Fort Campbell, Kentucky.

Eisenhower was disgusted that he had to order troops into action on American soil, but he felt secure in his authority to do so. In his proclamation, which committed the troops, he invoked provisions of the U.S. Code, including Chapter 15 of Title 10, Section 332, which specified that "if rebellion against the authority of the United States" made it impossible to enforce the law, the president "may call into Federal service such of the militia of any state, and use such of the armed forces, as he considers necessary to enforce those laws or to suppress the rebellion." When the Supreme Court reviewed the principle in 1879, it ruled as follows: "We hold it to be an incontrovertible principle, that the Government of the United States may by means of physical force, exercised through its official agents, execute on every foot of American soil the powers and functions that belong to it."

Accompanied by wailing sirens and flashing headlights, federal paratroopers in sharply pressed olive-green battle fatigues jumped out of trucks and half-tracks and assumed dress formation around the Central High School perimeter, M-1 rifles slung on their shoulders and entrenching tools stuffed in their belts. One thousand soldiers were in place by nightfall.

On the morning of September 25, Major General Edwin Walker, in dress uniform, sped up to the school and took command. He was a general's general, a tall, lean Texan who had served under Eisenhower as a commando in Europe during World War II, fighting in the Anzio invasion and in the conquest of southern France. Walker flatly disagreed with this operation, believing that American troops had no business getting involved in domestic peacekeeping, that was the job of civilian police only. Privately, Walker offered his resignation, but Ike refused to accept it.

General Walker and his officers huddled over a battle map and aerial photos of the assault zone, reviewing the tactical plan: paratroopers lining the street at intervals of three yards . . . a detachment, with rifles, in the hallway outside every classroom . . . troops not to enter the classroom unless a teacher calls for help . . . all Negro troops to be kept out of sight at the Little Rock University Armory until further notice . . . any group of more than three adults within a mile of the school to be dispersed . . . civilians to be treated politely and addressed as "sir" and "ma'am" at all times.

At 8:00 A.M., pockets of sullen white onlookers gathered around the school. An otherworldly silence prevailed, soon pierced by bursts of radio traffic on the troops' walkie-talkies. An army helicopter appeared low in the sky, buzzing the area in search of trouble. A pink-shirted boy jeered at the troops. "Why don't you tin soldiers go home?"

Coy Vance, a white seventeen-year-old student planning to study medicine, declared, "I'm not going to school with niggers, because they are inferior to us." The boy vowed, "If I catch one, I'll chase him out of the school." Bonnie Vance, his sixteen-year-old sister, chimed in, "If they didn't have soldiers in the halls the niggers would get murdered." Senior Tommy Dunn speculated: "I think that if they get chased in the halls enough they will leave by themselves. Don't they know we don't want them?"

Major James Meyers called up an army mobile public-address system and announced, "You are instructed to go to your homes peacefully. Disperse and return to your homes." The crowd wouldn't budge. Soon two platoons of infantrymen dog-trotted in formation toward the two biggest crowd concentrations. "Back!" a soldier yelled. "Back on the sidewalk!"

A sergeant barked the command, "Bayonets at the back of their heads, move 'em fast!" The paratroopers advanced, bayonets pointed out, and began pushing the crowds down the side streets. Forty-seven-year-old railroad worker C. E. Blake stood his ground and tried to grab a paratrooper's rifle. The trooper quickly flipped his rifle around and punched Blake over the eye with the rifle butt, knocking him to the ground. Nearby, Paul Downs of Springfield, Arkansas, got jabbed in the arm with a bayonet when he didn't move fast enough.

General Walker dispatched army station wagons, jeeps with mounted turret guns, and trucks packed with bayonet-wielding troops to pick up the black teenagers at a designated group-pickup spot and drive to the school at high speed to avoid possible snipers, under the watchful gaze of an escort helicopter. Then he ordered the white students of Central High to an assembly. The astonished teenagers passed bayonet-wielding Airborne troops and filed into the auditorium for an address by General Walker. There was dead silence as Walker took the stage.

"As an officer of the United States Army," General Walker announced to the wide-eyed students, "I have been chosen to command these forces and to execute the President's orders. . . . We are all subject to all the laws whether we approve of them or not, and as law-abiding citizens, we have an obligation in conscience to obey them. There can be no exceptions; if it were otherwise, we would not be a strong nation but a mere unruly mob.

"You have nothing to fear from my soldiers, and no one will in-

terfere with your coming, going or your peaceful pursuit of your studies," the general concluded. "They are seasoned, well-trained soldiers,
many of them combat veterans. Being soldiers, they are as determined
as I to carry out their orders." Walker strode out of the hall.

At 9:20 A.M., shouts erupted outside the school, "There they
come!" A U.S. Army station wagon raced through a security barricade
up to the front entrance of Central High, flanked by two jeeps stuffed
with helmeted troops. The black students got out of the wagon, six
girls in brightly colored dresses and with books under their arms, and
three boys in sport shirts, one swinging his books on a strap. The windows of the school were packed with white students quietly peering
down at the historic tableau.

Thirty paratroopers formed a protective bubble around the black
children as 350 soldiers stood at attention around the school. "Forward march," an officer called out. "We began moving forward," wrote
Melba Pattillo. "The eerie silence of that moment would forever be
etched in my memory. All I could hear was my own heartbeat and the
sound of boots clicking on the stone. Everything seemed to be moving
in slow motion as I peered past the raised bayonets of the 101st soldiers." That morning, Pattillo heard her colleague Minnijean Brown
say, "For the first time in my life, I feel like an American citizen."

Many white Southerners reacted with horror at the spectacle, and
Southern newspapers launched a chorus of outrage. Governor
Faubus, now riding a wave of popular support in Arkansas for his defiance, said in a TV speech, "We are now an occupied territory." "In the
name of God," he implored, "what's happening in America?"

In Marshall, Texas, a speaker at a Kiwanis meeting proclaimed the
Little Rock event "the darkest day in Southern history since Reconstruction." The Kiwanians then refused to pledge allegiance to the
American flag. Georgia's senator Herman Talmadge thundered, "The
South is threatened by the President of the U.S. using tanks and troops
in the streets of Little Rock. I wish I could cast one vote for impeachment right now." South Carolina's senator Olin Johnston proposed an
even more radical step: "If I were Governor Faubus, I'd proclaim a
state of insurrection down there, and I'd call out the National Guard
and I'd then find out who's going to run things in my state."

President Eisenhower himself was defensive, knowing that while
75 percent of Northerners in a Gallup Poll thought his Little Rock operation was right, only 36 percent of Southerners did. "No one can

deplore more than I do the sending of federal troops anywhere," he told a press conference after the deployment. At the same time, he pointed out, "the courts must be sustained or it's not America."

Inside Central High School, however, there were some hopeful signs. Melba Pattillo recalled entering her first class: "My heart skipped a beat as the classroom door closed behind me." Then she looked back and saw her bodyguard, a helmeted young soldier of the 101st Airborne, gazing through the door window, keeping watch over her. "Sunlight flooded into the room through a full bank of windows along the far wall," she wrote. "It was a beautiful morning."

During lunch, one of the black male students sat alone in the cafeteria with a glass of milk and a sandwich. Some white students nearby asked him, "Won't you join us?" The boy broke into an enthusiastic smile. "Gee, thanks," he replied, "I'd love to." They finished their meals together, eating and chatting.

The "Battle of Little Rock" was over nearly as soon as it started, without a single serious injury and without a shot fired.

CHAPTER TWO

The Warrior

■ ■ ■ ■

I considered myself an active duty soldier. I was at war, and everything I did I considered an act of war.

—James Meredith

A T AN AMERICAN AIR BASE on the outskirts of Tokyo, a U.S. Air Force staff sergeant named James Meredith read the international news reports of the Battle of Little Rock. He was enthralled by the drama.

For the politically conscious twenty-five-year-old, it was as if a giant door of strategy had been opened. For the first time in the century, an American president was forced to send combat troops into action to protect the rights of citizenship for black Americans. An insight that had been forming in Meredith's mind began to crystallize.

James Howard Meredith was a character so colorful and complex, he could only have sprung from the rich soil of Mississippi. He seemed to dwell inside a myth of his own design, a realm often remote and impenetrable to other people. He was an obscure loner who before his thirtieth birthday would engineer a stunning historical coup by mobilizing thousands of people to do his will, including the president and the Supreme Court of the United States. He was a supremely logical man whose reasoning would be misunderstood by practically everyone, a brilliant strategist who would be dismissed by many as being crazy. His sudden impact on Mississippi history would pack the explosive power of a social and political bombshell.

James Meredith was an intense, slightly built man of five feet seven inches, with piercing eyes. He was born in the heart of central Mississippi's hilly farm country in a place called Kosciusko, a town named for a Polish freedom fighter in the American Revolution. People who met him often found him an enigmatic, even mystical personality. "If I know what a mystic is, then James Meredith is a mystic," reported David Sansing, a University of Mississippi history professor. "He doesn't think like we do, he doesn't act like we do, he doesn't even hear the same sounds we hear." Historian Arthur Schlesinger, Jr., described Meredith simply as "a lonely, taciturn and quixotic man of courage and purpose."

Meredith boasted of a dazzling array of ancestors. Some of them seemed in symbolic collision with one another and even themselves, and some may have been connected to Meredith more in myth than physical reality. He claimed one great-great-grandfather who was crown prince of the African kingdom of Dahomey; and a Native-American great-grandfather, General Sam Cobb. "My great-grandfather was the national leader of the Chocktaw nation when it was dissolved," Meredith said of Cobb in a 2000 interview, "and that was why I always wanted to be a general. For twenty years he was in every major war against the Indians with General [Andrew] Jackson on Jackson's side."

Meredith also traced his lineage to a white great-grandfather, Judge J. A. P. Campbell, a colonel in the Confederate army who later, as Mississippi Supreme Court Justice, helped write the notorious white-supremacist 1890 state constitution. "Campbell was my father's mother's father," reported Meredith. "He had a white family and a black family. He spent the last twenty-seven years of his life with his black family. It was really not an uncommon thing in those days. He practically raised my father."

The most regal figure in Meredith's life was his father, Moses Meredith, a proud, fiercely independent farmer, the son of a slave, who, unlike the great majority of Mississippi blacks, was both a property holder and a registered voter. His commanding presence generated respect from everyone, especially James, who called his father Cap, short for "Captain." "Everything I have ever done in my life,"

Meredith explained, "has been a direct result of what my father taught me. I have continued on his mission."

Mississippi was a semi-sovereign empire of white supremacy, but Cap Meredith ran his eighty-five-acre property like a free and independent kingdom inside it. He and his wife, Roxie, steered all ten of their children through high school, and seven into college. Cap fenced off the family's property from neighboring white farms and minimized contact with outsiders, both black and white. "We were most isolated," said Meredith. "Our relationship with people black and white was totally controlled by my father." It was Cap Meredith's way of infusing pride and self-sufficiency in his children.

As a boy, young James Meredith roamed the fields and streams to catch grasshoppers and crickets to sell to fishermen as bait, and after school he plowed the fields with his father. At night sometimes he built a city in his dreams. He never could figure out where the city was, but he knew it was light-years from Kosciusko. When he was around twelve, he visited a white doctor's office and gazed up at a picture of the doctor as a star football player at the University of Mississippi. Meredith then had a young boy's dream of attending the football-powerhouse school himself.

Meredith didn't fully comprehend the gulf between the races until he was fifteen, when his family drove north to visit relatives. James took the train back with his brother. "The train wasn't segregated when we left Detroit," Meredith recalled in 1962, "but when we got to Memphis the conductor told my brother and me we had to go to another car. I cried all the way home from Memphis, and in a way I have cried ever since."

Meredith was among the first wave of black soldiers to serve in the racially integrated U.S. armed forces—he enlisted directly out of high school in 1951, just three years after Harry Truman's historic 1948 desegregation order. Meredith selected the air force because as a brand-new service branch formed after the war, it had no legacy of racism to overcome and had the best reputation among blacks for fair treatment. Meredith thought the desegregation of the military was among the most epochal developments in the history of black Americans.

Meredith was now in his sixth year in the air force, where he worked his way up as a clerk typist. He was known for being extremely meticulous, well organized, and frugal. He was said to grab unused typing paper out of the wastebasket to avoid wasting resources. In 1956 Meredith married Mary June Wiggins of Gary, Indiana, and she followed him to his posting in Japan. He planned to return to Mississippi after his final military hitch to study law, but his experience as a black noncommissioned American officer in Japan was a transforming one.

In the United States, Meredith always felt conscious of his racial identity. But Japan felt like another world. "Japan is where I got it all together as a man," recalled Meredith. He was amazed by the air of racial tolerance he experienced in the Japan of the mid-1950s, which was just emerging from American-occupation rule and was consumed with re-industrializing at a furious pace. "I never felt as free as in Japan," he declared. "You were first and foremost an American."

The racial turmoil of his home country, however, was rarely far from Meredith's heart. He had always been an intense student of race relations and spent many hours of anguish during his military service following the news of racial strife at home, to the point of developing stomach trouble. "I don't ever want to think I am 'well adjusted' as a Negro," he once quipped. When Meredith appeared before a military promotion board in 1954, rather than asking him about his job responsibilities, the colonels asked him his opinion of the recent Supreme Court decision ordering the desegregation of public schools in the United States. He told them in no uncertain terms of his support, and after they promoted him to staff sergeant, the colonels told him they were with him in the struggle but "the outcome will depend on you." From then on Meredith considered that statement a personal badge of responsibility.

As he walked along a Japanese road one day in September 1957, Meredith met a young Japanese schoolboy and the two began chatting about the Little Rock crisis, which had been given wide coverage in Japan. The boy was stunned to meet someone from Mississippi and couldn't believe that Meredith would want to go back to such a place. The encounter helped persuade Meredith that he should someday go back to his home state to fight for a better society.

In Mississippi, Meredith thought, the state system of white supremacy was so powerful and violent that traditional civil disobedience was doomed to ineffectiveness. "I really thought they were crazy," he later said about the tactics of the traditional civil rights movement when applied to his homeland. "I mean, they were out of their minds.

Anyone talking about going into Mississippi and dealing with a strategy of nonviolence, turning the other cheek, I think, these people got to be crazy."

Now, as the 101st Airborne patrolled the streets of Little Rock, Meredith speculated that white supremacy in his own state might be overthrown, but only if confronted with such overwhelming physical force and firepower.

"Little Rock," Meredith explained in a 2000 interview, "was a very, very big factor in my whole desire to break the system of white supremacy. I genuinely believed that the only way that we would get our full rights of citizenship was to get a greater military force on our side than Mississippi had, and there was only one force in the world bigger than that, and that was the U.S. armed forces. So when Eisenhower, who had been the biggest general in our history, committed the troops to support the rights of citizenship, that was what my objective was in the whole Mississippi scheme."

In July 1960 James Meredith was honorably discharged from the air force. He returned to Mississippi and registered for the fall semester at all-black Jackson State College, in the state capital of Jackson, to complete his studies toward a bachelor's degree in political science. The school was a showpiece in the state's failing public-relations campaign to deliver education for blacks that was "separate but equal."

Meredith might as well have landed on another planet. Until now, he had lived mostly in societies where white supremacy was irrelevant: a childhood in the isolated independence of his father's farm; nine years in the integrated U.S. Air Force; and three of those years stationed in Japan, where the concept of white supremacy was nonexistent. Suddenly Meredith was in the belly of the most segregated state in the nation, a society that one local white newspaper editor called a "jungle of hate."

At the dawn of the 1960s, Mississippi was both the poorest state in the country, with annual per capita income of just $1,233, and the state with the highest proportion of black citizens, approximately 43 percent. Radical white segregationists controlled the police, the media, and the state government; dominated the hearts and minds of much of the white population; and systematically eradicated the citizenship rights of black residents.

If you were black in Mississippi in 1960, the overwhelming odds were that you could not vote, could not hold office or serve on a jury, suffered substandard schools and housing, and were totally segregated from normal American life. There were no black sheriffs, state Highway Patrolmen or National Guardsmen. The token number of twenty-two thousand black voters in 1952 was beaten down by violence and terrorist threats to eight thousand in 1958. Racial violence against blacks, by white citizens and police forces alike, was a matter of established routine, especially when blacks attempted to organize politically.

A daring young black army veteran named Medgar Evers was in his seventh year as field secretary of the state NAACP, working with courageous black leaders such as Aaron Henry of Clarksdale, C. C. Bryant of McComb, and Amzie Moore of Cleveland, Mississippi. Acting as a one-man intelligence agency, Evers donned disguises to dash around the state investigating atrocities against black citizens. His wife and assistant, Myrlie Evers, reported that "affidavits testifying to the routine cruelty of white Mississippians toward Negroes piled up in Medgar's files. Each represented an hour, a day, a week of Medgar's life in a surrealist version of Hell."

The reports wove a monotonous montage of horror. In the Delta town of Belzoni on May 7, 1955, a Baptist minister and NAACP member named Rev. George Washington Lee was executed by gunshots to the head soon after he registered to vote. Three months later, Lamar Smith, a sixty-year-old black farmer who registered to vote and encouraged others to join him, was assassinated by gunfire in broad daylight on the courthouse lawn of Brookhaven. That August also brought the kidnapping, beating, and execution of young Emmett Till, an act so heinous it triggered worldwide revulsion.

There seemed to be no end to the nightmare. Reports of beatings and intimidation kept piling up in Medgar Evers's office. In 1958 Woodrow Wilson Daniels died of a brain injury after being beaten by a white sheriff, who was tried and acquitted. The next year, in Poplarville, Mack Charles Parker was charged with raping a white woman, dragged from jail, and shot to death by a mob, his body dumped into the Pearl River. In October 1959, Luther Jackson was shot to death by a policeman in Philadelphia, Mississippi. No charges were filed.

"A map of Mississippi," recalled Mrs. Evers, "was a reminder not of geography, but of atrocities, of rivers that hid broken bodies, of towns and cities ruled by the enemy."

Elsewhere in the United States, as the new decade began, African-Americans were beginning to challenge white supremacy with creative new tactics and mounting excitement. As the old-line NAACP continued to press legal assaults on Southern segregation, younger groups such as the Congress of Racial Equality (CORE) and the Reverend Martin Luther King, Jr.'s, Southern Christian Leadership Conference (SCLC) planned grass-roots action. In February 1960 four black college students in Greensboro, North Carolina, were refused service at a Woolworth's lunch counter, and their tactic of staying put until they were served triggered a wave of "sit-ins" and "pray-ins" around the country.

As a student at all-black Jackson State, James Meredith sharpened his growing political consciousness by helping to form a small secret society of campus intellectuals called the Mississippi Improvement Association of Students, or MIAS. Their weapon was the mimeograph machine, and their ammunition was leaflets announcing they were going to break the system of white supremacy. Before morning classes, Meredith and his comrades would write signs on all the blackboards, which read, "MIAS vs. BIAS: who are you for?" Under cover of darkness, they delivered "subversive" anti–white supremacy literature to targets around Jackson. They dropped leaflets on the doorsteps of politicians, the chief of the Jackson police, even the Governor's Mansion. They never got caught.

By now, James Meredith was sharpening a political philosophy that was extremely radical yet rooted firmly in that most basic principle of American civics—citizenship. To Meredith, the usual discussion of civil rights and integration seemed timid and incremental. Such concepts were insults to the simple question of whether or not he was an American citizen. "To me, a person is no better off enjoying nine of ten rights than they are none of ten," Meredith explained years later. "My thing is the whole hog; either all of the citizenship rights, or none. I have no quarrel with the civil rights people," he explained. "It is just simply that their objectives are just so minute compared to mine." Paradoxically, the concept of integration was never Meredith's goal. His objective was the total destruction of white supremacy.

Meredith began developing an almost messianic vision of destroying the system of white supremacy in Mississippi, believing this was his "Divine Responsibility." Gradually, a bold strategic stroke Meredith had toyed with in the back of his mind was taking center stage: following through on his boyhood dream and registering as a student at the state-supported University of Mississippi at Oxford, where no black students were ever known to attend.

Meredith chewed his idea over with his fellow activists at Jackson State, and one day he walked into the nearby office of Medgar Evers, introduced himself, and spilled out his thoughts. Evers, who in 1954 had unsuccessfully explored registering at the Ole Miss law school himself, had nothing but enthusiasm for Meredith's idea, and offered his support and the NAACP's legal resources when Meredith was ready.

The University of Mississippi was a multiracial, multiethnic institution that was open to almost every ethnic group on Earth. It hosted white, Hispanic, and Asian-American students, and welcomed non-white foreign-exchange students from countries such as Vietnam, Korea, Formosa (Taiwan), Pakistan, and India.

But the university had the absurd distinction of excluding just one group ever since it opened in 1848: The school refused to allow people of black African descent to attend. The state university of Mississippi was closed to 43 percent of the state's own population, despite the fact that it was financed in part by hundreds of thousands of black taxpayers. The majority of the members of the state's political structure and white population was dead set against letting blacks in, and resolved to block with overwhelming physical force any black who tried to enter the school.

"Ole Miss," as the school was known (the nickname was used by antebellum slaves for the white mistress of the house), was located west of the city of Oxford in north-central Mississippi, a placid community perched on a ridge between the Yockony Patawfy and Tallahatchie Rivers in the heart of the great Southern forest, on the very farthest western edge of the Appalachian foothills. It was a football-crazed institution, not an A-list school, but for generations of Mississippians, attendance was a crucial rite of cultural passage into the state's social and business elite. As Meredith observed, "It's better than Harvard at teaching you how to use 2 + 2 = 4 in Mississippi."

Almost half the Ole Miss faculty held doctorates or other advanced degrees, far above the average for American colleges and universities. Despite poorly paid professors and regular assaults by segregationist state politicians on academic freedom of thought, Ole Miss students equaled or beat national norms in most fields in graduate exams, and the school produced more Rhodes scholars than almost every other Southern university.

The school occupied a gently rolling landscape west of the town square of Oxford. At the heart of the campus was the Greek Revival–style Lyceum building, where wounded Union soldiers from U. S. Grant's invading army were billeted in December 1862. "William Nichols patterned the Lyceum after an Ionic temple on the Illysis near Athens," wrote historian David Sansing. "The campus was in a setting of great natural beauty, with the buildings arranged in a semicircle at the crest of a slight eminence." The white-columned Lyceum was named after the Athens garden where Aristotle taught, and it housed the offices of the school's dean and registrar.

The idyllic splendor of the Ole Miss campus sometimes inspired outsiders to rhapsodic prose. "There are magnolias scattered among the elms, oaks, redbud and dogwood trees," wrote visiting *Sports Illustrated* writer Joe David Brown in 1960, "and on flat and sultry days their fragrance is everywhere, just as sentimental novelists claim. Mockingbirds sing in the trees, and on quiet nights when the moon is riding high katydids fill the air with a soft keening, and lightning bugs blink everywhere."

In a state that celebrated the sport of football with sacramental intensity, the University of Mississippi was the holy shrine and tabernacle, home to some of the greatest playing in the country. "Inspired by Ole Miss, the whole state vibrates in a constant football flap," reported *Time* magazine in 1960. "Every Friday night the state is set aglow from the Gulf to the Tennessee border by the lights of high school games." The high priest of Ole Miss football was the legendary Coach Johnny Vaught, who lorded over the strongest coaching staff in the country and a squad of corn-fed homegrown players so massive that they looked as though they were wearing pads even when they weren't.

Visitors were often startled by the beauty of Ole Miss coeds, two of whom became consecutive Miss Americas in 1958 and 1959. Part of the charm of Mississippi women, wrote Joe David Brown, was "their dewy-eyed acceptance of their men as reckless and dashing creatures. If the women raise their voices at all, it is to squeal with delight or to feign terror at the accomplishments of the men."

East of the school, at the center of Oxford's Courthouse Square, was the white stucco Lafayette County courthouse, built in 1871, which was guarded by a thirty-foot-tall granite monument of a Confederate soldier gripping a long rifle. The statue was erected by Civil War veterans in 1907 and bore the inscription "They gave their lives in a just and holy cause." Union troops of General U. S. Grant's army invaded the square in December 1862 and stayed for only a few weeks, then returned in August 1864 on a rampage and burned down the old courthouse and much of the city. In 1962, the city was home to 4,700 whites and 1,300 blacks who attended legally segregated schools and used segregated public facilities, as did all Mississippians.

On the north side of the Square was John Leslie's Walgreen drugstore, where you could park yourself on a stool at the fountain section and buy a hamburger for twenty cents, a J. Hungerford Smith–brand chocolate hot-fudge sundae for thirty-five cents, and a large Coca-Cola for a dime.

A few blocks south of the Square was the sprawling estate of Rowan Oak, the home of Oxford's most famous resident, Nobel Laureate and Pulitzer Prize–winner William Faulkner, arguably the greatest writer America had yet produced. He would sit on a beat-up chair by a sunny window, inhale the fragrance of gardens rich with magnolias and wisteria, and conjure up epic tales of murder and betrayal and doomed ancient destiny on his old Underwood portable, tales modeled on the real-life characters of Oxford and Lafayette County. "And he didn't exaggerate in those stories, he toned them down if anything," quipped his buddy, attorney Phil Stone. "That's just Mississippi."

In the April 1954 *Holiday* magazine, Faulkner sketched the baroque wilderness of his ancestors in an article titled "Mississippi." "In the beginning it was virgin," Faulkner wrote of his homeland, "to the west, along the Big River, the alluvial swamps threaded by black, almost motionless bayous and impenetrable with cane and buckvine and cypress and ash and oak and gum; to the east, the hardwood ridges and the prairies where the Appalachian Mountains died and buffalo grazed; to the south, the pine barrens and the moss-hung live oaks and the greater swamps, less of earth than water and lurking with alligators and water moccasins, where Louisiana in its time would begin."

Faulkner strolled the side streets of Oxford swinging his cane, and sometimes stopped to hover on the edge of the Square. He would gaze at the courthouse, perhaps thinking up a new tale as he slowly packed his pipe with a rich tobacco blend lightened up with a pinch of Virginia bright. He always took his new manuscripts to Gathright-Reed's drugstore on the Square, where Mack Reed would drop what he was doing and hand-wrap the package for him for mailing to his New York publisher.

Some of the locals in Oxford were skeptical of Faulkner and thought he put on airs by dressing like a country squire, training horses on his front lawn, and generally acting aloof. An old friend once joked that Faulkner was about as popular as "a dead skunk in a sleeping bag."

At the university, where Faulkner once briefly served as postmaster before being fired for ignoring the mail in favor of scribbling out his stories, no black person was ever known to have attended the school as a student. Black faces on campus were common, but only as maids, janitors, food-service workers, and workmen.

In fact, though, a light-skinned black student from out of state named Harry Murphy, Jr., attended Ole Miss for nine months in 1945–1946 under the navy V-12 program without anyone realizing his race. He had several campus romances, ran track and field, and enjoyed punch and cake at church socials and square dances. He found it a charming place.

In 1950 a black artist named M. B. Mayfield became a janitor in the university's Fine Arts Center, and with the help of Professor Stuart R. Purser, the chairman of the art department, and his students, he sat in a broom closet during class and took notes as an unofficial student. He went on to become a renowned Mississippi artist.

In 1953 a black minister from Gulfport, Mississippi, named Charles Dubra applied to the law school armed with a master's degree from Boston University and the backing of both the University of Mississippi chancellor and the law school dean, but Ole Miss trustees rejected him on the technicality that his undergraduate degree was from an unaccredited institution. Few other blacks besides Medgar Evers had ever bothered to apply to the school, knowing they would automatically be rejected because of their race.

As he strategized with his allies, James Meredith could see some encouraging precedents for his idea of entering Ole Miss. Since the *Brown* decision in 1954, the public schools of Washington, D.C., Delaware, Maryland, West Virginia, Missouri, Oklahoma, Kentucky, and parts of Texas had begun desegregating. The state universities of

Virginia, North Carolina, Georgia, Florida, Texas, Louisiana, Tennessee, Arkansas, Missouri, Oklahoma, and Kentucky had all accepted black students or were in the process of doing so.

In February 1959 "massive resistance" to desegregation, a strategy articulated by a Democratic U.S. senator from Virginia, Harry Byrd, abruptly collapsed in his own state when fifty-three black students were admitted to eleven all-white Virginia elementary schools. The theory of massive resistance called for overwhelming white opposition to desegregation and carried the implicit threat of riots or other violent opposition if integration was forced by federal authorities. But in Virginia, no blood was spilled.

In the "deepest" Southern states of Alabama, South Carolina, and Mississippi, however, Meredith could see discouraging signs. As noted earlier, in neighboring Alabama in 1956, Autherine Lucy had to withdraw from the state university hours after arriving, in the wake of white riots. The school remained closed to blacks, as did the state university of South Carolina. Even those other Southern schools that were integrating were thus far accepting only token numbers of black students.

The most frightening precedents were in recent Mississippi history. In 1958 a black man named Clennon King arrived in Oxford and announced his intention to register at the university. King was an eccentric, controversial minister and former instructor at all-black Alcorn Agricultural and Mechanical College who triggered a student uproar and boycott in 1957 when he wrote a series of articles denouncing the NAACP and supporting segregation.

When he entered the Lyceum building, the Reverend King was escorted to an empty room and left alone for a while. University officials weren't sure what to do with him, since he refused to follow the normal process of filling out and mailing in forms and had brought some news reporters and photographers with him onto campus. Suddenly King began yelling for help, afraid his life was in danger. He shouted loudly enough for the reporters outside the building to hear, "They are going to kill me!" Mississippi governor James P. Coleman, who was monitoring the situation by phone, ordered state Highway Patrolmen to throw King off the campus. When King swore to keep coming back, Coleman ordered King packed off to the state mental institution, where he was imprisoned for twelve days. King soon fled the state.

In 1959 a decorated black former U.S. Army paratrooper named

Clyde Kennard tried to apply to all-white Mississippi Southern College. State officials charged him with allegedly helping steal twenty-five dollars' worth of chicken feed and packed him off to serve a wildly excessive seven-year term at the notoriously brutal Parchman Prison farm, where he developed stomach cancer.

But in 1960 James Meredith sensed reasons for hope and felt the time might soon be right for his own assault on Ole Miss. "Anybody who thinks all blacks were on one side and all whites were on another has another thought coming," he recalled many years later. "There were plenty of people in Mississippi who wanted to see change. Mississippi was the most aristocratic state in America by far. Very few people controlled most everything major. These people were always generally opposed to the hard-core white supremacy. But nobody got out of line with the white supremacy ideology since twenty-five years after the Civil War."

During the fall 1960 presidential campaign, instructors at Jackson State College planned a student debate to mark the televised debates between Democratic candidate Senator John F. Kennedy and Republican candidate Vice President Richard M. Nixon. When no students were willing to argue for the Democrats, who for generations had stood for segregation and white control in Mississippi, Meredith volunteered. "You've got to understand," Meredith recalled in 2000, "[in Mississippi] all blacks then were Republican. No one would take the Kennedy side of the debate. Consequently I had to learn everything about the Kennedy campaign, which I did, almost word for word."

Meredith carefully scrutinized Kennedy's speeches as well as the strong Democratic party platform on civil rights, and when Kennedy narrowly won the election, Meredith decided the time was now right to put his plan into action.

One day after watching the flickering black-and-white TV images of John Kennedy taking the oath of office on January 20, 1961, James Meredith sat down at his Smith-Corona portable typewriter and wrote to the University of Mississippi, asked for a brochure and an application, and in so doing, quietly launched a one-man revolution. It wasn't the Olympian rhetoric of Kennedy's inaugural speech that inspired Meredith; Kennedy didn't even mention civil rights for black Americans in his speech. "The objective," Meredith later explained, "was to put pressure on John Kennedy and the Kennedy administration to live up to the civil rights plank in the Democratic platform. It was an effort to force Kennedy's administration to either live up to it or suffer the public relations consequences of not doing what he was pledging."

"We are very pleased to know of your interest in becoming a member of our student body," read the letter from Ole Miss registrar Robert B. Ellis that came a week later. "If we can be of further help to you in making your enrollment plans, please let us know."

Meredith filled out the application and added a shocker of a footnote: "I sincerely hope that your attitude toward me as a potential member of your student body . . . will not change upon learning that I am not a white applicant. I am an American-Mississippi-Negro citizen." He concluded, "I certainly hope that this matter will be handled in a manner that will be complimentary to the University and the state of Mississippi."

Meredith explained he couldn't send the required five letters of recommendation from Ole Miss alumni in his home county, since they were all white and he didn't know any of them, so he enclosed recommendations of good character from five black citizens.

By now, Meredith had accumulated a briefcase full of college credits and was three semesters away from a degree. In eight years of part-time study in the air force, he took dozens of college courses and passed them all, including tough courses in subjects such as the Russian language. As he was rotated to different postings, he studied at the University of Kansas, Washburn University, Wayne University, the University of Maryland, and the U.S. Armed Forces Institute. He earned the Good Conduct Medal and an honorable discharge. One thing was certain—if his ethnicity was anything other than African-American, James Meredith would have been welcomed to Ole Miss with open arms.

Meredith dropped his application in the mail. Within days, the University of Mississippi summarily cut him off.

On February 4 the registrar sent a telegram: "It has been found necessary to discontinue consideration of all applications for admission" received after January 25. This was a brand-new technicality that was invented strictly to dispose of Meredith's application. The note said firmly, "We must advise you not to appear for registration."

Meredith expected this and quickly informed the Civil Rights Division of Bobby Kennedy's Justice Department in Washington, D.C., by letter: "It grieves me keenly to realize that an individual, especially an American, the citizen of a free democratic nation, has to clamor with such procedures in order to try to gain just a small amount of his civil and human rights."

Meredith also paid a courtesy call to the Federal Bureau of Investigation's resident field agent in Jackson. Meredith was well aware of the Mississippi government's practice of crushing dissidents, and he knew he might well need the might of the federal government to back him. He also knew he would need to draw national attention to his case, to avoid the underpublicized fates of people such as Clyde Kennard and Clennon King before him. "The objective," Meredith later explained, "was to make myself more valuable alive than dead."

At Medgar Evers's suggestion, Meredith had already written a letter on January 29 to NAACP counsel Thurgood Marshall in New York, asking for legal help from the group's famed Legal Defense Fund. "I am making this move," Meredith wrote Marshall, "in what I consider the interest of and for the benefit of: (1) my country, (2) my race, (3) my family, and (4) myself. I am familiar with the probable difficulties involved in such a move as I am undertaking and I am fully prepared to pursue it all the way to a degree from the University of Mississippi."

But there was one problem: The esteemed Thurgood Marshall could not believe any black person would be crazy enough to try to register at the University of Mississippi. The NAACP had no immediate plans for legal action on education in the state. Mississippi was so hopeless that it wasn't even on their target list. In fact, Evers had been exceeding his authority when he automatically promised legal resources to Meredith.

Marshall insisted on speaking to Meredith personally, to make sure he was sane and sincere. Meredith began speaking to Marshall on Medgar Evers's house phone, but grew furious at Marshall's incredulity—he thought his integrity was being questioned. Meredith cut off the discussion. He was going to move with or without Thurgood Marshall or the NAACP.

The journey might have died then and there. James Meredith had nearly infinite supplies of physical courage and mental determination for the struggle ahead and was very much the leader of this crusade in the making. But the NAACP had one thing he needed to succeed: a crack staff of battle-tested civil rights attorneys who could help him navigate the labyrinthine legal minefield that the state of Mississippi would force him into.

Medgar Evers stayed on the line, placated Thurgood Marshall, worked with Meredith, and kept the process going. Without Evers's intervention, Meredith's crusade would have ended.

At the NAACP Legal Defense Fund headquarters in New York, Thurgood Marshall walked into the office of Constance Baker Motley, a brilliant, methodical young associate counsel. Marshall dropped Meredith's letter on her desk, saying, "This guy's gotta be crazy!" Then he announced, "That's your case."

Motley asked, "Why me?"

Marshall joked that as a black woman, Motley was less prone to physical attack in the Deep South than black men, since many white men had black "mammies," or nannies.

Meredith welcomed the involvement of Motley and her NAACP associate Jack Greenberg, a white attorney who successfully argued the *Brown* case before the U.S. Supreme Court. For his part, Greenberg thought that "Meredith was a man with a mission. He acted like he was an agent of God." According to Motley, "We never would have brought suit in Mississippi if it wasn't for James Meredith. Meredith had to have a Messiah complex to do what he did." Medgar Evers later observed of Meredith, "He's got more guts than any man I know, but he's the hardest-headed son-of-a-gun I ever met. The more you disagreed with him the more he became convinced that he—and he alone—was right."

James Meredith now harbored dreams of joining the business and political elite of Mississippi, and in the early days of his campaign to enter Ole Miss, he declared to a white reporter who visited him at Jackson State that he wanted to be governor. "James Meredith is crazy," concluded the reporter. "That's the best way to describe it. I think he's got a screw loose somewhere."

Actually, Meredith was simply a man who was ten, or twenty, or forty years ahead of his time, like a man from the twenty-first century dropped through a time warp into America's racial prehistory. The prospect of living out his life in the Dark Age of a segregated Mississippi was simply unacceptable to him. James Meredith wanted the world, and he wanted it now. As he later explained, "I asked myself the question, 'Why should it be someone else?' If people keep placing the responsibility with someone else, nothing will ever be accomplished."

In a letter dated May 25, 1961, the University of Mississippi unequivocally rejected Meredith's application for what it hoped would be the last time, expecting that Meredith would fold his cards, give up, and go away. The registrar cited Meredith's lack of proper recommendation letters and, invoking a new technicality invented expressly to thwart Meredith, ruled that the school would not accept transfer students from institutions that, like Jackson State, were not accredited by the regional academic organization. "I see no need for mentioning any other deficiencies," Ellis declared. "Your application file had been closed."

Instead of walking away, Meredith packed his briefcase with color-coded files and on May 31, 1961, marched into the Meridian, Mississippi, courtroom of U.S. District Court Judge Sidney Mize, flanked by his lawyers and Medgar Evers and armed with a lawsuit.

Meredith's suit coincided with a fresh burst of civil rights action in the South in the first days of the new presidency. "The change of tide in Mississippi did not begin until 1961," wrote Mrs. Myrlie Evers. "Then, almost imperceptibly, Negroes took the offensive in the struggle for full citizenship." In March, nine students from Tougaloo Southern Christian College, a black private school, launched a sit-in campaign at the whites-only Jackson Public Library. A new regional grass-roots coalition called the Student Nonviolent Coordinating Committee (SNCC) announced plans for a voter-registration project in Mississippi.

The most dramatic episode unfolded in May 1961, when the tiny Congress of Racial Equality sent biracial teams of volunteers into Alabama and Mississippi to conduct a nonviolent test of Supreme Court decisions banning segregation on interstate travel. On Sunday, May 14, a Trailways bus carrying the first team of Freedom Riders was captured by a mob of nearly two hundred white men outside Anniston, Alabama, who firebombed the bus and beat the volunteers until Alabama state policemen opened fire with warning shots.

An hour later, a second team of Freedom Riders was attacked in a Trailways bus at Anniston. When the bus escaped to Birmingham and pulled into the terminal, a frenzied mob of Ku Klux Klansmen ambushed and beat the Freedom Riders with lead pipes, injuring reporters and bystanders as well. The local police had helpfully allowed the Klan a fifteen-minute interval to attack and escape. When the rides resumed on Saturday, May 20, a mob of almost a thousand whites launched a riotous, savage attack on the Freedom Riders at the Greyhound terminal in Montgomery. The attacks triggered worldwide headlines and compelled federal authorities to protect the travelers with National Guardsmen. When the Freedom Riders made it to Jackson, Mississippi, they were peacefully escorted by city police and state Highway Patrolmen directly into jail.

Against this tumultuous backdrop, James Meredith appeared in U.S. District Court in Meridian, Mississippi on May 31, armed with a suit petitioning the court to direct his admission to Ole Miss, charging that the university refused his application because of racial bias. Judge Sidney Mize, distressed, as many other white Mississippians were, at the simultaneous arrival of the Freedom Riders to the state, summoned Meredith's attorney Constance Baker Motley back to his chamber and asked, "Why did you have to come now?" Motley replied that she couldn't pick her clients or their timing.

For the next sixteen months, Meredith and the NAACP lawyers dashed around the state, often tailed by Mississippi state government investigators, relentlessly pressing their legal fight while state officials fought back with an increasingly desperate campaign of evasion, delay, and obstruction. "I considered myself an active duty soldier," recalled Meredith. "I was at war, and everything I did I considered an act of war." Meredith's spirits were buoyed by the fact that one of his lawyers was R. Jess Brown, one of only three black attorneys in the state. "He was one of the men that I admired the most," remembered Meredith. "He was the only black lawyer that would take those cases in Mississippi for many years. To me he was the important one."

Meredith's Byzantine legal struggle unfolded like a tale by Franz Kafka. On December 12, 1961, District Judge Mize ruled, ridiculously, that Meredith was not denied admission on racial grounds. On January 12, 1962, the U.S. Fifth Circuit Court of Appeals in New Orleans ruled the university's policy of requiring referrals from alumni was unconstitutional. On February 3, Judge Mize reheard the case and ruled against Meredith, on the absurd grounds that the school was not a racially segregated institution. On June 6, Meredith was briefly jailed on a bogus false-voter-registration charge.

The case stopped and started over and over again, and sometimes Meredith, who continued his studies at Jackson State, feared he wouldn't succeed. For inspiration he read a quote from Theodore Roosevelt that he'd clipped out and carried around for nearly ten years. "It is not the critic who counts," the quote read. "The credit belongs to the man who is actually in the arena, whose face is marred by dust and sweat and blood . . . who at the best knows in the end the triumph of high achievement, and who at the worst, if he fails, at least fails while daring greatly, so that his place will never be with those cold and timid souls who know neither victory or defeat." He read the quote over and over, hundreds of times.

At last, on June 25, 1962, the U.S. Fifth Circuit Court of Appeals found that Meredith was rejected "solely because he was a Negro," and ordered Meredith's admission for the fall 1962 semester. "A full review of the record," wrote Judge John Minor Wisdom, "leads the Court inescapably to the conclusion that from the moment the defendants discovered that Meredith was a Negro they engaged in a carefully calculated campaign of delay, harassment, and masterly inactivity." In a peculiar backhanded compliment, Judge Wisdom noted admiringly that Meredith seemed "just about the type of Negro who might be expected to try to crack the racial barrier at the University of Mississippi: a man with a mission and with a nervous stomach."

Between July 28 and August 4, 1962, Judge Ben F. Cameron, a member of the Fifth Circuit Court of Appeals, issued four "stays," or delays, of the injunction. The first three were overturned by the full Court of Appeals, and Meredith and his lawyers appealed the fourth all the way to the Supreme Court. On August 31, the United States Justice Department entered the case for the first time as a "friend of the court," and petitioned the Supreme Court to rule for Meredith.

Finally, the case of *Meredith v. Fair* (referring to Charles Fair, chairman of the state Board of Trustees of Institutions of Higher Learning) was approaching the highest court in the land, but, with time running out and the fall semester already starting at Ole Miss, the Court was still out of session for the summer. Meredith's fate was now in the hands of Supreme Court Justice Hugo Black, the judge responsible for overseeing the Fifth Circuit Court of Appeals.

Justice Hugo Black was a native Alabamian who always carried a copy of the Constitution in his pocket. In 1923, when he was a prosperous trial lawyer, he joined the Robert E. Lee Ku Klux Klan No. 1 of Birmingham, and stayed active in it for two years. He later repudiated the Klan, but in an interview he gave to the *New York Times* on condition that it would be published only after his death, he explained that most Klansmen then "were the cream of Birmingham's middle-class. It was a fraternal organization, really. It wasn't anti-Catholic, anti-Jewish or anti-Negro."

Justice Black consulted all of his fellow Supreme Court justices by telephone, and on September 10, 1962, Black announced that each one agreed with him that he should issue an order to vacate all four of Judge Cameron's stays, enjoin Ole Miss from "taking any steps to prevent enforcement of the Court of Appeals mandate," and allow Meredith to register. In response three days later, District Judge Mize also ordered the university to immediately admit Meredith.

Now, after a stubborn, methodical, year-and-a-half-long legal campaign, James Meredith and his lawyers had finally compelled the University of Mississippi to admit him right away, on the same terms as white students. And suddenly, although probably nobody but Meredith realized it, the mystical young strategist had succeeded in forcing three new allies to his side: the president of the United States, the U.S. Justice Department, and the most powerful military machine in history.

In a matter of days, they, along with the rest of the country, would all be running to catch up with James Meredith.

CHAPTER THREE

The Incendiary Man

■ ■ ■ ■

He was the greatest actor of our time. . . .

—Hugh Sidey on John F. Kennedy

IN SEPTEMBER 1962 JOHN FITZGERALD KENNEDY presided over a nation enjoying the final summer days of what historian Taylor Branch called "the last year of postwar innocence," the brief American interregnum between the booming consumer culture of the 1950s and the political chaos and social disorder that engulfed the country later in the 1960s.

The conflict in Vietnam was a distant, low-level crisis; the American military advisors there had yet to participate in a major battle. Although Wall Street was experiencing a slight slowdown, the U.S. economy was still roaring through its stunning postwar economic boom. The culture was powered by communications technologies that would soon vanish: carbon paper, mimeograph machines, stencils, computer punchcards, and black-and-white TV.

In Washington, D.C., inside the thirty-five-foot-long, twenty-eight-foot-wide workspace of the Oval Office, there dwelled one of the most popular presidents in history, a man described by his secretary of state, Dean Rusk, as "an incendiary man who set most of the people around him on fire," and by State Department official Pedro Sanjuan as being "like the sun: he radiated confidence and victory."

The American people were, by and large, besotted with their chief executive, with his energy, his ideas, his hauntingly beautiful family, and his seeming command of the job, and they rewarded him with Gallup job-approval ratings that lingered in a distant stratosphere of 70 percent and sometimes even 80 percent. They loved him when he succeeded, which was surprisingly rare, and they loved him even more when he failed, as when he mismanaged the disastrous proxy invasion of Cuba at the Bay of Pigs in April 1961 and his popularity shot up by eleven points. Even Kennedy thought it was incredible. He was only forty-five, and he seemed to be a computer-generated holographic image of the perfect president, striking handsome poses in Italian-cut suits and a perpetual Palm Beach tan, bellowing heroic speeches in his peculiar clam chowder–laced accent.

Every two weeks Kennedy seduced and conquered his people all over again through the alchemy of televised press conferences, toying with adoring reporters, grinning as he knocked their questions out of the ballpark, demonstrating his technical mastery of the world's most dangerous job.

Inside the White House, JFK chuckled, "this is a damned good job." He could barely sit still, snapping his fingers, darting around the White House grounds, pushing open the French doors of the Oval Office to breathe in the fresh air of the Rose Garden, firing off memos into his Dictaphone machine. Writer Gore Vidal, a onetime friend of John Kennedy's, sketched the president up close: "The outline is slender and youthful, but the face is heavily lined for his age. On the upper lip are those tiny vertical lines characteristic of a more advanced age. He is usually tanned from the sun, while his hair is what lady novelists call 'chestnut', beginning to go gray. . . . He is immaculately dressed; although, disconcertingly, occasional white chest hairs curl over his collar."

Kennedy, who in his life had never run an organization larger than a PT-boat and a small Senate staff, was an improvisational executive who dispensed with committees and staff meetings and preferred to fly by the seat of his pants and thrive on chaos as the world's problems tumbled into his office. His Oval Office atmosphere was electrically charged with wisecracks, spirited argument, and locker-room arrogance, enforced by a small army of worshipful assistants.

"He had this extraordinary ability," noted State Department official Philips Talbot, "of having a telephone conversation, of reading a newspaper and listening to some lackey in front of his desk, all at the same time." British prime minister Harold Macmillan snorted at Kennedy's breezy executive approach by claiming he spent "half his time thinking about adultery, the other half about secondhand ideas passed on by his advisers."

The sea-loving navy man's Oval Office was overflowing with nautical items: ship models, stuffed Cape Cod sandpipers, a whaling harpoon. On Kennedy's casually disordered desk were family pictures, tiny sculptures of a lion and polar bear, bookends of whales' teeth, a black alligator desk set from General De Gaulle, a model PT-boat, and a pen-and-pencil set that contained a secret trigger for tape machines that could record his visitors without their knowing it through tiny microphones scattered through the Oval Office and Cabinet Room.

Also on JFK's desk was an ashtray laminated with his own fingerprints, a teasing gift from FBI Director J. Edgar Hoover that also held a sinister meaning. The twisted, tortured old crime fighter held secret tapes and files on the president's private life dating back to the 1940s that could destroy Kennedy's career in a matter of minutes if made public. "J. Edgar Hoover," Vice President Lyndon Johnson growled to a few trusted journalists over cocktails, "has Jack Kennedy by the balls." In private, Kennedy was juggling a personal life that was a race with disaster.

Somehow, JFK was managing overlapping extramarital affairs and fleeting sexual experiences with a galaxy of women, constantly exposing himself to possible blackmail and national-security lapses. Amazingly, Kennedy had not yet gotten caught, in part because it was a different era in American journalism, when reporters protected a president's private life rather than tearing it apart.

One of the women involved with JFK, Judith Campbell, had also been mistress to Chicago Mafia boss Sam Giancana. Another, an East German woman named Ellen Rometsch, was suspected by the FBI of being both a high-priced call girl and a Communist spy. The president was propositioning and sleeping with secretaries, starlets, hat-check girls and hookers; generally behaving, remembered Secretary of the Cabinet Fred Dutton, "like God, fucking anybody he wants to anytime he feels like it."

The president was also concealing medical problems including venereal disease and Addison's disease, a failure of the adrenal glands that required him to take constant doses of cortisone, a drug that gives the user surges of confidence and sexual desire. At the same time, Kennedy was receiving highly dangerous multiple-drug "speed cocktails" injected by a physician named Dr. Max Jacobson (nicknamed "Dr. Feelgood") to give the president an energy boost. Dr. Jacobson dispensed amphetamines to a celebrity client list until his license was revoked in 1975 by New York State medical authorities, who found him guilty of forty-eight charges of unprofessional conduct, including manufacturing "adulterated drugs consisting in whole or in part of filthy, putrid, and/or decomposed substances."

According to White House Secret Service gate logs, Dr. Jacobson visited Kennedy in the White House some thirty times in 1961 and 1962. Although the precise amounts of amphetamines that entered the president's bloodstream are unknown, Jacobson later admitted that a typical dose for his clients was 25 milligrams. It was not until later in the decade that the dangers of amphetamines became fully understood, and the president could not have known that it was a highly dangerous psychoactive drug that, according to experts, can cause even first-time users to be confused, agitated, and likely to physically assault other people. A single dose as low as 50 milligrams, or just two times Jacobson's typical dose, can produce toxic psychosis with paranoid delusions and hallucinations.

Another one of Dr. Feelgood's celebrity patients was author Truman Capote, who once collapsed and was hospitalized after Jacobson's shots. The shots made him "feel like Superman," Capote explained. "You're flying. Ideas come at the speed of light. You go 72 hours straight without so much as a coffee break. You don't need sleep, you don't need nourishment. If it's sex you're after, you go all night. Then you crash—it's like falling down a well, like parachuting without a parachute. You want to hold on to something and there's nothing there but air."

Even if the drug is administered under proper clinical conditions, amphetamines force brain cells to relay signals faster, which creates euphoria, increased energy, nervousness, and changes in behavior and thought patterns. But Dr. Jacobson was not coordinating the shots with President Kennedy's other medicines, and he typically mixed his amphetamine shots with painkillers, hormones, vitamins, human placenta, and unknown other ingredients in a grotesque, cramped little office in New York. One patient explained Jacobson's procedure: "He took a syringe and made up a kind of cocktail from lots of vials, in different colors that were wheeled in like an hors d'oeuvres tray."

One night, Dr. Jacobson took one of his patients, fashion photographer Bob Richardson, to see the mysterious back room where his elixirs were formulated. "There were cauldrons and masses of rocks and things boiling around," recalled Richardson, who began seeing Jacobson in 1963. "It was like science fiction." In 1972, when he was under investigation by federal and state drug and medical authorities, Jacobson explained to *Newsweek* that magnetic fields, phosphorescent minerals, and ultraviolet rays were crucial to the mixing of his potions, which he also regularly injected himself with.

In June 1961 JFK secretly took Jacobson along to Vienna to shoot him up in preparation for his summit with Soviet premier Nikita Khrushchev, but Kennedy's performance in their closed-door meetings was by his own account disastrous. Attorney General Robert Kennedy was so concerned about the possible dangers of drug ingredients in Jacobson's elixirs that he wanted to have them tested by both the Food and Drug Administration and the FBI laboratory. JFK dismissed his brother's concerns with the crack, "I don't care if it's horse piss. It works."

In January 1961 John Kennedy had inherited a United States in which multitudes of black American citizens in the South still dwelled in a Dark Age of racial injustice, a de facto racial dictatorship in a number of states where they were terrorized from voting and forced into separate and unequal public facilities. Only a fraction of 1 percent of black students in the South attended integrated schools, and the number of blacks holding real political power in the entire nation could barely be counted on one hand.

Until he decided to run for the White House, the multimillionaire Kennedy had achieved nothing for black civil rights. Indeed, his entire twelve-year record in Congress was nearly devoid of any major accomplishments at all. But as a personality, as a speaker and as a campaigner, Kennedy was electrifying, and he owed his razor-thin election victory in part to strong support from those African-Americans who could vote, which he captured through several low-cost gestures.

First, Kennedy declared that discrimination in federally assisted housing could be eliminated with "the stroke of a pen," implying that he would issue such an executive order if he was elected. "The next President of the United States," argued Kennedy in a slap at the retiring Eisenhower, "cannot stand above the battle engaging in vague little sermons on brotherhood." At the Democratic Convention, the Massachusetts senator had pushed through a strong civil rights plank, and during his first televised debate with Vice President Nixon he spoke eloquently of the plight of minority children. Then, on October 20, 1960, just days before the election, Kennedy placed a sympathy phone call to a pregnant Coretta Scott King as her husband, the Reverend Martin Luther King, Jr., sat in a Georgia jail.

"No presidential candidate," observed historian Carl Brauer, "had ever before given such prominence to the cruel human consequences of discrimination." Civil rights leader Roy Wilkins noted that Kennedy "had a grace and a charm and above all an intelligence on this thing that immediately invited you in to commune with him on it, so to speak."

Black voters, accustomed to generations of presidential indifference to civil rights, were impressed, and they rewarded Kennedy with an overwhelming margin of their votes. Kennedy's election marked a stunning shift in black voting: In 1956 blacks voted Republican by a 60–40 margin, but in 1960 the split was 70–30 in favor of the Democrats.

But in the instant that he captured the Oval Office, John Kennedy shoved the issue of delivering full citizenship to black Americans toward the bottom of his priority list by not even mentioning it in his inaugural address. As a matter of principle and of patrician good manners, Kennedy was sympathetic to the distant theoretical goal of black civil rights, but it was a sideshow to his main concern: managing the worldwide ideological and military competition with the Soviet Union. JFK was preoccupied with superpower relations—mainly U.S.–Soviet tensions over Berlin and Cuba—and would not fully commit the presidency to the civil rights struggle. He was drawing criticism from many civil rights activists for moving too slowly. The time is not right, JFK told them in private over and over.

"What disappointed me most," wrote Kennedy's own civil rights assistant Harris Wofford, "was not so much the President's recurring decision to wait, for which he had reasons I understood, as the way he made the decision—each time hurriedly, at the last minute, in response to Southern political pressures without careful consideration of an overall strategy."

Kennedy saw civil rights abuses not as a national disgrace but as a propaganda embarrassment that damaged America's image in the world. "The President believed that segregation, like colonialism, was an anachronistic addiction curable by the steady advance of modern attitudes," wrote historian Taylor Branch in his epic saga of the civil rights years, *Parting the Waters*. "To him, this required the exercise of cool, detached reason in an atmosphere of public calm, which was incompatible with emotional demonstrations by either whites or Negroes."

Despite his muscular man-of-action campaign rhetoric, John Kennedy was a cold-blooded political technocrat with a brutally pragmatic view of presidential power, a philosophy that ruled out squandering political capital on lost causes. "There is no sense in raising hell, and then not being successful," Kennedy explained in an Oval Office discussion with reporters in December 1962. "There is no sense in putting the office of the Presidency on the line on an issue, and then being defeated." Another time he observed that "Every president must endure a gap between what he would like and what is possible."

Kennedy's extremely cautious approach to civil rights stemmed in part from his microscopic popular-vote margin; at only 112,803 more than Nixon's it was the smallest yet in history. JFK's enormous public popularity in office was slipping, from a March 1962 high of 79 percent in the Gallup Poll to a mid-September score of 67 percent, still very high compared to other presidents.

By background and temperament, John F. Kennedy was not conditioned to be a civil rights crusader. He was not a bigot, but he lived the pampered and spoiled life of the superrich, where black people appeared strictly as bit players hovering in the background, usually as domestic servants. His World War II years were spent in the notoriously segregated U.S. Navy, and during his career in Congress he largely ignored black issues other than paying lip service to his relatively small constituency of Massachusetts blacks. Like a great many American whites, he had no black intimates or business associates, other than the very occasional token black secretary or junior staffer. Almost every morning for the last fifteen years of his life, he was greeted by a pleasant black face, belonging to his valet George Thomas.

One overriding problem seemed to doom any new civil rights laws in the Age of Kennedy: in Congress, he faced a brick wall of conservative Republicans and Southern Democrats, a working majority that the president knew would torpedo any strong federal civil rights legislation he would care to propose. For now, any such legislation was a lost cause, dead on arrival in Congress.

"He had at this point, I think, a terrible ambivalence about civil rights," noted Kennedy aide and historian Arthur M. Schlesinger, Jr., about JFK's first year in the White House. "While he did not doubt the depth of the injustice or the need for remedy, he had read the arithmetic of the new Congress and concluded that there was no possible chance of passing a new civil rights bill." After one meeting with Kennedy, Rev. Martin Luther King, Jr., noted glumly, "I'm afraid that the fact is he's got the understanding and he's got the political skill . . . but the moral passion is lacking." King concluded that JFK's first year in office was "essentially cautious and defensive" and aimed at the "limited goal of token integration."

Another barrier to presidential action on civil rights was White House officials trying to shield Kennedy from taking risks on the issue, risks he was unlikely to take in the first place. "John Kennedy was not a convinced and devoted proponent of civil rights as a policy," recalled State Department official Pedro Sanjuan, who as Kennedy's campaign strategist on minorities in 1960 had helped deliver the crucial state of New York, and was now trying to break down racial barriers in the State Department.

"The White House staff was very seriously divided on the issue of civil rights," recalled Sanjuan. "The 'Irish Mafia' of Kenny O'Donnell [appointments secretary], Ted Reardon [cabinet assistant] and Larry O'Brien [congressional-affairs assistant] were focusing entirely on Jack—what's good for Jack, what's bad for Jack—and they couldn't care less about civil rights. Generally speaking they thought it was not a good idea. They thought it would get the president in trouble." Kennedy's closest White House aide, chief speechwriter and special counsel Theodore C. Sorensen, was much different, Sanjuan remembered, as was Cabinet Secretary Fred Dutton. "They were willing to recognize and to help those things that had merit anywhere, particularly in the civil rights area." But civil rights proponents could rarely penetrate what Sanjuan called the "ring of steel" of caution that surrounded Kennedy, an attitude that deeply penetrated the president's own mind.

When the Freedom Riders invaded the South in the spring of 1961, John Kennedy publicly supported their right to demonstrate, but privately saw them as "a pain in the ass" in the words of his Deputy Attorney General Nicholas Katzenbach, and nothing more. The president was furious that the Freedom Riders were embarrassing him on the eve of the Vienna summit with Soviet prime minister Nikita Khrushchev. "Tell them to call it off! Stop them!" he barked at an aide. "You're making my life difficult," Kennedy told the U.S. Civil Rights Commission when it wanted to hold public hearings on discrimination in Mississippi. "I would appreciate it if you didn't."

Kennedy sat on his "stroke of the pen" pledge to ban discrimination in federal housing and did nothing on it for nearly two years, as angry civil rights activists mailed boxes full of pens to the White House. To mollify the South, JFK appointed five segregationists to the federal bench, including one, William Howard Cox of Mississippi, who later referred to black civil rights activists as "niggers" and "chimpanzees."

While the White House was fervently dodging legislative action on civil rights, something astonishing was happening at the Justice Department, where President Kennedy had dumped the entire issue into the lap of his thirty-seven-year-old younger brother Robert Kennedy, the attorney general.

From the baronial splendor of his gigantic inherited office in Room 5115 of the Justice Department building, amid tennis sneakers and footballs and strewn crayon drawings by his children, Bobby Kennedy and his staff were doing something no other federal agency had ever done before. They were seriously encouraging, nurturing, and cooperating with the detonating movement for black civil rights. They did it sometimes reluctantly, angrily, and even petulantly. They did it in part because they wanted to control and slow the movement down, shut it up and grab as many black votes as they could without triggering a white Southern backlash—but they were doing it. And compared to every administration before them, this was a radical and revolutionary moment in American history.

RFK had run his brother's 1960 presidential campaign with brutal back-alley precision, and was rewarded with the job of the nation's chief law-enforcement officer, even though he'd never tried a single case in court. Robert Kennedy's mission in life now was to protect and serve his brother, in part by keeping what the president called "this God-damned civil rights mess" off his desk and, if possible, out of the headlines.

As young men growing up, John and Robert Kennedy had not been particularly close—the poised and aloof John was the polar personality opposite of the rumpled, pugnacious Bobby. But since the 1960 campaign, Bobby had become a one-man hit squad, idea factory, sounding board, and protective shield for the president. An unnamed top foreign-policy official told the *New York Times* that Bobby "has the President's confidence as no other human being does." The atmosphere between the brothers was intense, irreverent, informal, and fast-moving. The two communicated almost telepathically, finishing each other's sentences in their own verbal shorthand. Under Secretary of State Chester Bowles noted, "Management in Jack's mind, I think, consists largely of calling Bob on the telephone and saying, 'Here are ten things I want to get done. Why don't you go ahead and get them done.' "

In 1961, with the President's approval, the younger Kennedy embarked on a strategy of quiet, behind-the-scenes persuasion to try to get Southern officials to voluntarily comply with judicial desegregation, backed by the threat of legal action. To try to appease black demands, forty black attorneys were hired in the Justice Department, and the Interstate Commerce Commission was ordered to ban discrimination in interstate travel. Justice Department officials even held strategy meetings with civil rights activists and private foundations to launch the Voter Education Project, an effort to register black voters in the South, who would, it was naturally hoped, gratefully gravitate toward Democratic tickets.

Before 1961 Bobby Kennedy had no more interest in the violation of black citizenship than his older brother had. As he put it, "I wasn't lying awake thinking about the Negro in this country." But he quickly proved much more susceptible to the issue than the president. "Bobby was very different," argued Pedro Sanjuan, who was installed by the younger Kennedy in the State Department. "He was a man who had made an enormous transition from being a right-wing conservative when he was general counsel for the McCarthy hearings. Bobby was in the process of transitioning. He was changing. Bobby was much stronger than Jack was on civil rights. Bobby was conflicted; he had problems with how the push for civil rights was going to affect the next election, but Bobby was pushing and supporting, and he had instilled fear in the White House on the issue. He was sort of self-propelled in the direction of civil rights. He thought you had to do certain things because they were right."

The giant wall map in the Justice Department "War Room" was soon bristling with colored pins indicating civil rights legal action across the South. There were even a few pins stuck in the state of Mississippi, the heart of the empire of white supremacy and perhaps the most hopeless of cases, where only 5 percent of voting-age black citizens were registered. In August 1962 the Justice Department announced plans for a broad legal attack on voting barriers in the state.

At his side, the attorney general had an energetic, bustling team of shirt-sleeved lawyers helping him, bristling with Ivy League diplomas and supremely convinced of their own talents. They were not always as bright or as young as advertised—a number of them were past forty—but they were devoted like swains to serve their leader Bobby, and they all believed in the moral justice of civil rights. One of them, Burke Marshall, had been a corporate attorney for clients such as the Du Ponts and Standard Oil. Bobby put him in charge of the Civil Rights Division.

John Doar was a lanky thirty-nine-year-old Republican and Princeton grad from a small town in Wisconsin who joined the Civil Rights Division at the tail end of the Eisenhower administration and was held over by Kennedy, perhaps because he was the only Eisenhower appointee who seemed to have a pulse. He soon became a legend in civil rights circles as a combat lawyer in the trenches. As early as April 1961, he decided to personally investigate conditions in Tennessee and Mississippi, so he disguised himself in beat-up clothes, rented a car, and traveled hundreds of dusty miles through the countryside, interviewing black voting applicants and building cases against racist state officials.

The number-two man in the Justice Department was a huge, chuckling, casually disheveled chain-smoker and Rhodes scholar with the mellifluous name of Nicholas deBelleville Katzenbach, the deputy attorney general. His pedigree could not be more elite: scion of a leading Episcopal family in Princeton, New Jersey; son of a New Jersey attorney general; Philips Exeter Academy, Princeton, and Oxford graduate; editor-in-chief of the *Yale Law Journal;* law professor at the University of Chicago. On February 23, 1943, as Army Air Force navigator on a B-26 Mitchell bomber, he casually held on to his smoking pipe when his plane was shot down and the craft fell into the Mediterranean. Katzenbach was rescued by an Italian seaplane and spent twenty-seven months in Axis prison camps, escaped twice, was recaptured twice, and continued his studies by devouring four hundred books loaned to the prison library from the Red Cross and YMCA.

The Kennedy men thought themselves a cool, tough bunch of action men. Like JFK, most of them had been junior officers in World War II, and that bond united them in a spirit of "top-gun" teamwork, relentless self-confidence, and contempt for what they saw as the lethargic style of the somnolent Eisenhower years. They were unshakably loyal to the president and attorney general and showered them with blind faith and eighty-hour workweeks. In return, as long as they stayed loyal and didn't leak secrets to the press, the Kennedys backed them up, supported them if they screwed up, and treated them as partners rather than employees, expecting them to argue their cases and disagree with them as they saw fit.

But for all their talents, the Kennedy men suffered under a colossal misconception—they thought they could steer and control the movement for full black citizenship. They thought they could do it with brains, charm, diligence, logic, and back-room negotiation.

They did not know it yet, but they were already being swallowed up by the movement, a vast, unstoppable force propelled by people such as Rosa Parks, the Little Rock Nine, Medgar Evers, Autherine Lucy, Amzie Moore, Clyde Kennard, and Rev. Martin Luther King, Jr.

As of September 10, 1962, retired air force sergeant James Meredith was at the controls.

CHAPTER FOUR

We Shall Be Invincible

■　■　■　■

The south is armed for revolt. . . . These white people will accept another civil war knowing they're going to lose.

—William Faulkner, 1956

ON SEPTEMBER 11, 1962, the day after Supreme Court Justice Hugo Black ordered James Meredith's admission to the University of Mississippi, the Democratic governor of Mississippi was under siege in his own office, battered by a maelstrom of conflicting advice and feuding advisors as America's past and future collided on his watch.

Governor Ross Robert Barnett's piercing, hawklike gray eyes peered through Coke-bottle spectacles out his office window in the Mississippi State Capitol building toward the giant *Monument to Confederate Womanhood* amid the oak and pecan trees, where two angelic women nursed a wounded Confederate soldier as he clutched the rebel colors pointed down on the ground. "To the women of the Confederacy," the inscription read, "whose pious ministrations to our wounded soldiers soothed the last hours of those who died far from the objects of their tenderest love." The governor could have been thinking of his own mother and grandmother, both of whom married Confederate soldiers.

For sixty-four-year-old Ross Barnett, the vision of a Confederate republic was not a remote abstraction but a physical reality, a current in his own bloodstream, something he touched and heard in his own lifetime, in the not-too-distant echoes of his own father's voice. As a boy in Leake County, Barnett would sit on the porch under a china-berry tree and listen to his father, John William Barnett, tell tales of his years as a Confederate soldier, witnessing the siege of Vicksburg, having his horse shot out from under him at the Battle of Shiloh, and seeing his own father, Captain John Henry Barnett, return home from four years in the Confederate army in clothes riddled by Union gunfire.

The man sitting at the desk was described by *Time* magazine as "as bitter a racist as inhabits the nation." His cavernous office was fitted with Italian tile, a thick green carpet, a fireplace, and formal drapes. A wooden plaque on the desk read, "Ross R. Barnett, Governor," and next to it were a Bible, pens, and piles of papers. The Mississippi and U.S. flags stood behind the padded executive chair. The governor sported a shiny basic-black suit, a gray cowlick, and the dignified, reserved manner of a small-town mortician. One Mississippi newspaperman, Ira B. Harkey, Jr., of the *Chronicle* in Pascagoula, reported that when Barnett smiled, the effect "was as astonishing and repelling as a grin on the face of a vulture."

Perched high above Barnett's second-floor office, a giant copper eagle coated in 14-karat gold leaf soared atop the Mississippi Capitol dome, which dominated the skyline and seemed to tower over the state and its luminous, tortured history.

There, a few dozen miles to the southwest were the remnants of Brierfield Plantation, the eight-hundred-acre cotton estate built by Jefferson Davis in 1838. And there, at the northeastern corner of the state was Brice's Crossroads, where General Nathan Bedford Forrest defeated a Union force almost three times the size of his own command. To the north and west were the sprawling floodplain of the Delta country and the rich commercial lifeblood of the Mississippi River, where Mississippians had fought a hopeless David and Goliath campaign against the advance of General U. S. Grant's forces.

At Yazoo Pass, the rebels stopped Grant's entire floating army by blocking the channel with one sunken vessel, *The Star of the West*. At Yazoo City, the commander of the Confederate ironclad *The Arkansas* took on the whole enemy fleet, paralyzing Union operations in the region for three weeks.

But by May 1863, Grant's forces had surrounded the prize jewel of Vicksburg, forty miles west of the capital. After a six-week siege, the port city fell, a surrender that Grant considered the turning point of the Civil War. Nearly a hundred years later, rebel boys carved in stone stood atop countless Confederate monuments in town squares and village greens across the state, as if they were scanning the horizons for the federal troops that might come again some day to their twilight empire.

On the surface, Governor Barnett ruled a lush and tranquil land blanketed with luxuriant forests of virgin pines, tupelo, sycamore, persimmon, magnolia, holly, sweet gum, and hickory, from gentle foothills in the north to cypress swamps curtained with Spanish moss and Gulf Coast resorts in the south.

Deep in the Mississippi interior were haunted mansions, foot-stomping revival churches, and tin-roofed general stores selling fish bait, Moon Pies, and RC Cola. It was a semitropical country of blast-furnace summers and fire-and-brimstone religion, the only remaining "dry" state in the nation, without a single legal tavern or liquor store.

Barnett did not look like the elected chief executive of a one-party terrorist police state, nor did he resemble a man about to launch an insurrection against the U.S. government. He looked more like an old-fashioned country lawyer, which is exactly what he was before he became governor of Mississippi in 1960. He was dignified, courteous, and steeped in the courtly politeness of Mississippi. He was also one of the last great Southern-showman performance-artist politicians, a throwback to the time before the days of fancy sound systems, when a politician had to roar and holler at the county fair so that the folks in the back row could hear him.

As a young man, Barnett built up his savings in an old coffee can on a cupboard shelf by picking cotton stalks as a field hand, working as a schoolhouse janitor, operating an outdoor barbershop, and organizing a fourteen-piece brass band that played county fairs across the state, with Barnett playing the French horn.

In the summertime, to pay his college expenses, Barnett rode buses and trains through Alabama and Mississippi as a door-to-door salesman for Wearever aluminum products, dragging a pair of huge sample cases that held seventy-two pounds of cooking utensils, pots, and pans. He set up demonstrations for groups of housewives, un-folded a jumbo sales chart, baked a cake on top of a stove, then cooked a roast without using any water or grease. He'd have a little girl serve fresh-baked cornmeal cakes, then award a prize to the lady who could write down the two best reasons why every kitchen should be equipped with Wearever.

After graduating from the University of Mississippi law school, Barnett built up one of the biggest and most profitable law firms in the state, specializing in personal-injury damage suits against corporations. "He was not a brilliant lawyer," recalled onetime University of Mississippi law school dean Robert Farley. "He was a brilliant jury manipulator, but I don't think anybody ever accused Ross of knowing much law."

A good part of Barnett's clients were black, and he tackled and won many cases for poor blacks that most other law firms wouldn't touch. A tale was told of an old black man who was injured on the job and was asked, "What doctor do you want us to call?" He quickly replied, "I want you to call Doctor Ross Barnett!"

In 1959, on his third try for governor, Barnett was elected to lead the poorest state in the nation. He did so by promising the white voters of Mississippi that the state would be perfectly and perpetually segregated between whites and blacks, whom he publicly referred to as "niggers."

"I believe that the Good Lord was the original segregationist," declared Barnett. "Mixing the races," he explained, "leads inevitably to the production of an inferior mongrel." Another time he intoned, "The Negro is different because God made him different to punish him. His forehead slants back. His nose is different. His lips are different. And his color is sure different." Said Barnett, "If a Negro wants to make good, we'll go all out to help him, but God intended that we shouldn't mix."

The bulwark of segregation in Mississippi was the public-school system, which state officials claimed would achieve the vision of "separate but equal," with state funding of new black schools allegedly totaling $57 million in the late 1950s versus $29 million for new white schools. But all this achieved was an inefficient double-school system, where total per-student spending for whites dwarfed that for blacks.

Barnett left no doubt that he would defend segregation with physical force. "Nobody wants violence," he asserted in one campaign speech, "but red-blooded Southerners should not turn aside from a fight when such important principles are involved—a fight to preserve what we know to be right." He pledged, "Ross Barnett will rot in jail before he will let one Negro ever darken the sacred threshold of our white schools."

Barnett was described by then University of Mississippi history professor James Silver as "militantly stubborn, more negative than conservative, an inflexible racist with a mind relatively innocent of history, constitutional law, and the processes of government." On the campaign trail, Barnett was transformed from a kindly grandfather figure into a zealot of scorching defiance and ferocity.

"Friends," growled Barnett before one segregationist meeting after his election, "I am a Mississippi segregationist—and I am proud of it!"

"We must separate the men from the boys!" he thundered. "We must now identify the traitors in our midst! We must eliminate the cowards from our front lines! You did not elect me Governor to bargain away your heritage in a smoke-filled hotel room!" In a news film of the speech, as Barnett roars, you can almost feel the paint on the walls melt.

By 1962 Mississippi was gingerly trying to gain a toehold in the twentieth century, as new industrial projects sprouted up, from a missile-testing range on the Gulf Coast to a bustling shipyard at Pascagoula and new office towers in the languid capital city of Jackson, population 145,000, perched on the bluffs of the Pearl River. A high-tech project at the Jackson Coliseum allowed Jacksonians to go ice-skating on a scorching July 4 for the first time in history.

But Ross Barnett was heir to a political tradition that often cursed Mississippi with leaders of neolithic racism and appalling backwardness. Mississippi's governor at the beginning of the century was the "Great White Chief," James K. Vardaman, who proclaimed that the Negro was a "veneered savage," a "lazy, lying, lustful animal which no conceivable amount of training can transform into a tolerable citizen." "Why squander money on his education," he asked, "when the only effect is to spoil a good field hand and make an insolent cook?" With Vardaman's election as U.S. senator in 1911, the so-called redneck small farmers of the northeastern Mississippi hills seized political power from the patrician planters and aristocrats of the Delta, tightening the stranglehold of militant white supremacy.

Vardaman's successor, a screeching, pint-sized crank and Ku Klux Klan member named Theodore Bilbo, was even worse. As governor from 1916 to 1920 and 1928 to 1934, and U.S. senator from 1934 to

1947, Bilbo openly encouraged violence to keep blacks from voting. "You know and I know what's the best way to keep the nigger from voting," Bilbo brayed before audiences of desperately poor whites. "You do it the night before the election. I don't have to tell you any more than that. Red-blooded men know what I mean." Luckily, Bilbo noted, state law required voters to explain a state constitution that "damn few white men and no niggers at all can explain."

Bilbo in turn was followed by arch-segregationist U.S. senator James O. Eastland, who charged that the Supreme Court was "brainwashed by left-wing pressure groups." When inviting guests for a weekend at his estate, he'd jokingly tell them to "pick out a nigger girl and a horse!"

Many white Mississippians reacted with instant panic to the 1954 *Brown* decision outlawing racial segregation. "The south is armed for revolt," William Faulkner declared to journalist Russell Warren Howe of the *London Sunday Times* in 1956. "After the Supreme Court decision you couldn't get as much as a few rounds for a deer rifle in Mississippi," Faulkner reported. "The gunsmiths were sold out. These white people will accept another civil war knowing they're going to lose." Faulkner, like President Eisenhower, foresaw the real possibility of armed conflict. "The trouble is the North doesn't know that country," Faulkner explained. "They don't know the South will go to war."

Faulkner, like all white Americans, was trapped inside the hypocrisies and contradictions of race. He worked, laughed, rode with, and wrote about black people much of his life, and he hated the violence and oppression inflicted on the black race. He was against compulsory segregation, and that view branded him as worse than a Communist in the view of some whites. But he also was against immediate, "forced" integration, believing that blacks weren't ready for it and whites would never permit it.

Faulkner was also convinced that Northerners knew nothing of the South, and that this was extremely dangerous. Northerners, believed Faulkner, thought the Civil War proved to Southerners that they were wrong, when in fact it did no such thing, as he wrote in his "Letter to the North" published in *Life* magazine in 1956, because "the Southerner already knew he was wrong and accepted that gambit even when he knew it was the fatal one. What that war should have done, but failed to do, was to prove to the North that the South will go to any length, even that fatal and already doomed one, before it will accept alteration of its racial condition by mere force of law or economic threat."

Within four months of *Brown,* the Mississippi legislature passed a measure permitting the total abolition of public schools in order to block integration. In 1956 the legislature declared *Brown* "invalid" and enacted a "Resolution of Interposition," which required all state officials to "prohibit, by any lawful, peaceful, and constitutional means, the implementation of or the compliance with the Integration Decisions of the United States Supreme Court." It also established a "Sovereignty Commission" to "protect the sovereignty of the State of Mississippi, and her sister states from encroachment thereon by the Federal Government."

The Sovereignty Commission was one of the darkest blots on Mississippi history, a "thought police agency" that violated the most basic concepts of American democracy. For almost two decades it operated as a "private Gestapo," according to then state representative Philip Bryant of Oxford, using public funds for "cloak-and-dagger investigations that develop into character assassinations."

The commission fielded a staff of several full-time investigators, collected secret files on the political opinions of more than sixty thousand white and black citizens and made cash payments to a network of tipsters and informers, including black "collaborationist" spies. One of the black collaborators was Percy Green, publisher of the *Jackson Advocate* weekly black newspaper, who acted both as a spy and as a pro-segregationist propagandist for the commission.

"The tragic truth about this secret-police procedure is that it is advanced by well-meaning citizens," noted editor Oliver Emmerich of the *State Times* of Jackson. "It is being done in the name of patriotism." The *Tylertown Times,* a weekly in southeastern Mississippi, described the atmosphere as one where "neighbor informs upon neighbor, where state-hired spies fill files in Jackson with information on 'suspicious characters,' and self-appointed Junior G Men scurry about Mississippi keeping the campaign of hate and suspicion fed to a fever pitch."

As soon as he was sworn into office, Ross Barnett launched a crash program to try to attract new business and industry to his apartheid state, logging tens of thousands of air miles on out-of-state sales-promotion tours and regaling out-of-town investment prospects at the Governor's Mansion with breakfasts of grits, country ham, buttermilk biscuits, red-eye gravy, and Leake County molasses.

On Sundays Barnett taught Baptist Sunday school class, and during the week, he'd invite perfect strangers on the street to lunch at the Governor's Mansion, asking, "Hey, you wanna have potluck with me?" Barnett was once even spotted escorting a black family into the Capitol cafeteria (through the rear entrance) for a sit-down lunch as the governor's guest, although Barnett sat at another table. "He was nice to blacks," said one Barnett aide. "He just didn't believe in integration."

Barnett ran for governor promising that any citizen of Mississippi could see him any day without an appointment. "My door is always open," he declared. "Just kick open the door and ask for ol' Ross!" As a result, hundreds of citizens lined up every day to see Barnett, and he took special joy in parading schoolchildren into his office to shake his hand, sometimes 150 at a time. He regularly pressed twenty-dollar bills from his personal bank account into the hands of little old ladies and homeless people who besieged him with hard-luck stories on the street.

Barnett put in back-breaking hours, tried to balance the state budget every single day, and worked past nine or ten o'clock, sometimes locking the Capitol doors himself because he worked later than even the security guard. Mississippians chuckled at his periodic *faux pas,* like the time he addressed the Beth Israel Temple in Jackson by noting, "There is nothing finer than a group of people meeting in true Christian fellowship."

But by the fall of 1962, Barnett was in trouble as governor, locked in debilitating power feuds with the state legislature, overpromising jobs to supporters, and spending through a $34 million budget surplus while jacking up the sales tax on cigarettes. His popularity scraped bottom when it was revealed that he spent $312,000 of taxpayer funds to renovate the Governor's Mansion, including the installment of gold-plated bathtub-faucet handles.

Now, there was the potentially apocalyptic problem of James Meredith, who was armed with a federal court order that demanded his admission to the University of Mississippi. James Meredith might have the federal government on his side, but on Ross Barnett's side was a man who, at that time, had more power in Mississippi than the president of the United States.

His name was Bill Simmons.

If the Southern Rebellion of 1861–1865 had succeeded and the Confederate States of America had endured until 1962, the charming, brilliant William J. "Big Bill" Simmons might have been its ambassador to England or France, or even secretary of state. As it was he was now Ross Barnett's de facto secretary of war, his senior adviser, strategist, and speechwriter on race matters. On the subject of race, it was Bill Simmons, not Ross Barnett, who ruled Mississippi.

Bill Simmons was the forty-six-year-old chief of the most powerful and feared political organization in Mississippi, the Citizens Council, as well as national administrator of the multistate Citizens Council of America. He was a sophisticated, wealthy, full-time segregationist intellectual, with a body that towered like an oak tree and a face like that of a thickened Clark Gable. His office gazed down commandingly upon the Governor's Mansion across the street.

Just a few weeks after the Supreme Court's *Brown* decision in 1954, a group of enraged, determined white community leaders convened an emergency meeting in the bayou town of Indianola in Sunflower County, Mississippi, and formed the Citizens Council, a society sworn to uphold segregation. With Bill Simmons as its full-time administrator and Robert "Tut" Patterson from Greenwood as its executive secretary, the Citizens Council movement blossomed in Mississippi and spread like kudzu into Alabama, Arkansas, Florida, Louisiana, South Carolina, and Texas, as well as linking up with similar groups in Georgia, North Carolina, Tennessee, and Virginia. By the end of the decade, the Citizens Council movement claimed a total of 250,000 members across the South.

In a 2000 interview, Tut Patterson, a former Mississippi State football star and army paratrooper who was at the first founding meeting of the Citizens Council in 1954, asserted that "everybody in the South felt like we did, with very few exceptions. We had the very finest people; ministers, lawyers, judges. It was a very fine, high-class, patriotic organization. In a nutshell, what we were trying to do was to protect our rights under the Tenth Amendment—the right to govern ourselves, for instance to control our own schools." At the time, the Citizens Council was not at all a renegade force or historical aberration—it articulated the majority view of many white Mississippians, and many other white Americans for that matter, who thought that integration was a bad idea.

Like Ross Barnett, Citizens Council chief William Simmons was a child of the Confederacy. A distant ancestor was states' rights hero John C. Calhoun, the senator and vice president who in the 1840s articulated the theory of nullification, or the argument that a state could ignore a federal order it objected to. Simmons's grandfather George W. Simmons fought in the infantry at Vicksburg and his great-grandfather William Alexander Noble was killed at Shiloh in 1862.

Simmons graduated from Mississippi College, traveled widely through Europe, studied French literature at the Institute of Touraine in France, and in 1940 joined the British army Royal Engineers in Trinidad, where he witnessed what he saw as the failures of an integrated system. He returned to Jackson after the war to launch airline and energy ventures, manage his substantial family investments, and run the Citizens Council, which he hoped would be the spearhead of a national conservative revolt.

"The general aims of the Citizens Council," Simmons proclaimed, "are to preserve racial integrity and to further the cause of state's rights—that is, our dual-sovereignty form of government." He argued that "the average Negro brain has a cerebral cortex fourteen percent thinner than that of the average white brain."

Simmons's rhetoric was simultaneously soothing and inflammatory. "In our section, segregation works quite well," he explained to one Northern audience. "It consists of easily acquired customs and a pattern of correct behavior between the races which have evolved out of the demands of necessity and a respect for obvious race differences." Simmons admitted, "Segregation is not perfect, even as no human effort is perfect. But it works, and the South will keep it."

Unlike the Ku Klux Klan, which drew support from the poorest whites, the Citizens Council opposed violence and attracted top community leaders from the ranks of the middle and upper classes—doctors, lawyers, and businessmen recruited through the Rotary and Lions and Kiwanis Clubs. In the state capital of Jackson, Citizens Council members included the governor, the mayor, much of the police force, and a galaxy of business and civic leaders.

Critics dismissed the council as an "uptown Klan," but council leaders saw themselves as a bulwark against Klan violence and claimed credit for the fact that it was dormant in Mississippi. Citizens Council membership became so accepted a badge of civil distinction in Mississippi that political leaders added it to their campaign literature.

"The Council is infinitely strengthened in Mississippi by the fact that the state is still basically agrarian, made up of small communities and towns in which the dissenter can find few allies," explained Hodding Carter III in 1961, then editor of *The Delta Democrat-Times* in Greenville, and one of the few moderates willing to speak out. "It is almost impossible to find a business or professional man who is not at least a nominal Council member. It just isn't good business not to belong."

The council sponsored segregationist radio and TV shows, school essay contests, and propaganda mailings, and kept files on white citizens to eradicate any glimmerings of dissent. Among the organizations the council listed as subversive to the "Mississippi way of life" were the FBI, the Methodist Church, the Department of the Air Force, and the YMCA. The leading newspapers and TV and radio stations in Jackson were controlled by Citizens Council hard-liners, who kept up a steady drumbeat of segregationist editorials and slanted news coverage. Mrs. Myrlie Evers reported that "the blackout of TV news on civil rights had gone so far that network news programming originating in New York were systematically interrupted with signs indicating technical difficulties whenever the news turned to race."

Hodding Carter III explained what happened to those who resisted the council: "The dissenter is a 'nigger lover,' a 'nest fouler,' a 'scalawag' or a renegade white. When the charges are repeated often enough in Mississippi's present climate of opinion, they begin to stick, and the non-conformist becomes the local pariah."

One small businessman explained why he joined the Citizens Council: "Three men came to see me and asked me to join. One was my banker, who holds the mortgage on my house. One was my lawyer. And the third was my wife's brother!" The Citizens Council threatened dissenting whites with economic boycotts and had dissenting blacks fired from their jobs, tossed off their farms, and harassed by banks and utility companies.

One council sympathizer, a lawyer, explained bluntly, "What the niggers want is race mixing. Nigger men have a thing about white women. Look what happens when nigger soldiers go overseas. In the South we like niggers. The NAACP won't give a scrap of food to stray niggers but we do and we're glad to do it. Niggers have no morals. Half their kids are illegitimate. Now we just can't have our white children going to school with a pack of nigger kids!"

Federal judge John Minor Wisdom described Mississippi as living in an "eerie atmosphere of Never-Never Land," and the Citizens Council was turning the state's elementary and high schools into an upside-down world of racist education where children were nourished on state-sponsored racial hatred like mother's milk. Children were special targets of Citizens Council propaganda, and school libraries and textbooks were censored by council watchdogs.

Mrs. Sara McCorkle, the council's director of women's activities, reported "wonderful cooperation" from state school administrators in distributing hundreds of pro-segregation books with lessons like, "Negroes are lazy. . . . It is difficult to tell when they are lying and when they are telling the truth. . . . They will steal chickens, food, small sums of money, etc."

The official council manual for the public-school fourth grade taught, "God wanted the white people to live alone. And He wanted colored people to live alone. . . . Negroes use their own bathrooms. They do not use the white people's bathroom. The Negro has his own part of town to live in. This is called our Southern Way of Life. Do you know that some people want the Negroes to live with white people? These people want us to be unhappy. . . . God made us different. And God knows best."

Another grade-school lesson read, "Famous scientists say races are very different. The white man is very civilized, while the pure Negro in Africa is still living as a savage." A typical council essay contest–winner declared, "We in the South do not intend to obey men, however exalted their seats or black their robes and hearts. We intend to obey the laws of God and the laws of this country which are made in accordance with the Constitution. As long as we live, so long shall we be segregated."

"The closed society of Mississippi thus swears allegiance to a prevailing creed with over a hundred years of homage behind it," reported University of Mississippi history professor James Silver, himself a transplanted New Yorker. "Based on antique assumptions no longer tenable and on a legendary past," wrote Silver, "the doctrine of white supremacy is guarded by a bureaucracy, by ceaseless, high-powered and skillful indoctrination employing both persuasion and fear, and by the elimination, without regard for law or ethics, of those who will not go along."

The Citizens Council was financed in part with state tax funds passed through the Mississippi State Sovereignty Commission. Together, the Citizens Council and Sovereignty Commission enjoyed almost total control of state power. The result, argued James Silver, was that "the closed society of Mississippi comes as near to approximating a police state as anything we have seen in America."

The Citizens Council's takeover of Mississippi was completed in 1959 with the election of the council's hand-selected Democratic candidate Ross Barnett to the governor's chair. Barnett's office became a revolving door—Big Bill Simmons and his associates would stride in and press him on racial matters; his back would stiffen in resistance; then moderate advisers would cool the governor down. Barnett's moderate advisers, led by top Jackson attorney Tom Watkins, were against integration, but they saw the end was in sight and knew they couldn't win a pitched battle with the federal government. They especially feared the impact that such a battle would have on Mississippi's fragile business prospects.

But Barnett's hard-line advisers, led by Simmons, had both irresistible arguments and naked power on their side, as well as the hearts and minds of a great many white Mississippians. Simmons and the hard-liners railed for a "line in the sand—you shall not go an inch further" showdown. Not only did they see no other alternative, they actually thought it might work. "One of Mississippi's great problems," noted longtime Jackson reporter Bill Minor, "is that it can live in the world of unreality and believe it. They were living in a fantasy world."

Barnett thought that the segregationists in Little Rock were defeated in 1957 because they were too divided to mount a strong fight. Mississippi, on the other hand, was impregnable. "We're all standing together, we've all got the right attitude," Barnett told a reporter in 1961. "We won't be divided in Mississippi. We're gonna stand firm in our convictions."

William Simmons reasoned that the strategy of total rejection to integration in Mississippi had, so far, worked—it was eight years since the Supreme Court's *Brown v. the Board of Education* decision, and the state maintained total segregation by simply ignoring the order and avoiding federal enforcement action. If the federals were forced to withdraw from a showdown at Ole Miss, Simmons thought, the segregationist dream of "massive resistance," which seemed to absorb a fatal blow in Virginia three years earlier, could be resurrected as a viable strategy.

The tide of history seemed totally against the segregationists, and cracks in the dike of massive resistance were springing up everywhere. In the last year a wave of Southern cities peacefully integrated their schools: Atlanta, Dallas, Galveston, Memphis, and Tampa. Border states were moving toward total desegregation, and even the states of the upper South were moving to token integration. After white students went on a rampage in January 1961, the University of Georgia at Athens adjusted to the presence of two black students.

Just across Mississippi's southern border, segregationists were waging a death struggle in the regional supercity of New Orleans. In November 1960 Louisiana governor Jimmie Davis and state legislators tried to delay token integration. In response, federal judge J. Skelly Wright slapped a restraining order on the entire state legislature and ordered the entry of four black girls to formerly all-white elementary schools, the first public-school desegregation in the Deep South.

On March 27, 1962, the Catholic archbishop of New Orleans announced the integration of all Catholic schools in the diocese, and days later, a federal judge ordered the accelerated integration of public schools. In response, white parents pulled their children out of school. Segregationist leader Leander Perez cried, "Don't wait for your daughter to be raped by these Congolese. Don't wait until the burr-heads are forced into your schools. Do something about it now!" A mob of two to three thousand whites went on a rampage through downtown New Orleans, trashing storefronts and beating black citizens. Despite the violence, it was too late for the white supremacists. The floodgates of integration seemed to be opening for good.

In interviews many years later, in 1999 and 2000, William Simmons explained his strategic thinking at the time. He and his fellow Citizens Council leaders reasoned that the Kennedys dared not attempt a final assault on segregation in Mississippi by forcing the entry of James Meredith, because the people of Mississippi would simply never submit to integrating the university. There would be an insurrection first, a possible massacre, and the Kennedys would have to garrison tens of thousands of combat troops in Mississippi, too high a price to pay or even consider. Surely the Kennedys were smart enough politicians to know that.

If the Kennedys were stupid enough to try to execute the federal court order with real force, Simmons reasoned, they would find themselves inside a trap—an embarrassing, possibly bloody showdown from which the federals would have to withdraw, leaving an invigorated segregation movement behind. "Through it all," noted Hodding Carter III, "the simple, single Council line has been: if we will only organize, maintain our solidarity and fight the good fight, we can still win."

Together, Barnett and Simmons had a dream of creating a new "Dixiecrat" third force in American politics based in the Deep South, which would command enough electoral votes to be able, as a swing force, to decisively influence future presidential elections, as the Dixiecrats had tried to do in 1948. Their theory was that if they could persuade all 128 electors of the eleven Southern states to vote as an "unpledged" bloc, the presidential election would be thrown into the U.S. House of Representatives, where a Southern compromise candidate would be elected president.

In a surprising, forgotten historical twist, Barnett and Simmons in 1960 actually persuaded Mississippi's eight presidential electors to abandon the Democratic ticket of Kennedy and Johnson in favor of a protest vote for segregationist senator Harry Byrd of Virginia and the symbolic vision of massive resistance. Barnett condemned the Democratic Party's 1960 civil rights platform as "so horrible, so repulsive, so obnoxious, and so contrary to our form of government that I don't see how the people of the South can accept it."

Barnett's grandiloquent idea, wrote Mississippi journalist Bill Minor in 1987, was "that he could jam the presidential election machinery and force the two major party candidates to bargain with him on the civil rights issue. For a few brief moments during the night of the nip-and-tuck presidential race between JFK and Nixon on November 8, 1960, Barnett's scheme almost became a bizarre reality. Even Walter Cronkite was saying on TV late that night the Kennedy-Nixon battle was so tight that it could come down to the eight electoral votes controlled by Governor Barnett to decide the presidency." When the twenty-seven electoral votes of Illinois pushed Kennedy over the top, however, the election was over, but Barnett and Simmons's dream of a "third force" lived on.

Suddenly, the Meredith case was coming to a head, and a decisive integration clash was coming to the heart of Mississippi faster than anyone had expected. As his advisers debated the options, Ross Barnett revealed two weaknesses that are common to politicians, but would prove potentially disastrous in this crisis: He wanted everyone to love him, and he constantly changed his mind. "Barnett just couldn't tell these [Citizens Council] people no," said Bill Minor. "He was not a mean man. He was just stupid and easily led."

One legislator said of Barnett, "As a politician he's proved his word means nothing. He'll make rash promises with no compunction and he'll break them with even less compunction." Another politician noted, "It's the last man to get to him who wins."

A hard-line stance offered Barnett a highly seductive, powerful benefit: It could divert attention from his generally lackluster recent performance as governor. "Some politically astute observers do not believe the governor is a fanatic," reported *The Wall Street Journal*. "Rather they believe he is following a daring plan to recoup his ailing political fortunes."

For now, Bill Simmons was winning the battle for Barnett's public voice. The clinching argument would be dismissed as sheer fantasy anywhere except the deepest South, and even there, few people took it seriously. It was the thoroughly discredited states' rights concept of "nullification," or "interposition"—a state's alleged authority to ignore a federal law or court order if it was repugnant to the state.

The concept was based on the Tenth Amendment to the Constitution, which reads, "The powers not delegated to the United States by the Constitution, nor prohibited by it to the states, are reserved to the states respectively, or to the people." Since education is not mentioned in the Constitution, the theory went, the states alone should control it.

The theory of interposition, which was settled decisively by the Civil War, had since repeatedly been rejected by various federal courts. As recently as December 1960, in a Louisiana segregation case, the U.S. Supreme Court ruled, "The conclusion is clear that interposition is not a Constitutional doctrine. If taken seriously, it is illegal defiance of Constitutional authority."

Many white Mississippians, however, were living in a fantasy land, and the state power structure took interposition very seriously, making it the crux of their argument to refuse integration of all Mississippi public schools. To the governor's forces, recalled James Meredith, the crisis "was never about me—it was about states' rights." So Barnett dusted off the thoroughly bogus "doctrine" of interposition and made it his battle flag.

At 7:30 P.M. on the night of September 13, in a statewide radio and TV address to the people of Mississippi, in a speech handcrafted by Bill Simmons, Ross Barnett squinted at the camera through his thick glasses, threw down the gauntlet and came close to declaring war on the U.S. government.

The governor began by reading from the Constitution. "These are not my words," he intoned. "This is the Tenth Amendment to the Constitution of the United States."

If there were any doubts over the danger and scope of the crisis, Barnett cleanly smashed them: "I speak to you as your Governor in a solemn hour in the history of our great state—in a solemn hour indeed, in our nation's history. I speak to you now in the moment of our greatest crisis since the War Between the States. In the absence of Constitutional authority and without legislative action an ambitious Federal Government, employing naked and arbitrary power has decided to deny us the right of self-determination in the conduct of the affairs of our Sovereign State."

Barnett railed on as the leader of a sovereign empire under attack: "Having long since failed in their efforts to conquer the indomitable spirit of the people of Mississippi and their unshakable will to preserve the sovereign majesty of our commonwealth, they now seek to break us physically with the power of force.

"We must either submit to the unlawful dictates of the Federal Government or stand up like men and tell them 'NEVER!' The day of reckoning has been delayed as long as possible. It is now upon us. This is the day—and this is the hour. . . . I have made my position in this matter crystal clear. I have said in every county in Mississippi that no school in our state will be integrated while I am your Governor. I repeat to you tonight—NO SCHOOL WILL BE INTEGRATED IN MISSISSIPPI WHILE I AM YOUR GOVERNOR!

"There is no case in history where the Caucasian race has survived social integration," declared Barnett. "We will not drink from the cup of genocide. Mississippi, as a Sovereign State, has the right under the Federal Constitution to determine for itself what the Federal Government has reserved to it."

Then Barnett leaped into the final abyss: "Therefore, in obedience to legislative and constitutional sanction I do hereby interpose the rights of the Sovereign State of Mississippi to enforce its laws and to regulate its own internal affairs without interference on the part of the Federal government or its officers.

"With the help of Almighty God," Barnett concluded, "we shall be invincible, and we shall keep the faith!"

The government of Mississippi was now quickly sliding into a state of rebellion against the United States of America.

CHAPTER FIVE

Order of Battle

■ ■ ■ ■

This could be another War Between the States.
—Robert Shelton

A S PRESIDENT KENNEDY AND the attorney general absorbed the impact of Barnett's explosive interposition speech, an ugly possibility quickly dawned on them. To enforce James Meredith's federal court order, they would have to use physical force.

It now looked like Barnett might somehow try to physically resist the court order. He could put up a real fight, if he wanted to. He had more than 220 Mississippi Highway Patrolmen under his command, and in a worst-case scenario he could call on hundreds of local police, sheriffs, constables, and deputies as well as 250 armed fish-and-game wardens. As governor, Barnett was commander of an eleven-thousand-man National Guard and a small National Guard air force, but both could be instantly taken away from him and absorbed into the U.S. Army by a presidential order.

Judging from Barnett's incendiary rhetoric, it was now clear that federal personnel, acting as agents of the Fifth Circuit Court of Appeals, were going to have to walk Meredith through the process of registering at the university, which meant they would have to physically guard him against the inevitable white crowds, and push him through any barriers the governor might deploy.

The problem was that in 1962, the president of the United States had surprisingly few appropriate law-enforcement officers under his command. The FBI was out, because its mandate was strictly investigations, not enforcement. There was a scattering of other federal agencies who fielded police-style agents, like the U.S. Border Patrol, the Bureau of Prisons, and the Internal Revenue Service, but they had neither the training or experience for what the Meredith operation might require.

There was one small, neglected agency inside the Justice Department that might do the trick: the U.S. Marshals Service. It was far from an elite paramilitary force, but rather an underfunded federation of semi-autonomous political appointees scattered around the country, charged with federal-courtroom security, serving federal court orders, and transporting prisoners. There was a total of ninety-four U.S. Marshals and more than three hundred deputies, but they were so decentralized, they technically didn't have to obey a direct order from the tiny Chief U.S. Marshal's Office in Washington. One Border Patrol officer dismissed them all as "political hacks and courtroom hangers-on."

The chief marshal of the United States was a man who looked like he stepped out of a Damon Runyon story, a chunky Irish New York street cop named James Joseph Patrick McShane. He was built like a tank, had the crushed nose of the Golden Gloves boxing champ he once was, and the puffy face of a man who enjoyed booze in his off-hours. On the streets of New York he survived seven shoot-outs with gunmen and was awarded the police medal of honor. He worked for Bobby Kennedy as an investigator for the Senate Rackets Committee probing corruption in the Teamsters Union, served as chauffeur and bodyguard for Senator John Kennedy during the 1960 campaign, and, as a political favor, was rewarded with the post of U.S. Marshal for the District of Columbia in 1961. In April 1962 he was promoted to the post of Chief U.S. Marshal.

The U.S. Marshals were used in strength only once before in the century, and it climaxed in a near-disaster. During the Freedom Riders turmoil in 1961, Attorney General Kennedy sent a force of more than four hundred marshals, including McShane, to Alabama to provide security. On the sweltering night of May 20, the marshals found themselves guarding a mass meeting of fifteen hundred civil rights activists and the Reverend Martin Luther King, Jr., at the First Baptist Church in Montgomery.

A mob of thousands of whites laid an all-night siege on the church, firing rocks, bricks, and Molotov cocktails, charging in human waves and bashing against the front door. The marshals, who had no helmets and were armed only with sidearms, tear gas, nightsticks, and yellow "U.S. Marshal" armbands, valiantly defended the trapped civilians with their bare hands, eventually repelling the mob with tear gas.

With seconds to spare, the battered marshals were finally reinforced by Alabama National Guard troops and by Alabama Public Safety Director Floyd Mann, head of the state Highway Patrol, who despite his allegiance to the segregationist state government, impressed federal officials as a dedicated professional. The marshals were pulled out, and at the federal government's insistence, security was handed over to the Alabama and Mississippi National Guard and state police forces. Peace was maintained through the end of the Freedom Rides in August 1961, although in Mississippi, "peace" meant that arriving Freedom Riders were, in a compromise agreed to by the U.S. Justice Department, slammed into the brutal state prison at Parchman on orders of Governor Ross Barnett.

The Kennedys thought they'd learned several lessons from the fiery baptism of the Freedom Riders drama. First, they concluded that while federal marshals were effective in small operations (as they would be, they hoped, in escorting Meredith), they were too disorganized and badly trained to hold back a large force of rioters. Second, they decided that from now on, they would lean heavily on local and state authorities to maintain order in such civil rights cases and avoid sending federal forces in strength, to avoid inflaming white Southerners.

It was in this spirit that on Saturday, September 15, 1962, the attorney general made his first call to Governor Ross Barnett, to genially discuss, as he put it, "some of the details of how to work this thing out with this fellow [Meredith] coming in next Thursday [September 20]." It was the opening move of what would become a bizarre, tortured process of negotiation and miscommunication, as the wily old governor, whom RFK thought was "an agreeable rogue," danced around the boyish attorney general, and later the president, in affable confusion.

RFK reviewed the outlines of what he expected would happen: Meredith would appear at the school to register with a small escort of federal marshals, be turned down, then the case would go to court. "That will take about a year," the governor noted pleasantly. The two executives politely agreed to have their secretaries come on the line to take notes of their conversations, and to stay in touch as the Meredith matter unfolded.

Robert Kennedy was following what author Victor Navasky called "the code of the Ivy League Gentleman," which assumed that "reasonable men can always work things out." However, as Bill Minor noted, "Those who understand the swamp-fox cunning of Barnett, the country-style lawyer, can see in the conversations that the Ivy League code had no standing in Barnett's school of redneck logic." Over the next five days, a flurry of legal maneuvers bounced between the Justice Department, various courts, and university and state officials.

Meanwhile, Ross Barnett's melodramatic September 13 speech had sparked a powerful white backlash of anti–civil rights feelings in Mississippi and was transforming the governor into a Southern superhero. Congratulatory wires began flooding in from coast to coast. Inside the state, Barnett's stand against the federal government was igniting what Hodding Carter III called the average Mississippian's "peculiar love" for his state: a "defensive love, compounded of resentment, pride, and pity for what we are in comparison to what we once were."

The pro-segregation *Jackson Clarion-Ledger* proclaimed in a banner headline on September 15: PLACE ASSURED IN HISTORY FOR FEARLESS ROSS BARNETT. Verner Holmes, a member of the state college board, recalled that "every encouraging word from crackpots across the country was seized upon and regaled on the front pages to show burgeoning support for Mississippi's position." The state was being swept away by pro-segregation hysteria, and the frenzy was triggering the most dangerous of fantasies: On September 19 Mississippi state senator Jack A. Pace proposed to the Mississippi legislature "a petition to the United States Congress to sever relations between the Union and the state of Mississippi." His colleagues quickly pulled him out to lunch to cool him down.

Late on the night of September 19, Governor Barnett, flanked by two beefy Highway Patrol bodyguards, strode into a secret strategy meeting of the Board of Trustees of Institutions of Higher Learning in a conference room at the University Medical Center in Oxford.

The frightened board members were teetering on the verge of voting to let Meredith into the school—at least three were ready to vote that way, and some of the other nine were wavering. Several of the board members were privately contemptuous of Barnett and sensed that he might be leading them down a path to disaster.

Barnett began to pace the room like a caged lion, lecturing the officials on states' rights and the Tenth Amendment. An impatient board member interrupted, shouting, "We've got to know what's the legal way to keep him out. That's all we want to know, Governor!" Barnett replied, "The only way I know to keep him out is just don't let him in!"

When someone pointed out they would all be in contempt of a federal court, Barnett snapped, "Forget it, contempt means nothing! They won't do anything to you. Just don't let the word 'contempt' worry you."

Barnett now looked into the eyes of attorney Tally Riddell, a board member who was ready to vote in favor of honoring the federal court order. The two men's fathers had grown up across the creek from each other in Leake County. "Tally," the governor announced, "yo' daddy would turn over in his grave to know you are a nigger-lover and votin' to admit Meredith in this University!" The board members were in shock at the outburst. One later said he thought the governor "had done lost all of his common senses."

"You're just nothing but a yellow-bellied dog," Barnett told Riddell as he shook his fist at his face. "You're just as sorry now as your old daddy was!"

A stunned Riddell reached over the table, and said, "Ross, if you were nearer my age, I'd come across that table and I'd beat you to death!" Riddell started to stand up and then fell backwards into his chair.

Now Barnett turned on board member S. R. "Doc" Evans and launched into a similar attack. "Just a minute now, Governor," said Evans, "you're fixin' for me to hurt you. You ain't going to talk to me that way." As Evans grabbed a paperweight, Barnett stopped dead still, and noted, "You know, I believe you would!" Evans continued, "You're fixin' to put me in the penitentiary, because you ain't going to talk to me like that."

Suddenly someone called out, "Get a doctor, get somebody, get the heart outfit!"

Tally Riddell was having a heart attack in his chair.

The meeting broke up in confusion as Riddell was rushed to the emergency room.

The stage was thus set for the first of four increasingly bizarre and dangerous Kabuki-like public confrontations, as Ross Barnett and his little armies tried to physically block James Meredith and his federal escorts from entering the university. Meredith recalled, "My plan was to get federal troops on my side to help assure my rights as a citizen— I always knew that's what it would take." In this sense, Meredith's strategy was the opposite of the "passive resistance" philosophy of civil disobedience pioneered by Mahatma Gandhi and the Reverend Martin Luther King, Jr. It was a strategy of pure, overwhelming physical force. James Meredith had engineered the governor of Mississippi into a direct collision, not with James Meredith, but with the president of the United States.

On the morning of September 20, the day of his first attempt to enter the university, James Meredith woke up at 8:00 A.M.* at a safe house in Memphis. He watched Martin Luther King, Jr., on *The Today Show* and called his parents to check in with his two-year old son, who was staying with them for security purposes while Meredith's wife remained in Jackson, where she was a student at Jackson State.

After donning a brown suit and a white shirt, Meredith went to the home of NAACP attorney A. W. Willis to wait for the federal marshals. Eventually a small squad of marshals pulled up to the house in a borrowed unmarked Border Patrol car, led by Chief U.S. Marshal James McShane, now in charge of federal protection for Meredith. After hours of waiting for the final go-ahead from Washington, Meredith entered a decoy Border Patrol sedan, then performed an elaborate clandestine switch into a new car to shake off any pursuers, and the caravan took off headed south for Oxford, ninety miles away.

Inside Mississippi, state officials were scrambling desperately to block Meredith. At 12:25 A.M. that morning, the state legislature had

---

*Unless otherwise indicated, all times in this book are Mississippi time, which in September and October 1962 was two hours behind Washington, D.C.'s Eastern Daylight Time.

passed SB-1501, the "Meredith Law," which denied admission to any state school to anyone convicted of a criminal offense. Within hours, Jackson justice of the peace Homer Edgeworth found Meredith guilty of a bogus charge of falsifying a voter-registration application, sentencing him to a year in jail and a five-hundred-dollar fine. The Justice Department appealed to federal district judges to strike the order down.

At the little Oxford airport, Ross Barnett was asked by a reporter if he would desegregate the university. The governor responded, "Hell, no!"

At 3:25 P.M., with Meredith en route, a frantic board of trustees voted unanimously to try to wash their hands of the crisis and dodge federal contempt charges by appointing Governor Barnett "temporary registrar" of the school. Barnett would face off against Meredith, alone.

As Meredith's car crossed the border and passed the "Welcome to Mississippi" sign, the driver asked, "Do you think they mean us?" Meredith replied, "No, I'm afraid they don't." Meredith surveyed the serene landscape and remembered feeling as he always did when he entered Mississippi: It was "the most beautiful land in the country."

In Oxford it was a crystal-clear, warm, lazy day in the seventies, and the bucolic community seemed a most unlikely place for a clash between two governments. Oxford's Courthouse Square was like a *Back to the Future* movie set for a pretty American small town, though decorated with some startling flourishes from its insurrectionary past. The Confederate Savings and Loan Association was offering 5½ percent interest per year for a savings account. The Rebel Cosmetology College occupied an upstairs office just next to the Sears, Roebuck store, and not far away was the Rebel Food Center.

Blacks and whites congregated daily around the courthouse on segregated benches to play checkers, gossip, and watch the world go by. On Saturdays folks bought fresh watermelon, okra, and sweet potatoes from farmers in pickup trucks parked around the Square. At John Leslie's Walgreen drugstore, the local farmers and workmen joined doctors, lawyers, students, coaches, and professors every morning to argue politics. "States' rights?" someone would say, giving the signal to adjourn the coffee break. "We lost that fight a hundred years ago."

The white people of Oxford were probably no more and no less racist than those in any other American town, but their bluntness could startle out-of-town reporters, and as *The Times* of London's Civil War correspondent William Howard Russell noted a century earlier, even casual conversations in Mississippi had "a smack of manslaughter" about them. One local white man mused on Meredith's chances to a visiting *Time* correspondent: "We got some boys around here that would just love to come in and shoot him. Yeah, we got some boys around here all right." A white cab driver added, "I don't particularly mind seeing Meredith go to the University, he's a smart nigger. But you got to realize that the niggers we got in Mississippi just ain't like those you got elsewhere. They ain't ready for integration."

At the heart of white fears of integration was not states' rights, or constitutional arcana, but sex—the sexual hysteria and jealousy of the black man that gripped white Americans since slavery began. It was fear of the dreaded "miscegenation," or mixing of the races, that was railed against publicly but often practiced in private by many white males, who for generations had pursued black women.

The widely understood subtext to segregation in the deepest South was the assumption that under no circumstances would black males ever be allowed to sit on an equal basis next to white Southern schoolgirls, especially the pride of Ole Miss, the thousands of powdered, scrubbed, lipsticked coeds who paraded around the campus in fresh cotton dresses chatting about sororities, pinnings, and upcoming football glories.

"Supposing Ole Miss went somewhere and played a team that uses Negroes," Governor Barnett later explained. "We would have to have a return game with them in Oxford, or Jackson. After the game, there would be a social event. What would the Negroes do? They would attend. What would the Negroes do? Would they dance with white girls? Not in Mississippi. It wouldn't work and that's why we're staying out of it."

To white racists, James Meredith was about to personify their worst nightmare: a confident, attractive young black professional marching in to invade the holiest temple of white supremacy, simultaneously polite and defiant, not remotely afraid of physical violence, and, if anything, slightly bemused by the excitement he provoked as the eyes of the world media flocked around him.

At the university on September 20, hundreds of curious students were gathering on the grassy lawns. Some were dancing the twist to past the time. A freshman in a blue-and-red beanie asked, "When will the nigger come?" Soon nearly two hundred Mississippi Highway Patrolmen in Confederate gray took command of the area, blocking the crowds and providing a safe passage for Meredith to enter and, they expected, quickly leave after being refused admission.

The crowd swelled. The story was starting to attract national interest, and reporters from out of town milled around scribbling notes. A group of young men ran to the flagpole carrying a Confederate flag, and amid much cheering, began striking down the American flag. As the Stars and Stripes neared half-mast, a student leader dashed over and stopped them, arguing, "Too many Americans have died for this flag for us to pull something like that." He then made a point of telling a reporter from New York, "That does not represent the feelings of most of the students here or most of the people of Mississippi. Those people are not from around here. We are Americans first."

All of a sudden, at 4:30 P.M. James Meredith entered Ole Miss, his car sweeping up to the Continuation Center, a small auditorium where Barnett and school officials waited. By now the crowd was nearing the two thousand mark, and a chorus of boos and cries of "Go home, nigger!" erupted. Meredith stepped out of the car and looked at crowd for a moment with a furrowed brow.

Meredith was stunned. This was the first time anyone in Mississippi had ever called him "nigger" to his face. In a 2000 interview he explained, "I'd heard the word millions of times. Not only heard it, I used it a lot." But he'd never heard it directed at him. He attributed this in part to his isolated childhood, shielded by his father from white society.

Inside the building, Meredith faced off against the governor and announced, "I want to register at the University." With a performer's flourish, Barnett unfurled a fancy gold-sealed proclamation, and declared, "Using my police powers as the Governor of the Sovereign State of Mississippi, as well as my official academic powers as Registrar of the University of Mississippi, and acting in accordance with the formal legislative decree of Interposition granted me by the Mississippi legislature, I do hereby deny you, James Meredith, admittance to this University."

Barnett's dramatic performance impressed Meredith, reminding him of a movie in which Charlton Heston played President Andrew Jackson.

At 4:51 P.M., with no other options, Meredith and the federal men turned and made a hurried exit through the now hostile crowd. As he left, Meredith dryly wisecracked through a tight-lipped smile, "If Governor Barnett keeps this up, I may not vote for him." A student lunged out for him but was restrained by a Mississippi Highway Patrolman. Seeing Meredith's Plymouth peel off at high speed, the crowd was jubilant. Nearly five hundred spectators sprinted after the car in hot pursuit, nearly catching up before it blasted off to the north to flee the state.

The triumphant governor joined his closest advisers for a victory celebration at the Alumni Center. Barnett asked one of them how he would handle the situation. "I'd make them point a gun at me and tell me to move over," the man replied, "then I'd move over and say come on in." The group exploded in guffaws when Barnett declared, "That's exactly how far I'm going!"

Ross Barnett had faced down the president of the United States and beat him, at least for now. A hundred years ago, in December 1862, it took the Confederate army three weeks to surround General U. S. Grant and his Union army, cut off their supply lines, and force them to withdraw from Oxford. Today, Ross Barnett sent the federals back to Memphis in less than an hour.

That night at 8:00 P.M., the Justice Department hit Chancellor John D. Williams, College of Liberal Arts dean A. B. Lewis, and Registrar Robert B. Ellis with contempt-of-court charges for not facilitating Meredith's admission into Ole Miss, ordering them to appear in court at 1:30 P.M. the next day. The next morning, the officials traveled to Jackson, where they reviewed their slim-to-nonexistent options with the state's legal team. When Ross Barnett appeared, the group eagerly awaited the governor's victory plan, but all Barnett had to offer was a reminder to Chancellor Williams of his own pledge to be imprisoned over the issue.

"I hope you'll go to jail with me," Barnett told Williams. "If you stay with me in this fight, I'll see that the legislature doubles your salary." The chancellor was too shocked to answer. By now, the trustees realized the awful truth: The governor had no strategy.

In fact, Barnett had admitted as much to a university lawyer: "Of course I know interposition is invalid. I'm bluffing. But you wait and see. I'll bluff the Justice Department into backing down."

On the afternoon of Friday, September 21, U.S. District Court judge Sidney Mize in Meridian struck down the contempt charge against the university officials. But the next day, the Fifth Circuit U. S. Court of Appeals in New Orleans ordered the officials plus the whole board of trustees to appear in court Monday morning to explain why they shouldn't be held in contempt. By now, Tally Riddell was recovering from his heart attack.

Over the weekend, a Barnett supporter on the board of trustees issued a defiant statement: "I am prepared to be cited for contempt, I am prepared to go to jail, I am prepared to die. And I'm even prepared to go to hell."

In Washington, D.C., on Saturday, September 22, a ceremony was planned at the Lincoln Memorial to commemorate the one hundredth anniversary of the Emancipation Proclamation. President Kennedy decided to take the weekend off in Hyannis Port, but he left behind a tape recording to be played at the ceremony. "Despite humiliation and deprivation," the president said, "the Negro retained his loyalty to the United States and to democratic institutions. . . . It can be said, I believe, that Abraham Lincoln emancipated the slaves, but that in this century since, our Negro citizens have emancipated themselves."

At Robert Kennedy's Justice Department, someone had a brainstorm. The lonely, depressed vice president Lyndon Johnson, until now ignored inside the administration on civil rights and most everything else, could be dropped into Mississippi by plane to personally escort Meredith to the university to register. The sight of the huge Texas powerbroker standing at Meredith's side as they entered the school just might project the right image of strength to calm the situation. LBJ was game for the plan. Following the "code of the Ivy League Gentleman," RFK helpfully ran the idea by Barnett.

The governor shot it down. Apparently he wanted a more decisive confrontation.

From now on, Meredith would often be shuttled in and out of Mississippi by U.S. Border Patrol planes, alternating from federal strong points at Memphis to the north and New Orleans to the south, in complex, military-style maneuvers. One time, when Meredith's plane flew across Mississippi airspace, it was preceded by a decoy plane, in case the Mississippi Air National Guard tried to shoot it down.

. . .

On Monday morning, September 24, the members of the Mississippi Board of Trustees of State Institutions of Higher Learning stood sheepishly before the Fifth Circuit Court in New Orleans.

The furious federal judges accused the officials of "monkey business" in their refusal to admit Meredith. The judges quickly ruled that the board must revoke Barnett's status as registrar and admit Meredith the next day, or the trustees would be in contempt and the court would appoint a new board to order the admission.

Faced now with the immediate threat of going to jail, the trustees caved in within minutes, and all pledged to register Meredith by 4:00 P.M. the next day, Tuesday, September 25.

That evening, at 8:00 P.M., Burns Tatum, the chief of the University of Mississippi campus police force, got a call from Joe Ford, sheriff of Lafayette County (which included Oxford), and head of the county's Citizens Council. Acting on behalf of the Mississippi Sheriffs Association, Sheriff Ford asked Chief Tatum for permission to bring in equipment to dig up the streets and erect barricades at key entrances to the university. The sheriff also wanted to know whether or not Chief Tatum and the dozen or so men under his command would be available for duty to prevent U.S. marshals and James Meredith from entering the university.

Although the eighty-two Mississippi sheriffs were locally elected officials and not under Ross Barnett's direct chain of command, they were falling in lockstep behind the governor and had decided, as a group, to join the state's policy of resistance. As University of Mississippi history professor James Silver later noted of this time, "The closed society was operating efficiently and automatically, as it does in times of great stress, as if directed by some malicious Frankenstein."

Chief Tatum called university officials in New Orleans for guidance. The word came back; no resistance to the federal court order, no barricades, no digging.

The University of Mississippi was quietly withdrawing itself from the state's strategy of blocking Meredith with physical force.

The leader of America's oldest terrorist organization sat at his desk on the fourth floor of the Alston office building in Tuscaloosa, Alabama, his fair eyebrows furrowed, his blue eyes squinting as he sucked on a Pall Mall and pondered the Meredith case.

Robert Shelton was a crew-cut, slightly built, almost skeletal thirty-three-year-old former rubber-plant worker and Goodrich tire salesman who now ruled the most powerful Ku Klux Klan faction in the country, the United Klans of America. One journalist wrote that Shelton's "mind and soul have the inner efficiency of a medieval torture rack." Now, his blood was boiling.

It looked like the federal government was going to shove this Meredith deal down the South's throat. The sacred sovereignty of the states was at risk of being obliterated. So, he thought, was the chastity of Southern womanhood. But the people of the South would never stand for it, Shelton thought. And there was one group of Americans who could be counted on to stand up for what was right: the Ku Klux Klan.

The Imperial Wizard's desk was flanked by a Confederate flag on one side and an American flag on the other. A photo of his wife and three young children graced the table. On another table was a sword, a Bible, and a vessel of water, symbols of the Klan's self-professed "dedication to Christianity and justice." A purple satin robe decorated with a Maltese cross hung in a nearby garment bag.

Shelton was the commander of an "invisible empire" of secret symbols and comic-book sorcery that rose from the ashes of the Civil War to defend the white South by terrorizing blacks with torture and execution. The Klan ceremony of cross-burning was patterned after the ancient call to battle of the Highland Scots, and the movement drew on the distant tribal memories of the proud, cantankerous Scots-Irish settlers of the American South, whose forefathers were in perpetual rebellion against the authority of the British crown.

In the 1920s the Klan skyrocketed to national political power with a membership of almost 5 million, then collapsed during the Depression to less than thirty thousand. Robert Shelton returned to his native Tuscaloosa after a stint during the Berlin airlift as a sergeant in the integrated air force, convinced that the races should never mix, and he joined the badly splintered Alabama Klan. He later explained his reasoning for joining: "I saw nigra American soldiers going out with German girls. I realized that the federal government was using these frauleins as guinea pigs in an experiment in mixing the races. I realized also that something had to be done to maintain the purity of our races here in America, and that if we didn't do something about it, the Communist conspiracy would take over America."

Shelton was now resurrecting the Klan, his energy fueled by a rising white backlash to civil rights, especially among the poorest whites most vulnerable to black competition in the labor force. Though most Southerners had always rejected the Klan and its violent tactics, the resurgent organization was enjoying a burst of power, with more than one hundred thousand members in various factions spread across the South, especially in Alabama, Georgia, Louisiana, and parts of South Carolina, North Carolina, and Florida. But the Klan was dormant in Mississippi—the Citizens Council's hammerlock on the state was so smothering that dissent was almost totally crushed, and there was no need for the Klan's tactics.

Nowhere was the Klan stronger than in Alabama, where Shelton's United Klans of America conducted business largely out in the open and claimed a national mailing list of 2 million for its newspaper, *The Fiery Cross*. Shelton swept into cow-pasture "Klonvocations" in a CB radio–equipped Cadillac or a twin-engine Cessna, and consulted regularly with Governor Robert Patterson, whom the Klan campaigned for and helped win the 1959 election. Soon Shelton would upgrade to a nine-person executive Beechcraft airplane and build a lakeside Klan convention center complex in Tuscaloosa, complete with a two-thousand-seat auditorium, fifty-person Klan motel and private cafeteria.

The lifeblood of the Klan was violence and the threat of violence, and in the ten years following the Supreme Court's *Brown* decision, Klansmen of different factions conducted an orgy of terror against innocent civilian targets, perpetrating at least a dozen murders, thirty church burnings, and seventy bombings. In 1957 Klansmen in Birmingham, Alabama, abducted a thirty-four-year-old black man named Edward Aaron, castrated him with a razor, doused his wounds with kerosene, and passed around his testicles in a paper cup.

Imperial Wizard Shelton tried to turn the Klan in a new direction when he completed his takeover in 1961, publicly rejecting violence, emphasizing political organization and holding rallies in public, without masks. Every Christmas, in a gesture of grotesque irony, a local sheriff escorted uniformed Klansmen around town to give fruit baskets to needy black homes and pose for publicity pictures with terrified black families in their living rooms.

But the Meredith drama, unfolding just over Alabama's western border, presented the Alabama Klansmen with a mortal threat. If federal officials succeeded in forcing Meredith into Ole Miss, they would no doubt turn their sights next on the totally segregated school system of Alabama, especially the University of Alabama. Robert Shelton and his Klansmen discussed the Meredith matter at a strategy meeting, and decided that if they went to Mississippi to help defend Ole Miss, they would be armed and ready to fight.

The Imperial Wizard soon gave the order to his empire to mobilize for full-scale war. The word flashed across the South, over CB radios and phone lines and into backwoods meeting halls and truck stops and ham radio base stations. The entire membership of the United Klans of America was to move into "standby alert" status, and Klansmen should prepare to move on Oxford with shotguns and rifles.

As he pondered the Meredith case, a terrible idea occurred to the Imperial Wizard, and thinking back on it thirty-eight years later, he could still clearly remember what went through his mind.

"This could be another War Between the States," he thought.

In Washington, Bobby Kennedy figured Ross Barnett must by now have had his moment in the sun, so he decided to register Meredith on September 25, not at the Oxford campus, but at the office of the university trustees at the Woolfolk State Office Building in downtown Jackson.

But Ross Barnett had no immediate plans to capitulate; not with every passing hour lifting him higher and higher on new waves of power and adulation. It must have been an intoxicating feeling. So at noon on Tuesday, September 25, with James Meredith and the federals on their way, Governor Ross Barnett marched down the steps of the yellow-domed Capitol and across the street to the Woolfolk Building, flanked by a Highway Patrolman and a pack of aides. Marching behind them was a phalanx of fifty state legislators.

Barnett wore his trademark funeral director–style uniform: homburg, dark suit, black knitted tie. He marched slowly and grimly to his historic rendezvous, sharpening the theatrical effect for the swelling lunchtime crowd, who responded with an ovation. A disabled war veteran named Buddy Cooper carried a sign: "I fought for my country in Korea. Now, I will fight for my State here." Barnett strode into the Woolfolk Building and barricaded himself in the board of trustees office on the tenth floor. A battery of TV cameras was set up in the hallway. Not knowing when the federals were coming, the Mississippi officials waited all afternoon.

In New Orleans, James Meredith and his federal escorts prepared to fly to Jackson. Before departing, Meredith had to use a "colored" bathroom in the basement, to the embarrassment of his escorts. Then Meredith and his party boarded a luxury government Cessna 220 that would now be one of their main methods of travel. Meredith was guarded by James McShane and Justice Department official John Doar, whom Meredith in the days ahead would consider among the bravest men he ever saw.

At 4:34, Meredith and his escorts pulled up to the Woolfolk Building. Now there was a noisy crowd of two thousand people around the building, and they booed lustily as Meredith, McShane, and Doar strode into the building, flanked by Mississippi Highway Patrolmen.

On the tenth floor, Meredith and his party stepped into pure bedlam—lights, reporters, policemen. There, at Room 1007, to their total surprise, was Ross Barnett, standing in the doorway of the board of trustees office with one of his cherished proclamations, blocking them from going into the room with his own body.

As video cameras delivered a live feed to the national TV networks, Barnett stood squarely in the door frame and greeted them with a smile: "I am glad to see you again." Then he uttered a comic punch line of polite contempt to the ocean of white faces interrupted only by James Meredith, standing directly in front of him wearing a dark brown jacket.

"Which one of you is Meredith?" the governor asked.

The legislators behind Barnett, some standing on chairs, exploded in belly laughs. The crowds outside, glued to transistor radios, erupted in tidal waves of laughter. Ross Barnett had hit a comedy home run.

Chief U.S. Marshal McShane tried to hand Barnett a summons to appear before the Court of Appeals on a civil-contempt charge, but the governor refused to take it. Then he grandly read from the proclamation: "I, Ross R. Barnett, Governor of the State of Mississippi, having heretofore by proclamation, acting under the police powers of the State of Mississippi . . . do hereby finally deny you admission to the University of Mississippi."

After blustering for a time about the Tenth Amendment, he announced, "My conscience is clear." Then he handed the proclamation over to a stone-faced Meredith, suggesting, "It might be a treasure for you to keep. Take it and abide by it."

As the senior federal representative, John Doar asked Barnett, "You realize you are in contempt, don't you? Do you realize you are breaking the law?"

Barnett sneered, "Who are you to say that I am in contempt? That is up to the courts to decide." Behind him, various jeering legislators called out, "Get going! Take off! Vamoose!"

Finally, Doar queried, "I call on you to allow us to see Mr. Ellis and register Mr. Meredith. Do you refuse to let us go through that door?"

Barnett replied, "Yes, sir. I do so politely."

"All right, then," Doar concluded. "And we politely bid you good-bye."

As they retreated, Barnett called out with mock sweetness, "Come see me some time at the mansion!"

The packed room of Mississippi officials and lawmakers behind Barnett erupted in a joyous ovation. The governor had faced down the federals again and beat them. Jubilation broke out on the street. "Dixie" blared on car radios. Two women office workers danced a jig on the sidewalk.

Meredith and his escorts quickly walked out of the building through a cordon of Highway Patrolmen who were holding back a now openly hostile crowd. White onlookers shook fists and yelled piercing cries at Meredith: "Tell that to Bobby Kennedy and send him to see us!"; "Ross is the big boss!"; "You trashy black nigger!"

The federal car pulled away from the crowd, paced by a hysterically screaming white woman. But then Meredith caught a vision of who he was fighting for, a sight he would never forget: Standing on the corner was a group of five or six delighted black maids and workmen. They were waving proudly at him.

In the State Capitol that night, another extraordinary declaration of rebellion by Governor Barnett was read to the cheering legislature. Incredibly, it was a proclamation directing state officials to arrest agents of the U.S. government. If any federal official tried to arrest or fine a state official in performance of his official duties, the federal official was "to be summarily arrested and jailed," the declaration read.

At a victory meeting of the state legislature that same night, Representative E. K. Collins declared, "James Meredith will not enter the University of Mississippi as long as there are red corpuscles in bodies of true Mississippians! . . . We must win this fight regardless of the cost in time, effort, prestige and human lives!"

Also that evening, RFK called Barnett, who happily informed the attorney general that he had turned Meredith away. RFK replied that the federal party would take Meredith to classes at Oxford tomorrow, anyhow. Barnett professed surprise, figuring the battle instead would now go to a prolonged legal phase. "I am astounded—I don't know what I'll do—I can't go running all over the state of Mississippi [to keep Meredith out]," Barnett protested.

"Why don't you try it for six months and see how it goes?" RFK asked. "It's best for him not to go to Ole Miss," Barnett insisted. "But he likes Ole Miss," countered RFK. Barnett said he was "shocked" at the trustees' capitulation, and upset at Washington's disregard of Mississippi courts. The call ended with RFK bluntly declaring that Meredith was going in, and asking the governor to provide adequate security. A dejected Barnett said he would look into it.

Also that night, Robert Kennedy spoke to James Meredith for the first time by phone. "It's going to be a long, hard and difficult struggle," said the attorney general, "but in the end we're going to be successful."

Meredith's terse reply was, "I hope so."

The next morning, September 26, Barnett's representative Tom Watkins called RFK's assistant Burke Marshall to suggest that the U.S. Marshals escorting Meredith should push Barnett aside gently, since a show of force could save Barnett's face and allow him to stand aside with his dignity intact.

RFK and Barnett were soon on the phone again, and once again they got nowhere fast.

"As Attorney General," Kennedy grandly announced, "it is my duty to see that federal court orders are enforced."

"I am going to obey the laws of Mississippi," Barnett parried. "The U.S. Constitution is the law of the land but not what some court says."

The attorney general meekly pointed out, "Governor, you are a part of the United States."

Barnett then made an astonishing statement, a remark that cut through the fog of rhetoric to the heart of the issue. "We have been a part of the United States," said the governor, "but I don't know whether we are or not."

A presumably amazed Kennedy asked, "Are you getting out of the Union?"

Barnett grumbled, "It looks like we're being kicked around, like we don't belong to it."

Tiring of the word games, RFK signed off. "My job is to enforce the laws of the United States. I intend to fulfill it."

At the Governor's Mansion in Jackson, Mrs. Ross Barnett, a dignified, refined woman in pearl-frame glasses, offered her guests homemade ice cream in the family dining room as she marveled at a huge pile of telegrams offering support to her husband.

There was one from Amarillo, Texas: "Dear Governor Barnett: You're the only man I know of with guts enough to stand by your principles and refuse to sell your soul for a few votes. What can I do to help you?" From Jackson, Mississippi: "May God continue to give you wisdom, strength and courage to protect our heritage." Vicksburg, Mississippi: "The name of Ross Barnett will be inscribed in the pages of history with Lee, Jackson and Jeff Davis as a great Southerner."

An alarming number of citizens were not just writing letters and sending wires, but preparing to march into battle to support Barnett. In Alabama, Louisiana, and beyond, hundreds and even thousands of Klansmen, National States' Rights Party activists, and Citizens Councilmen were holding meetings, planning strategy, and sending out calls for volunteers.

Barnett had strong bedrock support from many rank-and-file white Mississippians, and amidst the militant frenzy it was impossible for the state's moderates to be heard. Karl Weisenberg, one of only two state representatives openly critical of Barnett, lamented, "The voice of the moderates in Mississippi is silent; it has been completely suppressed." A businessman explained, "It's fear. Fear of physical violence and fear of economic pressure by the Citizens Council."

For thirteen days Barnett and his government had flamboyantly defied the force and majesty of federal law. As RFK aide Burke Marshall recalled in a 1996 interview, "The Governor was in rebellion one moment and then again not, depending on who he was talking to."

On the central social issue of the day, Mississippi was fast becoming a breakaway republic.

At 9:00 A.M. on Wednesday, September 26, Lieutenant Governor Paul B. Johnson, Jr. stood in the road two blocks east of the main entrance to the University of Mississippi, wondering where on earth the governor was.

If Ross Barnett looked like a mortician, the cadaverous Paul B. Johnson, Jr. resembled one of his recently departed clients. He was a fierce-looking lawyer with a head shaped like a snub-nosed bullet, who had served as president of the Ole Miss student body and, as a captain in the Marine Corps saw combat across the South Pacific, including the Battles of Iwo Jima and Saipan. Like Barnett, Johnson was both a firm segregationist and a men's Bible class teacher. He was neither close personally to Ross Barnett or part of his inner circle, and he ran for lieutenant governor independently, as was the custom in Mississippi, in hopes of succeeding Barnett in 1964.

Johnson was the son of Mississippi governor Paul B. Johnson, Sr., who was a champion of education for both whites and blacks and was, by Mississippi standards, a moderate on racial issues. In 1940 he pushed through the state's first free-textbook law, and in the face of vicious opposition, he insisted that it apply to black students as well.

On this misty, murky morning in 1962, his son was standing at the head of a human barricade, vowing to block a black man from entering the state university, and to prevent the federal government from executing the law of the land on American soil. A distant statue on campus gazed toward the scene, a likeness of a Confederate soldier erected in 1906 by the local chapter of the United Daughters of the Confederacy. The bottom of he monument was inscribed, "To our Confederate dead—Whose valor and devotion made glorious many a battlefield."

Governor Barnett was nowhere to be seen. Barnett's plane was fogged in at Jackson this morning, so he had switched to a convoy of police cars and sedans, to accommodate a contingent of state legislators he had asked to come along. The Highway Patrol escorts were doing their best to speed the caravan north to Oxford in time to meet the federals. They might actually make it in time. The only trouble was the governor had to go to the bathroom.

They were making good time until they approached Calhoun City, when the chief executive ordered the convoy to stop at a gas station so he could grab a Coke for the road and relieve himself. But by the time Barnett concluded his business, jubilant townspeople were flocking around his car. Someone exclaimed, "Look—here's Ross!" The word got out fast, and more and more people swarmed and engulfed their governor in a wave of joy and congratulations.

Every time the convoy pushed forward to escape Calhoun City, a fresh crowd surrounded Barnett's car, and the convoy came to a dead stop. Time was running out, but the governor wanted to shake their hands and relish the pride and happiness in their faces. There were so many of them.

To a once-fading politician like Barnett, who had endured months of criticism and ridicule and even was booed at an Ole Miss football game two years back, this sudden, overwhelming adulation must have felt like heaven. He decided to linger awhile, so he could savor the sweet, golden beauty of it all.

In Oxford, an exasperated Paul B. Johnson scanned the horizons but there was still no sign of the governor. It looked like the lieutenant governor would have to handle the theatrics of the blockade himself.

An FBI informant inside the Mississippi police apparatus had relayed to his Bureau contact the details of an elaborate battle plan for today's showdown. The scheme was worked out by the Highway Patrol, the politicians, and the state's sheriffs, and, incredibly, it combined aspects of a Wild West showdown with the tactics of nonviolent resistance.

The Mississippi forces had blockaded the approach area two blocks east of the campus entrance with Highway Patrol cars and a skirmish line of twenty patrolmen standing in front. Blocking the road behind them, in a line across the wide street, was a battle formation of nearly fifty plainclothes Mississippi sheriffs and sheriff's deputies. Dozens more police were deployed nearby as reserves.

Expecting the marshals to advance on foot using a wedge formation, the Highway Patrolmen were ordered to link arms, two or three deep. If the marshals pushed through the first line, then the sheriffs and deputies were to keep their hands at their sides and try to repel the invaders with body blocks, a sure recipe for slapstick newsreel footage. If the federals pulled guns, the defenders planned to fall back and presumably allow the marshals and Meredith in.

The problem with this intricate scheme was obvious: If push came to shove, someone could easily start shooting, and a small bloodbath would erupt right in front of the news cameras.

At the Oxford University Airport, James Meredith and the federal marshals arrived by Cessna and were met by a special escort for the short drive to the school: a sixty-six-year-old man with the picturesque name of Tom Birdsong. Colonel T. B. Birdsong was Mississippi's commissioner of public safety and head of the state's 220-man all-white Highway Patrol. A World War I veteran, he had himself set up the state's first Highway Patrol from scratch in 1936. His men felt protective toward the colonel, as he was getting on in years and his eyes were going bad. He had to wear thick sunglasses all the time to protect his eyes from the glare.

The Highway Patrol was not a state police force, but a lightly armed road-safety patrol whose authority was usually restricted to federal and state highways. Among whites, the patrolmen had a reputation as effective crime fighters, but to blacks they were often seen as shock troops of racism. The forces with the worst reputation for racial brutality were the scores of locally elected, semi-autonomous sheriffs, constables, and deputies around the state, who were potentially more powerful and less disciplined than the Highway Patrol.

When the federal caravan approached the campus, the Highway Patrol escorts abruptly stopped and pulled over to a side street, leaving the Border Patrol car containing Meredith and his escorts to face the blockade alone. An alarmed Chief U.S. Marshal McShane ran up to Colonel Birdsong's car and exclaimed, "Wait a minute. Our agreement was that you would escort us *onto* the campus!"

Colonel Birdsong shrugged and said, "This is as far as we go. My orders are to escort you to the campus entrance, and that's what we've done."

A furious McShane unloaded Meredith and Doar to face yet another crowd-pleasing media spectacle. Reporters and photographers crowded around. It was 9:45 A.M. McShane and Doar approached Lieutenant Governor Johnson as police surged in close to defend him.

James Meredith stood at attention like a general reviewing the battlefield, gazing straight ahead and resolutely ignoring catcalls from the crowd. McShane stood nearly toe to toe with the lieutenant governor, and announced, "I want to take Meredith into the college and enroll him as directed by the Federal Court."

Johnson replied, "I am refusing him admission. I refuse, acting for and under the direction of Governor Barnett and the Governor's proclamation."

Justice Department attorney John Doar tried to serve court papers on the lieutenant governor. Johnson said through clenched teeth, "I will not accept the papers. I do this politely."

"We're going in," announced McShane.

"You aren't," parried Johnson. "We are going to block you and if there is any violence it will be on your part. Any bloodshed will be on the head of Meredith and the Federal Government."

McShane replied, "I'm only doing my duty as a United States Marshal. I would like to go in." He then placed his hand lightly on Johnson's arm, but instead of yielding, as Tom Watkins had said Barnett would do, Johnson dug his heels into the asphalt. If there really was an agreement to stand aside, Johnson either hadn't heard about it or wasn't playing along.

Johnson declared, "You are not going in."

The two sides melded into a kind of rugby scrum of pushing and shoving. To *Washington Post* reporter Robert E. Baker, it looked like Johnson and McShane "were shoving each other at the belt-line in a sort of weird and gentle belly dance."

McShane saw an opening at the left and danced over to lead Meredith and Doar through. Patrolmen stepped over to block them, their bellies jiggling. A deadly serious confrontation was devolving into a dangerous form of slapstick theater.

McShane asked the patrolmen blocking him, "Do you realize you are in contempt of the Federal Court?" Johnson chimed in, "He cannot enter the campus." The flummoxed federal officials started jotting down the names off the Highway Patrolmen's badges.

Doar made one last stab. "We want to call upon you for the last time to let this man in." No response was forthcoming.

Finally, outnumbered and outgunned, the federals turned and left. McShane had a grim parting word for the lieutenant governor: "We have a duty to perform and intend to do it." When the little green federal plane raced off into the gloomy sky, Meredith quipped, "Well, at least I'm getting in a lot of flying time."

The jubilant Mississippi troopers, sheriffs, and deputies let out war whoops of victory. For the third time, the Mississippi government went belly-to-belly with the federals, this time literally, and for the third time the federals retreated and fled the state. Perhaps Mississippi really was invincible.

Others weren't so sure.

Quietly, some white people around the state were having second thoughts about where things were heading, although most were too afraid to speak out publicly. One who did, board of trustees member Verner Holmes, had declared days earlier in a public statement, "I am not willing to go to jail if it will accomplish nothing. This would be ridiculous and ineffective." In Jackson, one state legislator decided that things were building up to where Americans could be shooting at Americans. He wanted no part of it, and decided to disassociate himself from the whole mess and stay away from Oxford. At Ole Miss, the president of the student body, law student Dick Wilson, announced succinctly that federal court orders are "explicit and need no other explanation."

"This is ridiculous," one student wearing a red-and-white freshman's beanie remarked to a visiting reporter. "How long does the state think it can keep this up?"

The next morning, Thursday, September 27, James Meredith and his federal escorts were back in Memphis, gearing up for yet another parade to Oxford, this time by land convoy with a beefed-up force of marshals. But James Meredith decided he had had enough. Without warning, as the caravan was about to take off, Meredith abruptly called a halt to the action.

"In order to prevail," James Meredith recalled in a 1989 oral history, "I had to get the federal government on my side, and that was the whole reason for making the maneuver to put the Kennedy administration under the gun with their promises. I was well aware of the contact between Ross Barnett and the Kennedys. Between them I was always sure the U.S. government was going to win."

However, Meredith admitted, "My greatest fear was a deal between

Barnett and Kennedy. I had no trust in either of them, and less trust for Kennedy than for Barnett, because the law barred Barnett from re-election, but I knew John Kennedy wanted to be reelected."

Meredith explained to the federal officials that they must go in with real force. At one point Meredith told a Justice Department man, "I question your sincerity." Meredith reminded the stunned government officials that every time they retreated, his citizenship became a laughingstock before Mississippi and a mockery before the world. We're not going anywhere, Meredith declared. As an individual citizen acting on his own, Meredith could make decisions and change tactics quickly.

The federal officials pleaded with Meredith's NAACP lawyers to talk him into going, but they supported Meredith's move, announcing, "We will advise him to make no further efforts to enter the campus until after the insurrection there has been put down by the Executive Branch of the United States Government."

The government men beseeched Meredith to reconsider, reminding him of all the energy that had been invested so far, and arguing that this time they had enough force to get the job done—they now had thirty marshals. "We know what we're doing," they said. "You've got to trust us." Seeing their determination, a still-skeptical Meredith reluctantly reversed himself and allowed for the operation to proceed.

The federal caravan started out from Memphis, and after elaborate car switches and decoy actions, the convoy of thirteen green U.S. Border Patrol sedans sped down Highway 55. A Border Patrol spotter plane flew above as a lookout and radio link to Bobby Kennedy's office in Washington, D.C.

Ever the swamp-fox negotiator, Barnett pleasantly badgered the attorney general by phone into having *all* the marshals draw their guns on him this time, not just McShane. Barnett would step aside, and Meredith would then enter the university, allowing the governor a face-saving photo opportunity of heroic defiance. "General, I was under the impression that they were all going to pull their guns," Barnett declared. "This could be very embarrassing. We got a big crowd here and if one pulls his gun and we all turn, it would be very embarrassing." RFK caved in and the deal was struck.

At Barnett's order, more than two hundred Highway Patrolmen

were blockading the Ole Miss campus entrances, armed with billy clubs, steel helmets, tear-gas masks, and police dogs. They were ordered to keep their guns in their cars.

The towering figure of Citizens Council chief William Simmons could be seen patrolling the campus entrance. To Simmons, it looked like his dream of a resurrected "massive resistance" movement against integration was springing to triumphant life in this solid wall of flesh of a united people. In this upside-down world, the federal government was a tyranny, invading their sacred soil to force a radical social experiment. The segregationists were defending the status quo, their "Way of Life," a system of segregation that was sanctified by the Supreme Court itself in its *Plessy v. Ferguson* decision in 1896.

Governor Barnett and Lieutenant Governor Johnson were suddenly faced with a mortal dilemma. They thought they had carefully choreographed a historic photo opportunity that would blaze in the history books forever: the two of them standing unarmed before the shock troops of the federal government, staring down the barrels of their guns, then manfully stepping aside to avoid bloodshed. But now things were out of control.

The city of Oxford was drifting into a state of chaos. There were people strutting with guns in the streets, and Ross Barnett and Paul Johnson could not control them. The comic-opera rebellion had blossomed into a full-scale people's uprising. Twenty-five hundred people swarmed around the university area and nearly one thousand students were massing at the campus gate.

A small team of plainclothes "observers" from Robert Shelton's United Klans of America quietly blended into the crowd, preparing intelligence reports for transmission to the Imperial Wizard in Alabama. The FBI had information that nineteen Klansmen from northeast Louisiana also were already in Oxford. As William Goodman, a young Jackson attorney, recalled, "There were so many scary people around who had come to town to see the show, armed with hunting rifles, shotguns, hachets and bricks."

Teams of civilian snipers were rumored to be lying in wait on the outskirts of the city to ambush Meredith. There was a chance that Meredith and his escorts would be shot to pieces before they got near the university, or that a shoot-out would erupt at the campus entrance involving dozens or hundreds of shooters firing around in a densely packed mob. Instead of starring in an epic photo, Barnett and Johnson would go down in history drenched in blood.

It had all gone too far.

Lieutenant Governor Johnson began touring the area in a police cruiser, trying to disperse the crowds by barking into a loudspeaker, "The nigger isn't here yet. . . . I plead with you. . . . Someone could easily be killed. . . . I beg of you to get out of this line of fire." But the pleas had no effect. Instead, the crowds seemed to keep growing.

At 1:50 P.M., Barnett and Johnson went to their headquarters office on campus and beseeched RFK by phone to call off the assault. RFK reminded the two politicians that if they disobeyed the court order, the federal judges would issue a bench warrant and have them arrested.

"General Kennedy," Johnson pleaded, "we cannot assure anybody that those people or someone maybe hotheaded won't start shooting." "We don't shoot Americans," Johnson explained, speaking for the Mississippi police forces. But, he said, referring to the gangs of armed civilians, "We've got some hotheaded people in this state who are in this group and we've got to have sufficient time to move them."

The attorney general pressed Barnett and Johnson to keep the peace, and the federal convoy still barreled on.

At 4:35 P.M., Barnett again appealed to RFK to stop the attempt. The caravan was now less than forty miles away from Oxford. "There is liable to be a hundred people killed here," asserted the governor. "It would ruin all of us," he begged. "A lot of people are going to get killed. It would be embarrassing to me." A flustered Kennedy replied, "I don't know if it would be embarrassing—that would not be the feeling."

Convinced finally of the possibility of a shoot-out, the attorney general relented, saying, "I'll send them back."

Inside the federal caravan, Meredith and the marshals were listening to the increasingly alarming radio news reports from Oxford. At Batesville, twenty-three miles west of Oxford, they found a deserted town—everyone from there, it seemed, had flocked to the university. Minutes later, the caravan received the command from the attorney general via radio relay from the spotter plane overhead. "Call it off. Turn back."

The caravan turned around and retreated back to Memphis.

At Oxford, night fell, and the segregationist forces rejoiced. The rebellion of the Mississippi state government was now backed by a popular insurrection. The federal government could not enforce the laws in one of its own member states.

In Mississippi, on the issue of race, the United States government had been overthrown.

CHAPTER SIX

In the Lord's Hands

A holocaust is in the making.

—Mississippi congressional delegation
message to the president pleading against
troop deployment, September 28, 1962

EVENTS WERE FLYING OUT of control. The force of U.S. Marshals alone was nowhere near strong enough to enforce federal authority in Mississippi anymore. It was time to press the button on the most awesome instrument of physical force the world had ever seen: the U.S. armed forces.

"We'd better get going with the military," Attorney General Robert Kennedy announced to his assistant Ed Guthman on Saturday, September 29. "Maybe we waited too long," RFK wondered aloud, amazed at the astonishing level of resistance and hostility building up in the South over the Meredith case. "I wouldn't have believed it could have happened in this country, but maybe now we can understand how Hitler took over Germany."

The Justice Department was hoping to make yet another attempt to force James Meredith into the university on Monday, October 1.

But now, the situation in Mississippi was looking increasingly dangerous to officials in Washington. Despite the ongoing telephone contact with Governor Barnett and his representatives, it not only appeared as if the state government was going to continue its rebellion, but FBI intelligence was indicating that the state would be supported in the streets by untold thousands of civilian volunteers from across the country.

On Friday morning, Ross Barnett had been hit with a frightful shock. The Fifth Circuit Court of Appeals issued an order giving him until next Tuesday, October 2, to register Meredith at the university, or face a $10,000-per-day personal fine. Barnett was a successful lawyer, but such a huge penalty could quickly wipe him and his family out, and this terrified him.

So Barnett, alarmed now at the inevitability of both violence and personal financial ruin, began desperately trying to somehow cool down the flames of the crisis without appearing to cave in to the federals. But this was an impossibly tall order, and Barnett was trapped by his own indecision and his inability to figure a way out of the mess he had helped create.

On Friday, September 28, the Mississippi State Senate approved a statement condemning the "police state and Gestapo methods" of the federal government. That night, on the Ole Miss campus, a giant cross wrapped in cloth and drenched in kerosene was ignited on a baseball diamond. Ten minutes later, an identical eight-foot-high cross was set ablaze while tied to the flagpole at the Lyceum at the center of campus. That same night, Mississippi's state Democratic chairman, Bidwell Adam of Gulfport, announced to a cheering crowd that he was quitting the national party because of its stand on integration.

The governor's office was being flooded with calls and telegrams from concerned citizens, racists, patriots, and crackpots across the United States, many with variations on the theme of "We'll bring our guns and fight." Barnett ordered his staff to respond, "Don't bring your guns; we don't want anything but peaceful action." He didn't say they couldn't come, though.

In Dallas, Texas, one man was watching the crisis with increasing fury. It was Edwin Walker, the conquering general of Little Rock in 1957.

In 1961 Walker resigned from the army after being reprimanded for indoctrinating his troops with right-wing propaganda and accusing Harry Truman and Eleanor Roosevelt of Communist tendencies. Now the career bachelor Walker was a darling of the extreme far right and a spokesman for the militant John Birch Society. As a measure of how radical Walker was, even Citizens Council chief Bill Simmons thought Walker was a right-wing extremist. Walker had recently run for governor of Texas and came in last in a field of six in the Democratic primary.

Something strange and terrible had happened to Edwin Walker's mind in the five years since Little Rock. If he was not a clinical madman by 1962, he certainly looked like one. His face twitched and froze in simian, glassy-eyed poses as he gave rambling, disconnected speeches to right-wing groups like the Citizens Council, speeches about fighting "war in the Fourth Dimension" and secret underground torture complexes beneath United Nations headquarters in New York. In a public letter to President Kennedy, he revealed the absurd depths of his incoherence when he warned the president that if he didn't blockade Cuba, American opinion "could rebel in revulsive repudiation of its traditional bounds against the untraditional escalation of intrusive and compulsive accommodation," whatever that meant.

At a December 1961 speech in Jackson attended by Governor Barnett, Lieutenant Governor Johnson, and Bill Simmons, Walker proclaimed, "I came here to meet the Communists on their battlefield right here in Mississippi. We are at war. Man your weapons and attack! Our objective is the defeat of the national pretenders and the professional power-mad politicians, and the Reds and pinks in every land."

Walker was now obsessed with the Meredith crisis, and on September 26, 1962, he issued a public battle cry for civilian volunteers to move on Mississippi. During a telephone appearance on a call-in radio show on Shreveport, Louisiana, station KWKH, he announced, "It is time to make a move. . . . We have listened and we have been pushed around by the anti-Christ Supreme Court. It's time to rise. To make a stand beside Governor Ross Barnett at Jackson, Mississippi. He is showing the way. Now is the time to be heard. Ten thousand strong from every state in the nation. Rally to the cause of freedom. . . . Bring your flag, your tent and your skillet." Walker concluded, "I have been on the other side in such situations in a place called Little Rock, and I was on the wrong side. This time I will be in Jackson, Mississippi, on the right side."

On Saturday, September 29, Walker landed in Jackson by private plane with a small band of Texas cronies and held a press conference on the tarmac. "I am in Mississippi beside Governor Ross Barnett," he announced. "I call for a national protest against the conspiracy from within. Rally to the cause of freedom. . . . There are thousands, possibly tens of thousands of people on their way to Mississippi from across the nation."

There really were thousands of Americans preparing to march on Oxford from coast to coast, both on their own initiative and in response to the general's call, though it was impossible to verify what was real and what was bluster. At FBI field offices throughout the region and beyond, rumors, informant's tips, and news reports were flooding in, indicating that the expected entry of Meredith on Monday, October 1, could result in mayhem and bloodshed. The intelligence was being flashed directly to Director J. Edgar Hoover, who was now personally directing the FBI's monitoring of the crisis, and relayed to his titular boss, Attorney General Bobby Kennedy.

In Los Angeles an FBI informant reported that one hundred volunteer armed fighters had pledged their services to General Walker and had already left for Oxford.

A tip came into the San Diego FBI office reporting that a group of 150 armed men was observed in an isolated desert area near an abandoned range in the Laguna Mountains. The unidentified men were spotted in cars, jeeps, and trucks containing high-caliber rifles, recoilless rifles, and a large radio. Fearing that there was some connection to the Mississippi crisis, FBI agents asked the San Diego County sheriff's office to investigate. Deputies in jeeps plunged into the mountains and canvassed the entire area, checking with fish-and-game stations, wardens, forest rangers, and deer hunters. They could not find a trace of the armed men.

Also in California, fifty citizens from Orange County, calling themselves the First California Volunteers, were reported in the local papers as having left for Mississippi on September 28 to stand against Meredith's admission. They carried an American flag, a state of California flag, and a "Christian flag." They sent a telegram ahead to Governor Barnett: "Hold fast and pray. We are en route to stand beside Gen. Edwin Walker in the defense of the sovereign state of Mississippi. Your fight is all America's fight."

In Gentilly, Louisiana, L. P. Davis, chairman of the local Citizens Council, fired off a cable to Walker: "You called for 10,000 volunteers nationwide for Ole Miss to fight against federal tyranny. Will pledge

10,000 from Louisiana alone, under your command. . . . They will come from all over the state. . . . I have been reliably informed that Mississippi already has 150,000 volunteers." Louisiana segregationist leader Willie Rainach also pledged ten thousand volunteers to Barnett.

In Miami, Fred Hockett, executive secretary of the Florida Citizens Council, pledged fifteen hundred armed men to rush to the defense of Mississippi. In Selma, Alabama, Sheriff James Clark of Dallas County announced that he and Sheriff Hugh Champion of nearby Chilton County were prepared to move into Mississippi with "posses" of up to five hundred men.

In Georgia, Calvin Craig, the "Grand Dragon," or state commander, of Robert Shelton's United Klans of America, declared that when the command was given, "a volunteer force of several thousand men would be on its way to Mississippi straight off." The FBI was picking up reports that no less than six hundred Klansmen from Alabama were already in Jackson, Mississippi, many checked in at the Robert E. Lee and King Edward hotels.

One cryptic report picked up by the FBI cited a ham-radio station in Kansas City broadcasting to a unit in San Francisco on 8.32 megacycles alerting "all Minuteman organizations, all ranger units, Illinois civilian control units, Washington militia," and other civilian organizations to stand by on alternate frequencies for more messages from Mississippi. Any involvement by the Minutemen would be especially alarming. The new ultra-right-wing terrorist faction was believed to be heavily armed and extremely violent. Its founder, Robert DePugh, was so radical he was expelled from the already radically conservative John Birch Society, and he was now planning a wave of bombings, bank robberies, and assassinations.

Across the state of Mississippi, town meetings were being planned for Saturday night to organize citizen caravans to go to Oxford. A source in Birmingham advised the FBI of a rumor of ten thousand citizens from Pascagoula, Mississippi, heading to Oxford to stand beside Governor Barnett. In Montgomery, Alabama, the National States' Rights Party, a far-right anti-black, anti-Semitic group with two hundred hard-core members, wired Governor Barnett with the claim that thousands of armed volunteers were ready to move when needed.

The same day, Saturday, September 29, the chairman of the Mississippi State Game and Fish Commission announced that his 250 supervisors and game wardens had been alerted to take part in the defense of Ole Miss. When these were added to the state's 82 sheriffs, 200-plus deputies, 200-plus constables, and 225 Highway Patrolmen, Governor Barnett could now field more than 1,000 armed men, not counting local police and civilian volunteers.

Agents of the state thought-police agency, the Mississippi Sovereignty commission, were operating in full-scale emergency mode. The Commission had six hundred thousand postcards printed up and addressed to President Kennedy, denouncing the federal government's "unnatural warfare" against Mississippi. A small fleet of private planes flew out of the Jackson airport on Saturday morning to deliver the postcards for distribution to weekend football crowds across the South, from Birmingham and Baton Rouge to Nashville, Dallas, and Columbia, South Carolina.

The most mysterious report of all was picked up by the FBI Milwaukee field office and relayed instantly to Director Hoover, who flashed an alert to agents in Chicago, Memphis, and New Orleans.

According to an FBI informant, a wealthy Barnett supporter in Mississippi had arranged for four P-51 Mustang Canadian surplus fighter planes to be flown from Wisconsin to an abandoned World War II B-17 airstrip in western Tennessee, then flown to Mississippi and placed at the disposal of Governor Barnett. Two of the P-51s were still military-style planes, and the other two had been converted into civilian models with "jump seats" installed behind the pilot seat. Three pilots had already volunteered to fly the planes. Director Hoover ordered his agents to run down the rumor immediately, but the agents couldn't confirm it.

In Washington the absolute worst-case scenario was stalking the president of the United States: To deal with the civil disorder that now seemed inevitable in Mississippi, he might have to send U.S. combat troops into action against their fellow Americans.

During the 1960 campaign, JFK had criticized President Eisenhower for vacillating in the 1957 Little Rock civil rights crisis: "There is more power in the presidency than to let things drift and then suddenly call out the troops," Kennedy charged. Kennedy Justice Department official Nicholas Katzenbach remembered that "the Kennedys thought that the one bad mistake Ike made was to send troops into Little Rock. They were determined not to send troops in, so that was the reason they worked so hard on Barnett."

But now John Kennedy had allowed events to drift toward an even more explosive outcome, and as his brother dueled indecisively by phone with Governor Barnett, the ghosts of the old South were rising from the clay soil and recapturing the state of Mississippi.

Beyond the obvious precedents of the Civil War and Little Rock, American presidents had deployed troops within the nation's borders a number of times before. In 1794 President Washington used federal troops to suppress the Whiskey Rebellion tax revolt along the Western frontier. When fifty thousand citizens rioted in Boston in 1854 as U.S. Marshals rounded up escaped slaves, troops were used to force the slaves onto southbound ships. President Grover Cleveland called out troops twice in 1894: in Montana to recover a train stolen by a gang of unemployed protesters called Coxey's Army; and in Illinois during the Pullman Strike. Woodrow Wilson dispatched the regular army to Colorado in 1914 to keep the peace during coal-mine strikes, and Franklin Roosevelt used troops in 1941 to seize the strike-afflicted North American Aviation defense plant in Los Angeles.

In July 1932 Herbert Hoover ordered U.S. Army chief of staff Douglas MacArthur to clear the nation's capital of the remnants of the Bonus Army, a force of veterans demanding immediate payment of their wartime bonuses, two of whom had been killed in a clash with city police on July 28. General MacArthur, sporting jackboots with spurs and flanked by a young Major Dwight Eisenhower, strutted eastward on Pennsylvania Avenue supervising an attack force of cavalry, tanks, infantry, and machine gunners. The soldiers advanced with drawn sabers and fixed bayonets, fired two thousand rounds of tear gas, and pushed the veterans out of the city. Dozens were injured in the clash, and an infant died from inhaling the tear gas.

Riots were nothing new to the American republic, either. In the 1834 city elections, the mayor of New York had to call in cavalry and infantry to suppress street battles among thousands of civilians. New York was the scene of the lethal Astor Place riot in 1849, when thousands of poor Irishmen attacked the Astor Place Opera House to protest the appearance of a famous English actor. The National Guard was called in, and twenty-two people died in two days of fighting. The savage Draft Riots in July 1863 plunged New York into four days of total anarchy, as several herds of ten thousand rioters each rampaged through Manhattan. The rioters, who were enraged by unfair draft laws, were finally subdued with musket and artillery fire by Union troops fresh off the battlefield at Gettysburg, but not before the riots killed at least one hundred people, including a dozen blacks.

Race riots, which were described by sociologist Gunnar Myrdal in his classic study An American Dilemma as "the most extreme form of extra-legal mob violence used to prevent Negroes from getting justice," erupted in East St. Louis, Illinois in 1917 (killing at least thirty-nine blacks and nine whites), and in thirty cities in 1919 (killing some forty-five blacks and twenty whites). "The breaking point," wrote Myrdal, "is caused by a crime or a rumor of a crime by a Negro against a white person, or the attempt of a Negro to claim a legal right."

The worst racial atrocity of twentieth-century America took place in Tulsa, Oklahoma, in 1921 when as many as three hundred blacks were massacred by armed white Tulsa citizens. The carnage was triggered by false rumors of an attack on a white female elevator operator, and saw the thriving thirty-four-block black district of Greenwood burned to ashes, leaving thousands homeless. The event was so horrific that it was purged from the history books for nearly eighty years.

In the "Zoot Suit Riot" of 1942, a mob of one thousand whites, acting on rumors of servicemen's wives being molested, rampaged through downtown Los Angeles, beating Mexican-Americans and blacks, causing many injuries but no fatalities. The following year in Detroit, on the hot Sunday night of June 20, a crowd of one hundred thousand blacks and whites sharing the integrated Belle Isle recreation area began shoving and scuffling, which blossomed into thirty hours of street battles that killed twenty-five blacks and nine whites. FDR was forced to send federal troops in to occupy the city for six months, and he also sent troops into New York the following month in the wake of a riot in Harlem that killed five and caused widespread property damage.

There were many reasons for John Kennedy to hate the idea of sending troops into Mississippi, not least of which was the midterm congressional elections just a few weeks away. As head of the Democratic Party, he presided over the party's exquisitely fragile, inherently unstable coalition of Southern conservative Democrats and Northern liberals. The coalition could implode over the issue of civil rights, and white Southern Democrats could defect en masse to the Republicans. U.S. troops had not been sent in action into the Deep South since Reconstruction, and the imagery of federal bayonets was sure to inflame some citizens to a hysterical pitch.

Politics aside, there was always the possibility that if soldiers were put into such an emotional, hostile environment with live ammunition, a massacre could occur and the president would be blamed for it. On Friday, September 28, seven members of the Mississippi U.S. congressional delegation raised this specter in a frantic cable to the president, pleading with him not to invade Mississippi, and warning simply, "A holocaust is in the making."

But President Kennedy had no choice. Never since the Civil War had a state officially "interposed" itself over federal authority, and this crisis was testing the very fabric of the federal system. So at the president's order, the Pentagon was preparing top-secret contingency plans for what could become the biggest domestic-peacetime show of military strength in the young republic's history.

In a move sure to infuriate the military brass, JFK deputized his brother Bobby to supervise the military buildup. It was a flagrant-enough violation of bureaucratic territory for Justice to oversee Defense. But worse, the young Bobby Kennedy's only military experience had been a few dreary months as a nineteen-year-old seaman, second class, on a warship drifting around the Caribbean after the end of World War II. His duties consisted mainly of chipping paint and swabbing the decks. Now he was overseeing the secretary of the army and the Joint Chiefs of Staff, with the concurrence of Secretary of Defense Robert Strange McNamara, who happily deferred management of this crisis to RFK.

The preliminary military planning had begun weeks earlier, in early September, when it looked as if the U.S. Army would be needed to set up a tent-city base in the Holly Springs National Forest north of Oxford to house U.S. Marshals and provide them with logistical support.

When Barnett made his interposition speech on September 13,

Bobby Kennedy and his Department of Justice team assumed that Mississippi state officials and police forces could try to block Meredith and the marshals, possibly triggering widespread public disorder, which would require a much larger military force. The army was planning for a variety of contingencies, from breaking up crowds and guarding the U.S. Marshals who were protecting Meredith, to inserting Meredith into the Registrar's Office by physical force, to seizing Governor Barnett himself.

Secretary of the Army Cyrus Vance and Major General Creighton W. Abrams, the army's director of military operations, began ramping up their plans, using the Millington Naval Air Station near Memphis as the staging area for what would soon become a gigantic invasion force. Under normal conditions Oxford was twenty minutes south of Memphis by helicopter and two hours by land convoy.

On Friday afternoon, September 28, the Joint Chiefs of Staff, along with RFK, had marched into the White House to brief the president on a Mississippi invasion plan. Two task forces, Alpha and Bravo, had been assembled and placed on twenty-four-hour alert. As the spearhead of Task Force Alpha, the first regular-army outfit to be sent into Mississippi would be a crack force of "riot-fighters" who were part of the 82nd Airborne Division based at Fort Bragg, North Carolina: a group of five hundred officers and men called the 503d Military Police Battalion.

Every once in a while the American military produces an outfit of such superb morale and superior training that it is remembered forever by the men who served in it in legendary terms. Such was the case with the 503d Military Police Battalion. It was a rough, highly trained group of men handpicked for both high intelligence and brute strength (their average height was five feet ten inches) who normally provided base security and policing duties at Fort Bragg, home to some of the toughest, hardest-partying GIs in the army, the Airborne paratroopers of the 82nd Airborne Division. The MPs had to be tougher. "If we weren't," noted one MP, Specialist Fourth Class William Mayes, a six-foot-five, sixth-degree black belt in karate, "we'd get our brains beat in" by the paratroopers.

The 503d MP Battalion was also designated as the army's elite riot-fighting outfit. For the past year, the MPs had been training intensively in mob control and the use of tear gas and rapid deployment, for the mission of crushing civil disturbances, which military planners expected could erupt in Asia, Berlin, or Cuba, if the United States invaded, or in the event of riots in the United States. As part of the army's rapid-response STRAC (Strategic Army Corps) force, the 503d was ready to load up and scramble into C-130 transport planes on two hours' notice, to be airlifted anywhere in the world.

By an ironic stroke of fate, one of the most perfectly integrated American societies of 1962 was being selected to invade the most segregated state in the Union. The 503d MP Battalion was, in the front ranks, a fully integrated force and a textbook example of the remarkable success of racial integration in the U.S. military, the policy instituted by President Harry S Truman in 1948. The 503d was made up of Northerners and Southerners, black and white, with many white Southern troops being commanded by black noncommissioned officers. There were eighteen-year-old white boys fresh out of segregated South Carolina high schools being bossed around by black World War II veterans from Newark, New Jersey. Yet there were absolutely no racial tensions in the battalion. In fact, no one had ever heard of any. One black sergeant, William Newton, remembered his white Southern troops as "so well disciplined that if you told them to get on a building and jump off, they'd do exactly that. They were super, an outstanding group of men. I never had such a sharp group."

There were many reasons for the 503d's interracial solidarity. One was that by being designated as an elite force often called to put on combat demonstrations for visiting brass, they were already one of the highest-morale bunches in the military. They were a special favorite of General Hamilton Howze, the Fort Bragg base commander and head of the Eighteenth Airborne Corps, which was comprised of both of the nation's two Airborne divisions, the 82nd Airborne and the 101st Airborne. Another reason was the simple fact that color blindness had become, by law, a governing principle of the 1 million–man U.S. Army. Blacks and whites bunked and showered and trained and chowed down together, and you either got used to it on day one or you could be thrown out of the service. It was that simple.

But two overriding factors guaranteed the spirit of the 503d: the character of its leadership and the chemistry between the officers and the enlisted men, from the top down. The battalion was commanded by Lieutenant Colonel John J. Flanagan, a combat veteran of jungle fighting in the South Pacific who grew up in Cliffside, New Jersey. A wiry man of forty, with hair beginning to turn gray, he was old enough to be the father of many of the battalion's young draftees. Some of the men nicknamed him "Father Flanagan" for his somewhat remote and austere demeanor, and when he sent them chiding memos to straighten out their paperwork, they were dubbed "Flan-o-grams." But he was a cool, sensitive, and methodical soldier and somehow one knew that when the bullets started flying, he'd do the right thing.

A dramatic personality counterpoint to Flanagan was the battalion's executive officer, forty-two-year-old Major Raymond Le Van, who reported to Flanagan. Le Van grew up in New Jersey and fought in many of the key battles in Europe, where he won three Silver Stars. He was a fearless, flamboyant soldier who seemed born for combat, and he had no problem bucking channels or bending the rules when necessary. One could easily picture him in combat with guns blazing and a grenade between his teeth, racing ahead of his own men.

Lieutenant Colonel Flanagan was given command of Task Force Alpha, which besides the 503d Battalion included tear-gas specialists from the 502d Chemical Company, the Fifteenth Field Hospital Detachment and its six ambulances, all from Fort Bragg, and the Thirty-first Army Light Helicopter Company from Fort Benning, Georgia. All together, Task Force Alpha totaled 689 officers and enlisted men.

The second task force, Bravo, consisted of 1,076 ground-infantry troops of the 2nd Infantry's "Indianhead" Division from Fort Benning, Georgia, commanded by Colonel Lucien Fairfax Keller. They had next to no riot training, and had to begin a crash program of training with gas and gas masks. Task Force Bravo planned to conduct a high-speed motor march to the Millington Naval Air Station at Memphis. The plan assumed that if they moved into Mississippi, they would be refused gas and oil by local merchants and that local police would not assist in traffic control.

The Pentagon was preparing three other task forces for possible action, using the air force base at Columbus, Mississippi, as a secondary staging area. The generals were even considering, as an absolute worst case, using combat paratroopers of the 82nd and 101st Airborne Divisions, the World War II heroes of D-Day and the liberation of Europe. Both the 82nd at Fort Bragg, North Carolina, and the 101st at

Fort Campbell, Kentucky, were close by air to Mississippi, and could be dropped in quickly if things blew apart in the state.

On September 25, the army had been asked by the Justice Department to begin contingency planning for the imposition of martial law in Mississippi, if necessary. This would enable civilians to be arrested and even tried by military personnel. The federal planners were hoping to avoid that extreme step, however, so to evade the restrictions of the Posse Comitatus Act of 1878, which prohibited the U.S. military from enforcing laws or arresting civilians within the country's borders, troops would only "detain" troublemakers and quickly hand them off to be formally arrested by U.S. Marshals.

One highly sensitive aspect of the invasion plan was especially troubling to the federal planners: Fully 20 percent of the troops being readied for deployment were black. According to the official Defense Department history of the crisis, during a meeting in Attorney General Robert Kennedy's office on September 27, General Abrams reported to RFK that "verbal instructions had been issued that when and if employed on a mission, Negro personnel would be withheld from committed units so that they would not come in contact with the civil population, in order to avoid unnecessary incidents."

There was no record of Robert Kennedy's objecting to this order, and if he had any objections, he quickly dropped them. In this offhanded closed-door decision, the attorney general of the United States signed off, in advance, on the resegregation of a sizable portion of the United States military.

It was fourteen years after President Harry Truman ordered the desegregation of the armed forces. Now the military had the go-ahead to pull several thousand black American soldiers out of action, off the front line of the struggle against racism itself, out of their outfits and hidden away in segregated holding areas, all because the sight of their black skin might upset the sensibilities of local citizens. It happened once before, in miniature, during the Army's Little Rock operation in 1957, when 114 black soldiers of the 101st Airborne Division were hidden away from view from the white civilian population. Now there were thousands of black troops involved.

James Meredith was risking his life to compel the U.S. government to commit to eliminate segregation in his home state. Now the federal government was about to reimpose segregation on a part of the U.S. Army in order to accomplish that mission.

. . .

Inside the 503d MP Battalion's headquarters office at Fort Bragg on Friday morning, September 28, the battalion's staff officers huddled around the desk of executive officer Major Ray Le Van. They were flabbergasted.

Outside, their men were preparing the battalion's 117 jeeps, 44 trucks, and 27,600 pounds of ammunition to be driven to nearby Pope Air Force Base and loaded onto giant air force C-130 transports for airlift to the staging point at Memphis.

In his hand Major Le Van was holding a piece of paper with the Eighteenth Airborne Corps letterhead on it, containing one of the most outrageous orders ever issued in the history of the U.S. Army. It was an order to separate all the black troops out of the battalion and leave them behind at Fort Bragg before moving out to Memphis.

The officers were sputtering a chorus of disgust. Major John Templeton exclaimed, "This takes the first sergeants out—this takes the platoon sergeants out! We can't function that way!" Almost half the platoon sergeants were black, as was half the motor pool and many other key personnel. This order would destroy the battalion's ability to function.

Captain George Baldwin, the communications officer who handed the order to Le Van, waited thirty-eight years to tell the story of what happened next.

Major Le Van snapped, "Who writes these things? What idiot did this? How do they think we're going to function?"

At that, Baldwin reported, Major Le Van "tore the order up and dropped it into a garbage can."

"We got eight written confirmations of the order," Captain Baldwin reported, "and we threw each one away."

In violation of direct orders approved by the attorney general of the United States, the 503d Military Police Battalion took off for action the next day with every one of its black soldiers.

Even as late as Saturday, September 29, the attorney general was still vacillating with the fantasy that the troops could be held back at their staging points and a beefed-up contingent of U.S. Marshals could be enough to force James Meredith into the university on Monday, October 1.

That morning, a force of 536 Deputy U.S. Marshals from across the country was converging on the naval air station at Memphis and undergoing crash riot-training. Of the regulars from the U.S. Marshals Service, there were 123; 97 were borrowed federal-prison guards from the U.S. Bureau of Prisons; and an additional 316 were hurriedly deputized from the U.S. Border Patrol, leaving much of the southern U.S. border unguarded from California to Texas.

When James Meredith was preparing to fly to Memphis for the final assault, a reporter asked him about the possibility of violence. Meredith replied, "It's just as impossible for me to imagine that fear could stand in the way of the education I want as it is for me to imagine not wanting that education. When I was in the service I felt that I was totally committed to any sort of call that might be made on me to protect my country. Right now I feel just as totally committed to ask for my right to the education that I want in my home state."

After Meredith arrived at the naval air station on Saturday, he looked out at the C-130s disgorging the crack troops of the 503d Military Police Battalion. He was impressed by how many of the men charging out of the planes were black.

At 1:35 P.M., Washington time, Saturday, RFK and Barnett conferred yet again by telephone. It was a typically courteous, desultory, and fairly ridiculous exchange; at one point RFK insisted, "Governor, he's going to the University of Mississippi." Barnett responded, "It looks to me, General, like such a foolish thing for him to keep his mind on that." RFK noted, "I think the courts have decided that."

Robert Kennedy was falling into quicksand. "What I was trying to avoid," he explained in a 1964 oral history, "was having to send troops and trying to avoid having a federal presence in Mississippi. In my judgment, what [Barnett] was trying to accomplish was the avoidance of integration at the University of Mississippi, number one. And if he couldn't do that, to be forced to do it by our heavy hand; and his preference was with troops. . . . He had people pulling and pushing at him from so many different directions that, I think, he just got himself into a bigger and bigger box. He eventually pulled me in with him."

Realizing he was getting nowhere with Barnett, RFK reluctantly decided to draw his biggest gun: the president of the United States. With his brother by his side in the Oval Office, President John F. Kennedy made his first call to the governor to try to charm Barnett out of the impasse. In fact, a cordial, gracious Ross Barnett had visited the president back in June, posing for pictures in the Oval Office with a delegation of Southern governors.

JFK flipped a secret switch on his desk. This triggered a red light on his secretary's desk, which was the signal for her to begin recording the call on a concealed Dictaphone. Several weeks earlier, John Kennedy had quietly installed the White House's first full-fledged secret-recording network (FDR, Truman, and Eisenhower conducted far more limited test recordings). It was a system of concealed switches, microphones, tape recorders, and Dictaphones that stretched through the Oval Office and Cabinet Room and into the White House mansion itself.

When the call was being put through to the Oval Office, the president announced jokingly, "And now—Governor Ross Barnett." Then he said, "Governor, this is the President of the United States—not Bobby, not Teddy." The attorney general wisecracked, "Go get him, Johnny boy."

Barnett came on the line, and JFK greeted him as a fellow chief of state: "I'm glad to talk to you, Governor. I am concerned about this situation down there."

Barnett replied, "Oh, I should say I am concerned about it, Mr. President. It's a horrible situation."

"Well, now, here's my problem," Kennedy offered. "Listen, I didn't put him [Meredith] in the university, but on the other hand, under the Constitution, I have to carry out that order and I don't want to do it in any way that causes difficulty to you or to anyone else. But I've got to do it. Now, I'd like your help in doing that."

Barnett affably retorted, "You know what I'm up against, Mr. President. I took an oath, you know, to abide by the laws of this state, and our Constitution here and the Constitution of the United States. I'm on the spot here, you know."

The president countered, "The problem is, Governor, that I got my responsibility, just like you have yours."

"Well, that's true," Barnett replied soothingly. "I realize that, and I appreciate that so much."

"Well, now here's the thing," offered the president. "The Attorney General can talk to Mr. Watkins tomorrow. What I want, would like to do is try to work this out in an amicable way. We don't want a lot of people down there getting hurt. We don't want to have a lot of people getting hurt or killed down there."

At the mention of Tom Watkins, the governor perked up with optimism. "Mr. Watkins is really an A-1 lawyer, an honorable man, has the respect of every lawyer in America who knows him. He's of the law firm of Watkins & Eager. They've had an 'A' rating for many, many years, and I believe that he can help solve the problem."

Barnett signed off with a sweet politician's farewell: "I appreciate your interest in our poultry program and all those things."

JFK, temporarily stumped for words, chuckled at the governor, then hung up. He then turned to his brother and kidded him, "You've been fighting a sofa pillow all week."

"He's a rogue," cautioned RFK.

At 3:15 P.M. President Kennedy and Barnett were back on the phone. JFK handed the phone to the attorney general, who told Barnett that he spoke with Watkins, who had no suggestions other than sneaking Meredith into registering at Jackson, while the authorities, media, and white mobs were preoccupied at the school's Oxford campus. The subsequent conversation was another exercise in futility, as the affable governor shadowboxed, slipped, and slid around the president with courtly congeniality.

Barnett solemnly declared, "I've taken an oath to abide by the laws of this state and our state constitution and the Constitution of the United States. . . . How can I violate my oath of office? How can I do that and live with the people of Mississippi? You know, they expecting me to keep my word."

JFK, sounding uncertain, said, "I know your feeling about the law of Mississippi and the fact that you don't want to carry out that court order. What we really want to have from you, though, is some understanding about whether the state police will maintain law and order."

"Oh, we'll do that," said Barnett. "They'll take positive action, Mr. President, to maintain law and order as best we can." But the governor backpedaled almost immediately, citing the difficulty of guaranteeing peace: "You just don't understand the situation down here."

JFK, increasingly exasperated and perhaps finally sensing that Barnett would resist to the end, snapped, "Well, the only thing I got is my responsibility. This is not my order, I just have to carry it out. So I want to get together and try to do it with you in a way which is the most satisfactory and causes the least chance of damage to people in Mississippi. That's my interest."

Once again, the chief executives had talked around and around each other and gotten absolutely nowhere.

Later in the afternoon, RFK and Barnett seemed to work out a tentative agreement for a decoy plan: Meredith would register quietly at Jackson on Monday while Barnett and Johnson were at Oxford standing heroically at the entrance to the university. A "surprised" Barnett would publicly attack federal subterfuge, but Meredith would be allowed into Ole Miss on Tuesday. Barnett said that law and order would be enforced by the Highway Patrol.

JFK and Barnett spoke again at 7:00 P.M. and agreed to the decoy operation.

JFK hung up thinking he had a deal.

In Jackson on Saturday night, forty-one thousand jubilant Mississippians packed the Memorial Stadium for the Ole Miss–Kentucky football game, forming a red, white, and blue sea of Confederate battle flags. Governor Ross Barnett proudly waved the flag of Dixie from his VIP seat. Many of the young men in the stands wore "keppie caps," the Confederate rebel military hat. When the teams retreated to their locker rooms for halftime, Coach Johnny Vaught's Ole Miss "Rebels" were beating Kentucky 7 to 0.

A jumbo screen flashed the words to the new state song "Go Mississippi!" as the one-hundred-piece Ole Miss band pounded out the frantic, upbeat tune: "Go, Mississippi, you cannot go wrong, / Go, Mississippi, we're singing your song, M-I-S, S-I-S, S-I-P-P-I!"

The multitude roared, "We want Ross! We want Ross!" and the world's largest Confederate flag was carried across the field. The governor of Mississippi strutted onto the field, and the crowd went nearly berserk in a delirious, sustained ovation.

Ross Barnett was being saturated with one of the most powerful crowd raptures ever given to an American politician. To one football fan, Captain Hassel Franklin of the Mississippi National Guard, it seemed like the stadium was going to collapse. It felt like a revolution was breaking out. To Ole Miss student Mary Lynn Hendricks, it seemed like the earth was shattering under her feet.

"You would have thought you were watching the Christians and the lions fighting in the Colosseum with the roar that went up," remembered Jackson attorney William Goodman. "It was like a big Nazi rally," an Ole Miss student recalled, adding, "Yes, it was just the way Nuremberg must have been!" Another spectator, E. L. McDaniel, felt that if Barnett gave the word, all 41,000 people would burst out of the stadium and march 170 miles north to Oxford to surround the university, and another 50,000 would join them on the way.

Barnett strode up to the microphone at the fifty-yard line with a furious expression on his face, thrust his clenched fist in the air, and held it up, his body a frozen statue of revolutionary defiance. Television cameras were broadcasting him in live close-up throughout the state. "Thousands of Confederate battle flags burst forth throughout the stadium," wrote journalist Bill Minor, "shimmering in the night like a forest fire running before the wind."

Barnett drank in the delirium and finally cried in a high-pitched voice that sliced the air like a saber, "I love Mississippi!" The crowd screamed in unison.

"I love her people!

"Our customs!

"I love and respect our *heritage!*"

That was all he said. The whole world knew what he meant. Barnett stayed there for a while, his fist aimed at the stars, drinking in the tidal waves of joy from his forty-one thousand subjects.

"That night," a student in the crowd later reported, "people would have been glad to die for Ross." Recalled H. M. Ray, then the U.S. Attorney for the Northern District of Mississippi, "Ross Barnett didn't know what he was doing. He really didn't realize the gravity of what he was unleashing."

Later that evening, one of Barnett's moderate advisers pleaded with him to just let the Meredith admission happen and be done with it.

"I can't do it," Barnett replied. "Did you see that crowd?"

Soon after the game, the cheers still ringing in his ears, Barnett phoned Robert Kennedy and called off the decoy plan. RFK was furious, but the two signed off amicably, with the agreement that the marshals would bring Meredith into Oxford on Monday morning, in full strength, with the Mississippi Highway Patrol on hand to help maintain order.

When President Kennedy learned of the collapse of the latest deal a few minutes later, he seemed to fear the worst might happen. So he ordered Task Force Echo to prepare for action. The force consisted of five hundred men of the 720th Military Police Battalion at Fort Hood, Texas, and the president ordered them to fly to the Memphis staging area immediately.

On the president's desk was the paperwork that would federalize the Mississippi National Guard. This force was commanded by Governor Barnett, but command could be transferred instantaneously to the president by an executive order. However, since the all-white Guard was comprised of local Mississippi men, most of whom were presumably pro-segregation or against immediate integration, the Pentagon was not sure how they would respond.

To find out, General Maxwell Taylor, the incoming chairman of the Joint Chiefs of Staff, was discreetly calling around to unit commanders of the Mississippi National Guard, asking them how they would react if they were called on to escort James Meredith onto the University of Mississippi campus.

One National Guard commander bluntly informed the general by phone that such an order would trigger the biggest exodus of AWOL troops the United States had ever seen. If he received such an order, the Mississippi commander declared, he would lead his own men out the door and out of the U.S. Army.

Based on this information, there was now no way for the president of the United States to know whether or not the eleven thousand men of the Mississippi National Guard would obey his orders.

As the clock approached midnight, the president was sitting at a long table in his second-floor study in the White House. Next to him was Assistant Attorney General Norbert A. Schlei. Kennedy took a pen and signed Proclamation 3497, which ordered the governor of Mississippi, state lawmen, and anyone else obstructing justice in Mississippi to "cease and desist therefrom and to disperse and retire peaceably forthwith."

"Is this pretty much what Ike signed in 1957 with the Little Rock thing?" asked Kennedy. "Essentially," said Schlei. The president asked, "Where do I sign?" He stopped before signing the date. "Is it past midnight?" he asked. Schlei checked his watch, and said, "It's just twenty seconds past twelve." The president also signed the papers that "federalized" the Mississippi National Guard and placed the force under his control, at least in theory.

The president switched off the table lamp, pulled his glasses off, tapped the table, and noted, "You know this was General Grant's table." Schlei was descending the stairs to brief reporters on the proclamation when he heard the president calling down after him, "Wait! Don't tell them about General Grant's table."

The president couldn't get to sleep right away, so he switched on his hi-fi set to relax.

In Oxford, the one-man FBI field office manned by Resident Agent Robin Cotten was drowning in a sea of rumors of armed Americans heading toward the city.

Until now, Agent Cotten's job consisted of the typical FBI criminal investigative work: car thefts, bank robberies, extortions, and kidnappings. At the time, Mississippi had such a relatively low caseload for the Bureau that it didn't even rate a field office, and the eight agents stationed in the northern half of the state all worked out of their homes.

Agent Cotten, who had a law degree from Southern Law University and was a graduate of the FBI Academy at Quantico, fell in love with Oxford when he was first stationed there in 1959, as did his wife, who plunged into the community's social life, joining the bowling league and all the ladies' clubs. Their son had just entered Ole Miss as a freshman. Suddenly, the Bureau's intelligence was indicating that Cotten's beloved hometown was about to be invaded by armed civilians who hailed from sea to shining sea. And he was the only agent on the scene.

"I need help! I need help!" Cotten pleaded by phone to his superiors at the regional office in Memphis. "Send more agents," he begged. "There's going to be some killing here!"

. . .

At 3:00 in the morning in Jackson, a strapping twenty-seven-year-old attorney was awakened by a persistent banging on his front door.

The attorney's name was Ross Barnett, Jr. He was the governor's only son. But he was also a second lieutenant in the headquarters detachment of the Mississippi National Guard, which had just been taken away from his father's control and absorbed into the regular U.S. Army.

Barnett opened the door to see one of his fellow National Guard officers standing under the porch light, telling him he had to report to the armory in Jackson, on orders of the president of the United States.

Ross Barnett, Jr., was about as close to his father as a son can be. In addition to continuing his father's law practice in the same office where his father had started business in 1926, he had lunch with the governor almost every day at the Governor's Mansion, and was very supportive of him politically.

"I loved my father, and I respected him immensely and would have done anything for him," the younger Barnett remembered in an interview in 2000. "I just hated that this came up. You just hate to be put in a position where you're in betwixt and between your duty and your loved ones."

Of his father's politics, the younger Barnett explained, "The majority of the [white] people of the state of Mississippi felt the same way my father did. The number-one plank in his platform was segregation of the races. That was all we knew down here. If you're used to doing something for years and years and years, and all of a sudden you've got to change, when change comes, regardless of what the change is, it disturbs people."

But that was all yesterday. As of midnight this morning, September 30, he was a federal soldier. "I'd taken an oath to uphold the laws not only of the state of Mississippi but the laws of the United States and to obey the commander in chief," Ross Barnett, Jr., explained. "Once you're federalized, you're under the command of the president of the United States."

As he went to the closet to put on his army lieutenant's uniform, Ross Barnett, Jr., told his wife, "I'm heading to the Armory. I've been federalized. I'm going to do my duty." There wasn't any argument; there wasn't anything for her to say except, "How can I help you get ready?"

The young officer drove through the deserted streets of his hometown toward the Armory. He was ready to ship out to Oxford or any-where else the army ordered him.

All across the state, through hollows and forests and swamps and hills, thousands of Mississippi boys and men were doing the same thing.

CHAPTER SEVEN

Though the Heavens Fall

■ ■ ■ ■

If rebellion was the certain consequence, we are bound to say, *"Justitia fiat, ruat coelum"*—Let justice be done, though the heavens fall.

—Lord Mansfield, chief justice of England, 1768

SUNDAY, SEPTEMBER 30, dawned crisp and clear in Oxford, the leaves on the old trees igniting in a yellow glow into a brilliant early autumn day. The morning was greeted with mockingbirds singing in the morning dew.

On the campus of the University of Mississippi, students were strolling around chatting about their football victory over Kentucky the night before, about homecoming queens and fraternity rushes.

At 9:00 A.M., a reporter from the *Chicago Sun-Times* named Hoke Norris was walking around the school grounds, jotting down notes on the local color. He was one of the first of more than three hundred reporters who were descending on Oxford today, getting into position for what was expected to be the big showdown over James Meredith the following day.

In front of the Lyceum building, Norris was greeted by two old farmers from out of town who pulled up in a pickup truck and asked where "that nigger" was going to be registered. One farmer predicted, "There's going to be shooting if they try to enroll that nigger. Barnett can't back down now." His buddy chimed in, "Kennedy can't back down either. How would it look if the governor of one state backed him down? The Russians could just come in and take over, then." The reporter watched the two farmers slip away, as they pondered the dilemma of two leaders in full collision. In a downtown restaurant, the reporter saw a local citizen shake his head gravely and declare, "We tried to lick the North once and got licked. I don't think we can do it now and I don't see why they don't know we can't. I'd like for the schools to stay like they were, but they ain't. We know that."

At St. Peter's Episcopal Church two blocks off Courthouse Square, the Reverend Duncan M. Gray, Jr., stepped to the lectern to preach the sermon at 10:00 mass.

Duncan Gray was the balding, bespectacled, slightly built thirty-five-year-old rector of St. Peter's. He was a fourth-generation Mississippian, a forceful advocate of racial justice, and one of the few white Mississippians willing to speak out against Governor Barnett. For the past eight years, Gray had been preaching in favor of compliance with the 1954 Supreme Court decision declaring segregated public schools unconstitutional. Gray was shielded to some extent from career disaster by the fact that his father, Duncan Montgomery Gray, Sr., was the current Episcopal bishop of Mississippi and had been since 1943, but the son's outspoken, courageous stand was still a dangerous one to hold in this place and time.

On this Sunday morning, Gray stepped to the lectern and delivered a fervent plea for sanity. "We do *not* have the right to defy and disobey the law when it is established and in force," he announced. "In trying to do this, we have brought upon ourselves the threat of *anarchy;* and, as Christians, we cannot and must not support this alternative to the democracy in which we live.

"We do not want troops in this state," declared Gray, "and we can be thankful that the Federal Government has been as patient as it has in not taking this step so far. However, we may well see troops here in the next few days. But when this happens we will have only ourselves to blame."

He concluded, "No university in the world would defend this position rationally, and no Christian Church in the world would defend it morally. . . . Surely, most of us realize by now that there can be only one resolution to this crisis: the admission of James Meredith to the University."

Duncan Gray later recalled the sudden impact of these words on his congregation: "When I told them that their Christian duty was to support the admittance of James Meredith, the church became deathly quiet."

Although Duncan Gray was a man of great courage, no one ever accused him of being a very good singer. Unlike some Episcopalians, he was not shy about joyously belting out a hymn like a Baptist, but he was often off-key and periodically buried the sound of his choir. This morning, as scattered armies gathered to invade his little city, the reverend sang the hymn "God of Grace and God of Glory" with his congregation. The lyrics seemed written especially for this day: "Lo! the hosts of evil round us, Scorn Thy Christ, assail His ways . . . Grant us wisdom, grant us courage, For the living of these days."

In Washington, D.C., John Kennedy attended 10:00 mass at St. Stephen the Martyr Church. Then he went to the Oval Office to prepare for a luncheon for Lord Home, the British foreign secretary, and to review drafts of a speech to the nation he planned to give that night to plead for peace in Mississippi. Restless as usual, Kennedy bounded up from his desk and through the great French doors for a stroll around the South Lawn of the White House.

A few blocks away, the attorney general was in his office at the Justice Department, flanked by Burke Marshall and other top lieutenants. When a call from Governor Barnett was put through at 12:45 P.M., the governor, true to form, backed away from the recent tentative agreements and proposed a brand-new, highly theatrical plan.

Barnett proposed to stand in front of a battle formation of five hundred unarmed Mississippi Highway Patrolmen, sheriffs, deputies, and unspecified "soldiers," and stare down and block the U.S. Marshals from entering the university, all in front of the world press, giving him an epic photo opportunity of heroic resistance to the federals.

"I will be in the front line," Barnett told the attorney general, "and when Meredith presents himself, I'll do like I did before. I will read a proclamation denying him entrance. I will tell the people of Mississippi now that I want peace and we must have no violence, no bloodshed. When you draw the guns, I will then tell the people. In other words, we will step aside and you can walk in."

This was too much for the attorney general, who feared a full-scale shoot-out and bloodbath. "The plan was riddled with unacceptable risks," recalled Justice Department official Ed Guthman, "including the distinct possibility that with one misstep the Appomattox-like melodrama would dissolve into armed conflict between state and federal forces."

The attorney general demurred. "I don't think that will be very pleasant, Governor. . . . I think it is silly going through this whole facade of your standing there, our people drawing guns; your stepping aside; to me it is dangerous and I think this has gone beyond the stage of politics, and you have a responsibility to the people of that state and to the people of the United States."

The governor still held fast to his dream of a sensational photograph. "I am not interested in politics personally," he claimed. "I have said so many times we couldn't have integration and I have got to do something. I can't just walk back." He insisted, "I have to be confronted with your troops," meaning several hundred federal marshals with their guns drawn.

Finally, the attorney general lost his patience and issued an ultimatum, threatening to reveal to the world his trump card—the full details of their secret negotiations to slip Meredith into the university, a move that both men knew could destroy Barnett politically with his pro-segregation supporters. "The President is going on TV tonight," RFK declared. "He is going through the statement he had with you last night. He will have to say why he called up the National Guard; that you had an agreement to permit Meredith to go to Jackson to register, and your lawyer, Mr. Watkins, said this was satisfactory, and you would let him fly in by helicopter."

A mortified Barnett exclaimed, "That won't do at all!"

RFK proclaimed, "You broke your word to him."

Barnett could hardly believe what was happening. "You don't mean the President is going to say that tonight?"

"Of course he is," said Kennedy. "You broke your word; now you suggest we send in troops, fighting their way through a barricade. You gave your word . . . you didn't keep it."

"Where didn't I keep it?" asked Barnett. "In what particular?"

The attorney general replied, "When you said you would make an agreement and that Meredith would come to Jackson; send everybody to Oxford."

"Don't say that," Barnett pleaded. "Please don't mention it."

"We have it all down," said RFK. This was a clear threat to reveal the details of the secret Kennedy/Barnett phone negotiations, recorded stenographically by RFK's secretary and electronically by John Kennedy's secret Oval Office Dictaphone.

The bluffing game of chicken that Ross Barnett had played with Bobby Kennedy for two weeks had reached a sudden climax. Now Barnett realized that there was no longer any way to prevent or delay the inevitable: James Meredith was coming into the university with the might of the federal government backing him up. There was no time left to maneuver.

Instead of the triumphant, immortal photo opportunity he yearned for, a hellish, bloody vision now appeared in Ross Barnett's mind. It was a picture of what would happen if Meredith arrived tomorrow, on Monday.

By then, Barnett later explained, he thought that as many as twenty thousand civilians would be in Oxford to block the federals; many of them would be armed, and hundreds of them could be shot dead in the streets. It would be a historic massacre, and he would be blamed for it. Even if it didn't happen in just that way, the president was threatening to destroy Barnett politically by revealing their secret phone negotiations. Ross Barnett was envisioning his own political execution in a sea of innocent blood.

The only way out Barnett could see now was to rush Meredith in as fast as possible, to short-circuit the inevitable people's insurrection before it could break out, before the tens of thousands of civilians who were planning to blockade Oxford could get there.

Barnett abruptly proposed, "Why don't you fly him in this afternoon?" RFK quickly consented, and the two agreed that Meredith would be flown in and installed on the Oxford campus that night, Sunday, with the Highway Patrol assigned to help keep order in preparation for Meredith's registration the next morning.

Barnett practically begged the attorney general not to go public with their agreement: "Please let us treat what we say as confidential? . . . I am sorry about the misunderstanding last night. I am extremely hurt over it really. I didn't know I was violating any agreement. Please understand me. . . . Please let's not have a fuss about what we talked about. . . . I hope you will consider my position here."

With the president's planned 8:00 P.M. speech to the nation in mind as a new deadline, the attorney general said, "If we get it straightened out by 7:30 tonight, the whole matter will be alleviated. . . . Let's get going."

Barnett now asked permission to continue his playacting of resistance: "If I am surprised, you won't mind or if I raise Cain about it?"

Signing off, the attorney general replied, "I don't mind that; just say law and order will be maintained."

With time running out, the president and attorney general decided to send an urgent telegram to Barnett to try to pin the governor down in writing. Citing the "breakdown in law and order in Mississippi," the president asked for a reply "at once" to the question of whether Barnett would help enforce the court order; if not, would he continue to block Meredith's entry, and, crucially, would the state police authorities cooperate in preventing violence? A reply never came.

RFK ordered a team of Justice Department men to scramble out of his office to a government JetStar and fly to Oxford to take charge of getting James Meredith placed on the Ole Miss campus. Leading them was Deputy Attorney General Nicholas Katzenbach. "Hey, Nick," RFK wisecracked to the departing Katzenbach with vintage Kennedy macho gallows humor, "Don't worry if you get shot because the President needs a moral issue." Of this scene, historian Taylor Branch observed, "This was the Kennedy panache—bright amateurs dashing cavalierly into semi-war."

Word of the new collapsed timetable was flashed to the U.S. Marshals at Memphis at midday. Suddenly, the marshals, who had been planning for an assault on the university on the next morning, now had to scramble to mobilize in less than four hours.

In the rush to mobilize the U.S. Marshals, nobody remembered to tell the most crucial player in the drama: the U.S. Army.

Right then, over twenty thousand U.S. Army military police, infantry, National Guardsmen, Airborne paratroopers, and helicopter pilots were standing by at staging areas across the region. But apparently the only troops aware of what was going on were the small advance contingent of 105 army engineers and drivers from the Seventieth Engineer Battalion from Fort Campbell, Kentucky, which was already positioned at Oxford, preparing a tent city and transport trucks for the marshals.

No one in the White House or the Justice Department remembered to tell U.S. Army general Creighton Abrams, the man in charge of the military forces at Memphis, what was going on, that the final assault on the university by U.S. Marshals was under way. The general would stay in the dark for the next five hours.

On Sunday morning, James Meredith had flown from New Orleans to the Millington Naval Air Station at Memphis, still assuming he would be going to Oxford the next morning, Monday. At midday, he grabbed a sandwich and a Coke and settled down to watch a football game on TV. As he witnessed the spectacular buildup of men and equipment at the air station, Meredith was both resigned to the course of events and confident in the outcome.

Meredith always knew it could come to this, that the beast of white supremacy might resist to the bitter end and have to be subdued by overwhelming force. But in a real sense, he had already triumphed; he had beaten the state of Mississippi in court, won the backing of the Supreme Court, and forced the Justice Department and the president of the United States to his side, along with their armies of attorneys and troops. He had maneuvered the president to a position from where he could not back down.

Today, Meredith was philosophical over the possibility of his own death in the imminent clash. "Many people express great concern about my life or death while I am involved in this struggle," Meredith told a reporter that day.

"If I must die for this cause," he asked, "then I have already been dead a long time, and of what value is life to a dead man?"

Compared to the slow strangulation of life under the heel of white supremacy, it was well worth dying in the attempt to be free.

At midday on that same Sunday, on a flight from Atlanta to Jackson, reporter Paul Guihard was also munching on a sandwich and drinking a Coke.

Guihard was a New York–based thirty-year-old staff correspondent for the French news agency Agence France–Presse and a stringer for the tabloid *London Daily Sketch*. By now, the Meredith case was attracting international attention, and reporters from around the

United States as far away as Honolulu were joining reporters from England and Europe, heading for Oxford to cover what could be an epic story.

Paul Guihard was a force of nature, a fun-loving raconteur who spoke perfect English and French and who had written and produced an avant-garde off-Broadway play in his spare time, an absurdist comedy called *The Deck Chair*. He was the son of a French father and an English mother, was raised in London, served in the British army, and had spent ten years working for Agence France–Presse. His mother recalled that "he was a born journalist who loved his job. He had wanted to be in newspapers since boyhood. He never wanted to do anything else."

A big, avuncular man with a fiery red beard and bushy mustache, Guihard would stand out as an outsider in Mississippi from a mile away. To a friend who warned him to be careful, he tugged his beard and said, "Hey, don't worry. I'm going to pose as a Kentucky colonel and cover this thing with a mint julep in my hand!"

On the flight to Jackson, the stewardess, trying to guess Guihard's business and accent, said, "Oh, I know, you're going down to the nigger thing!" Guihard smiled painfully, turned to his partner, photographer Sammy Schulman, and said in French, "These people. It'll take them a hundred years to start forgetting."

When they landed at Jackson, Guihard and Schulman rented a white car and drove to the huge Citizens Council rally then in progress in front of the Governor's Mansion. What he saw around the mansion was absolutely unreal, Guihard thought. In the street between the Governor's Mansion and the office building containing Citizens Council headquarters, the festive crowd had swelled to three thousand. It looked like a carnival.

Mississippi fight songs thundered from car radios. Citizens Council official John Wright leaned out the third-floor office window with a bullhorn, and announced, "It may be that an attempt will be made to seize Governor Ross Barnett from the mansion today. We want you to form a human wall around the mansion! Take your place around the sidewalks of the Governor's Mansion. Don't let anyone through!"

The crowd surged around the mansion, and women and children sat down on the steps and cheered, "Two, four, six, eight, we don't want to integrate!" Men in shirtsleeves stood on the sidewalk and formed a chain with linked arms. Red, white, and blue Confederate flags flew everywhere.

A man in the crowd declared, "If the marshals want to arrest Ross, they're going to have to come through me first!" Another announced, "I just got word that a caravan of armed volunteers from Alabama just arrived at the border, and they're headed to Oxford!" A man declared, "I'm with Barnett all the way, even if the troops come in. But frankly I don't think he's got a chance of winning." Another noted soberly, "Man, we wouldn't last five minutes in another war with the United States."

Paul Guihard pushed through the crowd and entered the bright, bustling office suite housing the Citizens Council national headquarters to borrow a telephone to call the story in to his New York office. On the glass door was a painted design showing the crossed American and Confederate flags with the legend "Citizens Councils" and "States' Rights—Racial Integrity."

The office was humming at a fever pitch, with phones ringing off the hook, answered with sugary sweetness by a pair of attractive secretaries. Large portraits of Robert E. Lee and Stonewall Jackson scowled down from the wall overlooking a display of racist propaganda booklets.

Guihard interviewed Citizens Council official Louis Hollis, who instantly liked the huge fellow, as did most everyone who met him. Anyone that nice would just have to be on our side, Hollis thought.

Guihard borrowed a Citizens Council telephone to dictate his story in French to his editor in New York. "The crowd laughed and sang under the warm autumn sun," he reported, "and it was apparent it hadn't the vaguest idea of the enormity of its actions." "The Civil War has never ended," Guihard concluded. Soon he and Sammy Schulman were in their car heading north toward Oxford.

Also in the Citizens Council office was its chief, Bill Simmons, who was gazing out his office window over the crowd on Congress Street. He swelled with pride at the unity and determination of his supporters. A squad of cheerleaders was leading cheers in the midst of the defiant crowd. "They won't give up," Simmons said to visiting reporter James K. Kilpatrick of the *Richmond News-Leader.* "They won't ever give up. They're the finest people on earth."

Like James Meredith, Bill Simmons was resigned to the possibility of violence over the Ole Miss crisis. Even if Meredith was forced into the university at gunpoint, he felt, the struggle would not end, and the fight would continue. Simmons believed that law and nature and justice were all on his side.

But if Meredith was allowed into the university, Simmons believed, it could fracture the system of segregation into total collapse. The floodgates would open, and integrated public schools, public facilities, and voting would all follow, bringing "race-mixing," rampant crime, and political chaos. To Simmons, this was the turning point, the line in the sand that could not be crossed. It was a cause well worth fighting for. Thirty-eight years later he explained, "We thought we were doing the right thing."

As the sun began falling on September 30, 1962, Bill Simmons said gravely, "It's in the Lord's hands." One day earlier, James Meredith's mother had said precisely the same words to the same reporter.

Across the street, inside the Governor's Mansion, Ross Barnett was, incredibly, continuing the totally confused comic opera of rebellion. He summoned four of the state's most powerful political officials to his office and appointed them as his personal representatives to go to Oxford that night and take charge of the state's defenses, not breathing a word to them about the agreement he was striking with RFK to install Meredith on the campus that same evening.

The governor's deputies were George M. Yarbrough, president pro tem of the state senate and the state's third-ranking officer; county judge Russell Moore; state representative C. B. "Buddie" Newman; and state senator John C. McLaurin. Barnett gave them a proclamation "to do all things necessary that the peace and security of the people of the State of Mississippi are fully protected."

Judge Moore believed that they were supposed to block Meredith and the marshals on the next day, Monday, like they had the past Thursday. "We thought we were going up there to get the defenses prepared," McLaurin recalled. "We thought we might all get killed." With this in mind, Buddie Newman scribbled out his last will and testament and had his colleagues witness it.

State senator Yarbrough ordered the Highway Patrol to converge on Oxford to take up defensive positions. Highway Patrol officials had already instructed almost the entire force, 200 out of 225, to report to Oxford on Sunday, except for one man in each district to check car ac-

cidents. Judge Moore used the Highway Patrol radio to alert seventy of
the state's eighty-two sheriffs to gather their deputies and rendezvous
at the Oxford courthouse at 10:30 that evening.

Hundreds of Mississippi lawmen were racing to Oxford. Almost
all of them assumed they were supposed to be blockading James Meredith and the federals.

On back roads and highways across the region, the first wave of
civilian volunteers was also setting out for what many felt could be the
South's last stand the next morning at Oxford. The road from Jackson
was already filling up with cars flying Confederate flags and signs
sporting slogans like "Mississippi: Toughest State in the Union" and
"Government of the Pope, by the Kennedys, for Meredith." One car
sported a pennant of a skull and crossbones.

A skinny, leathery Texan man of about sixty appeared in the Citizens Council office in Jackson, explaining he'd driven all the way from
Corpus Christi, "because the general asked us to come fight." He quietly asked where he could find General Walker. "He's gone to Oxford,"
said one of the office ladies. "I thank you kindly, ma'am," replied the
Texan. "I'll go on to Oxford, too."

At an airstrip near Tuscaloosa, Alabama, Imperial Wizard Robert
Shelton stepped into a single-engine Cessna with a small delegation of
lieutenants from United Klans of America headquarters. They took off
in a crystal blue sky and flew west toward Oxford.

That morning, in Pavo, Georgia, a radical right-wing activist
named Melvin Bruce sent a telegram to Governor Barnett: "I volunteer my services, arms and munitions to you as a combat infantry-
man and will serve under any officer that you might designate. I
would consider it an honor to serve under the patriot, General
Walker." He packed a suitcase, gassed up his green-and-white Nash
Metropolitan automobile, and set off on an all-day drive to Oxford.
In his trunk he'd stashed two rifles: a 6.6 Swedish Mauser and a 30.06
Springfield.

In Chattanooga, Tennessee, a policeman spotted a 1961 white
Ford convertible driving erratically and pulled it over. The car flew a
Confederate flag and was covered in slogans painted in brown shoe
polish, "Mississippi or Bust"; "Barnett's the Man"; "Keep America
White"; and "Long Live the South." The driver was drunk. The three
occupants explained that they had heard of Walker's call for ten thousand citizen volunteers and set off for Oxford. In the car the officer

found a .3030 Revelation model repeater rifle and a shotgun. He arrested the driver and impounded the car.

At about 3:00 P.M., a ragtag twelve-car convoy of twenty-six men, five women, and three children calling themselves the Citizens for the Preservation of Democracy left Prichard, Alabama, near Mobile and set off for Oxford, more than three hundred miles to the north. Some carried weapons. They all wore red armbands, packed enough clothes for several days, and painted "Alabama Volunteers" on their rear windows. They were tailed by a mobile TV truck, a sports car driven by a local newsman, and an FBI surveillance team.

The first planeload of 173 U.S. Deputy Marshals arrived at the tiny Oxford airport from Memphis at 2:25 P.M. They lined up in scraggly semi-military fashion beside the C-130 transport plane to pose for news photographers on the tarmac. Some of the marshals looked dazed and confused, since many of them had assumed this was another dry run and were told that this was the real thing only when they were airborne.

The hastily assembled squads looked for their equipment, some of which had been lost in the rush—thirty-six Border Patrolmen forgot their gas masks, and nobody could find the loudspeakers. Some of the marshals carried 1.5 caliber tear-gas guns; others just had gas grenades. The force had only a limited quantity of short-range tear-gas shells and hand-thrown-type grenades. They wore white steel helmets with "U.S. Marshal" inscribed in stencil.

"We were sent in unprepared," one marshal later remembered, "with nowhere near the equipment we should have had. The government didn't believe it could escalate the way it did." Their squad formations were already breaking down, since they originally drilled in teams to go to Oxford in buses, not planes. Most of the marshals carried Smith & Wesson and Colt .38 revolvers, but they were ordered to hide them holstered under their jackets to prevent civilian casualties.

A few people in the small crowd at the airport booed them. Otherwise, it was a tranquil summerlike afternoon. One marshal nonchalantly practiced his golf swing on the tarmac with his billy club. At 3:45 P.M. the JetStar landed from Washington and disgorged Deputy Attorney General Nicholas Katzenbach and the Justice Department team.

The marshals piled into seven army trucks for the short drive to campus, led by Justice Department officials in a Border Patrol car. As they were leaving the airport, Colonel T. B. Birdsong, head of the Mississippi Highway Patrol, pulled up to escort them. He was one of the only state officials who had yet been alerted to the RFK/Barnett deal to place James Meredith on campus that night, and he was now cooperating with the federals, although most of his men hadn't gotten the word yet.

Chief U.S. Marshal McShane stepped out of his car to greet Birdsong and confer briefly about the short motorcade to campus. McShane surveyed the scene and nervously noticed pockets of jeering spectators on the hillside, so he decided to strap on his steel crash helmet and don a combat vest containing a bandolier of tear-gas shells.

Colonel Birdsong, in sunglasses, shirtsleeves, and a fedora, looked like a man lost in a storm. McShane patted him reassuringly on the hand, gave him a tight, Irish cop smile, and ordered the procession forward. Somehow the marshals looked simultaneously ridiculous and threatening, stuffed helter-skelter into the open troop carriers like toy soldiers in dump trucks, their shirttails out, cigarettes dangling from their lips. During the slow parade to campus, dozens of people spontaneously gathered along the roadside. Some people cheered, while others yelled obscenities and insults. One man, surprised at the sight of the invading marshals, called out, "You know you're going to be carried out, don't you?" On a hill, a man and a small boy were waving a Confederate flag. A few civilian cars cut in and out of the convoy to harass the drivers.

Soon another plane descended into Oxford Airport, this one carrying three members of the governor's delegation: Judge Moore, State Senator McLaurin, and State Representative Newman. They were supposed to rendezvous with Yarbrough at the campus at 6:00 P.M. Not knowing about Barnett's deal with RFK, they gazed in shock upon the federal planes and trucks around the airport.

"It's completely occupied," Senator McLaurin said in disbelief. Then he thought, "Bobby and Jack jumped the gun."

CHAPTER EIGHT

The Gates of Bedlam

■ ■ ■ ■

All hell had to break loose. It did.

—James Silver, University of Mississippi
history professor

A T A FEW MINUTES before 4:00 P.M., the convoy of U.S. Marshals rumbled onto the campus of the University of Mississippi
and up to the pink-brick Lyceum building at the center of campus.

To Deputy Attorney General Nicholas Katzenbach, the Lyceum
seemed the logical destination, since it contained the Registrar's Office, which would be Meredith's first official stop on campus. Katzenbach told Colonel Birdsong, "I'd like to dismount these men right
here." Birdsong replied, "It's all right as far as I'm concerned."

One of the marshals' squad leaders, Deputy Marshal Clarence "Al"
Butler, surveyed the scene in front of the Lyceum and was struck by
how peaceful it was, occupied by only a few inquisitive squirrels on
this quiet Sunday afternoon. The campus was almost deserted, as
many of the students were returning from the football weekend in
Jackson, and the Highway Patrol was so far keeping all non-students
off campus.

Katzenbach entered the Lyceum building and found a small group
of university officials in the Chancellor's Office. They informed
Katzenbach that they had talked by phone with Burke Marshall in

Washington and talked him out of registering Meredith upon arrival, since they couldn't find the registrar and his files were locked. Besides, they argued, it would be inflammatory to register Meredith on the Sabbath day, and the students returning from the football weekend were already excited.

Since the timetable had been collapsed and rearranged, Katzenbach now had scores of battle-ready federal marshals and nowhere to put them. The nearby university gymnasium was filling up with incoming Highway Patrolmen who were using it as a temporary headquarters, and the tent city set up by the army engineers, only a few miles north at the Holly Springs National Forest, was too far away in case the marshals were needed urgently to protect James Meredith, who was being flown in shortly.

Katzenbach sized up the situation. He had nowhere to hide the marshals. For lack of any other plan, Katzenbach decided simply to line his men up around the Lyceum to secure it in preparation for Meredith's planned registration the next day. This spur-of-the-moment decision to set up a show of force was taken without any prior planning, without much thought at all. The marshals started forming a defensive semicircle around the entrance to the building.

Katzenbach had no idea he was creating the most provocative display anyone could imagine—hundreds of what looked like comic-book gladiators were surrounding the very heart of Ole Miss, defiling and desecrating it with their billy clubs and battle helmets and cigarettes. They were mobilized so abruptly that many of the marshals didn't have time to put on their business suits. Some were in jeans, some in sport shirts and khakis, and one marshal wore what looked like a Hawaiian luau shirt. Even the gas guns they held pointed up at the sky looked like stun guns out of a B science-fiction movie. They were unintentionally debasing one of the holiest temples of Mississippi pride.

The marshals were facing a tactical nightmare. Night would fall soon upon the Circle, an oval-shaped park covering several hundred yards adjoining the Lyceum's main entrance, with dozens of trees to offer perfect spots for guerrilla ambushes. Buildings were packed close together around the Circle, providing numerous perches for snipers. All told, there were hundreds of places to hide and attack the marshals.

No matter how far out the marshals extended a defensive perimeter, conditions would not improve, due to the dense layout of the campus. The campus borders were five miles long, straddling woods, fields, and residential areas that would take fifteen hundred troops in total to seal off.

An enormous blind spot overwhelmed their field of vision. Standing on the steps of the Lyceum, their view was almost totally obstructed by the densely packed trees of the Circle, which began just a few yards in front of them. The marshals would soon be totally exposed in the open, standing under the lights of the building, while anyone in the Circle's park would be in the dark and essentially invisible.

Looking back years later, Katzenbach acknowledged his mistake in lining the marshals up around the building: "We didn't have enough planning on it; we didn't know what we were doing nearly as well as we should have." In fact, he had no other choice. The only other logical place to put them would be around Meredith's dormitory, Baxter Hall, which was a few hundred yards to the west and behind the Lyceum, but this ran the risk of drawing throngs of students closer to Meredith once he arrived.

As the federal men set up a hastily improvised command post in the Lyceum, they realized that they had no special radio or phone hookup, no secure way of communicating with Washington. Katzenbach turned to Justice Department official Joe Dolan and said, "Get a line to Washington right away."

Dolan surveyed the layout and thought, "We don't want to use the University phones, they might cut us off." Spotting a pay telephone in the Lyceum hallway, Dolan dropped a dime in and asked the operator to call the White House and reverse the charges. When the White House operator accepted the call, Dolan issued an order to her: "We want to keep this line open all night. No matter what happens, don't cut it off."

At 5:00 P.M., General Edwin Walker appeared in a sedan at the campus main gate, wearing a fawn-colored cattleman's hat and a floral patterned tie. He had arrived in Oxford and checked into a hotel earlier in the day with a small retinue and issued a press statement: "As the forces of the New Frontier assemble to the north, let history be the witness to the courage and determination that calls us to Oxford to support a courageous governor. His lawful stand for state sovereignty is supported by thousands of people beyond the state's borders now on the way to join you at Oxford."

A Mississippi Highway Patrol officer blocked Walker's sedan and waved him away from the campus. Before turning around, Walker gazed longingly toward the Lyceum in the far distance, his view mostly obscured by the trees of the Circle.

In the sky over Oxford Airport, a single-engine Cessna was radioing a request to land. The air-traffic controller, now denying clearance to anything but federal government aircraft, refused permission. Imperial Wizard Robert Shelton and his Ku Klux Klan brass disappeared into the eastern horizon.

Word of the marshals' sudden arrival and seizure of the Lyceum building was flashing around the campus and beyond. Small pockets of faculty and students were already appearing on the Circle to inspect the bizarre scene. Students on dates strolled hand in hand into the Circle to see what was going on. A boy toddler of about three stood absolutely still, studying a news photographer.

Word of the marshals' presence was electrifying the campus, and hundreds of students and faculty began pouring onto the Circle. It was quickly becoming a campus "happening." The weather was perfect, and students lay down on the grass, laughing and having a good time. By 5:30 P.M., four hundred people had gathered near the Lyceum building. Mississippi Highway Patrolmen were blending in and out of the crowd, trying to push it back, but curious people started surging around them.

Local radio stations were broadcasting bulletins of the federal takeover of part of the university, helping to pull throngs of civilians toward the campus. Many people in Mississippi were hunters, and naturally carried a shotgun or rifle in the trunk, especially now, since the start of squirrel-hunting season was tomorrow.

One announcer declared bitterly that it reminded him of Pearl Harbor, "a sneak attack and on a Sunday." WLBT radio in Jackson, the state's number-one station, was broadcasting segregationist editorials at a fever pitch, and had dispatched a station wagon full of reporters and equipment to the campus.

More and more students were returning from the weekend, and as the crowd swelled, it got more boisterous. Seeing the marshals packed around the white-columned building, many students became enraged. "Most of us were unreconstructed rebels," then-student William D. Trahan explained years later. "We were fired up for reasons that had a lot more to do with the federal government than they did with James Meredith. One hundred years after the War we felt like we were still being treated like a conquered province."

Rumors ricocheted around the Circle: "Is he here yet?" "They're bringing him in tomorrow." "The Klan is waiting for him on all the roads. They're going to dynamite his car." One report had General Walker marching on the campus with thousands of people to help defend the school. Confederate flags were sprouting from everywhere, draped out of dormitory windows, on car antennas. A news helicopter floated overhead filming the blossoming spectacle.

The University of Mississippi campus police force was by now able to deploy six of its men around the scene, but they were widely dispersed and lightly equipped. They had only one squad car with one radio, no gas masks, no riot equipment, and no planning for what was about to happen. Still, they drifted around the Circle, trying to calm things down.

"I am just a little fuck," announced a boy who walked right up to the line of marshals. "Go ahead and shoot me, you nigger-loving son of a bitch!" The lad retreated and fell into a jovial conversation with a Mississippi Highway Patrolman. A student produced a three-by-five-foot Confederate flag on a long bamboo fishing pole and paraded up and down the line of marshals.

At 5:30 an announcement on the loudspeakers at the Student Union Building asked students to stay away from the Lyceum, but it had the opposite effect—new throngs of curious people flocked to the scene. Chancellor J. D. Williams and other school officials wandered nervously through the crowd, pleading for people to go back to their dorms. But without megaphones, their voices were lost and submerged in the rising buzz of the crowd.

The marshals stayed there, courageously lined up around the Lyceum, staring ahead, some smiling weakly to appear less hostile, others smoking cigarettes and chatting nervously to their comrades. They came from California to New Hampshire—regular U.S. Deputy Marshals mixed in with federal prison guards and U.S. Border Patrolmen. Ironically, a majority of them were Southerners themselves, from places such as Texas, Florida, Georgia, and South Carolina, and many of them personally had no use for integration. The longer the marshals stood there, the more bewildered and furious the spectators became as the Circle continued to fill up with onlookers.

More Mississippi Highway Patrolmen were speeding into Oxford, and they were being ordered by their commanders to lock their sidearms inside their cars to lower the risk of a shoot-out with the federals. But some patrolmen quietly refused and kept their guns in their holsters. Others didn't get the word. This was the second time in a week they were ordered to take their guns off, and they were seething about it. They had been a proud bunch of officers, and now, without their guns, they were little more than an unarmed school-safety patrol, with no way of defending themselves.

Until today they were a well-disciplined force protecting and escorting James Meredith in and out of his Kabuki confrontations with the governor, blocking his path and sending him and the federals right out of the state. Now, as the sun was setting, the Highway Patrol chain of command was completely falling apart. The man directing the Highway Patrol's movements in Oxford, Senator Yarbrough, had no idea that the governor had struck a deal with Bobby Kennedy to put Meredith on the campus that night.

The aging Colonel Birdsong, who would soon be battered with conflicting orders, was greeting incoming patrolmen with their new mission: "We're cooperating." But some patrolmen thought instead that the marshals had taken over and they were supposed to step aside. Some of the officers thought the whole deal was a political farce and wanted no part of it. Their loyalties were being severely fractured, and their sympathies were with the crowd. They also had no riot-control training and no riot equipment other than defective 1917-vintage gas masks that were no use against tear gas.

Suddenly, instead of blocking the marshals as they had done for more than two weeks, the Highway Patrolmen were supposed to help them install Meredith into Ole Miss. But many patrolmen assumed that the marshals were still an enemy force. As it happened, a number of marshals felt the same way about patrolmen. "What are you going to do if one of those marshals starts pushing you around?" one state officer asked his partner. "I'm gonna break his damn jaw if I can hit hard enough" was the reply.

U.S. Marshals asked Mississippi Highway Patrolmen for help

moving the crowd back. Some helped, others refused. One state patrolman replied that no one could control the crowd now. One marshal, Felix M. Aycock of San Francisco, reported, "When we asked them to hold the crowd back, the patrolmen just stood there and laughed at us." One Mississippi Highway Patrolman said, "Let the mob go ahead."

Another marshal asked a patrolman for help moving the crowd back, but the officer muttered, "To hell with you, you son-of-a-bitch, I didn't invite you down here." One patrolman spotted a kid busily hacking away at an army truck's tires with a knife and offered him advice on his technique: "Cutting the tread isn't going to do it; cut right into the sidewall—by the valve stem."

Someone sneaked up and plastered a "Kennedy Go Home" sticker on one of the army trucks, and a small Confederate flag was anchored on another. Inside the Circle, Mississippi Highway Patrolmen mingled and joshed with the students. One patrolman said, "We haven't spotted the black bastard." Then, at 6:00 P.M., the word came: "The nigger's on his way."

Sections of the crowd lurched forward. Some people were now in spitting range of the marshals, and began to do so. The jeering abruptly jackknifed into screaming.

"You fucking idiots," one embittered youth hollered at the marshals, "why don't you go to hell?" At 6:00 P.M., a crew-cut youth in a T-shirt waved a knife at the marshals, warning, "If you come over here I will cut you to ribbons." Some marshals tried to soothe the crowd, replying, "Go on home. Go to your dorm. Everything will be OK."

Boys in the Confederate uniforms of the Ole Miss college band, just returned from the big football game, paraded up and down the field, taunting the marshals. A boy in a Confederate uniform climbed up on a buddy's shoulders, pointed his bugle at the marshals, and began blowing cavalry charges. Then he played "Dixie."

Just after 6:00 P.M., eggs, pieces of gravel, and larger stones were hurled in the air toward the marshals. One gravel thrower wore a Confederate general's uniform. A wooden coat hanger flew over the marshals' heads. A cheer broke out, a mutation of the Ole Miss football cheer: "Hotty toddy, God A'mighty, Who in the hell are we? Flim flam, bim bam, white folks, by damn!" Crowd members began repeated attempts to set fire to the army trucks.

A boy ran up to the federal line, screaming, "Shoot me! Shoot me!" as pebbles and lit cigarettes flew toward the marshals. Stunned at the sudden size and ferocity of the crowd, Deputy Marshal Al Butler thought to himself, "We might be in for a little donnybrook here tonight." Alexander Koenig, a deputy marshal from San Francisco, recalled, "They stood there in their little blue beanies with their Southern girl friends by their sides and they called us every filthy name in the book."

Dusk was coming on strong now, and above the Oxford Airport, James Meredith descended from the heavens in his government Cessna. He disembarked to a frantic scene of marshals toting billy clubs, cameras flashing, scattered boos from onlookers, and a wildeyed Deputy Attorney General Katzenbach on hand to escort him onto campus. On the hill, a little boy and a man were still waving a Confederate flag.

James Meredith was stoic as always, wearing a suit, carrying a newspaper, and toting a briefcase. He looked like a young executive catching the commuter train.

Escorted by a Mississippi Highway Patrol car, Meredith was quickly and quietly whisked onto the campus through a side entrance and driven to Baxter Hall. A university official had suggested a roundabout route for Meredith to come in through, and by some small miracle, very few civilians noticed Meredith's arrival. Once inside the dorm, Meredith inspected his room, made his bed, and read his newspaper. A small team of marshals took up positions around his room, trying to draw as little attention as possible.

The chain of command on the federal side was also fracturing under the stress of imploding timetables and a bureaucracy stretched to the limit. General Creighton Abrams, the man in charge of the massive military buildup at Memphis, found out that Meredith had been flown to Oxford when a staff officer went out for a bite to eat and heard it on the news.

Increasingly larger groups surged onto the Circle and sang frenzied cheerleader calls: "Go to hell, JFK!"; "Where's that nigger?"; "The hell with the United States!" To some in the crowd it still felt like a football pep rally, except the opposing team was armed, dangerous-looking—and inches away, completely surrounded.

The crowd heckled and shoved closer as the marshals gritted and gripped their billy clubs, holding them up to deflect incoming rocks and other missiles. Somebody ran a Confederate flag up the campus flagpole, and the crowd roared until it got stuck halfway up the pole. Some people even yelled, "Heil Hitler!" "I'm going back to the dormitory," one student said, "this makes me sick."

The front of the crowd, now swelling toward one thousand, zeroed in on the U.S. Army truck drivers in front of the Lyceum, five of whom who were black. The drivers sat implacably in their cabs as youths hurled taunts and lit cigarettes at them. A student grabbed a fire extinguisher from the side of a truck and blasted its black driver in the face. The driver clutched his eyes in agony, earning the attacker a new ovation from the crowd. "Those things are cold," the boy exulted, returning to his friends. "I'll bet it froze his goddamned face off!"

Another youth heaved a burning hunk of newspapers on top of the truck, setting the canvas top ablaze. Voices in the crowd roared, "Let it burn!" The driver scrambled up to beat the fire out and was plastered in the back with flying eggs. A boy darted up to a marshal and flicked a cigarette into his face point-blank.

More false rumors erupted. One had federal marshals on the verge of arresting Governor Barnett on the campus. In fact, Barnett was in Jackson. Dozens of reporters and photographers were streaming toward the Lyceum, some with borrowed student passes, others sneaking around the Highway Patrol checkpoints.

Just after 7:00 P.M., when the checkpoint at one entrance was suddenly and inexplicably opened, *Detroit News* reporter Tom Joyce walked onto the campus. "I had not gone 100 yards inside," Joyce recalled, "before I sensed that real trouble was inevitable with the same certainty one feels when a thunderstorm is brewing on a humid August night. The clean-cut looking youths of a few hours before had been transformed into restive animals."

At the Lyceum, Deputy Marshal Al Butler approached Chief Marshal McShane, who was supervising the distribution of tear-gas equipment, and asked permission to fire tear gas. "Hold it off for awhile," said McShane, "and maybe things will ease up." They both realized they had no first-aid equipment.

Flashbulbs began popping from different directions. Off to the side of the Circle, a blur of flying fists erupted in the midst of a pack of one hundred crowd members, and a cameraman was slammed to the ground. His attacker ripped his camera away and held it tri-umphantly aloft, spurring a burst of applause.

Reporters and photographers became instant targets of the crowd's anger, especially representatives of the hated "Yankee press," whom some Mississippians thought were systematically biased against the state. Some local witnesses swore they saw reporters and photog-raphers directly exhorting the crowd to violence, saying things like, "You're just going to stand here and let 'em run over you like this? Do something!" One photographer on the edge of the crowd was quoted as asking a group of young men, "Can you create a disturbance so I can get some good pictures?"

Even if these incidents were apocryphal, the sudden presence of so many outside reporters and photographers and flashbulbs startled the crowd like a panicked beast, and just after 7:00 P.M. its rage lashed out at Hearst Movietone newsreel cameraman Gordon Yoder of Dallas. A crowd surrounded Yoder and his wife inside their station wagon a few dozen feet from the Lyceum. Hands darted into the wagon, grabbed his 35mm Bell & Howell camera, and launched it toward the marshals. The crowd kicked and rocked the car while ripping the wires out from under its hood and bashing the windshields in. The Yoders sat help-lessly inside.

One crowd member climbed halfway into the car to grab the newsman. A nearby student protested, saying, "Don't hit him, he didn't do anything." A boy stuck his head inside the car and screamed at Mrs. Yoder, a Jackson, Mississippi, native: "You nigger-loving bitch, you Yankee bastard!" Youths were stripping off the car's chrome orna-ments with their bare hands.

An Ole Miss coed asked her date, "Lord, Joe, what are they gonna do to that woman?" Replied Joe, "Kill her, I guess. She's a nigger lover, ain't she?" Finally, Mississippi Highway Patrolmen John McCauley and his partner Ralph Pennington pushed their way through the crowd, pulled the couple out of the wagon, and escorted them to safety in their patrol car, the station wagon barely missing them as it was flipped over by the crowd.

When a reporter from Chicago approached the Lyceum and switched on his tape recorder, a friendly student said, "If you value your life, I advise you to get out of here with your equipment. They've gone crazy here."

Newsweek photographer Dan McCoy was suddenly attacked by a gang led by a bloody-shirted football player who pummeled him to the ground with a right punch. McCoy got up and was flattened again. "For God's sake," he pleaded with four men in a sheriff's car, "get me out of here." They just sat there. "The students knocked me down again and started hitting me and working on me with kicks with the side of their feet," McCoy recalled. "I figured I just about had it. Then I felt some hands on my shoulders. I figured they were picking me up to hit me some more. But they were other students who had pushed them back. The big guy tried to come in again, but they rushed me into a building."

The crowd was metastasizing into a mob, and when it realized it could get away with violence, it grew bolder.

In the months since he took over as Chief U.S. Marshal, James McShane had been trying to prepare his men for this kind of situation, drilling them in riot control and mob psychology. He wanted to prevent the kind of disaster that nearly overwhelmed the marshals at the First Baptist Church siege in Birmingham in May 1961, when McShane saw an undertrained, badly equipped force of marshals nearly get run over. McShane even printed up a comprehensive *Riot Control Training Manual* for his men, which explained the four-stage sequence of how a crowd transforms into a riotous mob.

But by 7:30 P.M. at Oxford, all four stages had already occurred. Step 1, the "weakening of the forces holding a crowd in check," kept happening as the crowd got larger and the marshals' force proportionally smaller. Step 2, "a single piece of audacious violence successfully carried through," was achieved by the multiple attacks on journalists. Step 3, a "harangue by a fiery leader," was simulated by the impassioned announcers blaring anti-federal invective over the transistor and car radios. Finally, Step 4, "the appearance of a conspicuous and hated figure," was reached by the arrival of both the marshals and the word that James Meredith had come on campus.

The U.S. Marshals were now unprepared, thanks to a chain reaction of bad luck, oversights, and a collapsed timetable. To have any hope of coping with what was about to happen, they should have had a public-address truck, mobile telephones, bullhorns, walkie-talkies, floodlights and generators, oxygen equipment, police barriers, flak jackets, stretchers, first-aid equipment and medics, and backup supplies of gas. They had none of these things. On top of this, the Border Patrolmen, who made up the majority of the deputized marshals' force at Oxford that night, had no riot-control training at all except the few hours they had just gotten at Memphis.

Dick Wilson was a second-year law student and president of the University of Mississippi student body. Ever since the Meredith case began heating up earlier in the year, he had been planning with student and faculty leaders for trouble. They even had an ingenious crowd-control plan worked out.

As soon as a mob formed, Wilson and other student leaders would fan out and call out as many people by name as they could recognize, figuring that could defuse the anger of the mob by pulling people back into reality, especially upon hearing their own names. Between himself and the forty student leaders in his cabinet and extended cabinet, Wilson figured they could recognize a great majority of students in any campus crowd.

However, by the time the Ole Miss student leaders found out about the spontaneous mob forming at the Lyceum, it was too late. Many were just returning from the football weekend in Jackson. The mob had already reached a frenzy, and the Ole Miss students in the mob would soon be outnumbered by non-students.

When three men in the mob came within arm's reach, the marshals snatched them and turned them over to Highway Patrolmen. When the marshals turned their backs, the Highway Patrolmen released the men right back into the crowd. One disgusted Mississippi Highway Patrolman expressed his feelings loud and clear: "Let them kill the nigger."

A Highway Patrolman tried to move with a group of students around the side of the Lyceum. Bracing for an attack and assuming the Highway Patrol was on the verge of becoming a hostile force, Deputy Marshal Graham "Gene" Same from Indiana thought, "There's no way they're coming behind us." He blocked their path and called out, "Stay there or we'll gas you."

Sheriffs and deputies from all over Mississippi were also drifting onto the campus. The state's chain of communication with them was even more chaotic—their last orders earlier that day from Judge Russell Moore (acting, he understood, on the governor's authority) were to converge on Oxford to block the federal forces. At 7:10, an order was heard on the Highway Patrol radio, announcing that the federal takeover of the campus was complete, Meredith was on the campus, and that sheriffs and deputies should turn back and return to their home districts. But many of the lawmen were already in Oxford or on the campus.

One Highway Patrolman wandered through the crowd, trying to calm the students down, telling them, "Don't get caught up in a mob mentality." An older member of the Highway Patrol came over to a group of newsmen and said, "We are going to get you fellows out of here."

A man in the swirling mob screamed at a marshal from Texas, "You goddamn, Jew-looking, Yankee son-of-a-bitch, come night and we're going to kill you." A rock clipped a marshal's leg. "Next time we'll get you in the head," a voice shouted from the dark. Soft-drink bottles crashed against the Lyceum pillars, showering glass on the marshals. A big piece of ice flew through the air toward the federal skirmish line.

Mary Lynn Hendricks, a junior transfer student from Arkansas, shimmied up a tree in the midst of the mob for a bird's-eye view. There were people all around as far as she could see, and none of them looked like students to her—she figured they were "rednecks" from the surrounding areas. As the mob swirled ever closer to the marshals and flashes of violence erupted into fistfights, it felt to Hendricks like a war was about to break out. She jumped down from the tree and raced to her dormitory to take cover.

Charles Hargroder, a reporter for the *New Orleans Times-Picayune,* heard behind him in the darkness the unmistakable clicks of shotguns being loaded with shells. One thought overwhelmed him: "Get out of here."

Hundreds of curious onlookers from Ole Miss, from Oxford, and from surrounding towns were moving to the far edges of the crowd, and most of them hadn't the remotest intention of participating in a riot. Local radio stations were flashing bulletins on the situation, and many of the civilians were there simply to see history being made. But a violent hard-core wave of citizens was invading the campus as well, and it was thirsty for combat. The apocalypse was here and now—according to the news reports, James Meredith was somewhere close by, on the campus. One man in the crowd announced, "I would like to see blood all over this campus by morning."

At 7:25, an order was flashed over the Highway Patrol radio from an unknown person, ordering the force to withdraw from the university. Scores of patrolmen began pulling out in their squad cars, leaving the marshals to face the crowd alone. Some officers stayed, including at least a dozen around the Lyceum. More Highway Patrol checkpoints at the campus entrances were abandoned, and new pockets of outsiders surged toward the mob at the Circle.

When the Highway Patrolmen withdrew, the mob cheered, taking it as a symbol that anything went now that the Mississippi contingent had left.

At the front line of marshals defending the Lyceum, a beautiful coed screamed at squad leader U.S. Deputy Marshal Al Butler, "You rubber-nosed motherfucker, where's your wife tonight—sleeping with a nigger?" One youth came within arm's length of U.S. Deputy Marshal Gene Same and screamed, "Your wife's at home having nigger babies!" Highway Patrolman O. L. Hampton heard another marshal being taunted. "Your wife is sleeping with a nigger! She's liking it! You can't do anything about it!"

"They couldn't pay me enough to take that kind of abuse," Hampton thought.

Mississippi state senator Yarbrough, head of the governor's delegation and an imposing, powerful character, stormed into the federal command post inside the Lyceum, and declared, "I demand to know who's in charge here." He was escorted to Katzenbach and McShane. In between the two was the elderly Colonel Birdsong, who seemed totally adrift in a sea of confusion. Birdsong was pleading with Katzenbach, "I have not given the marshals police protection. I've been telling these people that all I've done is escort you onto the campus. Will you please clarify this?"

Senator Yarbrough told the federal men, "You have occupied this University and now you can have it. What happens from now on is the responsibility of the Federal Government. We are withdrawing the Highway Patrol."

Katzenbach exclaimed, "No, you can't do that! That would be a horrible mistake!" Yarbrough replied, "I want to avoid bloodshed, and to do so, we must withdraw the Highway Patrol."

Katzenbach told Yarbrough, "All law-enforcement officers must cooperate to maintain law and order. I want to be very clear about the fact that I think the withdrawal of the state troopers will not avoid violence, but will be the one decisive thing that will lead to violence." He continued, "Call the Governor. He'll tell you that the state Highway Patrol is meant to preserve law and order here. And he has promised that they would."

Yarbrough replied, "That is not my judgment. We will withdraw the patrol. It is just a question of when." In fact, they were already pulling out. As the state and federal officials bickered, the mob was lurching toward chaos, and few people understood what was happening—in the city of Oxford, Mississippi, law and order was completely breaking down.

By 7:30, it was almost totally dark as a convoy of fourteen vehicles carrying the next batch of incoming marshals from Memphis drove onto the Ole Miss campus and straight into the mob. When all his car windows were bashed in just inside the campus gate, one marshal was forced to bail out of his car and try to proceed alone on foot without any equipment. He was followed by a screaming mob all the way to the Lyceum.

In Jackson, Governor Barnett went on the air at 7:30 P.M. to deliver a typically confused statement simultaneously offering both surrender and defiance.

"I have just been informed by the Attorney General of the United States," said Barnett, "that Meredith has today been placed on the campus of the University of Mississippi by means of government helicopters [actually, he had arrived by plane], and is accompanied by Federal officers." Although many in the crowd already knew from news bulletins that James Meredith had arrived on the campus, this confirmation from the governor triggered a roar of outrage from people listening on radios.

Barnett offered a plea for peace cloaked in doomsday rhetoric: "Surrounded on all sides by the armed forces and oppressive power of the United States of America, my courage and my convictions do not waver. My heart still says 'never,' but my calm judgment abhors the bloodshed that would follow. I love Mississippi. I love her people. I love the 10,000 good Mississippians in the National Guard who have now been federalized and required to oppose me and their own people."

Barnett continued, "I know that we are now completely surrounded by armed forces and that we are physically overpowered. I know that our principles remain true, but we must at all odds preserve the peace and avoid bloodshed."

But the governor closed his speech with a doomsday flourish, using language that undermined his nonviolent message and could even be interpreted as a call to battle: "Gentlemen," he said, addressing the federal government, "you are trampling on the sovereignty of this great state and depriving it of every vestige of honor and respect as a member of the United States. You are destroying the Constitution of this great nation. May God have mercy on your souls."

At 7:40, RFK came on the Lyceum telephone line and ordered Katzenbach to tell Yarbrough that if he pulled out the Highway Patrol, the president, about to go on national TV, would tell the world about the secret phone negotiations. (JFK had delayed his speech from 6:00 P.M. Oxford time to 8:00 P.M., in hopes that the crisis would ease.)

Since Barnett had kept Yarbrough and most other state officials in the dark about the negotiations, Yarbrough didn't know what Kennedy was talking about, so he tried to call the governor, who was wrapping up his speech.

In minutes, RFK called Barnett, Barnett called Yarbrough, and Yarbrough gloomily announced he wouldn't withdraw the Highway Patrol. By now patrolmen were drifting back onto the campus. But precious minutes were burned away, and confusion was gripping the entire scene.

At 7:45, Chief Marshal McShane burst into the Lyceum and announced he was going to have to take positive action because the crowd was out of control and someone had just thrown a piece of long pipe at the marshals, narrowly missing one.

Colonel Birdsong, the Highway Patrol chief, responded cryptically that his hands were tied and he could do nothing. Besides, he noted, "We'll have to live here long after you people are gone." State representative Buddie Newman warned McShane, "You don't need to use tear gas—you're fixing to make a big mistake!"

When a Coke bottle filled with flaming gasoline exploded in front of the marshals, McShane decided he had no choice but to prepare to do battle: "Load your guns! . . . Gas masks ready. . . . Gas guns ready. . . ."

The marshals struggled to strap on their gas masks and held up their 1.5 caliber gas guns loaded with federal #203 short-range "blast dispersion" tear-gas cartridges. At the sight of the marshals preparing for battle, some people in the crowd fell back and scattered.

The cartridges were built for shooting at close quarters and fired a blast of a white powdered chemical called chloracetophenone, or tear gas, out about twenty feet. When vaporized in the air, the powder caused intense irritation in the eyes, choking, and a burning sensation on the skin. The effects usually wore off after a few minutes of exposure to fresh air or water. The gas was also supposed to help break up a mob by a dense smokelike effect that blocks rioters from seeing one another. Those marshals who didn't have the gas guns got ready to throw their gas grenades and smoke grenades.

A young man called out to the mob that the glass in the marshals' gas masks could be shattered by throwing stones and coins at them, and started demonstrating his technique by firing missiles at the marshals' eyepieces.

Still the marshals stood their ground.

Senator Yarbrough went out the front door, was horrified to see the marshals putting their masks on, and pleaded with McShane to reverse the order. McShane reluctantly ordered, "Masks off!" The crowd surged back toward the Lyceum.

From the Lyceum steps, Yarbrough pleaded with the crowd, "Please, please listen to me! I'm Senator George Yarbrough, and I represent the Governor. I'm on your side. I live just 40 miles from here at Red Banks. We don't want any violence. Get back off the street and, if you will, go back to your dormitories. All will be well! Please return to your dormitories!"

However, most of the people in the mob couldn't hear Yarbrough and, assuming he was a federal man, booed him. "We want Ross!" they yelled. "All right," Yarbrough responded. "If you clear the street, I'll bring you Ross."

Yarbrough went inside to tell John Doar he would ask the governor to fly up to Oxford to try and quiet down the mob. But Yarbrough demanded guarantees that Barnett would not be arrested. Doar phoned the attorney general, who shot the idea down, fearing that Barnett might inflame the situation.

In the warm night air, part of the crowd was chanting a lynch mob's refrain: "Let's get Meredith! Let's get Meredith!"

A rock knocked a marshal down. Deputy Marshal Butler angrily confronted his boss McShane, a man he loved like a father, saying, "Damnit to hell, Chief, how much of this are we going to take? How many people are we going to have hurt before we do something about it?"

On the edges of campus, a dozen FBI agents were rushing to get into position to infiltrate the mob. Resident Agent Robin Cotten had persuaded his bosses to send about a dozen men to Oxford to gather intelligence to back up the marshals, and several of them were young enough to pass as students. But everything was happening much too fast, and the FBI men had no riot-control equipment, just some field radios and unmarked cars. Seeing the fury of the swelling mob, some of the agents, already in civilian clothes, were frantically tearing off their ties and jackets to avoid being identified and attacked.

Also in Oxford at this moment was a small advance team of U.S. Army intelligence agents, pre-positioned to help plan for Meredith's expected arrival the next day. But they didn't get word of the collapsed timetable fast enough, and couldn't make it to campus in time.

As violence loomed ever closer, the crew inside a mobile TV truck from WMPS-Memphis debated what to do. They decided to try to get a remote broadcast going before 8:00 P.M. Minutes later, as the mob swirled around them, they locked up and abandoned the truck. Part of the screaming mob then flipped the truck onto its side and set it on fire. There would be no live TV images of what would happen next.

At this moment, campus policeman James Parks realized what was coming, but couldn't believe what he was seeing. "A lot of people are going to get killed in this operation," Officer Parks thought as he watched the TV truck burning, the marshals standing fast, and the screaming crowd undulating toward them. "There's going to be a lot of people dying here—no question."

The marshals now braced themselves under a fresh shower of rocks and pop bottles and kicked away Molotov cocktails that were detonating at their feet.

Chief U.S. Marshal McShane stood on the steps of the Lyceum, praying to himself he somehow wouldn't have to give the command to fire the tear gas. But he noticed Highway Patrolmen blending into the fifth and sixth ranks of the mob, and it seemed to him they were stepping aside to let the mob advance. It looked to McShane like the multitude, now numbering twenty-five hundred, was on the verge of charging and storming the Lyceum.

It looked the same way to Gene Same, the U.S. Deputy Marshal from Indiana who was standing on the southeast corner of the marshals' perimeter. The Highway Patrolmen he saw were stepping aside so that the mob could attack.

"Those goddamn Feds," yelled someone in a police uniform, "let's get them!"

A voice called out from somewhere else, "This is it."

"You're chicken," a youth jeered at the federal officers. "You wouldn't fire those damned things."

A two-foot-long piece of heavy pipe spiraled through the air and fell onto a marshal's helmeted head, knocking him down.

Finally, Jim McShane figured he had no choice. "All right, damnit—MASKS ON! Let 'em have it—throw the gas—GAS!—FIRE!" He pumped his fist up and down to give the firing signal. The order bounced down the line of marshals and around the Lyceum.

A few Mississippi Highway Patrolmen grabbed their World War I–vintage gas masks and started wrapping them around their faces.

While the marshals prepared to fire their weapons in Oxford, the president of the United States sat at his desk in the Oval Office, grasping sheaves of paper, surrounded by drop cloths and klieg lights and staring into a television camera. In a few moments he was to go live on national television to announce that James Meredith had entered the university and to plead for peace.

According to the unpublished personal journal of Dr. Max ("Dr. Feelgood") Jacobson, discovered by journalist Richard Reeves during the research for his 1993 book *President Kennedy: Profile of Power,* President Kennedy summoned Jacobson to the White House by private plane to shoot him up before his TV address that night. The young chief executive explained to the doctor, "This one is a ball-breaker."

The president sat still as the TV technicians signaled the countdown.

At Oxford the U.S. Marshals aimed their stubby gas guns point-blank at the heads and belts of the front row of the mob and squeezed the triggers.

David Henry, a pharmacy student from Gulfport, said, "It seemed like one man fired and then it rattled down the line. It sounded like machine gun fire."

The marshals ripped out the arming pull rings of their gas grenades and threw them as hard and as fast as they could heave them at the civilians. The semicircle around the Lyceum exploded in tear-gas blasts.

The Battle of Oxford had begun.

CHAPTER NINE

Demons Out of the Earth

▪ ▪ ▪ ▪

Turn your eyes to the immoderate past,
Turn to the inscrutable infantry rising
Demons out of the earth—they will not last.

—Allen Tate, "Ode to the Confederate Dead"

INSIDE THE LYCEUM BUILDING, U.S. Deputy Attorney General Nicholas Katzenbach was startled to hear the flurry of muffled explosions. He knew the mob was getting wild, but he thought they still had a chance to calm it down.

Outside, reporter John Harris from the *New York Journal American* saw "helmeted U.S. marshals, advancing like troops in combat, methodically firing tear-gas shells into fleeing crowds of screaming students and coeds." The hissing gas grenades sizzled through the air, skipped across the grass, and released great clouds of billowing, stinging, bittersweet fumes.

Within seconds, reported eyewitness journalist Richard Starnes, "the campus became an indescribable nightmare." The marshals were firing point-blank at the crowd but were hitting Mississippi Highway Patrolmen as well. In front of the building, Highway Patrolman Welby Brunt was hit in the back of the head with either a gas grenade or the hard wax padding fired out of the tear-gas guns, which could knock a man down if he was close enough. Patrolman Brunt fell down, then managed to crawl and stagger twenty feet. He fell down again, gas

poured into his lungs, and he drifted toward unconsciousness. Someone wearing a gas mask finally appeared and carried him off to an automobile.

Just before the firing, Patrolman John McCauley worried for the
safety of his boss Colonel Birdsong, and turned around to see Birdsong being hustled into the building. McCauley thought the colonel
was being arrested. At that instant, McCauley was hit under the eye by
the packing material fired out of a marshal's tear gas gun eight feet
away. His eyes and skin began burning, and he couldn't see. He wandered the field, choking and blinded, until a woman appeared and led
him by the arm to safety. He wanted to thank her, but she disappeared.

Patrolman Loy Gammel was in the street a few yards in front of
the marshals. It seemed to him, and to many patrolmen, that the
crowd was obeying them and the situation could be controlled. (They,
of course, were not the men being pelted with verbal abuse, spit, and
flying objects.) When the barrage erupted, a marshal threw a gas
grenade canister toward Gammel, and the handle somehow got
jammed in Gammel's pocket. Gammel ripped it out of his pants and
threw it back at the marshal, who ducked as the canister hit the wall
behind him.

On the south end of the line was Patrolman Charles Staten, who
had fought in the battles of Okinawa and Guam and was a sixteen-year
Highway Patrol veteran. In the confusion, he hadn't received the order
to disarm, and he had his service revolver strapped into his holster. A
marshal fired a blast of tear gas at Staten; something ricocheted off his
gun, and Staten dropped to the ground to escape the barrage, as did
many other patrolmen.

Another patrolman later realized it was a good thing he didn't
have his gun, as he would have opened fire on the marshals right then
and there. One of his colleagues kicked a tear-gas grenade and swore,
"God damn them marshals," as tears cascaded from his eyes. "I'd like
to come back here with some tear gas of my own and get them good."
Other patrolmen, blinded by gas, scattered off the field with packs of
students and crowd members in total confusion.

One team of Highway Patrolmen, upon hearing a rumor that
Birdsong had been killed by the federal men, charged toward their
squad cars to grab firearms and turn them against the marshals. Senator Yarbrough intercepted the officers, squelched the rumor, and ordered them to keep the guns in their cars.

Mississippi state legislator James Mathis described what he saw as he drove onto campus in a Highway Patrol car: It "was one of the most horrible sights that I ever hope to see in my lifetime. There were probably 1,500 or 2,000 people standing in front of the Lyceum Building, and around the Lyceum what I thought at first was a picture of some intruders from some foreign planet."

"The center of the campus was in mayhem," recalled the state legislator. "People were being shot, not over their heads, but directly, by tear gas. We rolled up our automobile windows in order to get through the center of action. The U.S. Marshal motioned for us to keep moving, which showed me from the outset that they did not want any assistance from the Mississippi Highway Patrol." As they drove around toward patrol headquarters in the gymnasium, he recalled, "I saw another sight that made my blood boil! The federal men were chasing persons around the Physics Building and shooting at them directly with tear gas barrages."

Standing near the mob was *U.S. News & World Report* correspondent Sterling Slappey, who saw a tear-gas canister rocketing through the air headed directly at him. "I tried to get away from it," wrote Slappey, "but it hit my heel and the impact sent me sprawling into the nearby shrubbery. As I fell, I saw another canister of gas strike a girl full in the face."

Furious Mississippi officials charged into the Lyceum to confront Deputy Attorney General Katzenbach. Their own officers were being shot down by tear gas. Highway Patrol investigator Gwin Cole cried, "That's the dirtiest trick I ever saw!"

Katzenbach pleaded, "I am terribly sorry about that. It is most unfortunate that the policemen were hit. The marshals weren't supposed to fire right from where they were standing. I am very sorry this happened. Please keep your men here."

Cole replied, "Well, you have just started a riot."

Then Cole bitterly addressed Chief Marshal McShane: "This is the most cowardly act I have ever seen done in my life by officers."

Senator Yarbrough ran out of the pay-phone booth and shouted that they shouldn't have fired, because he was trying to get the governor on the telephone.

"We're sorry, somebody jumped the gun," Katzenbach replied.

Grabbing the phone, Katzenbach was patched into the White

House Cabinet Room and told his boss, the attorney general, "Bob, I'm very sorry to report that we've had to fire tear gas. I'm very unhappy about it, but we had no other choice."

Robert Kennedy replied, "I think I should really go tell the President about it. He's just going on the air." RFK and Burke Marshall sprinted from the Cabinet Room over TV cables toward the Oval Office to tell JFK, but the president was just starting his conciliatory, now-irrelevant speech.

At 8:00 P.M., almost the exact moment Kennedy began speaking, a hellish carnival of violence had erupted at Ole Miss. Screams of terror came from coeds as the mob stampeded backward under the tear-gas barrage and fumes billowed out around the Circle. The area in front of the Lyceum was in total chaos. Bystanders, students, reporters, and faculty were scattering in all directions. President Kennedy's voice drifted across the mayhem on the campus from transistors, car radios, and dormitory TV sets.

"Good evening, my fellow citizens," Kennedy began. "The orders of the court in the case of *Meredith vs. Fair* are beginning to be carried out. Mr. James Meredith is now in residence on the campus of the University of Mississippi.

"This has been accomplished thus far without the use of National Guard or other troops—and it is to be hoped that the law enforcement officers of the State of Mississippi and the federal marshals will continue to be sufficient in the future. All students, members of the faculty, and public officials in both Mississippi and the nation, it is to be hoped, can now return to their normal activities with full confidence in the integrity of American law."

The president chose not to make a moral appeal for the justice of civil rights or full black citizenship, but to instead stress that "observance of the law is the eternal safeguard of liberty." He proclaimed, "Americans are free, in short, to disagree with the law—but not to disobey it. For in a government of laws, and not of men, no man, however prominent or powerful, and no mob, however unruly or boisterous, is entitled to defy a court of law."

In a direct repudiation of Ross Barnett's recent crusade of "interposition," Kennedy warned, "If this country should ever reach the point where any man or group of men, by force, or threat of force, could long defy the commands of our courts and Constitution, then no law would stand free from doubt, no judge would be sure of his writ and no citizen would be safe from his neighbors."

After saluting the eight other Southern states who had admitted students "regardless of race," the president pointed out that "neither Mississippi nor any other Southern state deserves to be charged with all the accumulated wrongs of the last 100 years of race relations. To the extent that there has been failure, the responsibility for that failure must be shared by us all, by every state, by every citizen."

Still unaware of the fighting that had already exploded at Oxford, JFK closed his speech with a now-fruitless appeal to Mississippi pride. "You have a great tradition to uphold, a tradition of honor and courage, won on the field of battle and on the gridiron as well as the university campus. You have a new opportunity to show that you are men of patriotism and integrity. . . . The eyes of the nation and all the world are upon you and upon all of us, and the honor of your university and the state are in the balance. I am certain that the great majority of the students will uphold that honor. There is in short no reason why the books on this case cannot now be quickly and quietly closed in the manner directed by the court. Let us preserve both the law and the peace, and then, healing those wounds that are within, we can turn to the greater crises that are without and stand united as one people in our pledge to man's freedom. Thank you and good night."

As President Kennedy's speech ended, scores of furious, choking Highway Patrolmen were surging into their temporary headquarters at the university gymnasium. They felt they'd been double-crossed; they were fulfilling their duties and maintaining order, but the marshals opened fire on them. "They began shooting without even telling us!" raged one officer.

Some patrolmen were demanding a counterattack on the marshals and some were grabbing their rifles and shotguns. "Let's get them Feds," one trooper proposed. "Let's take care of them sons of bitches," demanded another. Colonel Birdsong entered the gym and was confronted by an officer who declared, "We can whip them!" Birdsong countered, "We sure can whip them, but we can't whip the Army, the Navy and the Marines, and they're coming!"

Colonel Birdsong called his men into a huddle and said, "Boys, I'm going to call the Guv for instructions." In the meantime, he ordered his troopers to lock up their guns in their patrol-car trunks. When some of the men hesitated, he barked, "Put your guns away in the trunk. Take 'em off now. Now!" The patrolmen did as they were told.

In downtown Oxford, former general Edwin Walker was chewing on a thick steak at the Mansion Restaurant with a young aide as John Kennedy's image flickered on the TV screen by the bar.

Walker got up, went to the television, bellowed, "Nauseating!" and turned off the set. Several diners, recognizing the celebrity in their midst, applauded him. An eighteen-year-old waiter asked the general for his autograph. One man walked over and declared proudly, "I will take care of the General's tab."

Walker finished his meal, strode out of the restaurant, and, flanked by a few of his cronies, set off by car for the short drive to the campus of the University of Mississippi to see for himself what was going on.

At the Circle, one student saw four fleeing girls ambushed by a marshal firing gas directly in their midst. "Two of the girls were able to stagger on, the other two collapsed from the fumes," the student recalled. "The marshals pursued the students to the Confederate statue and completely cleared the Circle, smashing student cars with night sticks and gun stocks and clubbing students who were overcome by fumes."

After they galloped down into the Circle, the marshals beat their nightsticks on the ground and drifted back to the Lyceum, hoping the worst was over. They were already outnumbered by at least four to one and backed into a defensive position, but perhaps this burst of strength had broken the back of the mob. Instead, the fragmented, enraged mob was re-forming to attack, and quickly transforming into a ferocious guerrilla army.

Ted Lucas Smith, a Mississippi-born correspondent for the *Memphis Commercial Appeal* who was helping to load a wounded Mississippi Highway Patrolman into an escape car, noticed his friend Charlie Caldwell of WMCT-TV Memphis switching on his newsreel-camera light and starting to film the scene.

"The light from his camera was a deadly invitation to the wild crowd to come over and smash the camera and do him bodily harm," reported Smith. "Already, expensive cameras of all kinds were littering the area in front of the Lyceum, and thousands of feet of ruined film was scattered about like confetti and many photographers were bleeding and limping and begging for their lives. I ran up to the crowd approaching Charlie and pled with them to leave him alone, claiming he was sort of one of us, from the Memphis station. . . . He eased back into his car as if any quick movement would indicate fear and invite a killing frenzy. He sped off with rocks peppering his car."

Rumors broke out in the darkness, most of them false. "They've got machine guns!" "We killed six of them!" "They shot a coed! She's dead!" The "dead" girl was identified as Ann Gillespie, a junior from Laurel, Mississippi, with sparkling green eyes. In reality, she was perfectly safe, and nowhere near the scene.

Just before 8:30 P.M., the bulk of the mob, recovering from the shock of the initial assault, coalesced into a mass formation and surged toward the Lyceum. A young man carrying a Confederate flag on a staff screamed, "Let's move in on them! Go as far as you can! . . . Let's force them to fire all their gas and then we'll kill them!"

Teams of rioters scurried over to the construction site of the new Science Building at the eastern edge of the Circle. There, a rioters' paradise awaited them—a fresh supply of thirty thousand loose bricks, each of them a deadly weapon.

Boys trundled the missiles in tennis nets and wheelbarrows onto the battlefield, one of them announcing, "Get your ammo here!" The rioters broke the bricks in half and launched them toward the Lyceum. Ragged formations combined and charged forward to launch rock barrages, then retreated.

A boy holding an empty pop bottle was observed by *New York Post* reporter Stan Opotowsky. The boy, leaning back in a perfect pitching stance, told his buddies, "Y'all get ready to run." Opotowsky recalled, "He heaved the bottle and it crashed to the street at the feet of a U.S. marshal. Four marshals spun around and fired their guns: poppety, pop, pop, pow. There were flashes of light, the white smoke of tear gas, and the students ran and stumbled and hurdled a fence in headlong flight from the stinging fumes."

As flying rocks pummeled their ranks, the federal marshals scrambled behind army trucks for cover and pumped tear gas into the night sky. In the turmoil, the marshals' squad formations fell apart, and the smoke and noise prevented them from communicating with one another.

Rioters broke into the Chemistry Building next to the Lyceum, emerged with beakers full of acid and began lobbing them at the marshals. One hit squad leader Al Butler, burning his arm from hand to elbow. Waves of other rioters collided into the marshals' formations, and the marshals began fighting for their lives. It was almost pitch black around them, and they could barely see through the bulky gas masks and thick smoke.

Deputy U.S. Marshal Seibert Lockman from North Carolina found himself trapped in front of the Lyceum, facing a crowd that was lunging at him with pieces of sharp metal and cracking him on the head with bottles. The six-foot, 215-pound, judo-trained Lockman brandished his billy club with two hands and swung it like a baseball bat at the rioters' heads. When the mob pressed in closer to within hand-to-hand range, he switched his grip to the middle of the baton and lashed out to the left side, then the right. Left, right.

Lockman repeated a chant in his mind as he beat down his attackers, "Hit him in the head, gut, groin, knock him down . . . head, gut, groin, knock him down." It was working: The rioters were dropping like tenpins. One man charged at him with a broken beer bottle; Lockman smacked him down and watched him tumble over onto his own weapon, the rioter's face absorbing the fall on the jagged glass.

Nearby, another marshal was flailing at rioters with a one-handed baton grip. "That ain't worth a damn," Lockman called out in the voice of experience. "Use two hands!"

Dan Pursglove, a twenty-nine-year-old U.S. Border Patrolman and now deputized marshal, suddenly found himself flat on his behind with his feet straight out and wasn't sure how he got there. He thought, "What the hell you doing down there, Pursglove?" Then he looked between his legs—his genitals had been hit full-force with a brick. He got up to his feet, madder than hell, so mad that he was almost ready to unholster his .38 service revolver and start shooting into the mob. He was certain they were going to have to shoot their way out of there eventually.

"If I'd a stood still, they'd a hung me for sure," remembered Deputy U.S. Marshal Thomas W. Irvine. "I got hit on the shoulders, in the back, on the hip, in the knee, on the head. If somebody had asked me where I wasn't hit, I couldn't have told 'em."

Already the breeze was playing tricks on the marshals, pushing the gas fumes from east to west, away from the mob and back toward the Lyceum. The smoke blocked their views of incoming Molotov cocktails, iron pipes, rocks, and shattering glass. "Sometimes you just couldn't see the things coming," reported Deputy Marshal Willard McArdle. "They'd cut loose with a rebel yell and cut loose on us."

The rebel yell had not been heard in combat in the United States for ninety-seven years, but it shrieked up from the crowd with a terrifying force. The writer Shelby Foote once described it as a combination of a "foxhunt yip mixed up with a banshee squall." A Civil War Union soldier recalled with dread the "peculiar corkscrew sensation that goes up your backbone when you hear it." Deputy Marshal McArdle reported, "If you've ever heard one of those yells you'll never forget it."

"I was more frightened at Mississippi," recalled McArdle, a World War II veteran, "than I was at Pearl Harbor or any other time during the war." Years later, student body president Dick Wilson recalled what he witnessed from the Student Union building: "It was like watching the last battle of the Civil War."

A carload of incoming federal prison guards from Terre Haute, Indiana, flew down from Memphis, drove onto campus, and straight into the mob. They slapped on their gas masks and braced themselves as they drove through a gauntlet of rocks and bricks toward the Lyceum. When they got there, every window in the Border Patrol car was broken. As they jumped out of the car, they were surrounded by rioters, whom they had to beat back with nightsticks.

Out at the Oxford airport, a team of incoming federal prison guards from El Reno, Oklahoma, heard that the marshals were out of tear gas and about to be overrun. As a unit, they volunteered to drive a panel truck filled with tear gas and gas masks to the Lyceum. They crashed through a blockade of concrete and wooden benches at the university entrance.

"We were led onto campus by a Border Patrol car," reported one of the guards, "encountering attempts to stop us by approximately 2,500 civilians and a Mississippi Highway Patrol car. The civilians bombarded the vehicle with Coke bottles, bricks, and other objects, breaking both front windshields and the left door window. The dents in the panel truck were too numerous to count." The rioters threw their weapons from point-blank range, nearly climbing onto the truck's fenders.

Once they got to the Lyceum, the El Reno guards fanned out on the front line and fired a barrage of two-hundred-yard-range gas projectiles, which temporarily slowed down some of the rioters' advance.

At 9:02 P.M., the FBI monitored an order being flashed on the Highway Patrol radio frequency from an unidentified voice ordering the troopers to withdraw from the campus and assemble at a rally point a mile west of the university, near Kiamie's restaurant and bowling alley. Scores of patrolmen ran to their cars, grabbed their shotguns, and loaded their revolvers back in their holsters. In a dramatic display of flashing red lights, a convoy of more than one hundred cars snaked past the Lyceum and down the Circle, pulling off the campus in a great bumper-to-bumper procession.

The entire force was withdrawing from the battle. One car tried to run over a pair of marshals, and a patrolman yelled, "All right, you son-of-a-bitches, you asked for it, and now here it is!" On the way off the campus, some patrolmen stuck their heads out their windows and shouted various encouragements to the mob: "Kill the bastard!"; "Go kill that son of a bitch!" Some of the officers were crying from the tear gas as they yelled. "Where you going?" a voice in the crowd asked a passing patrol car. "Are you coming back?" A Highway Patrolman answered, "Yeah, we'll be back. Give 'em hell, boys. Keep it up."

Inside the Lyceum building, Nick Katzenbach confronted Highway Patrol chief Colonel Birdsong: "Your men are pulling out. Get them back." Birdsong replied, "Your information must be wrong. They are not leaving." It was hard to coordinate his men, Birdsong explained, because they were being tear-gassed.

Katzenbach proposed, "If they want to get away from the gas, let them go down to the entrances and set up roadblocks." But Birdsong countered, "They can't do that. And now that they've been gassed, I'm not sure that they are willing to."

Now all the entrances to the campus were wide open, and outsiders were pouring in. A huge fat man with beady eyes announced to the crowd in the Circle, "We've come to hep y'all." Students from high schools and colleges around Mississippi were mixing together with roughnecks converging from across the region.

They carried the weapons of a spontaneous, improvised insurrection—clubs, hunting knives, blackjacks, tire chains. Other rioters with squirrel guns, shotguns, .22s, and high-powered rifles were on the way.

Mildred Quarles, a black Oxford resident who lived near the Ole

Miss campus, looked out her window into a "pure hell" of people flocking toward the school. "People waving sticks—the most horrible-looking people you have ever seen, from Alabama, Louisiana, Texas. Those people were terrible. I'd never seen people like them before. They were just going crazy."

As soon as the Highway Patrol pulled out, a new wave of rioters charged toward the Lyceum with pipes and bricks.

A horrified student watching the conflagration said, "I can't believe this is happening at Ole Miss."

On the edge of the Circle there appeared a diminutive, bespectacled figure gazing in shock at the raging battle.

It was Rev. Duncan M. Gray, Jr., the rector of Oxford's St. Peter's Episcopal Church. When he heard news reports of the trouble breaking out on campus, the young father of four snapped on his minister's clerical collar and raced to the scene to offer help, along with his colleague Rev. Wofford Smith, the Ole Miss chaplain.

What Duncan Gray saw before him was "pure bedlam," he remembered, a hallucinatory swirl of screaming, tear-gas shots, charging rioters, and Confederate flags. Within moments, he realized what he had to do. He decided to plunge directly into the riot and try to stop it, armed only with his clerical collar.

Gray stepped into the path of the rioters, facing them with his back to the Lyceum, his hands outstretched, pleading with the mob to stop its attacks. The sight of a white minister's collar caught rioters completely off guard, and seeing the balding, professorial-looking little minister approaching them, some stopped dead in their tracks.

He was using his body as a human shield. "He didn't see it as courage," his wife, Ruth, later explained. "Duncan just didn't know any better. He was a priest, and that was what a priest did on that day. For him it was as much a part of his vocation as lifting the chalice in the Eucharist that morning."

One bewildered rioter who was leaning back to fire a brick was confronted by Gray, who commanded him, "Give me your brick, son." The rioter looked at Gray like he was insane, and the minister repeated, "Give me that brick." The rioter complied and then wandered off the field with a bewildered expression.

It happened over and over: Reverend Gray and Chaplain Smith

moved from one rioter to another, talking them into surrendering their weapons. The pair collected armfuls of rocks, concrete pieces, bricks, and metal pipes and trotted them back into a growing pile in the YMCA building.

In fact, Gray understood why the crowd was going berserk. They had been brainwashed, he thought. "Think of the freshman today at Ole Miss," he explained in a sermon a few weeks later. "He was only 10 years old when the Supreme Court's decision on segregation was handed down—and a senior today was only 13. Theirs is the generation that has been exposed to textbook and library censorship, mandatory essay contests on white supremacy, and a massive propaganda campaign against the Federal courts. . . . Who could really blame them when the Governor of the state himself was in open rebellion against the law; a living symbol of lawlessness?"

Tonight, Duncan Gray accosted even the wildest of the rioters, saying, "Please go on back to the dormitories. You're hurting the university, you're hurting the town, and the state. What you're doing is wrong." Incredibly, many of the students were responsive to the appeals. "Some of the students were almost in a daze," recalled Gray, "and were brought back to reality when you confronted them."

But there were far too many rioters and not enough ministers on the battlefield, so Reverend Gray and Chaplain Smith decided to split up to cover a wider area.

Just after 9:00, two students were hit by stray birdshot. Assuming they were being fired on by the marshals, the wounded students dashed into the YMCA building to tell Chaplain Smith. The minister crossed the battle lines waving a white handkerchief and entered the Lyceum to beg the marshals to stop shooting the students. In the blood-spattered Lyceum halls he was told that the federals did not have any shotguns.

Outside, the rioters were calling for a parley. Marshal Floyd Park and Chaplain Smith walked out of the Lyceum together to face the mob. The minister frantically waved a white handkerchief as the marshal shined a flashlight on his clerical collar and shouted, "Here's your priest. He will talk to you."

The mob temporarily suspended its assault and formed a north-south line facing the Lyceum. "Why are you attacking these men at this point?" the chaplain asked the rioters. "Because we want to get Meredith," someone replied. Smith replied, "To my knowledge, Meredith is not in this building." He argued that they had no right to attack these innocent marshals—they were policemen just like the policemen in any hometown. One student, a senior and a member of the football team, said he would try to reason with the mob: "All right, I'll talk to them."

He stretched his arms out to the assembly and shouted, "Here's the deal. The marshals will stop using tear gas if we stop throwing rocks and bricks."

After a few silent moments, voices in the mob called out, "Give us the nigger and we'll quit!" and, "We want Meredith!" Then someone tossed a brick in the air toward the nearby marshals, a marshal responded with a blast from his tear-gas gun, and the battle reignited into full-scale conflict. Chaplain Smith wandered off in a state of despair. "They just wouldn't listen," he said. "They're getting worse."

At 8:40 P.M., a white rented Chevrolet was nearing the campus. Behind the wheel was reporter Paul Guihard, and in the passenger seat was his Agence France–Presse photographer Sammy Schulman.

Minutes earlier they had been on the highway nearing Oxford, listening on the car radio to President Kennedy finishing his speech. When the president announced, "There is in short no reason why the books on this case cannot now be quickly and quietly closed in the manner directed by the court," that seemed to signal an end to matters. Assuming that the crisis was ending, Guihard said, "Oh, hell. The story's all over, but we might as well go up and clean it up." During the long drive up from Jackson, Guihard had talked with Schulman, reflecting on his life: his beginnings in the newspaper business, his ambitions to become a playwright and actor.

A Mississippi Highway Patrolman stopped Guihard's car at the university entrance and announced, "I can't guarantee your life or property if you drive in." Guihard nodded and drove in to park the car. In the distance, Guihard and Schulman could hear sounds of pandemonium. As they walked toward it, a group of friendly students told the two to hide their cameras, because "some bums up there" were smashing them. The two journalists decided to split up to cover more ground. "I'll see what's doing," Guihard told Schulman, "and see you back here in an hour then."

In that instant, the mob surged toward them, running away from the charging marshals. Guihard walked in the direction of the Lyceum and was swallowed up by the crowd. Photographer Flip Schulke, who was crouching in some bushes to protect himself, saw Guihard and called out to him to be careful and get down. A British army veteran, Guihard replied with typical good-natured aplomb, "Oh, I was in Cyprus—this is nothing!"

Paul Guihard then stepped into oblivion. A few minutes later he was found by some students, sprawled on his back in an unlighted area near a clump of trees 12 feet east of the Ward dormitory, bleeding to death. The spot was about 165 yards northeast of the Lyceum building. He died minutes later.

The FBI later recovered a slug from Guihard's back and found it to be a .38 Special lead bullet of the Peters or Remington brand, fired either from a .38 Smith & Wesson revolver or a .357 Magnum Smith & Wesson revolver, which also could fire .38 ammunition. Both weapons were standard police guns, and also were widely available to civilians.

The identity of Paul Guihard's killer remains a total mystery to this day. No witnesses ever came forward, and investigations by the FBI, the Mississippi Highway Patrol, the Lafayette County sheriff, and a Lafayette County grand jury could not turn up any suspects or witnesses to the shooting. No one ever came forward claiming to see who shot Guihard.

There was one faint clue to the nature of Guihard's shooting. By studying the wound and the entry hole in Guihard's brown jacket, the FBI laboratory in Washington, D.C., determined that Guihard was shot from a distance of less than one foot. It appeared that Paul Guihard's death was not a stray shot—it was a summary field execution. Guihard had made it to a spot within twelve feet of the building's east wall. He was not far from the front entrance to the building, where he might have been headed to escape the gas, but by now his killer may have been marching or ordering him to go to the unlighted area. For some reason Guihard stopped, the bullet was fired into his lower back, penetrating his heart, and the young reporter fell down on his back next to a flower bed, his feet resting on the sidewalk.

Guihard was within five hundred yards of huge concentrations of law-enforcement officers—more than four hundred federal marshals; over two hundred Mississippi Highway Patrolmen and other state police forces—and a crowd of more than twenty-five hundred civilians. Yet no clues to the identity of his killer ever emerged.

There are fleeting glimpses of Guihard's movements, but they are so obscured by darkness and smoke and the passage of time that they may be mirages. Rev. Duncan Gray saw a shadowy figure pass near him at this time, moving close to a group of adult civilians near the YMCA building. The civilians were gathered around a car, using a two-way radio, asking for people to come and bring guns. Gray later recognized Guihard's photo in news reports, and he believed that Guihard may have run afoul of that group of civilians.

A few weeks after the shooting, on October 26, 1962, a Mississippi Highway Patrol investigator interviewed a Mrs. Aubrey Harris, who at 9:00 P.M. was visiting her daughter at Ward Hall. She told the investigator that she went to the scene where Guihard was lying, and a group of five or six students was standing around him. The body was still warm and had a pulse, she reported, and people were trying to summon an ambulance. "While she was with the body," the investigator's report stated, "two male students came by and stated to her that about 15 to 20 minutes past they saw this particular subject running from the grove [the investigator meant the Circle] in the direction where he was found. They were referring to the park area in front of the Lyceum. . . . They also stated that the marshals were shooting tear gas toward the subject."

In one of many speculative possible scenarios, based on this fragmentary clue, Guihard, who may not have had time to size up the situation, could have been inadvertently bounding west toward a group of charging marshals, and then abruptly veered north and east when he realized what was happening, running to get away from them. The marshals, fighting for their lives inside of suffocating gas masks they could barely see out of, sometimes inside thick clouds of their own tear gas, could easily have mistaken Guihard for a large, potentially dangerous adult rioter, and seeing him abruptly run away from them, they might have blasted tear gas toward him or even begun chasing him. Another witness, Mrs. James Taylor, a Tupelo high-school teacher who was visiting her daughter at Ward Hall, reported to the Highway Patrol in an October 28, 1962 interview that she saw marshals firing tear gas in the immediate vicinity of Ward Hall at some point after 8:00 P.M., although she wasn't specific about the precise time.

In interviews conducted by the FBI and Mississippi Highway Patrol weeks later with hundreds of marshals, reporters, students, faculty, and other eyewitnesses to different parts of the riot, no other clues or evidence of any kind appeared to support this or any other scenario of the nature and intent of Guihard's movements, who moved with him, or who shot him.

Both the FBI and the Mississippi Highway Patrol turned up several witnesses to the immediate aftermath of Guihard's shooting, and the records of their interviews provide an outline of what happened next. Within minutes after his shooting, Guihard was discovered by a small group of students, one of whom who had heard him moaning in the dark, through a dormitory window. They found the mortally wounded Guihard moving slightly, with a faint heartbeat, his body still warm. Because he was shot in the back and was lying face up, they could not see any wound and they assumed he had had a heart attack from the gas. They removed his glasses, massaged his heart, and covered him with a blanket while someone called an ambulance to take him to Oxford Hospital. The small university infirmary was closer, but no one was sure there was a doctor on duty there, and they thought he'd have a better chance of survival in the more fully equipped hospital.

Minutes ticked by, but the ambulance couldn't navigate onto the war zone of a campus. Eventually a group of students carried Guihard in blankets into a car to drive him to the hospital, but he had already expired.

Guihard's killer has never been identified, let alone arrested or prosecuted. With his fiery red goatee and tall, bulky build, Guihard not only stood out, but was clearly an outsider from far away and might have been mistaken as a "beatnik" type. He may not have hidden his camera yet, which could have identified him as a hated journalist. Either perception could have been lethal for him.

Later in the evening, a sloppy-looking young civilian in blue jeans was seen standing in front of the Fine Arts building with a pistol, possibly a .38, squeezing off fast shots toward the marshals, aiming high for head or upper-body shots. Perhaps Guihard encountered him on his flight from the Lyceum.

The killer could have been a renegade Mississippi law-enforcement officer, perhaps one of the many armed sheriff's deputies wandering the campus that night. It is unlikely that the murderer was a Mississippi Highway Patrolman, since the entire force was gathering in the previous half hour at the gymnasium on the other side of the Lyceum, prior to withdrawing from the campus en masse by car.

There is even the remotest possibility that the shooter could have been a federal marshal. In the smoke and chaos of full-scale combat, a marshal might have mistaken Guihard for a rioter running away from the vicious attacks at the Lyceum, and in the process of subduing him, somehow panicked or was startled in the dark and smoke and gas and squeezed off a shot, accidentally or in anger.

No eyewitnesses to Guihard's execution ever came forward, no suspects were ever identified, and no murder weapon was ever found.

The always jovial Guihard could have just said the wrong thing to the wrong person, something as simple as identifying himself as a journalist when challenged by an armed rioter. On this night, that was more than enough to get you killed.

At the same time that Paul Guihard was heading to his doom, not far away a dazed-looking man from Texas wearing a cowboy hat was walking toward the battle.

CHAPTER TEN

The Silent Pillar

▨ ▨ ▨ ▨

He stood a foe, with all the zeal
Which young and fiery converts feel,
Within whose heated bosom throngs
The memory of a thousand wrongs.

—Lord Byron, "The Siege of Corinth"

FORMER U.S. ARMY major general Edwin Walker stepped under a lamppost on the edge of the battle and stared glassy-eyed into the chaos. Flying columns of young rioters and counterattacking federal marshals were crisscrossing the field, charging into and out of thick clouds of tear gas.

General Walker had arrived on the campus at 8:43 P.M. and hovered in the darkness, silently observing Chaplain Smith's aborted peace parley with the marshals and rioters. Now, as the streetlight illuminated him, Walker was being recognized by small groups of rioters who shook his hand and asked for his autograph. One boy proudly showed him his bloody T-shirt.

"Look," someone exclaimed, "now we have a leader! We have a leader now!" One man asked, "General, will you lead us to the steps?" The general nodded. Then Walker and a small group started marching toward the Lyceum, but they were quickly blocked by a sustained volley of tear gas from the marshals. So they turned east and walked past the trees, heading toward the Confederate monument guarding the entrance to the Circle.

Voices queried, "General Walker, sir, why don't the marshals quit?"; "General Walker, sir, where are the thousands of supporters you said were coming?" When told the riot had been under way for an hour, Walker responded, "Keep it up all night. We've got more people coming."

Rev. Duncan Gray, who was still trying to talk rioters out of their attacks and was running armfuls of bricks and other weapons into a pile in the YMCA building, spotted the commotion and recognized the general. The minister pushed his way up to Walker, grabbed his arm, and beseeched him to help stop the fighting: "Please help us stop this. You can stop this. You certainly can't let them do this—this is terrible!"

General Walker twisted and turned to try to get away from Gray, now trotting beside him. "Take your hand off me. I can't do anything about it. Get away from me. Who are you and what are you doing out here?"

Gray replied, "I am rector of the local Episcopal church. This is my home. I care very much about this university and this town. They are being destroyed. I am trying to stop the rioting. This is not your home—you are not helping here at all. General, I beg you, please help us get the students to go home and stop the rioting. They identify you with their cause. They will listen to you in a way that they won't listen to me."

Walker retorted, "I'm not here to stop what they're doing. They have every right to do what they're doing, and I'm here only as an observer, I'm not here to stop it." Finally, he disgustedly asked, "You're an Episcopalian, aren't you?" When Gray told him yes, Walker announced, "You're the kind of Episcopal minister that makes me ashamed to be an Episcopalian." Walker and his entourage then marched down to the Confederate monument.

There a crowd of more than eight hundred was milling around after scattered, uncoordinated attacks had failed to dent the marshals' defensive line. A part of the swelling crowd was chanting, "We want a leader! We want a leader!" As if on cue, there was General Walker. A roar of applause went up as the general was recognized. "When word of his identity spread," reported *St. Louis Post-Dispatch* correspondent Tom Yarbrough, people "moved toward him as if attracted by a magnet. It was as if he played some magic music on a flute, so eager were these people to see him."

The general walked up to the Confederate monument to the heroes of Lafayette County that guarded the entrance to the Circle, the symbolic heart of the university. The statue was inscribed with a passage from Byron: "They fell devoted, but undying; / The very gale their names seemed sighing: / The waters murmured of their name; / The woods were peopled with their fame; / The silent pillar, lone and gray, / Claimed kindred with their sacred clay; / Their spirits wrapt the dusky mountain, / Their memory sparkled o'er the fountain; / The meanest rill, the mightiest river, / Rolled mingling with their fame for ever."

The passage was from Lord Byron's epic poem "The Siege of Corinth," which told the story of an accidental disaster that occurred while a governor was negotiating to surrender his city. The poem was based on a climactic incident in 1715 during the long conflict between the Ottoman Empire and Venice over control of the Peloponnese, when Giacomo Minotto, the Venetian governor of the city of Corinth, was facing attack from an overwhelmingly superior force of Ottoman Turks and decided to negotiate a capitulation. But while the negotiations were under way, the Venetian ammunition dump accidentally exploded, killing scores of Turkish guards and triggering the massacre of six hundred Venetian soldiers.

General Walker stepped onto the base of the monument and the crowd fell silent. With glazed eyes and a strange sleepwalker's demeanor, Walker harangued the crowd in his disconnected, rambling, often confused way. "I want to compliment you all on the protest you're making," Walker bellowed slowly. "You have a right to protest under the Constitution. Any bloodshed here tonight is on the hands of the federal government. . . . Don't let up now. You may lose this battle, but you will have to be heard."

Reverend Gray, seeing the harangue from the YMCA, raced over, struggled through the crowd, climbed up onto the base of the statue, and worked his way around it until he was next to the general, who was in the midst of his oration. Gray held on to the statue, his minister's collar reflecting in the faint glow of a street lamp, and tried in vain to persuade Walker to cease speaking, or better still, call a stop to the violence.

Instead, Walker looked at Gray with contempt and declared, "There is an Episcopal priest here who wants you to go home. He makes me ashamed to be an Episcopalian!"

The crowd erupted in fury, and a voice cried, "Let's kill the minister!" Hands reached up and pulled Gray off the monument into a flurry of flying fists. Gray was being pinned to the ground and beaten when an argument broke out in the crowd. "No, no, no," said one person. "Let's don't hurt the preacher." The man beating Gray replied, "Let's kill the son-of-a-bitch."

Watching helplessly nearby was University of Mississippi professor William Willis, who thought he saw tears in Duncan Gray's eyes. The tears were not from fear or from the tear gas, Willis thought. Duncan Gray was weeping because his heart was breaking. Within moments, Gray was shielded by an unidentified deputy sheriff who had waded bravely into the crowd, and the minister was escorted back to the YMCA building by friendly students.

"Protest!" bellowed the general, resuming his rant. "Protest! There is no stopping point! You must be prepared for possible death! If you are not willing to pay the price, go home! This may be a lost cause but continue fighting and show them what you're made of. Many people from out of state are heading toward Oxford. Tens of thousands of individuals are coming to help us and we have to win."

General Walker was finishing his speech when a tear-gas projectile landed nearby. "Governor Ross Barnett is your governor," Walker said. "Stand by your governor. Charge!" He stepped down from the statue and faced the Lyceum, a spontaneous army forming around him of battalion strength.

General Walker had led men into battle before, against Hitler's Wehrmacht in Italy and France, and in 1957 he had commanded the peaceful capture of Little Rock, Arkansas, by the 101st Airborne. Tonight, the tastes and sounds and smells of combat were all around him again, and he was surrounded by boys as young as sixteen and seventeen, some wearing bloodstained shirts and improvised tourniquets over their wounds and wet bandannas around their faces to wipe their eyes and to defend against the tear gas.

"Lead us, General!" a voice rang out. Walker's harangue was a turning point for the battle: It ignited the first massive coordinated charge toward the Lyceum. Up to that point, there had been many charges, but they were made by relatively small groups. Fifteen or twenty would run up with bricks and bottles to throw, followed by twenty-five or thirty, but they were coming from different directions with little or no coordination or organization. Now the mob moved as a mass formation.

Reverend Gray, determined to the last, went onto the battlefield yet again to intercept the advance, beseeching the rioters: "Is this America? This is all wrong. You should act like human beings, not a bunch of animals. Please don't do this. Please return to your homes." The clergyman was trying to stop the forward motion of the riot with his own flesh, placing his body between groups of rioters and the Lyceum. "Go home, this is terrible," Gray called out. "We shouldn't be doing this, violence is not the answer!"

The rioters lashed out at Reverend Gray, comparing themselves to Hungarian freedom fighters. "They were in tears," recalled Gray, "and they were certain that the federal government was persecuting them and they were standing up for human freedom." One man even chased Gray with a shovel, but Gray outran him. From this point on, the minister noticed a sea change in the character of the mob. The rioters were even more ferocious and determined now, and he was able to disarm far fewer of them than before.

The mob surged around Gray toward the Lyceum, and the riot was pushed over the edge. After Walker's speech, said Gray, "all eight hundred or nine hundred people around the monument moved as a body toward the Lyceum. Things just went from bad to worse after that." As the massed and unified mob neared the flagpole near the middle of the Circle, the general called out, "Get the fire truck!" One rioter thought Walker looked like "he might have been riding up Broadway in a ticker-tape parade. He never flinches or dodges or pays the least attention."

As the crowd approached, the beleaguered line of marshals fired a long barrage of tear gas. In a cloud of burning chemical smoke, Walker disappeared. The mob faltered and then fell back. An anonymous voice ordered, "Regroup!"

General Edwin Walker now began patrolling his headquarters zone between the Confederate monument and the flagpole near the center of the Circle, dispensing tactical advice and encouragement to the boys who flocked to him as if he were a Civil War commander. "Keep it up!" Walker told them. He stooped over to consult with a boy who was struggling with a Molotov cocktail, then took a moment to explain the perfidy of the New Frontier to several bystanders. Inches away, a boy pitched a missile toward the marshals and the riveted general followed its arc with a slight movement of his head.

At the flagpole, an excited youth asked, "What if we find the power plant and cut off their lights?" The general replied, "Fine, but do you know where it's located?" Someone else asked, "Couldn't the marshals just quit when they know we're right?" Walker agreed. "They should drop their badges and just turn around and desert."

"Do you think you'll get all those volunteers we read about in the paper, General?" asked a very young-looking boy. "If they haven't been fooled into thinking it's all over and turning back now that he's [Meredith] on the campus," replied the general. "They'll be here tomorrow, all right."

"General Walker, I fired expert in the Army," announced a fat young man, adding, "I could shoot out those marshals' lights from anywhere in this grove." Walker replied, "No, you'd better not do that. That could be too dangerous. You've already got your bloodshed, and they used tear gas. That is the kind of protest we needed."

"General Walker," another rioter proposed, "couldn't we rush 'em? We have a lot of supporters. Do you think they'd shoot to kill?" Walker answered, "Better not try that." Perhaps sensing that reporters and other witnesses were close by, mixed into the crowd, Walker was now tempering his comments with statements against the violence he was helping unleash.

"I'm going to tell people what's going on here tonight," Walker assured the crowd. "As soon as I get to a radio, I'll get on the biggest network and tell what's going on here. You're making news all over the country."

Later on, at about 10:45 P.M., Walker gave another speech at the base of the Confederate monument, to a group of 150 to 200. It was a typically confused, disjointed, slow-motion oration that triggered both boos and cheers from the perplexed crowd: "I'm not advocating violence but continuing protest against force. . . . If you can't help us you might as well go home. . . . This is not the proper route to Cuba. . . ." His words trailed off and soon the crowd did, too, returning to the business at hand, which was war.

In interviews nearly four decades after the battle, members of that mob spoke about their experience, reflecting on why they were fighting the federal marshals.

One of them was a then Ole Miss sophomore and naval reservist named Pascal Townsend, who described himself as "a typical Mississippi boy raised in the Delta." He reported that many people by now knew that James Meredith was not inside the Lyceum. He explained he wasn't fighting James Meredith, because he believed "he had a right to go to school if he wanted to." It was the marshals that he hated.

To Townsend, "It was not an issue of integration. It was an issue of brute force coming in and trying to abuse me and mine." He recalled, "As far as we were concerned the marshals were just scumbags. Just the dregs of humanity they sent down there, just like the Gestapo. That's exactly how we felt. They were just like Hitler's Gestapo. I still feel that way. They looked like racketeers in the movies, thugs they sent down to beat people up, to rape us. We figured they were from Washington, D.C. They looked like East Coast thugs, big brutes. We felt like they'd invaded our homes. We weren't trying to kill them. We wanted to make them pay. We wanted to hurt them so damn bad they'd leave us alone."

Townsend recalled a two-man team of rioters who set up an ambush for the marshals. One youth would taunt the marshals at close range, then quickly retreat past a tree where his partner waited. When a marshal passed, the hidden youth would swing a baseball bat full force at the marshal's head, flatten him to the ground, and then retreat.

Another mob member, an Ole Miss freshman from Greenwood, Mississippi, explained his motivation simply: "I didn't want the black guy in there. I would have been happy if they'd have killed every fucking marshal there. Plus that nigger. I still feel that way. I felt they were cramming this deal down the people of Mississippi's throat." He heard rumors that the marshals had already killed ten to twenty people, but he felt in no danger until he was halfway through the Circle, when a blast of birdshot hit him in the face, stomach, hands, and arms, taking him out of action. They were mainly surface pellet wounds, and he was sure they came from the Lyceum, since he was hit flush forward. (Although federal officials denied any shotguns were deployed by marshals at Oxford, at least one news photograph shows a federal marshal patrolling the area in front of the Lyceum holding up a shotgun, and an FBI report quotes a deputized federal prison guard referring to riot shotguns that his squad brought with them.)

The wounded freshman's older brother, a sophomore, also was peppered with birdshot when he was in front of the Lyceum picking up a hot tear-gas canister to throw back at the marshals. He caught pellets in the forearm, wrist, and hand. But the wounds just made him madder. Now he was ready to whip the whole damn world. "If they're going to shoot at me," he thought, "then I'm going to put some misery on them." The boy stayed out for hours fighting the marshals, sometimes with his bare fists, eluding capture. "If I had to go do it over again," he said in 2000, "I probably would have fought a little harder."

Inside the human attack wave was former Eagle Scout Nathan Clooskey and three fellow students from Itawamba Community College in Fulton, Mississippi. The TV and radio stations were broadcasting bulletins on the crisis all day, and the excitement sounded irresistible to the boys. This would be something that would be written about in the history books, they figured, so they jumped into a 1955 Chevy and headed for Oxford to have a look. They had planned to be spectators, but they immediately blundered into the conflict and willingly became a part of it.

"I was an immature eighteen-year-old college freshman," explained Clooskey. "One of the things that influenced us was the fact that even the rural police departments were getting their dogs ready and arming themselves to go down and defend Ole Miss against Northern oppression." Like Townsend, Clooskey saw the enemy as the federal government, not James Meredith. "It wasn't black and white racial prejudice we were feeling," said Clooskey, "but governmental oppression." The students drove onto the campus and walked right into the mob regrouping at the Confederate statue. General Walker was haranguing the crowd like a football coach. Confederate flags were waving above the mob. "Walker would give us a rousing speech and we'd all go charging the marshals. They'd let us have the tear gas, everybody would go running back, he'd speak to us again, and several hundred of us would go charging again."

Clooskey saw people falling all around him from the gas and the marshals' baton charges, but somehow he felt he was completely safe and invincible. With a huge Confederate flag fluttering ahead of him, Clooskey felt like he was inside a Civil War movie.

In a burst of complete lunacy, the state's leading radio and TV station, WJDX/WLBT, was broadcasting Confederate war songs as the battle raged. The station had correspondents reporting from the scene at Oxford, and they were doing their best to report the facts of the riot. But in Jackson, after cutting away from the on-the-scene reports, the

station's segregationist management was inflaming the riot by spin-
ning "rebel" recordings, providing a demented, rousing, pulse-pound-
ing soundtrack to the riot. The musical mayhem drifted throughout
the Mississippi countryside, into the homes of frightened citizens, into
the car radios of civilian volunteers moving on Oxford, and into the
ears of rioters and spectators at the battle.

What they heard was the music of total war: "Fear no danger, shun
no labor, / lift up rifle, pike and saber, / To arms, to arms, to arms in
Dixie! / Shoulder pressing close to shoulder, / let the odds make each
heart bolder, / To arms, to arms, to arms in Dixie!" Then there was the
"No, No, Never" song, written especially for the Meredith crisis:
"Never, never, never, never, No, never! / Ross is standing like Gibraltar,
we shall never, never, falter. . . ." Then a joyous coed chorus belted out
the tune "Go, Mississippi!" the new state song and football anthem.

The years melted away, and suddenly it was 1861 again and Jeff
Davis was president, and the Confederate army was unvanquished,
and the dream of an independent Southern republic was almost as
alive as tomorrow morning, consecrated in blood and bullets and the
glory of gallant, golden-haired young heroes. The transistor radios
cheered the rioters on with songs of vengeance: "I can take the hide off
the Yankee that stole ol' Abner's shoes . . . The Yankees took me prisoner, and if I get parole, / I'll go right back and fight 'em, I will upon
my soul."

When he was serving in the air force, James Meredith had read a
spellbinding book called *The Mind of the South,* written by a brilliant,
tormented North Carolina newspaperman named Wilbur J. Cash, who
committed suicide soon after the book was published in 1941. It was
one of the most influential books Meredith ever read, and for him it
seemed to unlock pathways of exploration and understanding of
white psychology. In a sense, the book also explained what was happening that night at Oxford.

In the book, Cash wrote of "the sentimental cult of the Confederate soldier" that sprang up across the South after the Civil War. Southern men, he wrote, "exhibited a striking tendency to build up legends
about themselves and to translate these legends into explosive action—to perform with a high, histrionic flourish, and to strive for
celebrity as the dashing blade." From birth, young men were saturated
with the quasi-religious symbolism of the Southern "Lost Cause," and

Cash wrote that "every boy growing up in this land now had continually before his eyes the vision, and heard always in his ears the clamorous hoofbeats, of a glorious swashbuckler, compounded of Jeb Stuart, the golden-locked Pickett, and the sudden and terrible Forrest . . . forever charging the cannon's mouth with the Southern battle flag."

Ninety-nine years before, on the afternoon of July 3, 1863, a group of University of Mississippi students had raced up a slanting field in Pennsylvania toward the dazzling, doomed vision of the "High Water Mark of the Confederacy" on Cemetery Ridge at Gettysburg. They were the remnants of Company A of the Eleventh Mississippi Volunteer Infantry Regiment, known as the "University Greys," who in 1861 had marched out of Oxford with some fifty University of Mississippi students and one hundred other boys and men from Lafayette County. After fighting their way through Harpers Ferry, the First Battle of Manassas, Seven Pines, Bull Run, and Antietam, there were only thirty-one of them left.

If the Greys and the twelve thousand Confederate troops beside them could break through the wall of Union flesh and cannon holding Cemetery Ridge, hoped General Robert E. Lee, they might split the Union Army of the Potomac in two, march on Washington, D.C., and demand terms for peace. Historian George Stewart wrote, "If we grant—as many would be ready to do—that the Civil War furnishes the great dramatic episode of the history of the United States, and that Gettysburg provides the climax of the war, then the climax of the climax, the central moment of American history, must be Pickett's Charge," which was named for Virginia's General George Pickett, who commanded the Confederate troops on the right flank of the assault.

Despite being pulverized by the most savage artillery barrage the Northern Hemisphere had ever seen, at 3:30 P.M. a handful of Mississippi troops made it all the way up to Brian's Barn on Cemetery Ridge, the northernmost point on the field reached by the Confederates. Private Joseph G. Marable planted the Eleventh Mississippi's colors at the stone fence before being wounded and captured, and despite a temporary breakthrough by several hundred other Confederates at the Angle and a clump of trees a few dozen yards to the south, the desperate, disorganized, and poorly planned charge was crushed.

Of the thirty-one University of Mississippi Greys who reported for action that morning, nine were dead, twelve had been wounded, and ten more wounded were taken prisoner. On that day the unit suffered 100 percent casualties. Not one of them ever went back to school at Oxford. From that turning point forward, the Confederate cause was in perpetual retreat all the way to the surrender at Appomattox.

In the years that followed, Pickett's Charge became the supreme iconic moment in the theology of the Confederate Lost Cause. "For every Southern boy fourteen years old," wrote William Faulkner in *Intruder in the Dust*, "not once but whenever he wants it, there is the instant when it's still not yet two oclock on that July afternoon in 1863, the brigades are in position behind the rail fence, the guns are laid and ready in the woods and the furled flags are already loosened to break out and Pickett himself with his long oiled ringlets and his hat in one hand probably and his sword in the other looking up the hill waiting for Longstreet to give the word and it's all in the balance, it hasn't happened yet, it hasn't even begun yet. . . ."

In Oxford on the night of September 30, 1962, roving bands of Ole Miss students and others were unconsciously reenacting a Pickett's Charge in miniature, and few of them could have known that they, too, were inside a turning point in history.

At the now-unguarded north campus gate on Sorority Row at 9:45 P.M., large groups of civilians were flooding onto campus. At the University Avenue entrance, outsiders were streaming in on foot, and teams of rioters were building makeshift barricades across the street, made of construction material, ripped-up concrete benches and drinking fountains, garbage cans and ping-pong tables.

A team of rioters broke into the campus fire house, cranked up the school's little old fire engine and rolled it into the Circle. The truck charged toward the marshals, a mass of rioters trotting behind, then veered over to a fire hydrant. The mob connected the fire hose and launched geysers of water toward the marshals, further defeating the tear gas. The marshals charged down the field, took out their pistols, and fired holes into the hose to put it out of action, creating ghostly water fonts in the dark. Their comrades ripped out the wires under the truck's hood with their clubs and retreated to the Lyceum.

Tear gas was drifting into six nearby dormitories, Garland, Dupree, Barr, Howry, LaBauve and Odom Halls, forcing students to flee outside. "Some boys were screaming," reported senior Dorothy Coco, "begging to be let into our dorms to escape the stinging fumes but they were not let in. Then the gas came into our dormitory. We were choking and our eyes and faces were burning. . . . We went out to the practice field and laid down on the grass to escape the fumes." Some students swore that Falkner Hall, a boy's dorm, was deliberately gassed by marshals who threw two tear-gas canisters into the hall and wedged one in the door, forcing the complete evacuation of both wings.

University of Mississippi junior Mary Lynn Hendricks spent the night looking out her dorm window, her nose pressed against the glass watching the battle.

"It was like looking into your worst nightmare," she remembered, "or a small window into Hell."

CHAPTER ELEVEN

The Guns of Midnight

■ ■ ■ ■

I have a rendezvous with Death
At some disputed barricade. . . .
At midnight in some flaming town

—Alan Seeger

DEPUTY MARSHAL GENE SAME kept a tight grip on his gas gun as he charged east through the Circle with some of the men from his squad. So far he'd fired only a couple of bursts, and he was conserving the few rounds of gas he had left. "No point in wasting it," he thought.

Behind him, the Lyceum building was enveloped in a glowing, un-earthly toxic curtain of tear-gas clouds that danced and shifted with the soft Southern breezes, its columns illuminated in the haze of its exterior lights, the only light left now that all the street lamps had been knocked out by the rioters. The clock on the Lyceum was approaching 10:00 P.M.

Just when Deputy Marshal Same thought they'd pretty well cleared out this area of the Circle, a group of rioters charged directly toward the marshals. Same stepped forward, leveled his gas gun, and fired a burst toward the rioters' formation. Something hit him in the neck. He heard what sounded like a big *splat*. That was the last thing he remembered before he hit the grass.

A slug fired by a hidden sniper, flying on a downward angle, had just entered Same's throat, severed his jugular vein, ripped through a cluster of nerves, ricocheted off his collarbone, ranged down through his lung, and lodged in one of his back ribs. The missile was either double-aught buckshot or a slug from a .22 rifle. Blood began gushing from his neck in a thick fountain. He was picked up by three of his fellow marshals, who hustled him into the front door of the Lyceum, and laid him down on the tile floor of the main hallway. Same's blood spurted up onto the wall.

The Lyceum halls were already littered with wounded, retching bodies. There wasn't a single doctor in the building and almost no medical supplies. Marshals were lying against the wall, constructing makeshift splints for their broken arms and legs out of their own billy clubs, gently probing their buddies' wounds to check for broken bones. A *Life* magazine correspondent jotted in his notes, "The cacophony of battle—explosions, shots, crashes, yells—thunders outside. Twelve marshals lie broken and suffering along the blood-spattered corridors inside, nearly obscured now and then in the swirling clouds of tear gas. Others are collapsed, weeping inside their gas masks."

Marshals were shouting in despair through their gas masks, which often prevented them from identifying one another's faces and voices. One cried, "My God, how are we going to hold them back with this little force?" Another exclaimed, "We don't have enough gas masks to go around!"

"This man has been shot," said an unidentified marshal standing over the unconscious Gene Same. "They've got a shotgun out there. Where's a doctor, this man is dying." Another replied, "We're trying to get one."

"Try, hell," said the marshal. "This man's dying!"

"My God, this guy's dead!" a voice called out.

"No, no, get me a goddamned first aid kit," a voice ordered. U.S. Border Patrol inspector William Dunn of the Chula Vista, California, station had been standing ten feet away when Gene Same was shot and had helped carry him inside. Though he wasn't a doctor, Dunn had two years of pre-med training. Tonight he had to become a combat field medic. He was Gene Same's only chance of survival.

Dunn leaned over the wounded marshal and inspected the deep puncture wound near the center of his throat. It was hemorrhaging badly, so he pressed on the wound with his fingers to stop the bleeding. Same was having great trouble breathing, which Dunn correctly diagnosed as being caused by blood pouring into the trachea.

One furious marshal confronted Deputy Attorney General Nicholas Katzenbach and asked permission for the marshals to return fire with their pistols. "No, I won't give the order to shoot those kids," Katzenbach replied.

"Then you just come over here," the marshal screamed, "and tell me what we're gonna do. Look at that man with his throat shot out. We've gotta have troops!"

A few hundred yards away, inside the athletic dormitory, Miller Hall, Coach Johnny Vaught was checking his team roster while players stuffed towels around the windows to keep out the tear gas. Coach Vaught had locked his Rebel football players inside the building to keep them safe and out of trouble. "We have got to band together," he announced to his squad. "We must keep our poise. We have to show the people of the United States just what we are down here. We're not a bunch of radicals. The only way is through our football."

For one player, a powerfully built star fullback from Greenwood, Mississippi, named George "Buck" Randall, the excitement was too much. Randall had no strong political views one way or the other; personally he didn't mind too much if James Meredith wanted to attend the university. He hadn't even been following the Meredith drama in the news. He just had to see what was going on. He slipped out the back door of Miller Hall and headed for center of campus.

When Randall got to the Lyceum, he ran straight into a barrage of bricks and bottles. Before he knew it, he was grabbed by campus police chief Burns Tatum, who hustled him into the Lyceum to take cover. In moments a horrified Buck Randall was staring at the injured marshal Gene Same, who was lying in a spreading puddle of blood as marshals toiled frantically over him.

Correctly assuming Randall was a student, Border Patrolman Richard Dick screamed at him, "You see him? He's bleeding to death! This is what you people are doing, you are killing us! This man is going to die! And you people are responsible for it! You go out there and tell those bastards they've killed a man."

Deputy Marshal Al Butler stepped inside to check on Gene Same's condition. When he saw how badly the marshal was wounded, the enraged Butler ripped off his helmet and gas mask, strode up to Katzenbach and Chief Marshal McShane, and screamed, "Are you fucking people ready to call in the troops yet?" McShane gently ordered Butler back outside, and Butler, having made his point, quietly obeyed.

Spotting the burly form of football star Buck Randall, Jim Mc-Shane had an idea, and he pulled Randall over for an urgent man-to-man talk. "Look, you'd better go out there and try to disperse this crowd," the lawman told the student, "or we're going to start killing people—we're just not going to have our people shot. Tell these people to disperse now, or we're going to start shooting—students and all." Those words, "students and all," scared Buck Randall to death. By now, he was hearing bullets slapping against the front of the building a few feet away.

Buck Randall decided to go out into the darkness, step into the line of fire, and try to stop the riot. His actions were witnessed by marshals, students, and reporters.

When asked about it nearly two generations later, Randall thought back to that night and explained why he did what he did next. He had hardly ever talked about it since, in part because he wasn't the sort of person to boast about something like that. "At that moment, it was just something I thought I had to do," Randall explained. "Just like playing football, when you got a certain assignment, you've got to carry it out. It happened so fast. I didn't have time to think about Meredith or anybody—I was thinking about people getting killed out there, and I wanted to stop that if I could. I just did what Marshal McShane told me to do."

Chief Tatum and Chief Marshal McShane stuck Randall out the Lyceum's side door and the gridiron warrior walked east into the Circle with his hands up in the air. It felt to Randall like he was inside a total war zone, and he saw what seemed like thousands of people in the distance. It was 10:15 P.M. in Oxford.

Randall stepped to the base of the flagpole inside the Circle, waved his hands and hollered, "Gather round, come on over here." He kept hollering until several hundred members of the mob flocked around the flagpole. He recognized only a very few Ole Miss students in the mob.

"I saw a marshal shot," Randall yelled as loud as he could. "I saw blood everywhere. I don't know if he's dead or dying but there's blood everywhere and they are mad. The marshal told me if y'all don't disperse now, leave the Lyceum and get away from here, they're going to start shooting."

Some people in the mob recognized Randall. Said one: "He's an Ole Miss football player. We'd better listen to him." Randall pleaded, "Stop this. We don't want to kill anybody!"

A voice in the crowd yelled, "Propaganda! Let's charge the building again!" Other voices began cursing Randall. The brawny young man persisted, "We'd better leave here—work it out some other way!"

One of the hecklers announced, "Let's pull this son of a bitch down off of there."

At this, Randall snapped, "Bring your ass on. If you want some of me, just come on!" There were no takers. Randall's five-foot-ten-inch, two-hundred-pound body was a deadly weapon on the football field, and as a fellow student later explained, "He was the biggest, baddest football player there was. Nobody wanted to mess with Buck."

"When I was on the flagpole," Randall remembered, "bullets were hitting the top of it—ding, ding, ding." When he figured he'd done all he could at the flagpole, Randall moved to another section of the Circle, stood on top of a bench and repeated his performance. Then he crossed over to another part of the Circle, stood on top of a table and did it again, and did it yet again down near the Confederate monument. Randall kept on yelling, "Y'all go home!"

"I just went from pillar to post, all around," Randall explained. He was heckled and cursed a lot as he continued his mission, but he noticed some people in the mob dispersing and wandering away.

Other Ole Miss students were also fighting for peace that night in their own ways. The vast majority of them were simply refusing to join in the riot. Some were acting as volunteer bodyguards to usher reporters to safety. An anonymous army ROTC cadet slipped over to the locked rifle closet and pulled out the firing pins of all the training rifles in case the rioters broke in. At the Sigma Nu fraternity house, the chapter president, a square-jawed twenty-year-old from Pascagoula named Trent Lott reportedly spent the whole night dispatching phone calls and runners to order all his 120 fraternity brothers away from the riot. He was solidly against integrating the university, but he wanted his boys out of danger. None of them got hurt, and only one was detained briefly by marshals on the scene of the riot.

But the battle was intensifying, and it looked like it was about to claim its next victim. Inside the besieged Lyceum building, Border Patrol inspector William Dunn rolled the horribly wounded Gene Same over on his side to drain the blood away from his mouth and trachea and to prevent strangulation. The victim was showing symptoms of severe shock, with a weak, fast pulse and shallow, rapid breathing. Dunn kept his right hand on Same's throat and counted off the pulse rate with his left. Finally, Gene Same's body surrendered and decided to die. His heart stopped, as did his pulse and his breathing.

Dunn wouldn't give up. He turned Same's head to the side and gave him mouth-to-mouth artificial respiration while massaging his heart with his left hand. A half dozen marshals kneeled around them, grabbing the few gauze pads they could find. Someone was on the phone pleading frantically for a doctor. "Send somebody, we've got a man dying in here!"

Deputy Marshal Same still had no heartbeat. The mouth-to-mouth wasn't working. Dunn instructed another marshal to apply artificial respiration through back pressure while Dunn controlled the hemorrhage and continued the external heart massage. Finally the heartbeat returned. Then Same began breathing on his own.

Gene Same's mind briefly drifted back to consciousness. He didn't know where he was. He could hear frantic voices saying, "I haven't got any pulse, can't find a pulse"; "Do it by the numbers, there, you've got it!" But moments later he lost consciousness, and his heart again stopped. Dunn and the other marshals were able to revive him. Minutes later, his heart stopped again. Again he was revived.

A civilian ambulance tried to fight its way to the Lyceum to evacuate the marshal, but it was trapped by a swarm of rioters who tried to turn it over, forcing it to abandon the attempt and flee. Finally a Mississippi National Guard ambulance arrived in back of the Lyceum.

Deputy Marshal Same was bundled in a makeshift stretcher of blankets and hauled out the back door into the Jeep. Everyone who saw him leave figured he was a dead man. Dunn hurriedly instructed the Guardsman riding in the back how to control the marshal's hemorrhage and apply artificial respiration and external heart massage.

As the ambulance pulled away from the Lyceum, a well-aimed Molotov cocktail spiraled through the air and exploded on the ambulance's roof, setting it ablaze. The next thing Gene Same remembered, he was lying flat out inside the ambulance, feeling rocks slamming against the vehicle. Soon he was hearing voices: "Oh shit!"

"What's the matter?"

"I think I passed the road to the airport! I've got to turn around. . . . No, I haven't, here it is."

Gene Same fell back into oblivion as he was driven onto the tarmac at the Oxford Airport and loaded into the same small plane that had taken James Meredith into Oxford five hours earlier. The seats were ripped out so that Same could be laid down. Once they were airborne, he came to again as an oxygen mask was wrapped around his face. Someone said, "Breathe in."

"He's not going to make it," Same heard the voice say. "I can't find any pulse." At this, he blacked out. Sometime later, he heard, "We're going to lose this boy, he's not going to make it!" Then Same felt something bouncing around the inside the airplane. He sensed that the oxygen had run out and someone had thrown the empty tank down in fury.

The voice hollered to the pilot for more speed. "He's had it, he's not going to make it!" By now Same was figuring he was about gone, too. Someone touched his forehead, and he again slipped off into unconsciousness.

Much later, he woke up in the hospital at the Millington Naval Air Station at Memphis. A doctor asked him for his blood type, address, and next of kin, and told him that when he woke up he would have a tube in his throat and not to worry about it. The marshal heard a navy doctor arguing, "This isn't right, we shouldn't have that man in here, he's not military."

"Don't worry about it, Doc," muttered the deputy marshal before sliding yet again into unconsciousness. "I won't sue you."

Deputy Marshal Gene Same died and was reborn four times in one night. In the end he survived. His shooter has never been identified.

Back on the front lines, the marshals had just about run out of tear gas, the only means they had to keep the rioters at bay.

"We've got to have more gas," one marshal demanded of Nicholas Katzenbach.

"We don't have any more right now, but we're working on it" was the reply.

"We've got to have it now," the marshal shouted. "My men are getting slaughtered out there!"

The marshals were pumping out tear gas faster than they could get reserves ready. McShane and the Justice Department officials were pleading for more tear gas to be flown down from Memphis, but the supplies were running so low there that marshals were commandeering crates of gas bombs from the 503d Military Police Battalion's supply. Two hours into the chaos, the riot was abruptly shifting into full-scale combat.

The marshals could hear a shotgun blasting away in the distance, and it was soon joined by the rhythmic "pow-pow-pow" of a .22 automatic. Before long, gunfire seemed to be coming from everywhere. "We were now alone," recalled newsman Ed Turner, "the crowd roaring louder with each barrage, the campus filling up with reinforcements from three states and no guard at the gates to stop them."

Across the region, cars and trucks full of armed and unarmed fighters were surging toward Oxford from all directions, especially from segregationist strongholds in adjacent Alabama and Louisiana. A few scattered Mississippi Highway Patrolmen were blocking potential rioters from the campus, but one patrolman was observed telling a carload of outsiders, "We can't let you in here but if you break into small groups you can sneak in across the railroad tracks."

Civilian volunteers armed with rifles and shotguns were flocking into the campus and taking turns opening fire at the Lyceum and the marshals, who now became the bull's-eye of a demented public shooting gallery. Over the next hours, snipers and muzzle flashes were reported at roofs and windows of the YMCA building, the Fulton Chapel, the Peabody Building, the Confederate statue, and scattered in the shadows around the Circle.

At 10:00 P.M., Deputy Marshal Al Butler reported to the deputy attorney general: "Mr. Katzenbach, that's not a riot out there anymore. It's an armed insurrection."

On the edge of campus, FBI agent Robin Cotten saw dozens of civilians carrying shotguns and long rifles as they jumped out of pickup trucks and ran up the hill toward the center of campus. Agent Cotten figured the campus was now swarming with Klansmen. He was extremely concerned for the safety of his son, who was an Ole Miss student trapped somewhere on campus. The FBI agent didn't know how to get his son out of there. In fact, the young man was pinned down on an upper floor of the YMCA building, directly underneath a sniper. "Every time the ambulance would pull out of there," Agent Cotten remembered, "I'd run by and see if it was my son inside."

What Cotten was witnessing, among many other things, were the beginnings of a Ku Klux Klan rebellion, with scores of out-of-state armed Klansmen converging spontaneously on Oxford. They were acting on their own initiative without orders from their leadership. There hadn't been time for that.

A rattletrap school bus with Louisiana plates pulled in behind the Ole Miss football stadium. Inside the bus, a sound system was playing a tune called "The Cajun Ku Klux Klan": "You niggers listen now, / I'm gonna tell you how, / To keep from being tortured, / When the Klan is on the prowl, / Stay at home at night, / Lock your doors up tight, / Don't go outside or you will find, / Them crosses aburning bright." A team of five stocky men disembarked with a beer cooler and picnic supplies. One of the men asked a student where the action was. Another announced that they had brought machine guns.

Hardy Stennis, a student who was observing the chaos, saw four armed men in cowboy hats and western wear walking toward the Lyceum. Stennis asked them, "Where are you fellows from?" The reply: "Louisiana." Stennis queried, "Well, what in the world are you doing way up here?" One gunman answered, "We come to help out!"

"Now, watch," Stennis lamented to a friend, "these people have no business here, and Mississippians and our student body are going to get blamed for what they do."

One sniper crouched down behind a pile of bricks near the construction site of the new Science Building. He shot his rifle three or four times, then trotted to a new position. Another shooter lay down in a flower bed close to the marshals and fired on them with a .22 automatic, squeezing out strings of twenty-five and fifty rounds from there and from a spot at the northwest corner of the YMCA building. When he blasted out a light near the Lyceum, the crowd cheered.

"We come to help kill the nigger," a pair of well-dressed men announced to a student. The men said they came from the nearby town of Batesville, and one had a light rifle shoved in his coat and a pint of booze in his pocket. He offered to share it with a rioter, asking, "Want a drink?"

One rioter clutching a shotgun climbed up a tree in front of the Lyceum and began firing at the marshals. A young man from southern Mississippi sprawled down flat on the grass fifty yards in front of the Lyceum, firing a squirrel gun. He paused to exclaim to a nearby acquaintance: "God damn, this is war!"

At 10:00 P.M., Ted Lucas Smith, a young local stringer for the *Mem-*

phis Commercial Appeal, noticed three acquaintances from his hometown of Oakland, Mississippi, strolling by him, each one toting a shotgun. They were about twenty-five years old, and not students. "They walked straight into the curtain of tear gas boiling around the front of the Lyceum," Smith recalled. "Their silhouettes raised the guns in unison and unloaded five rounds each into the tear gas. . . . Then they calmly turned and walked back past me, down the hill toward the football field, saying nothing."

On the other side of the firing range, anyone standing outside the Lyceum was a sitting duck, unable to see the snipers. Early in the riot, a forty-two-year-old staff reporter for the Associated Press named Bill Crider was wandering around in the foggy darkness "like a damn fool," he recalled, trying to figure out what to write about. He barely knew where to start. Crider was based at the AP Memphis office and usually covered Tennessee state politics, not the world's most dramatic beat. Tonight, Crider found himself in the epicenter of what felt to him like a revolution breaking out.

Out of nowhere, Crider remembered, it felt "like some giant hand reached down from the sky, clubbed me and laid me flat on my face." As he fell, he saw muzzle flashes from a shotgun. Two pellets of double-aught buckshot had pierced his back muscles, one on either side of the spine. An anonymous voice yelled, "Somebody's hit!" A team of marshals came over with their guns drawn, hoisted Crider by his arms and legs, and hustled him inside through the front door of the Lyceum. There he waited, hoping a doctor would show up as his wounds trickled blood.

Also in front of the Lyceum, a federal prison guard from Atlanta was holding a lit flashlight when a sniper zeroed in on him with a shotgun. He caught six pellets in the stomach and chest, and a seventh flew through his gas mask and punctured his forehead. He was patched up with the few first-aid supplies inside the Lyceum, and then he volunteered to go back outside on the firing line, where he stayed all night. Another Atlanta prison guard felt two blasts striking the right side of his head and chest. The eyepiece of his gas mask was cracked by a shotgun pellet, and another pellet pierced his chest. Yet another marshal was hit in the earlobe with double-aught buckshot, spun around like a top, and fell to the ground as pellets slammed into the wall behind him.

Border Patrolman Dan Pursglove was sprawled on the Lyceum

floor, bleeding from a shotgun pellet wound in his right thigh. "Damnit, Dan," he thought, "you've spent four years in the Marine Corps, a year in Korea, and ten years in the Border Patrol, now some fellow Americans are going to be your demise." As the night raged on, one thought increasingly dominated his thoughts: "I wonder if I'm going to see the light of day."

Deputy U.S. Marshal James K. Kemp was a thirty-six-year-old father of three from Nashville, Tennessee. "I was a gunners mate in the Navy," Kemp recalled soon after the riot, "and after my ship went down, I was in the Atlantic Ocean for about an hour." But the riot at Ole Miss, Kemp shuddered, "was the worst thing I've ever been in."

Nicholas Katzenbach grabbed the line to the White House, and finally pleaded for a military rescue.

"For God's sake," he said, "we need those troops!"

Inside the White House Cabinet Room, a stunned John Kennedy was listening to the bulletins of disaster being phoned in from the Lyceum at Oxford.

When his televised Oval Office speech to the nation ended, before 8:30 P.M. Oxford time (10:30 P.M. Washington, D.C., time), the president sat down at his place at the huge Cabinet Room table, reached underneath it, and flipped a hidden switch. This activated a double-deck Tandberg reel-to-reel recording machine that was hidden in a six-by-eight-foot locked storage room underneath the office of Mrs. Evelyn Lincoln, Kennedy's secretary.

Kennedy had ordered the Secret Service to install the secret room tape recording system during the previous month, about the same time he ordered his secretary to patch his Oval Office phone line into a Dictaphone recording system. Why Kennedy installed the recording systems is unknown, but Mrs. Lincoln speculated that he may have wanted to collect material for his memoirs, and also to create an exact historical record of conversations so that his own officials couldn't later distort them.

The Oxford emergency was the first crisis to be captured by Kennedy's new recording system. The president was flanked by his brother, the attorney general; his chief speechwriter and special counsel, Ted Sorensen; Justice Department civil rights chief Burke Marshall; and by two soldiers of the so-called Irish Mafia, congressional-affairs assistant Larry O'Brien and appointments secretary Kenny O'Donnell.

The attorney general aside, none of Kennedy's men knew he was taping them through tiny microphones hidden in the walls around them.

On the tapes, which would not be released for twenty years, the atmosphere veered between the usual wisecracking ebullience of the Kennedy team and the helpless realization that the White House had completely lost control of the crisis. The president, explained RFK in a 1964 oral history, "was torn between an Attorney General who had botched things up and the fact that the Attorney General was his brother." RFK called it "a terrible evening, because people were being shot."

Early in the evening, the attorney general was mumbling in a stream-of-consciousness fashion: "We have control over the air. If you have gas, you got a pretty good operation going. They got five hundred marshals. You see, they're sitting there, and they're throwing iron spikes, and they're throwing Coke bottles, and they're throwing rocks." An unidentified voice said, "This reminds me a little bit of the Bay of Pigs." RFK groaned, "Yech!" At this, another voice quipped, "Especially when Bobby said we'd provide air cover!"

Later, RFK asked on the open line to the pay phone in the Lyceum, "Is the gas coming in there?" The president muttered, "How do we get the gas in and out of there?"

JFK attempted a few feeble wisecracks. "We have riots like this at Harvard!" His aides chuckled. "Where is Nick [Katzenbach]?" the president asked. "Is he up in the attic?" More laughter. Later on, JFK quipped, "I haven't had such an interesting time since the Bay of Pigs."

"How's it going down there?" Robert Kennedy asked his beleaguered press aide Ed Guthman, who was trapped inside the building. "Pretty rough," Guthman replied, "it's getting like the Alamo." Then Kennedy cracked, "Well, you know what happened to those guys, don't you?" Guthman, who would later title his book about the Kennedy team, *We Band of Brothers,* knew that this mock-fatal teasing remark was RFK's way of empathizing with him and the other men the attorney general may have inadvertently sent to their doom tonight. It worked. Guthman cheered up.

When word was passed to Robert Kennedy that reporter Paul Guihard had been killed, the attorney general began worrying about the public relations impact. On the line with Guthman, RFK rambled, "They tell me the fellow from the London paper was killed. Well, they found him in back of some dormitories. . . . What are we going to say about all this, Ed? We're going to have a helluva problem about why we didn't handle the situation better."

RFK reported to the president, "General Walker's been out there, downtown, getting people stirred up." JFK mused aloud, "General Walker, imagine that son of a bitch having been commander of a division up until last year. And the Army promoting him."

As the riot intensified, the president and attorney general agonized over whether to authorize the marshals to return fire with their pistols to avoid being overrun, or to defend James Meredith. At Baxter Hall, a small team of marshals wearing battle helmets was standing outside James Meredith's room with their guns drawn.

When the riot began, it wasn't clear to James Meredith what was happening, so he scanned a newspaper and fell asleep around 10:00 P.M. The shouting and gunfire woke him up several times, but he felt unconcerned. "My job had been finished," he later explained. "My job was to get the federal force on my side." One thing was going right during this night of horrors: Very few rioters were attacking Baxter Hall. Deputy Attorney General Nicholas Katzenbach's impromptu diversion plan seemed to be working.

James Meredith and the forty marshals at Baxter Hall were hanging by the slenderest of threads—they were connected to the Lyceum only by a single car radio, had a limited gas supply, and one determined charge by the mob could easily overwhelm them. In fact, Meredith didn't know it, but things were so precarious now that the president was not ruling out the possibility of packing him into an escape helicopter and flying him out of Mississippi.

"I think they have to protect Meredith now," Robert Kennedy announced into the telephone, giving the marshals approval to fire pistols if Meredith's life was threatened. "They better fire, I suppose. They gotta protect Meredith. . . . Is Meredith all right? . . . I think they can fire to save him. Now, can you hold out for an hour there? Can you hold out if you have gas? Is there much firing? Is there any way you could figure a way to scare 'em off?"

Hearing this conversation, JFK confirmed to RFK that the marshals were not to fire back under any conditions except to save Meredith's life. The attorney general instructed an unidentified federal official at Oxford: "Get somebody that's up there that knows how important it is to keep Meredith alive . . . it should be somebody that you know. And stay right by Meredith and shoot anybody that puts a hand on him."

When a small team of rioters briefly attacked Baxter Hall with a barrage of bottles, the federal officials feared that an all-out assault on the dormitory was beginning. The attorney general announced to the men in the Cabinet Room: "They're storming where Meredith is." Now the president wavered helplessly between standing fast and trying to evacuate Meredith, thinking out loud: "Help necessary. You better try to stick and hold the line and then I suppose get him in the car and start to see if they can—may not be able to move him out, I suppose."

JFK aide Kenneth O'Donnell noted ominously, "You don't want to have a lynching." An unidentified voice reported, "The marshals are now going to start firing." But the attack on Baxter Hall vanished almost as soon as it started, and while the area around the dorm was relatively calm, war was still raging around the Lyceum.

The president had to find a way to take charge of the disaster, and fast. As the clock approached 10:00 P.M., Oxford time, JFK put a call through to Governor Barnett to beseech him to get the Highway Patrol back on the job.

At the Governor's Mansion in Jackson, an exhausted Ross Barnett was in a state approaching total shock. He never thought things would fall apart this horribly. Barnett's hands were shaking so violently that he couldn't pick up the phone.

Across town, the switchboard at Mississippi Highway Patrol headquarters was flooded the entire night with Americans who wanted to join in the insurrection. Colonel Birdsong's assistant Charles Marx stayed up the whole night answering the calls, telling people to stay home.

"People were calling in from across the nation wanting to volunteer their services," Marx recalled in a 2000 interview. "They asked where to report, where to bring their arsenals and weaponry to join the revolt. There were serious people who wanted to join the 'rise of the South.' There was a drunk from Louisiana who said he'd bring ten thousand people." The calls even came from the far western states of Wyoming, Montana, and Nevada. "Who do we report to?" asked one caller from California. "We have vehicles and munitions. We can furnish aircraft for air support. We're ready to go to war."

Ross Barnett was hunkered down in a small study in the mansion, a portrait of despair. Outside the study's door was a larger meeting room, which was filling up this night with a churning coterie of perpetually bickering advisers.

Citizens Council hard-liner Louis Hollis had interpreted Barnett's 7:30 speech as a capitulation and hurried across the street to confront the chief executive. "Governor, everybody thinks you've surrendered," a teary-eyed Hollis implored. "Everybody in the office is crying. You've got to tell them you haven't surrendered." The hard-liners argued if Barnett got on the air now to issue a final call to battle, enough reinforcements would arrive to force the marshals out. Tom Watkins and other moderate advisers fought back with all the arguments they could think of.

Charles Clark, a young Jackson attorney who was serving temporarily as special state assistant attorney general for the Meredith case, barged into Barnett's study. It seemed to Clark that Barnett might be on the verge of overruling the moderates and returning to the TV studio to issue a call to arms. Clark addressed the governor: "Do you know what's happening? People are being killed at Oxford! Governor, what I suggest you do is get on the radio right now and do anything you can to calm those crowds down and tell them to go home."

Barnett listened intently to Clark's impassioned plea. "Governor, you need to stop this. You ought to tell the people of Mississippi that the United States Army is capable of putting anybody into the university physically and that they should not resist. They should go home." Barnett graciously thanked Clark and soon returned to his study as his aides continued bickering. Clark left the room. He had done the best he could.

Incredibly, Ross Barnett had been able to shield the Citizens Council hard-liners from the fact that for the last fifteen days he had been consorting with the Kennedys over putting James Meredith into the university. Tonight, he was able to continue the deception by taking the incoming call from JFK away from the Citizens Council men in his interior study, accompanied only by his twenty-nine-year-old daughter Ouida Barnett Atkins.

When his daughter put the receiver into Barnett's trembling hand, the governor now saw a supremely audacious opportunity—with all hell breaking loose at Oxford, he might get JFK to issue an emergency order to pull Meredith out of the university. Barnett would announce the withdrawal himself. If he could pull this off, Barnett would be anointed by segregationist multitudes as virtually the Second Coming of Christ, as both peacemaker and conqueror.

John Kennedy, who was recording the call on his Dictaphone, didn't want to play along, but he couldn't dismiss the idea of evacuating Meredith entirely either, because for all he knew the mob might soon be close to killing Meredith. In fact, he had a rescue helicopter standing by to pluck Meredith and McShane out of Mississippi, but in this chaos such a rescue might not be feasible. They might not be able to find a safe place to land, and Meredith might be killed before he even could get to the chopper.

Kennedy told the governor, "We can't consider moving Meredith as long as the, you know, there's a riot outside, 'cause he wouldn't be safe." Barnett asked uncertainly, "Sir?"

"We couldn't consider moving Meredith if you, if we haven't been able to restore order outside," replied Kennedy. "That's the problem, Governor."

Barnett, seeing his main chance, tried to prepare his trap by proposing helpfully, "Well, I'll tell you what I'll do, Mr. President. I'll go up there myself."

The president asked, "Well, now, how long will it take you to get there?"

Barnett ignored the question and continued, "And I'll get a microphone and tell 'em that you have agreed for him to be removed."

JFK, instantly realizing where Barnett was going, cut him off firmly, snapping, "No, no, no—now, wait a minute. How long—wait a minute, Governor! Now, how long is it going to take you to get up there?"

Barnett drawled, " 'Bout an hour."

"Now, I'll tell you what," said Kennedy, floundering for an exit, "if you want to go up there and then you call me from up there. Then we'll decide what we're gonna do before you make any speeches about it."

"Well, all right," replied the governor with equal cluelessness. "I mean, whatever you, if you'd authorize—"

The president was tap-dancing in place, unsure of where to turn: "You see, we got an hour to go, and that's not, we may not have an hour. Won't it take you an hour to go up there?"

The two chief executives were playing chess with pieces of dynamite, not knowing which wrong move could set off a massacre, or in Barnett's case, his own political extinction.

Barnett abruptly mentioned the false news reports of Patrolman Welby Brunt's death, saying, "This man has just died."

Kennedy queried, "Did he die? Which one? State police?" Barnett declared solemnly, "A state policeman."

"Yeah, well you see," Kennedy rambled, "we gotta get order up there, and that's what we thought we were going to have."

Perhaps sensing Kennedy's despair, Barnett tried to jump in for the kill: "Mr. President, please. Can't you give an order up there to remove Meredith?"

At this, the president exploded, almost shouting, "How can I remove him, Governor, when there's a riot in the street, and he may step out of that building and something happen to him? I can't remove him under those conditions. Let's get order up there, then we can do something about Meredith."

Barnett offered obligingly, "We can surround it with plenty of officials."

JFK brought the call to a sudden end: "We've gotta get somebody up there now to get order, and stop the firing and the shooting. Then you and I will talk on the phone about Meredith."

Barnett signed off with an avuncular "All right."

When Barnett put the phone down it looked like he still had a chance of expelling Meredith from the campus.

The president stepped into the Cabinet Room and reported to his brother, "He wants us to move him. And I said, 'Well, we can't move him if the situation's like this.' And he says, 'Well, we'll take care of the situation if you move him.'"

"I can't get him out," his younger brother protested. "How am I gonna get him out?"

"That's what I said to him," said the president.

When the president and the governor came back on the line awhile later, the two were still cordially at cross purposes, trying to manage a conflagration they had lost control of hours before. Barnett assured President Kennedy that he could arrange the logistics of an evacuation: "What we were talking about, we wouldn't have any trouble. Do it tonight, you know."

JFK, still playing along, replied, "Yeah. Well our people say that it's still a very strange situation. They wouldn't feel that they could take a chance on taking him outside that building."

Kennedy pressured Barnett to get his police into action against the snipers. "I hear they got some high-powered rifles up there that have been shooting sporadically. Can we get that stopped? How many [Highway Patrol] people have you got there? We hear you only got fifty."

"Well, I have approximately 200 there now, Mr. President," Barnett said, although the patrolmen were still standing off campus, away from the battle. "I'm doing everything in the world I can."

"That's right," said Kennedy. "We've got to get this situation under control. That's much more important than anything else."

As Kennedy tried to stop the battle by remote control, Barnett wanted to share his feelings with the president: "Mr. President, people are wiring me and saying, 'Well, you've given up.' I had to say, 'No, I'm not giving up, not giving up any fight. I never give up. I have courage and faith, and we'll win this fight.' You understand. That's just to Mississippi people."

The infinitely patient young chief executive addressed Barnett like he was an eccentric elderly uncle: "I understand. But I don't think anybody, either in Mississippi or any place else, wants a lot of people killed."

"Oh, no, no," said the governor.

"And that's what, Governor, that's the most important thing," said Kennedy.

Barnett agreed, "I'll issue any statement, any time about peace and violence."

"Well, now here's what we could do," Kennedy proposed. "Let's get the maximum number of your state police to get to that situation so we don't have sporadic firing. I will then be in touch with my people and then you and I'll be talking again in a few minutes about, see what we got there then." They signed off.

For the president, there was only one option left, and it was the one he had to fear the most: federal combat troops. Nicholas Katzen-

"The south is armed for revolt," warned the Nobel Prize–winning writer and Oxford resident William Faulkner in 1956. "These white people will accept another civil war knowing they are going to lose." *(Carl Mydans/TimePix)*

The Oxford Court House, defended by the statue of a Confederate soldier. *(Corbis)*

U. S. Air Force veteran James Meredith launched a one-man revolt against white supremacy and triggered the greatest constitutional crisis since the Civil War. *(Corbis)*

Time called Governor Ross Barnett "as bitter a racist as inhabits the nation." On the eve of the final battle in Oxford, he absorbed the delirious rapture of a crowd of forty thousand white Mississippians in Jackson going berserk. *(Francis Miller, TimePix)*

William Simmons, chief of
the Citizens Council, an
all-powerful group of white
community leaders sworn
to uphold segregation.
(AP/Wide World Photos)

John F. Kennedy: One of the most popular presidents in history,
he presided over America's final summer of postwar innocence.
(Corbis)

The president wanted "this God-damned civil rights mess" kept off his desk, but he and his brother Attorney General Robert F. Kennedy blundered toward disaster at Oxford. *(Corbis)*

Lieutenant Governor Paul B. Johnson and Governor Barnett stride to a showdown with the federals on September 20, 1962, in Oxford. *(AP/Wide World Photos)*

Imperial Wizard Robert Shelton, the most powerful Ku Klux Klan leader of the late twentieth century, commander of the United Klans of America. *(Corbis)*

The Lyceum, symbolic heart of the University of Mississippi and epicenter of the insurrection. *(U.S. Army)*

Nicholas Katzenbach, number-two man at the Justice Department, was sent to take charge of federal forces at Oxford with no tactical plan, no field intelligence, and no time. *(AP/Wide World Photos)*

U.S. Marshals land at Oxford on the afternoon of September 30. They had been told their mission only in midflight, and they were mobilized so abruptly that much of their equipment was lost. *(AP/Wide World Photos)*

Marshals seize the Lyceum after 4:00 P.M., Sunday afternoon. Some three hundred marshals soon faced a mob of more than two thousand white civilians. *(Flip Schulke, Corbis)*

The crowd swells as dusk approaches and a chain reaction of errors combines to unleash a riot. *(Corbis)*

Combat explodes: As tear gas is fired at 8:00 P.M., marshals try to push the mob back. Soon they are fighting for their lives in hand-to-hand combat. *(Lynn Pelham/TimePix)*

Paul Guihard: one of three hundred reporters who flocked to Oxford from around the world. His murder would forever remain a mystery. *(Agence France-Presse)*

Duncan M. Gray, Jr., rector of Oxford's St. Peter's Episcopal Church, presiding at William Faulkner's burial, July 1962. Gray tried to stop the Battle of Oxford with his bare hands, armed only with his clerical collar. *(AP/Wide World Photos)*

Mississippi Highway Patrolman Welby Brunt being evacuated after sustaining injuries in the federal tear-gas barrage. Mistaken reports of his death triggered the start of an armed revolt by the Mississippi Highway Patrol. *(AP/Wide World Photos)*

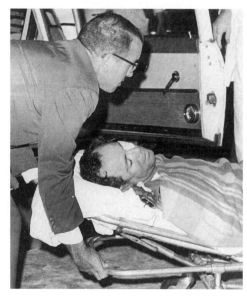

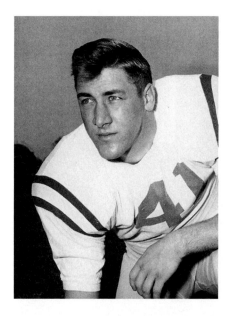

George "Buck" Randall, star full-back for the Ole Miss Rebels: He tried to stop the riot as bullets flew over his head. *(Courtesy University of Mississippi)*

U.S. Marshals and GIs with a suspected rioter near the front door of the Lyceum. *(AP/Wide World Photos)*

As the crisis flew out of control, JFK ordered an enormous invasion force of more than thirty-one thousand combat troops to crush the rebellion and recapture the state of Mississippi. *(John F. Kennedy Library)*

The Mississippi National Guard were among America's most forgotten and gallant heroes. The fate of hundreds of civilians rode on their shoulders as they attempted an impossible rescue. *(AP/Wide World Photos)*

Troops of the 503d Military Police Battalion, the army's riot-fighting SWAT team, conducted a helicopter assault on an Oxford that had collapsed into anarchy. They were a fully integrated force, with white Southern boys serving under black sergeants. *(Courtesy Michael G. Hardy)*

Major Raymond Le Van, 503d Military Police Battalion: A combat-tough World War II veteran, he led the first rescue convoy into Mississippi at the trigger of a .50 caliber machine gun. *(Courtesy Mrs. Raymond Le Van)*

U.S. Army Military Policemen storm into Oxford at first light, Monday morning, October 1, their M-1 rifles loaded and locked. *(Donald Urbrock/TimePix)*

Military police charge into Oxford: The blurred figures at upper right are state highway patrolmen who have been forced aside by federal troops at bayonet point. *(AP/Wide World Photos)*

Troops of the Second Infantry "Indianhead" Division enter the town square of Oxford as the riot moves from campus to downtown, 8:00 A.M., October 1, 1962. (*AP/Wide World Photos*)

Lieutenant Charles Shockley, a young black Second Infantry officer, led his rifle platoon onto the Oxford Town Square and straight into the riot. (*Courtesy Charles Shockley*)

Wearing steel flak jackets, the infantrymen absorbed showers of missiles thrown by their fellow Americans. "The dignity of the Negro soldiers has been little short of inspiring," marveled one witness. *(Robert W. Kelley/TimePix)*

Riot leader Edwin Walker, former army general and now right-wing fanatic, is surrounded by Second Infantry troops on the town square. *(Corbis)*

As thousands of army troops dropped into the little city of Oxford, James Meredith coolly filled out his registration forms. A stunned Registrar Robert B. Ellis stands at attention. *(Corbis)*

Meredith triumphant: The young strategist delivered a death blow to "massive resistance" and engineered a turning point in American history. *(Francis Miller, TimePix)*

bach was on the phone pleading for them; the federal marshals in Oxford were being shot down like rabbits, and it appeared that the state of Mississippi might be sliding toward some form of civil war.

No American president had faced a domestic military crisis of this magnitude in almost a century. The previous week, *Time* magazine had called the Meredith case the "gravest conflict between federal and state authority since the Civil War." Now it had become potentially the most dangerous.

For President Kennedy, the hazards were enormous. Soldiers could accidentally kill or be killed by their fellow American citizens, and a chain reaction of bloodletting could ensue. A powerful white backlash could be triggered, one that could paralyze progress on civil rights. The country could be disgraced in the court of world opinion. The white South could crack off of the Democratic Party and give the Republicans a dominant share of power in future elections. White "massive resistance" to integration could be reborn.

Still, Kennedy had no other choice now. U.S. combat troops had to rescue the federal marshals and James Meredith, recapture and reestablish federal sovereignty on Mississippi soil, crush the insurrection, enforce the federal court orders, and force James Meredith into classes at the University of Mississippi at gunpoint.

Just before 10:00 P.M., the president issued the order for the U.S. Army to launch a military invasion of northern Mississippi to restore law and order, starting with the riot fighters of the 503d Military Police Battalion.

He ordered a message flashed to the commander of the troops in Memphis: "This is a direct order from the President of the United States to General Abrams: I want him to move out now, ready or not."

But the president had waited too long. Things had already fallen apart in Oxford, blood was flowing on the streets, and the regular army was ninety miles away.

Somewhere, somehow, a miracle had to happen. And it had to happen in the next few minutes.

CHAPTER TWELVE

History Will Not Forget You

■ ■ ■ ■

Stand fast, Mississippi!

—Colonel Jefferson Davis
at the Battle of Buena Vista

CAPTAIN MURRY C. FALKNER answered his phone at the Oxford National Guard Armory, a mile east of the university. It was 9:50 P.M.

On the line was Deputy Attorney General Nicholas Katzenbach, telling him that on behalf of the president of the United States he was ordering Falkner to convoy his men to the university and surround the Lyceum.

Katzenbach didn't have time to wait for the regular army MPs, who were still at Memphis. The Lyceum was about to be overrun, and the marshals were on the verge of opening fire on the mob with live ammo. He had to take the chance that local Mississippi men, National Guardsmen, would risk their lives to save the federal officers and restore order to the campus.

"Chooky" Falkner was the exuberant, charismatic thirty-three-year-old Oxford agent for the Lamar Life Insurance Company. As the nephew of Nobel Laureate William Faulkner and the son of John Faulkner, also a noted author, Chooky Falkner was a scion of Oxford's royal family (he used the original spelling of the family name). He was also the commanding officer of the Oxford-based Troop E, Second Squadron, 108th Armored Cavalry Regiment of the Mississippi National Guard. When the riot started, Falkner's two officers and seventy-one enlisted men were the only federal military presence already inside Oxford, besides the small contingent of regular army engineers and drivers.

Falkner's Troop E was a group of part-time soldiers, local boys and men who trained twice a month and several weeks in the summer. The average private made less than a hundred dollars a month. In normal times, Troop E and the eleven thousand men of the Mississippi National Guard were a state militia under the command of the governor. Their motto was "Stand Fast, Mississippi!", the phrase uttered by Colonel Jefferson Davis to his Mississippi troops at the Battle of Buena Vista during the Mexican War.

Sometimes people joked that the Guardsmen were "summertime soldiers," but in wartime, or if federalized by the president, as John Kennedy had done at midnight this morning, they became part of the regular U.S. Army, subject to the same hazards and responsibilities.

Chooky Falkner assumed that JFK had federalized the all-white National Guard to neutralize eleven thousand armed Mississippians and remove them from Barnett's command. Earlier that Sunday, Falkner had gathered his men at the Armory, loaded their vehicles, raised the American and Mississippi flags, and posted a sentry at the door to chase reporters away. By early Sunday evening, almost all of Falkner's men were accounted for, and morale was high. They thought they had it made—they had cots, blankets, mattresses, a radio, and television, "the works."

Given the level of extreme hostility between the state and federal governments, Falkner guessed that his outfit might be ordered away from Oxford to remove them from any federal efforts to force James Meredith into the university, and to prevent any unauthorized attempts by state officials to mobilize the Guard to support Barnett instead.

Although he had voted against Barnett, Chooky Falkner was politically conservative and like many of his men and many white Mississippians, he strongly opposed the way the federal government was handling the Meredith case. At their evening meal, Falkner and his troops laughed in disbelief when they heard a report that a large contingent of U.S. Marshals was arriving at the Oxford airport. "Surely the

Federal Government would not take this means to cram the issue down our throats," Falkner thought.

By 9:00 P.M., Falkner reported, "I had a troop on my hands eager to join forces to preserve segregation and States' Rights." The Guardsmen were getting their cots ready for a good night's sleep when rumors of a riot on campus began reaching the Armory, along with false reports of up to six dead students. An Ole Miss coed called in asking for information on how to counteract the effects of tear gas, which was flowing into her sorority. Falkner flipped through his army manuals but couldn't find anything to help her.

A car screeched into the Armory parking lot, and a federal marshal raced inside to ask Falkner for as many gas masks as he could spare. Falkner ordered one of his men to fill up a duffel bag with masks for the marshal, but, perhaps thinking of the Mississippi students supposedly murdered by the marshals, the soldier refused. Falkner issued the same order to another Guardsman, but he refused as well, so Falkner had to do it himself. After the marshal left with the masks, Falkner called all his men into formation.

One of the men, Harold "Happy" Antwine, was an Ole Miss student who lived with his wife in the married students' housing on campus. On the night of September 30, he was in his National Guard uniform standing at Captain Chooky Falkner's side. Antwine remembered the mood among Troop E's men in a 2000 interview: "We were on the side of the students in the university. We thought we were being invaded. It was hard for us to realize that we were part of the invasion."

Corporal Antwine described what happened next. "This is a court-martial offense," Falkner told the two soldiers. "You disobeyed a direct order." Addressing the whole formation, Falkner declared, "We're now federal troops. You're federalized. It had better not happen again." If it did, Falkner promised, he'd launch a court-martial.

When Katzenbach had called in with the order, Falkner replied that his men had only a few hours of riot-control training, but they'd assist as best they could. Katzenbach asked how fast they could get to the Lyceum. Falkner told him they could pull out in ten minutes and get to the campus in fifteen. As the Guardsmen fell into formation, Falkner called his immediate superior, Lieutenant Colonel J. P. Williams, at squadron headquarters in Ripley to confirm the unusual order. "I just got the craziest chain of command," Falkner said, explaining the presidential command that had just managed to bypass the entire U.S. military command structure. "Better do it," Williams noted, "JFK is the commander in chief." Williams then ordered Falkner to leave his ammunition at the Armory, presumably to reduce the risk of civilian blood being spilled.

The Guardsmen didn't realize it yet, but they were being sent into combat with unloaded weapons. The seven-vehicle convoy lined up in administrative march formation: Falkner's command Jeep, two more Jeeps, a pair of two-and-a-half-ton trucks, a three-quarter-ton truck stuffed with troops, and a trail Jeep carrying his executive officer.

Katzenbach called again at 10:00 P.M. to confirm that the men were ready to mobilize. He wasn't sure they would obey. Falkner replied, "Yes sir, all men are loaded on the vehicles," except the five-man cook detail, which Falkner ordered to stay behind to guard the Armory, the ammo, and his two Walker Bulldog M-41 training tanks. "Are you positive?" the deputy attorney general asked. "Yes, sir," said Falkner. Katzenbach ordered Falkner outside to check that his enlisted men were loaded and would obey the order to come to the Lyceum. Falkner did this, ran back, and reported in the affirmative.

Normally, Falkner would have rolled the truck tarps down, but there wasn't time. So Captain Chooky Falkner and his little all-white band of part-time Mississippi "summertime soldiers," now regular troops of the U.S. Army, loaded out of the Armory and began the journey to campus to prevent a massacre.

Inside one of the trucks was twenty-seven-year-old Loyd Gunter, whose regular job was on the checkout line at the Kroger supermarket in Oxford. Tonight he was a specialist fourth class, in the U.S. Army. "I'll tell you the truth," Gunter recalled in an interview almost forty years later, "there were some mixed feelings in the bunch about going out there. We had one loudmouth in the truck who said, 'I'll tell you one damn thing, when we get out there, I'll get out there and help them sombitches throw bricks!' " He hastened to add, "It wasn't everybody who felt that way."

Falkner had no intelligence on the riot from Katzenbach or anyone else, just fragmentary news reports. As the convoy pulled onto University Avenue, without really knowing why, Falkner abruptly stopped the procession and ordered all his men to don their gas masks, just in case. As soon as they got under way again, civilian vehicles raced past the convoy, cursing, screaming, and honking their horns.

As they barreled west, Falkner reflected on Katzenbach's questioning of his men's loyalty. He mused, "This was a great National Guard unit and the thought never occurred to me that they wouldn't follow." Falkner's parents lived in a house near the campus by the University High School, and as they approached, Falkner recalled, "I caught a glimpse of my daddy standing out in front of the house. I reached over, gave the horn a honk, and passed on by."

On July 21, 1861, Chooky Falkner's great-great-grandfather Colonel William C. Falkner, commanding the Second Mississippi Infantry Regiment at Manassas, led a charge toward the Union lines with a stylish feather jammed in his hat. A Confederate general saw him and called out to his troops, "Men, follow yonder knight of the black plume and history will not forget you!"

Tonight, as the National Guard convoy entered the campus of the University of Mississippi, Falkner realized he, too, was about to crash into a wave of full-scale combat. Throngs of people lining the streets began yelling curses and throwing rocks at the Guardsmen.

Corporal Antwine was driving the lead command Jeep into the campus with Captain Falkner in the passenger seat. Ted Lucas Smith, correspondent for the *Memphis Commercial-Appeal,* saw them enter campus: "I clearly remember seeing one boy standing on the opposite curb with a huge piece of concrete raised over his head, ready to throw. The convoy was easing along. It seemed they didn't expect what they suddenly got. The boy with the concrete slab waited until the jeep pulled even with him and he threw with all his might. The concrete smashed into the officer and literally knocked him almost out of the jeep on the driver's side. He saved himself with his uninjured left hand, pulling himself back into the jeep.

"Most of the bricks and concrete were missing their mark and crashing into the group on the opposite side of the road," Smith reported. "I saw one boy take a brickbat right in the face and he went down hard, blood splattering high in the air."

Corporal Harold Antwine recalled, "They knocked both windshields out of the Jeep. They bent my steering column with a brick. They were brick impacts from people standing twelve feet away and throwing as hard as they can. They riddled the canvas all to pieces until there wasn't any canvas left."

"I could see the mob in the Circle and the Lyceum Building," Falkner reported in his after-action report of the incident, which he wrote in May 1963. "It appeared the Circle was full of people and the street on which we were to drive was a sea of people. The only lights were from the Lyceum and the glow from a burning automobile. As we passed the Geology building and the Confederate Statue, a two-by-six piece of lumber was thrown at my jeep. Fortunately it missed its target! From here to the Lyceum building was absolute Hell! People would not move out of the street. They threw bricks, concrete, everything and anything they could find—including words.

"If there had been any doubt as to whether the men would follow me," recalled Falkner, "there was none now. I was indubitably sure I had their support. A person loose in that mob, wearing a uniform, would have been dead. Now we were all concerned with a matter of self-preservation." Falkner later quipped, "It's hard to feel brotherly love toward someone who is trying to kill you."

"Don't stop for anything!" screamed Captain Falkner to Antwine. "Put that thing in second gear and don't slow down!" After their Jeep dodged around a rioters' barricade of concrete benches, Falkner recalled, "I noticed something white coming toward my face from the right of my jeep. Reflex action, I threw up my left arm to shield my face. This missile broke three bones and cut my wrist." From somewhere, a sniper fired a bullet into the radiator of Falkner's Jeep.

Guardsman Loyd Gunter suddenly realized they were trapped in a sea of fellow Southerners who were trying to kill them. "When we crossed that bridge," Gunter remembered, "man, there was just people everywhere. That grove was full of people hollering and cussing—I never heard such language in my life. They were throwing bricks, chains, bottles, everything they could get their hands on. When we ran that blockade, we wound up getting 28 men injured going in. Any of us who didn't know which side they was on, that made up their damn mind right then."

Word rippled through some people in the mob that the incoming troops were Mississippi Guardsmen, but this did nothing to dent the crowd's fury. Voices called out, "Leave it to the marshals, Mississippi boys!" and, "Go back to the Armory!" As rocks and bricks showered the convoy, a gas-masked Guardsman popped his head out of a truck and called out desperately, "Hey, we're Mississippi National Guard!" Among the replies from the crowd were "Fuck the Guard!" and "Nigger-lovin' son of a bitches!"

The Guardsmen had no tear gas and no ammunition and were

traveling through a crowd that outnumbered them by at least ten to one. The mob formed a solid wall, slowed the convoy down, and brought it to nearly a dead stop. The Guardsmen were being swallowed up by a human ocean.

Inside one of the two-and-a-half-ton trucks was twenty-one-year-old sergeant and squad leader Lannon Franklin, who was the state representative for Lafayette County in the Mississippi legislature, as well as a sophomore at Ole Miss. He was terrified as he felt bricks raining against the tarpaulin sides of the truck from all directions, and he thought for sure every man in that convoy was terrified, too.

Like Sergeant Franklin, many of the Guardsmen were Ole Miss students or Ole Miss alumni. Captain Falkner himself had attended the university. "Don't throw it at us," one Guardsman called out, "we don't want to be here either!"

The little caravan plowed through a gauntlet of concrete benches, bottles, and Molotov cocktails toward the Lyceum. "The number three jeep in line hit one of the benches," remembered Captain Falkner, "a two-and-one-half-ton truck got another, and the trail jeep got the third one. This only provided more ammo for the mob. All vehicles took a terrific beating from the debris that was thrown. My driver and several other men were hit as we drove on toward the Lyceum."

As they approached the Lyceum, one of Falkner's men popped his head out of the truck, and, in a frantic attempt to identify themselves, called out the locally famous Ole Miss "Hotty Toddy" football cheer. Before he could finish the cheer, bricks rained into the sides and back flaps of the truck. When Lieutenant "Bo" Metts stepped out of his Jeep, a sniper blasted three rounds through the windshield into the seat where he had just been sitting.

When he first saw Falkner and his men coming to the rescue, Deputy Marshal Al Butler felt it was like the Fourth of July. It made him want to stand up and wave the flag and sing. The marshals let out a great cheer and charged forward to cover the Guardsmen's arrival with a tear-gas salvo. It was 10:10 P.M.

By the time they reached the Lyceum, seven of the Oxford Guardsmen had to be carried into the building. The supply sergeant was hit by gunfire, and an enlisted man had glass fragments in his eye from a shattered gas-mask eyepiece.

When he jumped out of his truck, Guardsman Loyd Gunter was

greeted by a federal marshal who said, "I never thought I'd be glad to see the goddamn Mississippi National Guard, but you're some good-looking sons of bitches." The marshals had only a few minutes of tear gas left.

But the federal officers soon realized an awful truth: While the arrival of the Oxford National Guard might save the building from being overrun and the civilians and marshals inside from being slaughtered, the combined strength of the federal forces was still too small to take the offensive.

Falkner reminded Katzenbach that his men had only a few hours of riot training; he also told him they had fifteen bayonets and no ammunition, not even enough numerical strength to fully surround the Lyceum. So the Mississippi Guardsmen started lining up around the Lyceum, filling in gaps in the marshals' lines.

Katzenbach handed Captain Falkner a bullhorn and asked if he would try to reason with the mob. Nursing his shattered arm, Falkner stepped out of the front door of the Lyceum with the battery-powered bullhorn and six volunteers and walked across the street into the Circle, shouting that they were Mississippi National Guardsmen. Abruptly, the bullhorn cut out and died, and the crowd rushed them, cursing and throwing rocks and bricks. The marshals blasted a volley of tear gas, enabling Falkner and his men to move back to the Lyceum perimeter.

Falkner got a new bullhorn, a new group of volunteers, and went out to face the crowd again.

"We're from Mississippi," Falkner announced. "We live here. Now y'all get out of here!" But this just made the mob madder. Again they were cursed and stoned by the mob, and the Guardsmen had to return to their lines under cover of tear gas.

One rioter appeared with a big drum of gasoline and yelled, "Get your gas here, boys!" Teams of rioters lined up to fill their Molotov cocktails, and as they hurled the bombs toward the Lyceum, several of the rioters thought proudly of the newsreel footage of Hungarian students fighting Soviet tanks in 1956.

In front of the Lyceum at 10:53, Deputy Marshal Al Butler heard a motor crank up somewhere down at the far end of the field. He heard a metallic clang and the clanking of treads. Captain Falkner studied the haze with a sudden terror—the rioters must have broken into the

Armory, overwhelmed the five cooks he left on guard, and hijacked his two training tanks.

"They're bringing up tanks!" a voice called out. Instead, out of the gas clouds came a bulldozer headed straight toward the Lyceum, followed by a sizable portion of the mob, giving out rebel yells. The bulldozer charged forward, its blade pointed up as a shield against flying tear-gas canisters. The crowd was wailing an inhuman cry, sounding like a pack of hunting dogs yelling after a raccoon.

Butler waved the signal to charge, and the marshals galloped toward the crowd, firing a ragged barrage of tear gas. The rioters fell back, choking and vomiting; the driver of the dozer jumped off, and it ran into a tree. Deputy Marshal Carl Ryan of Indianapolis jumped on the dozer to get at the controls, dropped the blade, moved the machine close to the federal line, and swung it around to face the rioters with its lights on.

The U.S. Marshals at the Lyceum were trapped in a nightmare, as were the arriving National Guardsmen.

"We were getting our asses shot off," noted Justice Department official Ed Guthman. "Every time the front door opened," recalled Border Patrol inspector Richard Dick, "shots were fired toward the door. We'd have to crawl on our bellies in and out of the door." Prisoners were being hustled through the door and propelled past gauntlets of billy clubs down to a makeshift holding cell in the basement.

The federals were surrounded and vastly outnumbered by the rioters, so they had no chance of taking the offensive. They couldn't all retreat inside the Lyceum for fear of being overrun and possibly burned alive. The team of marshals guarding Meredith at Baxter Hall was dangerously small. The federals couldn't withdraw Meredith—not only would it hand Barnett a triumphant victory, but there was no way to get him out safely as long as the riot raged. All they could do was hang on for dear life and pray that more army troops would rescue them in time.

The scene inside the Lyceum did indeed resemble the Alamo. Under a sign that said "Welcome to Ole Miss," wounded and choking marshals were scattered through the bloodied hallways. Marshals choked down coffee, cigarettes, hot dogs, and sauerkraut, the only battle rations available. Wounded Associated Press reporter Bill Crider wandered around taking notes as blood trickled down his back. Three full hours into the battle, there still wasn't a doctor on the scene.

A few blocks away, a thirty-two-year-old general practitioner was at his home on South Lamar Street, eating dinner with his wife. He had just delivered a baby at the Oxford hospital, and he was still in his scrubs.

Dr. Lloyd Gerald ("Gerre") Hopkins was a country doctor who handled everything from runny noses and broken bones to major surgery. He grew up in a town called Walnut in Tippa County. His mother died when he was five, and he was raised by a black woman his father hired to run the house. In his work, Hopkins saw up close the ties of blood fellowship that bound blacks and whites together despite the iron grip of state apartheid. Hopkins was not a political activist, but he was probably typical of many educated white people in Mississippi who thought, as Hopkins did, that separation of the races was "absolutely ridiculous" because blacks were connected to whites in the most intimate ways of daily life.

In the middle of his dinner, Dr. Hopkins heard a knock at the door. Standing on his front porch was Colonel T. B. Birdsong, head of the Mississippi Highway Patrol, asking him if he would come to the Lyceum and help take care of the wounded marshals and civilians piling up in the building. Colonel Birdsong had been dashing in and out of the back entrance of the Lyceum, and seeing the bloody mess inside, he decided he personally had to somehow get a doctor in there. "We need to get you out there," Birdsong explained simply.

Dr. Hopkins pointed out that he'd just delivered a baby and had to check on the mother. "Can't the doctor at the school infirmary handle it?" he asked. No, Birdsong replied, there were too many wounded and they couldn't get them out of the building. On the way out to campus, Birdsong offered, he could drop Hopkins in to the hospital for a quick check on the new mother. Sensing Hopkins's disbelief at the situation, Colonel Birdsong put the squeeze on the young doctor. He knew Hopkins's father, Lloyd, and invoked his personal friendship with him: "Lloyd would be very much in favor of you responding to this. He would do this kind of favor also because he's that kind of fella.

"We've really got to have you," the old crime fighter implored on the doorstep, "because we just don't have anybody else to go. We've got to have you go." Hopkins gave his wife a hurried farewell and took off in the backseat of Birdsong's sedan, a state trooper on either side of him.

Dr. Hopkins quickly realized that he had no medical supplies.

"Everything's at the hospital," he told Birdsong, "I've got to go get some supplies." The squad car drove to Court House Square, veered east on Van Buren Avenue and pulled up to the Oxford hospital.

As he burst through the front door, Dr. Hopkins was already running through a mental checklist of the supplies he needed to improvise a combat field hospital with no surgical equipment, no operating room, and no nurses. He peeked in on his patient holding her newborn baby. "I'm OK," she declared. "Are you sure you're all right?" Hopkins asked. "Oh, I'm just fine," she said sweetly.

Dr. Hopkins alerted a team of nurses to start filling up a giant three-by-three-by-three-foot Kotex box with all the supplies they could grab. Since Kotex sanitary pads were sterile and highly absorbent, Hopkins figured they'd make good pressure dressings for wounds, so in they went. Then he gathered up all the emergency wound packs he could find, along with plaster-of-Paris material for making splints, emergency surgery kits for small wounds and lacerations, an abdominal-surgery kit, six vials of tetanus toxoid as a booster for macerating puncture wounds. It all went into the box, which was now overflowing.

Hopkins trotted out to the squad car, jammed the box in the backseat, and the sedan blasted off toward University Avenue and the campus. Hopkins carried the box on his lap—it was so big he couldn't see over it, so he peeked around it. After they crossed the bridge onto campus, Birdsong saw upside-down burning cars blocking the road. "Take a right," he ordered. They sped helter-skelter over grass and sidewalks.

Near the girls' dormitory Ricks Hall, they drove straight into a row of concrete posts holding up a security chain, busting the car's radiator. Birdsong barked, "Cut right in front of that building and GUN IT!" As they cut across the front of Ricks Hall and passed the Fulton Chapel, steam was blowing up from the smashed radiator, so the driver had to stick his head out the window to see where he was going.

"Gun it!" Birdsong again ordered, and they hit another series of concrete posts by Peabody Hall, severed the security chain, bounced over a culvert, crossed the street, and screeched to a halt in the back of the Lyceum building.

The two Highway Patrolmen squeezed Dr. Hopkins out of the car by his armpits, picked him up off the ground, Kotex box and all, and hustled him into the rear entrance of the Lyceum, his feet never touching the ground. It was the same door Gene Same had been evacuated through just minutes earlier. The policemen ran back to their car and fled, fearing that they'd be fired on by the U.S. Marshals.

Hopkins surveyed the human wreckage choking the Lyceum hall-ways, put his box down and walked down the hall, trying to jam open office doors so that he could set up an emergency-aid station. All the doors were locked shut. "I've got to have somewhere to set up a hospi-tal station and I've got to have running water," he thought. But where?

Stepping over the blood and the wounded, he turned the corner and there it was. The ladies' room. There were few if any ladies in the building tonight, and here was running water. The only trouble was, a sniper who seemed to be shooting from the top of Peabody Hall was methodically blasting away at the windows and stairway right next to the room. Still, it would have to do.

Dr. Hopkins dragged in the Kotex box, set up his one-man surgery station in the rest room, and went to work. He went out and con-ducted a quick walk-down of the hall, picking out the people he thought had the most life-threatening injuries.

"Who is bleeding?" he asked the wounded men. "Who has a gun-shot wound? Who has a stab wound? Do not all talk at once." To the less severely wounded, he said, "I'll get you next. Do not come down and stand in the hallway because somebody is shooting through the window and it's going right above where I'm working. So just stay in the hallway where you are; it's the safest place in the house."

"I've been shot," said one of Hopkins's first patients, Associated Press reporter Bill Crider. "Am I dying?" He was still bleeding from the buckshot wounds in his back. "Well, no," Hopkins reported as he dug one of the pellets out. He couldn't figure out where the other pellet had wound up. It was buried too deep, so he left it in and patched Crider up by wrapping long bandages clear around him. Crider went out to patrol the halls and continue taking notes for his story, shirt off, a giant bandage wrapped around his torso.

Dr. Hopkins worked alone through the night, treating gunshot wounds, brick injuries, scratches, and broken limbs. He may have treated as many as a hundred patients: marshals, National Guardsmen, injured civilians, and rioters. He was too busy to keep a log. At one point, when Hopkins was running low on supplies, a university offi-cial named George Street appeared. He had heard of the wounded people trapped in the Lyceum and volunteered to help.

As the University of Mississippi's director of development, George

Street had been following the school's anti-Meredith line, but tonight he became a quiet, unsung battlefield hero. Dr. Hopkins enlisted him as a medical quartermaster, running supplies down from the campus infirmary. Over and over, George Street slipped out the back door, dashed through the hedges and up Magnolia Drive, dodging the rioters as he hustled medical supplies back to the Lyceum.

At one point, the pay phone just outside the ladies' room was ringing off the hook, and Dr. Hopkins angrily grabbed it, declaring, "Look, damnit, we're having a riot. Get off the damn telephone, you're bugging me!" A voice said "Just a second, the attorney general would like to talk to you." Hopkins said, "OK."

Robert Kennedy came on the line, extremely apologetic for interrupting Hopkins's work, looking for anyone who could tell him what was going on. The attorney general asked, "Is there anyone else I can talk to so you can go back to your work?" Answered Hopkins, "No, not a damn soul but a bunch of people who are all beat up."

Kennedy asked Hopkins to just take a second and tell him what was going on, so the doctor gave him a quick report, then got back to treating the wounded.

CHAPTER THIRTEEN

A New Civil War Has Begun

■ ■ ■ ■

What is taking place here at the University is completely unbelievable. This is 1962, and because one Negro has been admitted—or is about to be admitted, it seems—to Ole Miss, a new Civil War has begun, exactly one hundred years after the big one.

—University of Mississippi English professor Gerald Walton, diary entry, October 1, 1962, 1:30 A.M.

A T THE EASTERN EDGE of the Circle, two best friends were watching the riot in total amazement.

The summer of 1962 had been a beautiful time for Ray Gunter and Charlie Berryhill, who had grown up together in and around Oxford and were best friends since grade school. Ray had matured into a soft-spoken, friendly twenty-three-year-old man who his friends said was full of curiosity and liked excitement. He was a slender, quiet young man with brown hair, brown eyes, and a shy smile that made people feel warm when they saw it. His new job as a jukebox repairman earned him fifty dollars a week and enabled him to drive a new pickup truck.

Ray and his young wife, Virginia, were settling in to a new four-room house and expecting their first baby any day now. Ray was great friends with Virginia's father, who at first resisted the idea of his daughter quitting high school to marry Ray at sixteen, but developed a strong affection for him.

Ray Gunter's passion was drag racing. That summer, Ray and Charlie and their wives launched the new Como Drag Strip in Como,

Mississippi, running drag races on Sunday nights. Ray and Charlie organized the drag strip, and Virginia and Peggy ran the concession stand, which yielded a tidy profit from folks who came from clear across northern Mississippi to see the races, as many as four hundred to five hundred at a time. The Gunters and Berryhills felt like they had a really good thing going.

At noon on this day, Ray and Charlie had gone dove hunting in a cornfield south of town, then returned around 5:00 P.M. to join Virginia and Peggy for a backyard barbecue. The news broadcasts were reporting excitement on the Ole Miss campus, so Charlie asked his buddy, "Ray, you want to ride out there and see what's going on?" Ray replied, "Yeah, might as well, but we can't get on the campus." Charlie said, "Oh yeah, I can." He was referring to the pass he had as a workman employed by the University of Mississippi.

Earlier that day, Virginia Gunter had seen scores of cars flocking around the university, none of them from Mississippi, some from as far away as California. She wasn't closely following the political crisis, but she had an uneasy feeling about it, almost a premonition of something bad happening. She pleaded with Ray not to go. But Ray thought it would be OK, and he wanted to pick up some parts for his truck at the gas station, which was on the way. At 6:30 P.M. the two young men parked on campus and walked toward the edge of the Circle.

For the next four and a half hours Ray Gunter and Charlie Berryhill stood transfixed by the spectacle raging before their eyes. Like many spectators, they never lifted a finger to join in the protests or the riot. They hadn't the remotest idea that something like this would happen. They had gone there strictly out of curiosity to see what they could see, and now history was out of control before their eyes.

Just before 11:00 P.M., Ray and Charlie were still on the eastern side of the Circle, about 220 yards southeast of the Lyceum, near the southwest corner of the construction site of the new Science Building, riveted by the drama raging in the distance. They had a good view, as they were standing on top of some twenty-inch-high drainage tile that let them see over the crowd's heads.

Charlie Berryhill was thinking he'd never seen anything like this, even in the movies. It was unreal, like being inside a World War II movie with John Wayne, or a cowboys-and-Indians epic. When the National Guard convoy was attacked as it entered the campus, Ray and Charlie's jaws dropped in astonishment. "Oh, God, we got trouble here," said Charlie. "They're throwing it at our own guys. I can't believe this; they're fighting our own brothers!" Ray agreed, saying simply, "My God."

Whenever the marshals advanced east in the Circle, Ray and Charlie moved back to a safe distance behind a building. Now it was late, and they were getting ready to leave. They would have quite a tale to tell their children and grandchildren, of a night when history was made before their eyes.

This was a night when time itself seemed to warp and collapse upon itself in the darkness and smoke, playing tricks with fact and memory. Civil War historian Carol Reardon warned that "the student of history must be wary of memory's introduction of the fog of war. Myth and history intertwine freely on these fields, and some of their tendrils always will defy untangling."

What happened next remains a complete mystery to this day, and fragmentary glimpses of what may have happened were sometimes remembered differently by different witnesses. Some patterns of evidence did not emerge until decades after the event, when raw FBI files of eyewitness interviews were finally unsealed.

At about this time, some minutes before 11:00 P.M., the fire truck that had earlier been disabled by the marshals suddenly reappeared and charged toward the Lyceum, veering left to run a high-speed half lap around the Circle and back up through the park to charge the marshals again. Border Patrol inspector Richard Dick remembered that "we thought we had disabled it two hours earlier by breaking off the spark plugs and pulling all the wiring loose with nightsticks. But they rewired it and had it running again, making passes down our flank, trying to run over us. The crowd would follow the truck toward us, the truck would turn, they'd fall back, and we would charge out and push the rioters back on the field."

Simultaneously there was a great deal of activity around the front of the Lyceum building. Marshals were firing tear-gas weapons, creating a cacophony that sounded like gunfire. A churning hard core of fifty to one hundred rioters was close by the Lyceum, attacking the marshals from behind bushes and trees, and sometimes in formations out in the open. On the south side of the Lyceum, rioters emerged from the adjacent Chemistry Building tossing makeshift chemical bombs that immediately burst into flames, and marshals were scurrying around trying to put out the resulting grass fires.

Once again, the fire engine sped directly toward the marshals standing in the street in front of the Lyceum. Deputy Marshal Al Butler grabbed the handrail and hoisted himself onto the truck in an attempt to stop it, but the driver swerved sharply to the left and sent Butler tumbling head over heels onto the grass.

Moments later the truck charged out of the darkness for a third attack on the marshals. In response, to defend themselves, some U.S. Marshals were forced to open fire with their service revolvers, despite explicit orders not to do so from the president and attorney general.

The marshals assumed the fire truck was trying to run them over and kill them, and as it came around for its third charge toward their skirmish line, several opened fire on it. A voice called out from the federal ranks, "Shoot the tire!" In the chaos of the evening, some marshals remembered the shooting as early as 10:00 P.M., some as late as midnight. But evidence from FBI eyewitness interviews in the weeks immediately after the event strongly suggests that bullets were flying from federal guns just after eleven, from .38 caliber service revolvers or .357 Magnums, which could also fire .38 ammunition.

A U.S. Deputy Marshal from Atlanta told an FBI interviewer in late 1962 that "as the truck swung past parallel to the front of the Lyceum Building and still on the grass, I was between the truck and the building. As I stepped back out of the way I drew my revolver and shot five times at the engine and tires in an effort to disable the truck and stop any further attempts to run over the marshals. I was fifteen or twenty feet from the truck when I shot at it and it passed in front of me. I was shooting from west to east and I believed that I had hit the truck with all five shots."

Other marshals opened fire at the truck. A Border Patrolman from Oceanside, California, fired three rounds at the truck's tires. He saw a marshal from Richmond, Virginia, shoot two or three shots at the rear tire. A U.S. Deputy Marshal from Charlotte stood in front of the truck and fired his Smith & Wesson .38 at the hood of the truck, then stepped aside and shot at the gas tank from four feet away. He remembered marshals on his left and right firing as well. A deputy marshal from Mobile, Alabama, shot at the tires and at the engine.

At least fourteen shots were fired by a minimum of five marshals toward the fire truck. The truck eventually stopped, and the marshals charged it, capturing the driver, a skinny, blond-haired young man dressed in a white sailor suit, who later identified himself as an off-duty U.S. Navy sailor stationed at the Millington Naval Air Station at Memphis. A fracas ensued as two federal prison guards dragged the sailor by his heels toward the Lyceum, and the rioter was buried in a flurry of flying billy clubs. He was later seen bleeding profusely from a gaping head wound, sobbing and begging, "Don't hurt me. I'm just a baby."

Some of the shots fired by the marshals at the fire truck were aimed in an eastward direction, in the direction of where Ray Gunter and Charlie Berryhill were observing, though the precise timing of the shots can't be determined down to the exact second, or even minute.

"That wasn't tear gas popping," Charlie Berryhill said to Ray Gunter at some time around 11:00 P.M. "They were .38s popping. Those are live rounds. We ought to get our asses out of here." Ray agreed. "Yeah, you're right," he said. Ray's hands were in his pockets, and he was facing west toward the Lyceum. They took one last look.

At this time, one witness told the FBI, he saw a group of sixty to seventy-five rioters running toward Ray and Charlie, away from the Lyceum, with marshals in pursuit. Another bystander, George Buffaloe, was an Ole Miss junior who was working part-time in the Biology Building, and had stepped outside to observe the drama. He was standing near Ray and Charlie. He heard a whistling sound and dropped to the ground, thinking it was a tear gas shell. It seemed to be coming from the general direction of the Lyceum building.

Charlie had already jumped off the drainage tile and was moving behind the building, heading for his car to drive himself and his best friend home. But he looked back and didn't see Ray. He went back and found Ray slumped down in a sitting position, as if he had slipped, with his head toward his knees. Charlie grabbed Ray, saying, "Let's go. What the hell's wrong with you?" Then he noticed blood coming from the center of Ray's forehead. "Somebody help me," cried Berryhill. "This man's been shot! Help me!" Ray had been hit in the forehead by a stray copper-coated lead bullet of Western or Winchester brand, fired probably from a Smith & Wesson–type .38 caliber revolver.

There were no figures of authority to be seen anywhere, no police, no ambulance. Charlie and a couple of bystanders carried Ray by the arms into a car and drove off to the Oxford hospital. On the way to the hospital, Ray Gunter died in Charlie Berryhill's arms. Like Paul Guihard's murder two hours earlier, Ray Gunter's death has remained unsolved to this day.

To determine if federal marshals had anything to do with the deaths of either Ray Gunter or Paul Guihard, the FBI later tested 450 weapons carried by Border Patrolmen, federal prison guards, and U.S. Deputy Marshals on the night of the riot. FBI technicians could not find a gun with riflings that matched the bullets recovered from Guihard or Gunter. The Bureau could not, however, rule out the possibility of a switched gun among the regular U.S. Deputy Marshals, for which there were no prior records to compare. At least one regular marshal quit before his personal gun could be checked.

If the bullet that killed Ray Gunter came from a marshal's gun, it was without question an accident—a warning shot aimed over the heads of the crowd or a missed shot or ricochet from one of the shots fired toward the fire truck. There was no way the shooter would have known he hit Gunter. If it was a marshal's bullet that accidentally killed Ray Gunter, the blame would reside not with the marshals, who were firing in self-defense, but with the rioters who were trying to run the marshals over with the fire truck. In a larger sense, the responsibility resided with the federal and state politicians whose negligence placed the marshals in such a horrific predicament.

Any theory of the identity of Ray Gunter's killer, like any regarding Guihard's, is pure speculation. As with the Guihard killing, Ray Gunter could have been shot by anyone with a .38 or a pistol that could shoot .38 ammunition. A number of local law-enforcement officials were prowling the campus that night, and one of them could have fired a warning shot of his own, either at the mob or the marshals. Additionally, at least two civilians were spotted firing handguns that night, and Gunter could have been hit by a ricochet from one of them.

Ray Gunter's wife, Virginia, pregnant with Ray's first child, was startled awake with a strange feeling. She called her father and told him, "Daddy, Ray's gone, and I'm worried to death." A newsman soon called her and told her that Ray had been fatally injured.

In the middle of the night, Charlie Berryhill drove east on Highway 6 to tell Ray's parents what happened. He had no one to help him, and he didn't know what to say. They had known Charlie since he was a boy. He was almost like a son to them.

Ray's brother John T. Gunter was later told of Ray's death by one of his brother officers on the University of Mississippi campus police force, who came to his house to break the news. It was John's night off.

. . .

Some time after 11:00 P.M., about twenty Oxford National Guardsmen were filling in the line in front of the Lyceum and bracing themselves for a frontal assault from the approaching mob.

A nearby marshal asked another how many tear-gas grenades he had left. The reply: "One." The marshals popped their last missiles into the sky, but the mob kept drifting forward. A marshal stepped back and said to National Guard sergeant Buford Babb, "OK, Sarge, it's all yours."

Like a predator, the mob sensed that the defenders had hurled their last gas and surged forward for the kill. "Here comes the damn mob," remembered Oxford National Guard Specialist Fourth Class Loyd Gunter (who was no relation to Ray Gunter). "We were standing out there and we didn't have any ammunition. Here they come. They get closer and closer. They start throwing bricks. We were under the streetlights. You couldn't see those bricks coming out of the dark."

The mob pushed to the curb of the street directly in front of the Guardsmen. They were just a few yards from the Lyceum steps. Right now, the Oxford Guardsmen, armed only with cold steel and guts, were the only thing standing between the rioters and the marshals, reporters, and civilians trapped inside the Lyceum building. If the Guardsmen wavered or broke formation, the mob would likely storm the building, the marshals would have to open fire at close quarters, and scores of people would die. In a pitched battle the rioters might even reach Baxter Hall, where Meredith was.

This was the high-water mark of the "second Confederacy," the long twilight empire of white supremacy that ruled much of the South since the late-nineteenth century. If the mob attacked and overwhelmed the Lyceum's defenders, a bloodbath could occur and the dream of "massive resistance" might be reborn.

The Oxford National Guardsmen were not fighting for segregation or integration, for states' rights or Ross Barnett or John Kennedy. They weren't fighting for James Meredith or the U.S. Marshals. They had a duty to perform, to save lives, to save their school, and to save their city. They stayed on the line because they were now regular U.S. Army troops, and they knew that an American soldier obeys orders and when necessary faces his own death without debating the fine points.

Sergeant Babb looked around for an officer but couldn't see one. He thought, "Well, only one thing to do."

He called out the command, "Fix bayonets!"

The Guardsmen pulled their bayonets out of scabbards and clicked them onto the rifles. As they did this, they let out an ear-piercing squall at the top of their voices, a scare tactic they learned during their brief riot training.

The Oxford Guardsmen gripped their M-1 rifles and squinted through their gas masks. They were local boys and Ole Miss students standing next to Korean War combat veterans as brother soldiers. Their guns were empty.

They snapped into the long guard position, stomped forward three steps, thrust their steel-tipped weapons out fully extended from their bodies, and let out another bloodcurdling holler. They stood there shoulder to shoulder, less than twenty soldiers facing a force many times their size, their hearts pounding like jackhammers, their bayonets pointing at the mob.

Guardsman Loyd Gunter was planning to swing and thrust his weapon if the mob realized they had no ammo and decided to charge. "I can beat the hell out of 'em with this rifle," Gunter thought to himself. "I figure I can get five or six of 'em with this bayonet before they get me."

"We're not playing," Sergeant Buford Babb remembers thinking as he held on to his weapon, still thrust out toward the crowd. "You can come across that street if you want, but we're not playing. We're not going to stand here and let you hurt us or the marshals. We're not going to let you burn down the Lyceum building or tear it up."

Five minutes passed. Then fifteen. "It seemed like forever," explained Babb in 2000. They stood there as long as they could stand it. The Oxford boys were holding the line. "The bayonet is a very good deterrent," Babb explained. "When you're looking at cold steel, and it's shoulder to shoulder, it gives you a second thought."

At last the rioters hesitated at the sight of the grimly determined Guardsmen. Finally the crowd decided not to charge the building en masse and melted back into the shadows toward the east side of the battlefield. Even though the back-and-forth combat resumed shortly, the Guardsmen had won a crucial victory.

. . .

Shortly before midnight, the exhausted voice of Ross Barnett reappeared on the radio.

Barnett decided not to make the battle-cry speech his radical segregationist advisers were calling for. If he had, Barnett thought, James Meredith would have been torn to shreds and thousands would have been killed. In fact, he had the power to unleash a bloodbath, and he chose not to pull the trigger.

But Barnett also chose not to make a clear, unambiguous plea for the fighting to stop at Oxford. Instead of a call for peace or a cry to battle, Barnett delivered a defiant statement that seemed designed to protect his political future by clarifying his 7:30 P.M. statement: "Some reports interpreting my statement tonight as altering my stand are positively untrue and wholly unfounded. My friends, I repeat to the people of Mississippi now, I will never yield a single inch in my determination to win the fight we are engaged in. I call upon every Mississippian to keep his faith and his courage. We will never surrender."

As Barnett was giving his speech, Lieutenant Governor Paul B. Johnson was in the passenger seat of a Highway Patrol cruiser blasting north from Jackson toward Oxford, pushing speeds of more than one hundred miles per hour.

Johnson had been dispatched by Governor Barnett to try to restore some order to the chaos in Oxford. Things were completely out of control already, but Johnson was even more worried about what would happen tomorrow morning, when he believed thousands of radicals from all over the South would descend upon the little city.

When Johnson pulled into Ole Miss, he stopped in at the Continuation Center on the eastern edge of campus to confer with the handful of state officials still on the school property. During the meeting, the lieutenant governor looked up to see an apparition in the doorway.

There, standing at attention, was the figure of a seventy-year-old farmer in overalls, clutching a Civil War–vintage "Long Tom" rifle, the kind that had to be loaded through the muzzle with gunpowder and a lead ball. They called it a Long Tom gun because it was so long it took a tall man to hold it. Somehow the farmer had wandered onto campus and learned of Johnson's whereabouts.

"Where you want me to go?" the old man asked the lieutenant governor. "I want to enlist!"

Johnson sized up the farmer and his weapon, which was so old

that it could have been used against the federals in the last War Between the States. Johnson asked, "Will it shoot?"

"It'll shoot. It really will!" declared the elderly volunteer. "My pa
give me this gun. I'm ready to fight!"

"I'll tell you what you do," the lieutenant governor coolly ordered
the volunteer. "You check that gun in over there in the corner." But the
farmer soon vanished.

Paul Johnson rounded up Colonel Birdsong and Highway Patrol
inspector Gwin Cole and headed through the combat zone for an
emergency conference with the federals inside the Lyceum. On the way
over, the sounds of gunfire and combat made Johnson feel like he was
back in the South Pacific, jumping from foxhole to foxhole.

At the Lyceum, the lieutenant governor faced down Nicholas
Katzenbach and John Doar and demanded that the marshals stop
shooting tear gas. Then, he proposed, the Highway Patrol could come
back on the campus and help the marshals clear the campus.

No, Katzenbach argued, the gas would have to continue as long as
it was needed. Someone then suggested that the Highway Patrol could
instead redeploy at new roadblocks around Oxford to block outsiders
from coming into the city. While they had no training or equipment
for handling a riot, they specialized in traffic control and roadblocks.

Katzenbach seized on the idea, saying, "Governor, if you can do
this it will be more help than you can give us any other way." Johnson
agreed.

But as these words were being spoken, at the Highway Patrol temporary rally point at Kiamie's restaurant and bowling alley on the
northwestern edge of campus, a new armed insurrection was erupting
among the troops of the Mississippi Highway Patrol. The scene was
described many years later by no fewer than six eyewitnesses, including five state troopers and a state legislator. According to their testimony, in the parking lot behind Kiamie's, scores of furious Mississippi
Highway Patrolmen had gathered, some of them choking from tear
gas, some cursing and swearing vengeance upon the federal marshals.

One patrolman announced he wouldn't mind if the marshals got
bullets in the backs of their heads. "Let's go and clean things out!" demanded one officer. The officers were whooping and hollering in fury,
many of them ready to go back on campus and fight the marshals.

The furious Highway Patrolmen were enraged for many reasons.
In the past two weeks, they had been used as photo opportunities in

the charade of blocking the federals. Rumors were rife among the men that some secret political deal was being made with the federals by Governor Barnett, a deal that involved guns being pointed at them, rumors that were not far from the truth. Today, their weapons had been taken away from them, and they had been receiving conflicting orders all the while.

At 8:00 P.M. Highway Patrolmen had been shot in the back, knocked down with tear-gas blasts and gas grenades fired by federal marshals, which the patrolmen believed was a deliberate ambush. Now, rumors were circulating that Lieutenant Governor Johnson and Colonel Birdsong were under arrest by federal officers at the Lyceum.

Worst of all, reported former Highway Patrolman Charles Staten in a 2000 interview, "We thought Welby Brunt was dead. Word was he died on the plane." Rumors had been circulating all night that Patrolman Brunt had been mortally wounded in the initial tear-gas barrage, and false reports of Brunt's death had been broadcast on local radio stations. In fact, Brunt had been evacuated by plane and was recovering from an overdose of tear gas in a Jackson hospital, but most of his brother officers did not know this yet.

Suddenly, a potentially disastrous collective decision was made by scores of state troopers. The policemen decided to storm the federal marshals' stronghold at the Lyceum and retake the campus at gunpoint. They were going to go into battle, with their guns blazing if necessary, and liberate the reportedly imprisoned Paul Johnson and Colonel Birdsong. They had no tactical plan; they were acting on blind impulse. Details of scene were confirmed in 2000 by eyewitnesses, including a Mississippi state representative and several surviving Highway Patrolmen.

"It had been decided to go back to fight the marshals," explained former Patrolman Staten. "The decision had been made to go back on campus. We were beginning to load up and start up our engines. Almost all the patrolmen were going back to fight and shoot." For his part, remembered Staten, "I was ready to start shooting."

As a voice called out, "Load up!" the troopers grabbed their 12-gauge Remington 97 shotguns, loaded their pistols, and piled into their squad cars. The night air was slashed by the roar of nearly a hundred squad cars starting their engines.

The Lyceum was a few minutes away.

For the first time since 1865, armed federal and state forces were about to enter full-scale combat on the battlefield. Given the circumstances, the Highway Patrolmen had a good chance of wiping the marshals out. A surprise night attack on the exhausted marshals at the Lyceum by nearly one hundred and fifty determined state troopers with rifles and shotguns would probably be over in a few minutes, with the Highway Patrol the victors.

At the exact moment the first Highway Patrol sedans were pulling out of Kiamie's parking lot to attack the marshals, a squad car containing Lieutenant Governor Paul Johnson and Colonel Birdsong pulled up to block the immense police convoy.

A short while earlier, a senior Highway Patrol official named Dave Gayden had watched the brewing insurrection-within-an-insurrection at Kiamie's and concluded the only way to stop it was to get Johnson and Birdsong out there to show themselves in person and prove that they were unharmed and not under arrest. A radio message from the officials wouldn't suffice. The Highway Patrolmen might think it was made under duress. Gayden raced to the Lyceum and summoned the two men.

The sight of the unharmed Johnson and Birdsong was welcome to the state troopers, but not enough to stop their forward motion. They still wanted to storm the campus. So the lieutenant governor faced his men, scores of furious warriors, some still choking from the gas lingering in their lungs, some clutching their weapons, all ready to enter combat and settle this matter right now. The bullet-headed politician began the most important speech of his life.

"Don't go up there fighting with those federals," Johnson ordered. "We cannot fight the might of the whole federal government. They'll have everything down here on us.

"We cannot fight the federal government," he repeated. "There's nothing we can do. The best thing we can do is try to keep people off the campus. What we're going to do is go to all the entrances and take up positions around the campus and set up roadblocks on the highways. We're going to keep as many people off the campus as we can."

Finally, the presence of the determined little lieutenant governor giving his impromptu speech was enough to calm the Highway Patrolmen down and bring them back to their senses. After a day of pure pandemonium, the policemen at last had a clear set of orders. Many of the Mississippi Highway Patrolmen now did exactly as Johnson ordered, setting up roadblocks around the school and around Oxford, searching cars, confiscating weapons, and blocking hundreds of armed rioters from reaching Oxford. There were still wide gaps in their perimeter of roadblocks, and civilians were still streaming in. But if the Highway Patrol hadn't gone into action, Paul Johnson later asserted in a Citizens Council propaganda film, "there wouldn't have been a marshal left standing."

Some Highway Patrolmen just took themselves out of the action, withdrew out of town, and stayed there until the next morning. "At that time," reported one of the officers, "we wasn't much interested in listening to orders." But none of the policemen went back to campus to fight the marshals.

It did not go into the history books, and none of the men would talk publicly about what just happened until the very end of the century.

But Paul B. Johnson, Jr. may have just stopped a massacre.

Another wave of armed Mississippians was closing fast on the Lyceum after midnight, early on the morning of Monday, October 1, not to do battle but to enforce peace, on direct orders from the president of the United States.

They were 165 fresh National Guard troops of the 108th Cavalry Regiment's Second Squadron, the first units that could get to Oxford fast enough to reinforce the men of Oxford's Troop E. These Guardsmen came from two nearby towns: eighty-five men of Troop G from Pontotoc, commanded by Captain Hassel Franklin; and an eighty-man howitzer battery based in Water Valley, commanded by Captain Billy Ross Brown.

When Captain Franklin was escorting his men out of the Pontotoc Armory, he was startled to hear a sharp explosion toward the back of the twelve-vehicle convoy.

"What was that?" asked Captain Franklin. "One of the trucks was just shot!" came the reply on the radio. A sniper had blown a hole in the vehicle's canvas side with a shotgun.

The Guardsmen were being shot at before they could even pull out of their hometown.

"Let's move," Captain Franklin ordered. "Let's get the hell out of here."

As they barreled west toward Oxford, Captain Franklin was sitting in the front Jeep with his captain's bars on, and he felt like he was going to a parade, except that the caravan was being taunted and buzzed by a dozen civilian cars flying rebel flags, some trying to run him off the road.

Checking in at the Oxford Armory, Franklin got his orders from Colonel James G. Martin, the 108th's commander: Find General Walker, arrest him, and report to Nicholas Katzenbach at the Lyceum. Also at the Armory, Troop G linked up with Captain Billy Ross Brown's howitzer battery and at midnight, both outfits set out west on University Avenue in a long convoy toward campus. The soldiers were carrying scabbarded bayonets, M-1 rifles, ammunition in their pockets, and orders to load only on an officer's command.

Colonel Martin raced ahead in a Jeep to scout the route and found what he later called "an uncontrollable, vicious mob." Martin concluded that, in his words, "It would be impossible to disperse this mob with anything less than firepower."

As the convoy came over the top of the hill at South Lamar Avenue and University Avenue to approach the university, Captain Franklin and his men suddenly found themselves in the middle of a gauntlet of civilians lining the streets with baseball bats and other weapons, some screaming the greeting "Go home, you nigger-loving sons of bitches!"

Captain Franklin was a local Mississippi businessman, a graduate of Mississippi State, a native son of Tupelo, and the sixth-grade classmate of one of Mississippi's most famous crown princes—Elvis Presley—and the mob thought he was a federal soldier sent in to, as many had put it, "shove this deal down our throats."

Also in the convoy was Captain Billy Ross Brown, commander of a Second Squadron's howitzer battery. He was a farmer, an Ole Miss grad, and a sixth-generation Lafayette County man. Earlier that night he had told his troops their mission was to protect the university. Every last one of them loaded up and followed him into Oxford.

As the convoy rolled over the top of the hill into the mob, it was too late to escape. They couldn't back up, and there was no other way to go, so the Guardsmen plunged ahead into the maelstrom.

A flurry of brickbats fell onto the Jeeps and trucks, and the drivers could see Molotov cocktails flying toward them. Once they crossed the railroad bridge onto campus, rioters pounced onto the convoy, bashing in almost all the windshields with bats. Captain Franklin distinctly saw Mississippi Highway Patrolmen sitting on a squad-car fender laughing at the scene.

Franklin's original mission, to seize General Walker, was now out of the question. There was no way Walker could be found. Now the Guardsmen's mission was to stay alive.

Rioters were reaching in and trying to pull the soldiers out of their open Jeeps, who were protected only by a safety strap. Pointing toward the Lyceum, Franklin told his Jeep driver, "Wide open! Look straight ahead and get there!"

Out of nowhere, a bearded man landed in Captain Franklin's Jeep and started swinging at his head with a lead pipe. The Jeep raced ahead, dodging rioters and trees in the Circle as Franklin struggled with his attacker. A bullet flew into the Jeep's radiator. The bearded rioter cracked Captain Franklin's chin with the pipe and laid it out to the bone. Franklin managed to kick his attacker in the chest and out of his Jeep, watching as he tumbled eight feet into the darkness.

Elsewhere in the convoy, Captain Billy Ross Brown braced himself as a rioter fired a metal hose connection at his head from point-blank range. It created a deep dent in his steel helmet. If Brown hadn't ducked, he would have been killed.

Captain Franklin dismounted at the Lyceum and ordered his men to line up along the north side of the building. He could see U.S. deputy marshals getting mauled with chunks of concrete. Racing inside, Franklin felt like he was on the wrong side of a firing range. Bullets were whizzing through the front door, blood was everywhere, and wounded marshals were groaning on the floor. He thought, "I've got to find someone who can tell me what the hell I'm supposed to do."

"Where's Mr. Katzenbach?" he demanded. Franklin was led to an office where the deputy attorney general was sitting with phones hanging off both his shoulders, holding court with a group of reporters.

Captain Franklin introduced himself through his gas mask. Katzenbach replied, "Good. Captain, we're proud to see you. People have broken into the Chemistry Building and are stealing all the acid and chemicals and throwing it on the marshals. I want you to go secure the Chemistry Building."

"Sir," replied Captain Franklin, "we barely made it in. There's no way to get out unless we lock and load—that's a solid mass of people."

Katzenbach, who didn't want to take chances with live ammunition, said, "No way."

The phones started ringing, and the conversation drifted off as Katzenbach talked to reporters and someone announced the attorney general was on the phone.

Captain Franklin walked the hall, his gas mask still on. "Man, this is unreal," he thought. "He doesn't know what he's doing. It's pure chaos. We're on our own."

Franklin went outside, where his troops were hunkering down behind vehicles, shrubs, and trees. Bullets were whistling by and richocheting off the street. Fires were starting in the grass and shrubs, and one of the Guard truck tarps was blazing.

Franklin announced to his men, "This is a war." Now he was afraid of a mass killing of his soldiers.

In the chaos of this night, various Guard units got different orders regarding their weapons and ammunition, everything from leaving their ammunition at their armories to putting ammo in their pockets but not loading. Franklin had been ordered to keep his weapons unloaded, but to be safe he brought along a locked safe full of M-1 and .45 ammo.

"I'm not going to let these fools kill my people," Franklin said. "I'm going to protect my men." He ordered a first sergeant to break out the ammo and distribute it to his sergeants and lieutenants, so that the enlisted men could load quickly if necessary. As he loaded his .45, Captain Franklin told his men, "Look, guys, we got a job to do. Just stay here. If there's a major problem, we'll protect ourselves. I assure you of that."

Suddenly Franklin noticed his gas mask was filling up with blood. He thought he was bleeding inside somewhere.

"God, I've been hit!" he cried. "I've been hit! Feel me!"

His first sergeant frantically felt around Franklin's back and stomach but couldn't find a wound. Then Franklin jerked his gas mask back and what felt like a quart of blood spilled out. It was from the wound from the lead pipe he sustained on the way in. Only now did the National Guard officer realize that his jaw was busted wide open.

Nearby, Captain Billy Ross Brown drove a small team of Guardsmen toward the athletic field about a thousand yards away. Their plan was to light up the field with their headlights so the army helicopters flying down from Memphis could touch down on campus. But Brown's truck barreled into a solid wall of people charging toward him. The only way the Guardsmen could get to the ball field was if they ran over the mob. Instead, the driver jerked the truck into reverse as the mob chased him backwards.

The truck peeled away with the mob still chasing it. Now the troops were cut off from the Lyceum as well. Captain Brown knew a side road to the Oxford Armory that bypassed the riot-choked University Avenue, so he led his men that way.

In the night air, Billy Ross Brown could see in the distance what looked like thousands of people swarming toward the school that he loved.

CHAPTER FOURTEEN

A Wall of Fire

■ ■ ■ ■

Keep going! Keep going through the fire!

—Lieutenant Donnie Bowman, 503d Military
Police Battalion, 2:00 A.M., October 1, 1962

A T 10:00 P.M. ON SUNDAY NIGHT, Captain Bill Peters of the
503d Military Police Battalion's Company B was in a dead sleep
under clean sheets in the temporary officers' quarters at Millington
Naval Air Station at Memphis, until he was shaken by a highly excited
corporal.

"Wake up, Captain! Wake up, sir!" exclaimed the soldier. "They're
rioting in Mississippi—we gotta go!"

Captain Peters had been sleeping off a drink he had had at the officers' club with his fellow officers earlier that night, when the president's speech ended and it looked like the crisis was over.

At the base gymnasium, the battalion's five hundred enlisted men
and noncommissioned officers had been packed in cheek by jowl next
to their duffel bags, sleeping right on the hardwood gym floor. Now
their officers were hustling them into action, kicking them out of the
sleeping bags. "Wheels up—we're going to Oxford!"

Nearby, Brigadier General Charles Billingslea was activating the
Oxford rescue plan. Billingslea was a towering six-foot-four, forty-

eight-year-old paratrooper and World War II combat veteran who was recently appointed commander of the Second Infantry Division at Fort Benning, Georgia. He was wearing combat fatigues, a dapper neck cloth, and a big gold buckle on his pistol belt. Today, Billingslea was the army's senior field officer for the Oxford operation, and all the army troops and Guardsmen reported to him. He, in turn, reported to army operations chief Major General Creighton W. Abrams, who was running the buildup in Memphis.

In classic bureaucratic fashion, the invasion of northern Mississippi was lurching forward in fits and starts in response to a series of sometimes conflicting orders from different federal officials.

As soon as the riot in Oxford began, General Billingslea got orders from the Pentagon to prepare to move the entire National Guard 108th Cavalry Regiment toward Oxford to reinforce the marshals. Then, at 9:33 P.M., Oxford time, Secretary of the Army Cyrus Vance in Washington ordered Billingslea to begin moving military police units to Oxford to back up the marshals. Thirteen minutes later, the order was countermanded by a direct call from the president, who ordered Billingslea to instead fly to Oxford, size up the situation, and report directly to him before committing regular army troops.

But nineteen minutes after that, before he could leave for Oxford, Billingslea was ordered by Secretary Vance to move troops directly onto the campus. At about the same time, Deputy Attorney General Katzenbach was ordering Captain Falkner and the Oxford National Guard from the Oxford Armory to the campus.

The military command structure was in complete chaos. General Billingslea and his men were now reporting to the president, the secretary of the army and the Justice Department, as well as to Billingslea's superior officer Maj. General Abrams at Memphis. Communications were clogged, and changing orders were coming in so fast that Billingslea's staff couldn't write them down quickly enough. An immense, highly complex military operation was being collapsed, rearranged, improvised, and micromanaged all in one evening.

General Billingslea decided to split Task Force Alpha into two groups. An advance rescue force of 117 men from the 503d Military Police Battalion's Company A were ordered to scramble into helicopters to conduct a mobile airborne landing at Oxford to reinforce the marshals and National Guardsmen and try to control the riot. The

MPs would form a perimeter around the Lyceum until the rest of the battalion, Companies B and C, arrived by land convoy.

At 11:50 P.M., nineteen single-rotor Sikorsky Mojave helicopters stuffed with MPs began lifting off for Oxford in three-minute intervals. Inside the aircraft, battalion commander Lieutenant Colonel John Flanagan, Company A's commander Captain Fred J. Villella, Jr., and their men struggled to open boxes full of chemical-gas grenades, using unwinding keys to get them out of boxes like sardine cans. The MPs stuffed the grenades into their pockets and checked their M-1 rifles, riot shotguns, and gas masks as the choppers sliced through the night sky.

Inside the helicopters, all was quiet as the officers reviewed mental checklists of orders and equipment, and the enlisted men were left to their thoughts. They knew they were flying into a chaotic situation, and they had little intelligence on the riot, but they had the greatest confidence in themselves and one another. For months and months, the MPs had trained for precisely this kind of event. They came from across the United States and from a multitude of backgrounds, but every man in the battalion agreed on one point: They were the best-trained riot fighters the world had ever seen.

Inside one helicopter, Specialist Fourth Class Melvin Lambert's feelings were so torn that he was sick to his stomach. Like many of the MPs, he was a white Southerner, born in Stanley County in central North Carolina. Decades later he explained his conflicted emotions. "I felt like a Yankee soldier invading the South. I thought, 'What am I doing going into the Deep South?'"

Lambert thought of his twelve grand-uncles, all of whom served in the Confederate army as North Carolina state troops. He thought of one in particular, Caleb Wiley Lambert, who served three years in the brutal prisoner-of-war camp at Point Lookout, Maryland. But at the same time, he knew he had a duty to perform.

As the helicopters penetrated Mississippi airspace, they became the first regular American combat troops to enter Mississippi in action status since the last Union troops withdrew in 1877.

A U.S. Army H-13 reconnaissance helicopter had flown ahead of the MPs' armada, and sometime after midnight it was hovering slowly over the University of Mississippi, scouting for a safe place near the Lyceum to land the advance strike force of the 503d's riot fighters. All the chopper pilot could see was pitch darkness and the chaos around the Lyceum. He circled lower and lower, struggling to find a secure landing zone. He couldn't see one. The pilot radioed back to Memphis that there was nowhere to land on the campus.

The marshals, civilians, and Guardsmen trapped at the Lyceum heard the throbbing roar of helicopter rotors groaning louder and louder, then abruptly speed up and grow fainter as the craft flew away. A sobered Deputy Attorney General Katzenbach and Chief U.S. Marshal McShane huddled up to prepare a worst-case scenario. They agreed that if the mob broke into the building, they would try to evacuate everyone through the back door and rush back to Baxter Hall for a final stand.

In the splendid impotence of the White House Cabinet Room, the president of the United States was yelling into the phone at frazzled Secretary of the Army Cyrus Vance.

"Where's the Army?" Kennedy shouted at Vance. "Where are they? Why aren't they moving?"

During Kennedy's entire presidency, through an apocalyptic nuclear crisis, a bungled invasion of Cuba, a failed summit with Soviet Premier Khrushchev, and crises in Vietnam, Laos, Berlin, and the Congo, the attorney general had never seen his brother as furious as he was now.

The hapless Vance was ensconced at the Pentagon, overwhelmed by a cyclone of conflicting flash reports from the field, all of which he was promptly relaying to the president. At 10:24 P.M. the MPs were still on the ground; at 11:02 the troops were airborne; at 11:47 the earlier report was deemed wrong—they hadn't taken off; by midnight the MPs were lifting off.

"Damn Army!" exclaimed Attorney General Kennedy, "They can't even tell if in fact the MPs have left yet!"

The president was enraged at the seemingly slow pace of the army rescue, not realizing the GIs were doing their best. "They always give you their bullshit about their instant reaction and their split-second timing," JFK fumed, "but it never works out. No wonder it's so hard to win a war."

John Kennedy was not the first American president to try to run a battle by remote control in real time from the White House. During Civil War battles exactly a century earlier, Abraham Lincoln camped out in the adjacent War Department's telegraph office around the clock, peering over the cipher operators' shoulders as instantaneous reports came in from the field. In August 1862, a Colonel Haupt described troop movements and the sounds of cannons booming to the president during the Second Battle of Bull Run. The following month, when Lee's army escaped after the battle of Antietam, Lincoln angrily fired off telegraphic orders to the slow-moving General George B. McClellan to pursue and "destroy the rebel army if possible."

But today, a hundred years later, another president was ranting and raging because he could not even establish contact with his commander in the field. From midnight, the time General Billingslea arrived at Oxford in a Caribou aircraft, until nearly two hours later, the president could not speak directly to him. The general was moving so fast he was outrunning the Army Signal Corps' ability to set up secure radio and telephone gear.

"People are dying in Oxford," the president sputtered in a radio flash to General Abrams at Memphis, in the hope that he could relay the message to Billingslea. "This is the worst thing I've seen in 45 years," he fumed. "I want the military police battalion to enter the action. I want General Billingslea to see that this is done. You are to proceed to the campus forthwith." The message eventually caught up with Billingslea at the Oxford airport at almost 1:30 A.M.

The over-optimistic army brass had promised the president a one-hour response, but three hours had passed since JFK's first order to deploy, and the MPs were still not at the Lyceum. RFK later griped, "The evening would have been quite different if the troops had gotten there at the time that they were supposed to have gotten there. The Army had botched it up."

But in fact, it was the Kennedys who had botched things up, and royally, by dithering with Ross Barnett for weeks and then suddenly activating an army-invasion plan late at night when it took extra time to get the men and their gear ready in the confusion and darkness. At least twenty minutes were wasted by the MPs having to locate and reload tear-gas supplies, since they had been ordered to release their initial supply earlier that night for airlift to the marshals at Oxford. The abrupt switch of landing zones from the university campus to the miniature Oxford airport burned away much additional time, as the nineteen choppers had to separate safely and land one at a time to un-load the MPs, who then had to reassemble and reload into vehicles to take them to the combat zone.

At 12:30 A.M. on Monday, October 1, the lead helicopter of the in-vasion armada carrying 117 men from A Company of the 503d Mili-tary Police Battalion was finally touching down at the Oxford airport. This was one of the first air-mobile operations in history, and it was being staged on an American city.

On the tarmac, General Billingslea was on the verge of panic, screaming at the MPs over the helicopter noise to hurry into forma-tion and get to the campus. When he grabbed one MP officer and shouted, "Go, go, go!" the officer pointed out that the choppers were still landing: "Sir, I don't have all my men here yet!"

The incoming MPs were met by Oxford National Guard Lieu-tenant Robert Crowe, who had been dispatched by Captain Falkner to link up with General Billingslea. The battalion's officers huddled around a vehicle's headlights and studied a map of the university as Crowe explained the layout of campus and the movements of the ri-oters. They agreed that the MPs would enter the campus through a secondary entrance, Rebel Drive, enabling them to bypass the worst of the mob as they approached the Lyceum. Luckily, somebody in the navy had thought ahead: Four gray navy buses were standing by to re-lay the MPs to the Lyceum.

Unlike the largely disarmed National Guardsmen, the MPs were traveling with full firepower. Each enlisted man wore a .45 on his pis-tol belt and carried the army's workhorse semi-automatic service rifle, the clip-loaded M-1, along with bayonets and magazines carrying a total of 180 rounds per man. As an additional show of force, sixteen of the MPs carried pump-action riot shotguns with eighteen-inch bayo-nets and a total of five hundred shells. They had a grim purpose: to non-fatally injure and stop as many rioters as possible by firing pellets of light shot in a wide arc.

Lieutenant Donnie Bowman of Company A was a towering, cool young Texan who commanded the platoon that would spearhead the operation. In his pocket he carried a presidential proclamation order-ing the mob to disperse, which he planned to read through a bull-horn. As the MPs filed into the buses for the ten-minute ride to the campus, Bowman asked General Billingslea who would give him the authority to fire back if they were fired on. The general replied, "Lieutenant, the president says to use whatever force is necessary to control this riot."

In the back of Lieutenant Colonel Flanagan's mind was a blood-curdling thought: a nightmare image of American soldiers shooting at one another. Even though Oxford National Guard Lieutenant Robert Crowe joined the MPs at the airport to guide them to the campus, Flanagan had no idea whether the rest of the Mississippi National Guardsmen were going to join the MPs or open fire on them.

The campus was coming into view now. Given the risks and the unknowns, Flanagan decided to take no chances, ordering his men to "lock and load!" In another bus, when Captain Fred Villella and Lieutenant Bowman issued the same order, one frightened private accidentally blew an M-1 round through the roof of the bus, scaring the living daylights out of everyone, including the driver, who swayed the bus abruptly while ducking.

It was 1:35 A.M. when the convoy pulled up to the edge of the campus and unloaded, but the drivers had accidentally pulled up to the wrong entrance, the main campus gate at Sorority Row. Now the MPs would have to march up through a little valley, up a long hill, and skirt closer to the main body of rioters, a half-mile march. Driving the buses onto the campus was out of the question—they could be blockaded by the rioters, and a few well-aimed firebombs could trap the MPs inside an inferno.

When the grim and fairly terrified troops dismounted the buses, they were accosted by a handful of Mississippi Highway Patrolmen stationed at the entrance. One grabbed a black MP, slammed him against the bus, shone a flashlight on his face and said, "What are you doing down here, nigger?" The private's fellow MPs quickly shoved the patrolman to the side.

One state patrolman taunted the soldiers, "I guess y'all are gonna go up there and shoot them women and children!" National Guard officer Crowe snapped back, "There aren't any damn women and children up there—there are bad guys up there!"

In the distance, Lieutenant Colonel Flanagan could see hundreds of roughnecks roaming the campus, so he ordered his men to strap on their gas masks and fix bayonets on their rifles, which were already locked and loaded. One of the platoon corporals, Melvin Brown, was delighted to put on his gas mask. Brown was a black soldier and one of the only men in the battalion who grew up in Mississippi. He thought for sure the MPs would have to fight their way through both the National Guard and the Mississippi Highway Patrol, and he knew the sight of invading black troops in combat gear would worsen the rioters' frenzy. In a gas mask he would be a less visible target.

Lieutenant Bowman fanned his assault platoon into a wedge formation. This was a classic riot maneuver, a show of force designed to intimidate a mob with the sight of troops stomping forward in a flying-geese formation as they thrust their bayonets forward and back.

"We don't know what's up there," Bowman announced to his soldiers, "but no matter what happens, we are going through. I'm gonna read the president's riot proclamation ordering the mob to disperse. If they don't, we're gonna go through 'em. Fire above their heads first. If they don't break apart, fire down at their feet. If that doesn't work, the shotgun squad will fire point-blank, 'cause we are going through them, regardless of what happens."

Just behind Bowman's platoon, traveling in a fixed column, was the second platoon, commanded by a fearful Lieutenant John Migliore. He wasn't much worried about his own safety—he was flanked by a solid wall of firepower—but he was extremely afraid of firing on civilians. He even imagined his own court-martial, complete with a grieving mother on the witness stand, wailing, "My little Billy would never throw rocks at federal military policemen—why did you shoot him?" If his men opened fire, Lieutenant Migliore figured, he would be hung from the highest tree. So he ordered his troops not to open fire unless he gave the order, and he would personally direct the shots, pointing out the targets.

In ghostly silence, the two formations of MPs ascended toward the heart of the campus, toward the surreal glow of burning cars and tear-gas clouds. As they marched toward the top of the hill and university chancellor John Davis Williams's residence, a small group of quiet spectators complete with a baby carriage created a false sense of security. News of the arrival of black soldiers was already flashing around Oxford. On the edge of campus, someone shouted, "They're bringing in nigger troops with rifles!"

Inside Chancellor Williams's residence, an emergency 2:00 A.M. meeting of the school board of trustees was just starting when the military-police troops approached. The meeting included Chancellor Williams, board president Thomas Tubb, board members Charles Fair and S. R. Evans, and the chancellor's assistant and former FBI man Hugh Clegg.

When the gas-masked MPs passed by in their slow riot shuffle— stomp, bayonet thrust; stomp, bayonet thrust—someone in the group noticed that there were black troops in the invasion force. At this, the board members were so infuriated that they immediately began trying to telephone their two U.S. senators, James Eastland and John Stennis, to use their influence to demand that Negro troops be withdrawn. The school officials thought their presence would incite even more violence.

As the lead V formation of MPs negotiated a right turn onto a dark road, a wall of flames suddenly exploded up from the road just fifteen feet ahead of the troops. A river of gasoline had been ignited by a team of hidden rioters.

Lieutenant Bowman yanked up his gas mask and yelled back to his men, "Keep going! Keep going through the fire! We're gonna go marching through it!" The troops had no idea what was on the other side of the fire. Company A's commander, Captain Fred Villella, thought that if a single MP opened fire, it could trigger a chain reaction of firing, and scores of people might die.

The MPs stepped into the wall of flames, and as they passed through to the other side, they stayed steady and held their formation. As the second MP formation marched through in column formation, Molotov cocktails spiraled toward their ranks. "We saw two sheets of flame about the size of our small house fall among the troops," observed University of Mississippi history professor James Silver, who was watching from the side of the chancellor's house. "They hardly got out of step."

Norbert Schlei, a Justice Department official trapped at the Lyceum, watched in amazement: "You could see the troops marching along in cadence. . . . The flames went up and the troops just went clonk, clonk, clonk right through the flames." One of the rioters marveled, "Molotov cocktails and bricks are flying through the air, and the cocktails hit the ground right in the middle of the MPs, spewing fire all around, and the MPs never even break step."

Rocks banged against the soldiers' helmets, and one Molotov cocktail scored a direct hit on an MP's head, but didn't explode. "I saw one marching soldier fall wounded," recalled reporter Donald Tate, who saw the GI's buddies pull him away "as the firebombs bounced around them."

The troops closed in on the perimeter of buildings near the Lyceum, moving toward the Circle. The MPs marched right around a roadblock of burning cars, and the soldiers never stumbled or even looked around. "Sometimes," one rioter recalled, "when the fire hits right in the middle of them, the ranks will move out to the left and right, like a drill team on a football field changing formation, and then, when they have passed the fire, the ranks will close up again. That's all. The fire was everywhere in the air and on the ground, the crowd yelling, the darkness all around. That's the U.S. Army for you. I reckon you'd say it was awe-inspiring."

The countless hours of riot training and physical conditioning at Fort Bragg were paying off handsomely for the MPs. They looked invincible and unstoppable. The spectacle of the MPs' grand entry onto the campus made at least one rioter think the troops were going to "kick ass and take names." He gave up and went home.

The marching MPs heard the crackle of rifle fire, and the flaming wreckage of overturned cars illuminated the landscape as bright as day. "I could not believe what I saw," remembered Lieutenant John Migliore. "I could not believe I was on the campus of a university in the United States of America." As he marched ahead, Lieutenant Donnie Bowman was stunned at the ferocity of the attack by his fellow Southerners. "I can't believe this is America," he thought. There was no way he could read the presidential proclamation to the crowd, not in this chaos.

Off to the left, a mass of rioters was forming in the distance and battalion commander Lieutenant Colonel Flanagan thought, "Sure as hell we're going to have to start shooting at people." He was ready to give the order to unleash the riot shotguns as soon as any of his men were set ablaze by a Molotov cocktail, since they were wearing so many straps they couldn't quickly get out of their clothes.

Flanagan lifted up his mask and, choking, called out, "Just take it, men. Take it! We're almost there. Take it, men. . . . Take it. . . . That's it. . . . Take it. . . . We're almost there. . . ." As the MPs finally stomped into view of the Lyceum, the embattled marshals let out a joyful cheer. Staff Sergeant Mack Mullins never heard so much applause in his life. A voice from inside the building cried, "They're here! They're here!" It was 2:15 A.M.

While the MPs were filling in the ranks of the Guardsmen and deputy marshals surrounding the Lyceum, Sergeant John Shook of the 503d heard a sharp voice with an unmistakable Boston accent barking through a field radio that had been placed on the building steps. "I want you to clear that campus," the voice demanded. "I sent that god-damn MP battalion down there and I want those people pushed off that campus. And now. And if they can't do it, I'll get somebody else to do it!"

Captain Fred Villella of the 503d soon heard a similar disembodied voice coming from the speaker, ordering, "Katzenbach, take that battalion and clear that riot!" Neither soldier could tell if it was the president or the attorney general, since their voices sounded so similar, but both were sure of one thing—the voice belonged to one of the Kennedy brothers.

Captain Villella realized that whichever Kennedy the voice belonged to, the speaker was mistaken. The whole 503d MP battalion was not yet on the scene, only the advance rescue force of A Company. Villella pointed out to battalion commander Flanagan, "I only have 117 men—B Company and C Company aren't here yet." The rest of the battalion was still hurtling down from Memphis by convoy.

Even counting the available Guardsmen and marshals and the MPs, the federal forces were still outnumbered. If they counterattacked now and were forced to unleash their firepower on the mob, a historic massacre could result. Villella's judgment was to wait until more National Guardsmen arrived. Flanagan and Billingslea agreed, and instead sent a team of twenty-four MPs to back up the marshals defending the sleeping James Meredith at Baxter Hall, and another team to protect the power plant.

At 2:30 A.M., Oxford time, General Creighton Abrams at the Millington Naval Air Station phoned President Kennedy to relay a report from General Billingslea that the rest of the MP battalion would arrive by convoy in two hours, by 4:30 A.M. It seemed to the president that the battle was concluding, so he went to bed at 3:30 A.M., Oxford time (5:30 A.M., D.C. time). Before he fell asleep, he made a last check with his men in the Cabinet Room, and signed off by ordering, "I want to be called if anything happens."

For the MPs at the Lyceum, it was now their turn to stand fast out in the open air and take a beating from the swirling, invisible guerrilla bands in the darkness beyond them. Thousands of civilians and rioters were still surging around the university, with an unknown number of reinforcements moving in on the country roads toward Oxford.

On the front line, Lieutenant Donnie Bowman soon got fed up watching his men dodge rocks and Molotov cocktails. He decided to quietly launch a two-man probe and counterattack toward enemy lines. Bowman asked one of his sergeants, "You got any tear gas-grenades?" The sergeant opened up his field jacket, which was overflowing with the baseball-sized weapons. "Come on with me," Bowman ordered. The two crept down the field, deep into the no-man's-land in the wooded Circle, and began pulling the grenade levers and hurling the missiles as far as they could throw them, trying to push the insurrectionists back out of range of the Lyceum.

In the reflected flame light of a burning car, one herd of rioters was conducting a war dance as they cried a bloodcurdling mixture of animal shrieks and rebel yells. A U.S. Deputy Marshal standing on the steps of the Lyceum said quietly to a reporter, "If I were Meredith, I'd be ashamed to go to school with these sorry bastards."

By now, more National Guardsmen from the 108th Armored Cavalry Regiment were speeding to the rescue from other nearby towns in northern Mississippi, from Holly Springs, Tupelo, Senatobia, Batesville, from every town that had a National Guard outfit. In central and southern Mississippi, Guardsmen of the 155th Infantry "Dixie Division" were falling in, too, in towns with lyrical names like Laurel, Aberdeen, Brookhaven, Magnolia, Corinth, Natchez, and Iuka, and in James Meredith's hometown of Kosciusko.

Eleven thousand Mississippi boys and men had jumped into battle gear, reported to their armories, and answered their nation's call. It was an all-white force, and few of the Guardsmen supported the politics of the mission they were being sent on. Many of them were deeply conflicted and resentful about it, and until tonight their hearts would have been with the rioters in spirit, if not in tactics. "This is the trashiest deal I ever heard of," one unnamed enlisted man told his local newspaper. One of his colleagues agreed. "We don't like this idea at all. If he [Kennedy] had asked for volunteers, I don't think he would have gotten the first one."

Yet there was not a single case of anyone refusing to do their duty. Across the state of Mississippi, all eleven thousand National Guardsmen were deciding that on this night they were Americans first and that the law was the law. They were obeying orders. "We've been federalized, and that's it," Captain George Lang told a local reporter in McComb. "We're trained to be soldiers and this unit will do what I tell them." A fellow Guard officer summed it up: "We have no choice. We have our orders and that's that." Another soldier agreed. "When you've got to go, you've got to go. It doesn't matter what my wife thinks."

In northwest Mississippi, 108th Cavalry Third Squadron commander Major William Callicott was loading his troops into a convoy at the armory in the town of Senatobia. Callicott, in civilian life an insurance man as well as a Mississippi state representative, figured the Guard had been federalized as a way of neutralizing eleven thousand men who might fight on the other side for all anybody knew.

As civilians, some of Callicott's men had been part of the mob that blockaded James Meredith and the federal forces at Oxford three days earlier, when the marshals were forced to turn back before they reached Oxford. Now, some of the soldiers were refusing to move.

"Major, we're not going to go," said one enlisted man. "We refuse to go."

Callicott replied, "No, you're in the army today. You don't refuse anything."

"Well, I'll just go to jail and stay in jail," the Guardsman said. "No," Callicott responded, "you're going, and you'd better shut your mouth and get on that truck. You'd better shut up and do what I'm telling you to do."

Another soldier chimed in, "I was over there Thursday trying to keep him [James Meredith] out. Now I've got to go back and try and get him in?"

"You got no choice," the commander declared. "You're in the army today, and you're going to do exactly what I tell you."

That ended the conversation. The men obeyed. From then on, Callicott had no disciplinary problems at all.

Just as the convoy was pulling out, Sheriff Bill Williams pulled up in a state of panic. He had just gotten got back from Oxford.

"Oh, my God," the sheriff despaired, "they're shooting—there are two or three already killed. You won't believe what's happening." Probably referring to a tear-gas attack, the sheriff reported, "I just saw this pretty girl shot in the face."

The Guardsmen were already scared to death, recalled Major Callicott, having heard reports of a mob approaching five thousand at Oxford. But the sheriff's panicked report, he said wryly, "really pepped us up."

On the way to Oxford, Major Callicott's convoy linked up with other National Guard units in little towns along the way, and by the time the long convoy arrived at the northern gate of the University of Mississippi, he had a force of well over two hundred men.

Callicott looked into the faces of his men and saw expressions of absolute terror. He felt exactly the same way. "I served two years in World War II," explained Callicott many years later, "in England, France and Germany, 1943 to 1945, and I never was as terrified as I was going onto the campus that night. It was the fact that I knew there had to be some local people from my hometown probably over there in that mob. That's what really worried me. If we killed anybody it could be my next-door neighbor."

But as he dismounted his men from their trucks at the Sorority Row entrance on the northern border of campus and they struggled with their gas masks, Callicott decided he could not send them into combat with unloaded weapons, regardless of what his orders were. So Callicott broke out the ammunition and told his men to carry it in their pockets but to not load their weapons yet. "I'm sorry," Callicott confessed many years later, "but I loaded mine and I'm afraid all the men loaded theirs, too."

Major Callicott lined his men up in columns of threes and sixes and announced, "If you have to shoot, shoot high, shoot low, 'cause you may be shooting your next-door neighbor."

The National Guardsmen marched up the hill into battle, and soon they were sweating and gasping for air inside the gas masks. "Two hundred and fifty of us entered the campus," Callicott remembered. "We were already scared to death. We marched up Sorority Row on foot, three abreast. We'd had a small amount of riot training, but tonight, with all the lights shot out, in the dark, with gas all around, and local folks on the other side, we had men who were absolutely petrified."

As he led his men into the darkness, Callicott's mind narrowed into a few thoughts: "Get in, get this mob out of here, and get out." Callicott recalled, "We marched onto the campus, and a group of students rolled a brand-new car out of the middle of the road in front of us and set it on fire. They broke up all the concrete benches on the campus, and were throwing chunks of rock and concrete and hitting us upside the head."

As they marched past the YMCA building, the troops, still holding their fire, were greeted with a barrage of steel pipes heaved from building windows and from street level. The pipes hit the asphalt and bounced up to face level and knocked some of the soldiers flat on the ground. The mass formation finally reached the Lyceum and fell in next to their fellow GIs.

And still the National Guardsmen came, from towns like Itawamba, Fulton, Nettleton, Belmont and Baldwyn; from Tishomingo County, Prentice County, and Ross Barnett's ancestral Leake County. They were privates with impossibly young faces, wearing battle gear two and three sizes too big for them, corn-fed high-school boys who lived with their parents and milked cows before sunrise, standing alongside sergeants who were battle-hardened Korean War vets. One outfit, a howitzer battery of the 108th Cavalry, was commanded by Captain Bob Griffin, principal of Nettleton High School. Today, he was leading some of his own seventeen- and eighteen-year-old students into battle.

This was one of the secrets of the Mississippi National Guard's perfect performance that night: the very structure of the Guard itself. It was organized on a town-by-town basis: Neighbors served with neighbors, storekeepers with customers, ministers with parishioners, brothers with brothers. These were the strongest bonds of unit cohesion and duty and fellowship, and guaranteed that the GIs wouldn't let one another down. What made the experience all the more terrifying for these early waves of Guardsmen was that they feared that some of their own neighbors or classmates might be on the other side trying to kill them.

Just as Major Callicott's Third Squadron troops were nearing the Lyceum, troops of the 108th Cavalry's First Squadron were simultaneously approaching the campus in convoy from the east along University Avenue, led by squadron commander Lieutenant Colonel Guy J. Gravlee. "The situation," according to a November 1962 National Guard report, "was still like a scene from Dante's *Inferno;* pitch dark, several thousand men and youths milling around among the trees on the Circle and Grove and among the University streets."

Lieutenant Colonel Gravlee of Tupelo, a thirty-nine-year-old who in civilian life headed up the family business, Gravlee Lumber Company, was riding with Major Oscar Megginson in a Jeep at the head of the convoy. Normally, senior officers would be riding behind the lead elements, but Gravlee thought the sight of his uniform and all the vehicles following him "would kinda sober that crowd up."

It didn't work out that way.

Colonel Gravlee's driver, PFC Jerry Mears, had to smash the Jeep through a roadblock of lumber and concrete as the mob bombarded the convoy with hand-thrown missiles. Then the convoy passed through a flurry of Molotov cocktails, which set one of the truck tarps ablaze.

"We literally had to fight our way onto the campus," explained Captain Bob Griffin in 1999. "They dropped a concrete block onto the cab of one of the trucks. It fell through the canvas and hit between the driver and the assistant driver. If it had hit one of them it would have killed him. I was in a Jeep, and a brick smacked me on the right leg. People broke out most of the windows in our vehicles. I've been continuously amazed that more people weren't killed. We had boys who had just got into the Guard, and had no training. Our vehicles were stopped and surrounded by rioters. Our weapons were locked and loaded, and each man had a clip of live ammo. I'm amazed we didn't shoot."

In 1999, Guy Gravlee explained why he thought his men performed as they did, even though most of them had a grand total of exactly one day's training in riot control. "They were like me; they didn't want to go over there and get involved in this thing because we had to live here and do business with some of these people. But they were disciplined. A number of the noncommissioned officers were veterans of World War II and Korea. They took over and did their duty. They were magnificent leaders."

When they jumped out of their trucks near the Lyceum, the First Squadron Guardsmen were getting hit with tear-gas canisters. The gas was coming from U.S. Deputy Marshals who were trying to fire over their heads and cover them as they dismounted, but it was falling short and dropping inside the soldiers' ranks instead.

The soldiers frantically strapped on their gas masks to defend against the friendly fire. Some of the troops, forgetting to immediately blow and clear the masks, were staggering to their knees choking for breath. Their officers ran around and held their young troops as they screamed instructions to them. "We were having to go around and check that everyone could breathe as we tried to form the skirmish line," Captain Griffin recalled. "We could hear twenty-two-caliber bullets hitting the trees above us, and in the meantime the crowd was moving in on us."

General Billingslea welcomed the incoming Guardsmen with a crisp greeting: "Glad to see you. I think we can get something done now." An exhausted deputy marshal told one of the Guard officers: "If y'all hadn't come, we couldn't have held out much longer."

The arrival of the 108th Cavalry's First and Third Squadrons, when added to the Second Squadron that had arrived earlier, meant the regiment was complete, with more than five hundred men. When combined with the force of 117 MPs from the 503d's A Company and the two hundred or so federal marshals who were still battle-ready, Billingslea at last had a force capable of taking the offensive against the rioters.

The mass formation of federal officers and troops formed a helter-skelter skirmish line, creating almost a complete circle around the Lyceum. Incredibly, the uninjured Oxford National Guardsmen of Troop E were still in the line of fire, quietly and stubbornly holding their ground since being the first troops to enter the combat zone five hours earlier. They had never been relieved. They were still standing fast.

A military policeman told Troop E's Sergeant Buford Babb, "You people fall in behind us, and we're going to run 'em off campus." Sergeant Babb replied, "We're not falling behind anybody. We'll join with you, but we're not going behind you or anybody else." In the counterattack being planned by General Billingslea, Troop E was supposed to be held in reserve at the Lyceum, but its troops were instead spontaneously lining up with the assault formation, itching to take on their tormentors lurking in the pitch black.

A National Guard officer called out, "Soldiers, load and cock your weapons!"

From somewhere in the darkness, deep in the line of National Guardsmen, came an astonishing call. It was a voice yelling a line from the new state song, a song that until this moment had been automatically connected to support for Ross Barnett and eternal segregation and the defiance of federal law. Loud and clear, the Guardsman's voice said, "Let's go, Mississippi!"

The order rippled around the building, "Forward march." The circle slowly surged out in all directions. Another voice called out, "Charge!" and parts of the line rushed forward in disorganized fragments.

Seeing the wave of advancing soldiers, most of the mob quickly fell back in all directions and melted away from the center of campus. Before he fled, one of the rioters planted a little rebel flag at the base of the Confederate monument. A Mississippi National Guardsman stopped a group of escaping rioters, grabbed a Confederate flag from one, and stomped it into the ground.

Some troops seized straggling rioters and trotted them at gunpoint back to the basement of the Lyceum. One of Troop E's enlisted men grabbed a rock and was about to hurl it at the civilians until ordered to halt by an officer. It was the only ammo he had had all night.

Troop E's Loyd Gunter remembered seeing a rioter close by bending over to pick up a brick to throw at the troops. One of his sergeants, Gunter recalled, "double-timed over, took his bayonet, and he stuck that guy right in the ass with that damn bayonet. That guy let out a bloodcurdling yell, and he cut out of there screaming and hollering. He stuck that thing up about four inches up his rear end." Explained another man from Troop E, "Hell, we'd been shot at and had bricks thrown at us all night. We was pissed off mad."

At the eastern edge of campus, Troop E's Lieutenant Robert Crowe was chasing a rioter down the sidewalk, swinging his .45 by the muzzle trying to clobber him with it, but the rioter was a half a step faster and outran him. Then another officer saw two Guardsmen from a different unit forcibly restraining a captured civilian brick-thrower. After a night of being shot at and attacked, the officer was in no mood for clemency. "Carry on," he told the soldiers.

Just beyond the university grounds, at the corner of University Avenue and South Fifth Street, the men of Troop E stopped. They were ordered to hold at the school's entrance and go no farther, but the troops were eager to charge a new concentration of rioters that was forming just beyond their perimeter. A 108th headquarters officer told Lieutenant Crowe, "We need to talk to these people [the rioters]."

"My people were mad," recalled Crowe. "The Oxford boys were mad as hell. They would have killed somebody if they got their hands on them."

"Hell, Major, you talk to them," Crowe told his superior officer.

"We've been fighting them all night, and I ain't about to talk to them. I'll run them off this damn intersection if you want me to. I'll fight 'em, I'll move 'em, but I ain't talking to them."

"Lieutenant," replied the major, "you're relieved."

"Yes, sir," said Lieutenant Crowe, who rounded up Troop E, put them in a column of twos, and proudly marched them back to defend the Lyceum building.

They and their brother U.S. Army troops, National Guardsmen and Military Policemen alike, had saved the University of Mississippi. They had fought their way through hell, held their fire, prevented a massacre, stood their ground, and broken the back of the revolt. They were restoring peace and law and order to a piece of American soil that had fallen into anarchy.

But the battle was not over. Like an intractable prairie fire, it was flaring back to life on the edges of the battlefield, and in the city of Oxford itself.

On the north edge of campus, Captain Hassel Franklin and the men of the 108th Cavalry's Troop G, Second Squadron, were ducking as live rounds of small-arms ammunition were being fired toward them from the darkness. Cars passing along Highway 6 were taking potshots at them as they tried to set up a roadblock and conduct a security sweep at the Sorority Row entrance to the school. Hysterical mothers and fathers were appearing at the entrance trying to get their daughters out of the sorority houses.

Captain Franklin took out his .45 and shot out the two nearby streetlights to give his men some cover, but the shooting continued. So as the clock approached 5:00 A.M., Captain Franklin ordered, "Dig in!"

"We were digging foxholes," explained Franklin, "because we were still getting shot at from cars passing along Highway 6." A university administrator who lived in the house whose yard they were tearing up came out and said, "Captain, this is private property. Don't be digging in my yard!"

Captain Franklin replied, "Sir, you get back in the house. We're going to dig wherever we want to. My men are being shot at, and we're going to dig in."

On the way out of the campus, Captain Franklin's National Guard troops had captured several prisoners, but lacking radio contact with

General Billingslea at the Lyceum, they didn't know what to do with them. "Put their arms behind them," Franklin ordered his men, "and tie them up with anything you can find."

They put the captives down into a ravine, made them lie down, and put a guard over them. "Later on that morning," Captain Franklin related, "we did some improvising and got some logs and confiscated some wire, and we made us a little pen. Eventually we had fifteen to twenty prisoners from all over the state." When the Guardsmen stopped a sports car driven by some Mississippi State students, they found four M-1 rifles in the trunk. The weapons had been stolen from the Mississippi State Army ROTC arsenal.

One civilian, a man of about sixty, came staggering down the street toward Troop G's checkpoint. The man, who seemed to Captain Franklin to be a "redneck type," was crying. "I felt sorry for him," Franklin explained, because "he looked like he'd been in a war for six months, with his eyeballs turned wrongside out."

"Fella," asked Franklin, "what in the world are you doing up here?"

"Captain, you won't believe this" the man weeped, "but I was sitting on my front porch, in a swing, in Philadelphia, Mississippi, and a couple a buddies drove by and said, 'Come on, get in the car. We understand they're doing a lot of pushing and shoving up at Ole Miss. The feds are up there. Let's go up there and watch 'em push and shove. Let's watch them get that nigger out!' I didn't have any more sense than to get in the car with 'em. We got us a case of beer on the way up here."

The man had a white shirt on, but he was so dirty it looked like he'd come out of a coal bin, and he was soaked in tear gas. "I've been running all night long," the man despaired. "I've been gassed, I've been shot at. I've run from one side of this campus to the other, and everywhere I go, somebody's getting shot at."

"Captain," the crying man vowed, "I'll tell ya, if I could ever get home, I'll never leave again. Just put me somewhere safe. I'll promise you if I ever get back to Philadelphia, I'll never leave it again in my life."

Captain Franklin sat the man down and treated him to a can of army C-rations.

At midnight in Memphis, at the same time the 503d Military Police Battalion's Company A was lifting off in the choppers, their colleagues in Company B, Company C, and headquarters staff were rumbling out of Millington Naval Air Station in a long land convoy of Jeeps and trucks, headed south on Highway 51 toward Oxford. The caravan was commanded by Major Raymond Le Van.

The MPs didn't know how to get to Oxford, so they commandeered a pile of free road maps from a Gulf station on the outskirts of Millington. MP William Mayes remembered, "As military police, we were used to patrol duties and high-speed chases, and it all clicked. We all thought like military police: cautious, alert to possibility that innocents might get hurt. Morale was extremely high, like it always was with the 503d."

It was a long convoy of 161 vehicles, led by two sweeper scout Jeeps racing a half mile ahead, followed by fifty patrol Jeeps, with sirens wide open, carrying three MPs each, armed with .45s and M-1 rifles. Following them were small quarter-ton trucks, followed by heavy trucks at the rear. Machine guns were mounted on the front of the trucks.

As the convoy came up to a walled levee just south of the Tennessee-Mississippi border, on the outskirts of a town called Walls, a scout Jeep radioed back to convoy commander Major Le Van: "Stop the convoy—we've got Highway Patrol blocking the road!"

Some twenty-five Mississippi State Highway Patrolmen were blocking the highway with six patrol cars. They were under orders by Governor Barnett not to let any outsiders into the state. With comic-opera determination, they were grimly interpreting this order to include the U.S. Army.

Major Le Van sped up in a Jeep, jumped out, walked toward the patrolmen, and announced, "Move these cars off the road immediately."

A Highway Patrol commander stepped forward and declared, "We are under orders by the governor of Mississippi not to let any vehicles pass. Turn your convoy around. You are not going through."

Le Van replied, "I am under orders by the president of the United States to proceed to Oxford. Now get out of the way."

The patrolman countered, "I said you are not going through."

Le Van snapped to the rest of the patrolmen, "All of you—clear your asses off the road right now so you don't get hurt. We are the United States Army, and we are going through." The patrolmen didn't budge.

Le Van walked back to the convoy, where his officers had gathered with a team of rifle-wielding troops standing at attention behind them.

"All right, bring up heavy trucks," Le Van ordered. "Break out all the mounted guns, put a man behind each one. Gimme six Jeeps with machine guns. Clear the east lane of the highway a half a mile back."

Le Van then ordered that two of the "deuce-and-a-halfs" be brought up. He ordered the drivers, both privates, out, and replaced them with two of his officers, First Lieutenant Joseph Cooke and Captain George Baldwin. "Now I'm gonna give them a time limit," said Le Van. "When I say go, you open them up and haul ass right through the patrol cars." Le Van then ordered up the communications truck, which had a public-address system.

MPs and trucks raced around and soon the Highway Patrolmen were staring into enough firepower to start a small war—six Jeeps with .30 caliber machine guns and five heavy trucks with .50 caliber guns, flanked by teams of MPs with high-powered rifles. And all the guns were pointed straight at the Highway Patrolmen, across what now was a de facto international frontier.

Le Van climbed up on top of the communications truck, placed himself at the trigger of a .50 caliber machine gun drilled into a 360-degree swivel mount, pointed the gun at the patrolmen, and announced into the microphone, "I represent the president of the United States. You have two minutes to move your asses out of the way, or I'll blow you off the road. Starting now. A minute fifty-nine—fifty-eight. . . ."

For a while, everything was still. The patrolmen stood their ground. Policemen faced policemen across the frontier.

Major Le Van signaled to the drivers to fire up their engines.

He announced the final countdown: "Five . . . four . . . three . . . two . . ." Le Van called over to the trucks: "Go!"

As their trucks flew toward the Mississippi lawmen, MPs Baldwin and Cooke were pushing sixty miles an hour. The patrolmen jumped in their squad cars and gunned their cars off the road as the U.S. Army charged into Mississippi.

The convoy finally approached Oxford before 4:00 A.M. At the Oxford city line, the convoy was greeted by yet another Mississippi Highway Patrol roadblock. Major Le Van demanded that the patrolmen move the cars that were parked across the road.

The patrolmen, standing on the side of the road, threw Le Van the finger. One muttered, "Goddamn Yankees." So Major Le Van called up one of the deuce-and-a-halfs and ordered it to push the police cruisers out of the way, telling his troops, "Crash it and keep going. If they fire, you fire back." The truck pushed the patrol cars aside, and the convoy proceeded into the city of Oxford.

The sight of federal troops, especially black troops, enraged the rioters milling in thick pockets around Oxford. "He'll be with your sister," they jeered at the white GIs, referring to the African-American troops.

The convoy now drove straight into a guerrilla trap. Rioters had moved the road signs to Ole Miss so that they pointed the wrong way. The convoy unwittingly skirted past the northern entrances of the campus and neared a narrow underpass beneath an Illinois Central Railroad trestle bridge. It was a perfect ambush spot, and the area was swarming with hidden rioters, who opened fire on the convoy with hand-thrown missiles.

Specialist Fourth Class Bill Mayes's Jeep was one of the first to go under the bridge. The rioters pushed the rear axle and the differential of an automobile off the bridge onto his vehicle. It slammed right down on his front hood, and the Jeep veered off of the road into a ditch. Seeing that Mayes was black, the rioters on the overpass bombarded him with rocks and bottles. Mayes and several other MPs dashed up to the overpass, chased the rioters off, and secured the bridge.

Now the convoy headed in the wrong direction toward the center of town where rioters were waiting, taking cover on second-floor windows and on top of buildings.

One of the MPs in the convoy, a Virginia-born specialist fourth class named William Parris, had grown up reading the stories of William Faulkner. As his Jeep slowly passed around the town square, he was startled to find himself looking up at the fabled courthouse, the allegorical heart of Faulkner's fictional Yoknapatawpha County. In *Requiem for a Nun*, Faulkner wrote, "But above all, the courthouse: the center, the focus, the hub; sitting looming in the center of the county's circumference like a single cloud in its ring of horizon. . . ." In the midst of the immense military show of force, William Parris thought, "I wonder what Faulkner would think of this."

As the caravan snaked around William Faulkner's beloved Courthouse Square, rioters on second-floor porches began tossing bucketfuls of human excrement onto the heads of the American soldiers. The trapped MPs were bombarded with falling trash, garbage cans, and the contents of chamber pots. They ducked and dodged the debris as it rained into their vehicles. The rioters, sensing correctly that the MPs were under orders not to shoot if they could avoid it, intensified their attack and surged toward the convoy, which had by now lurched to a stop. Seeing the rioters closing in, Major Le Van called out the order, "Load shotguns!"

The order bounced down the convoy. Soon the crowd froze at the sight of a long line of towering MPs in battle dress rising up in their open Jeeps, slapping rounds in their riot shotguns and jacking the rounds into the chambers. The noise of the loading shotguns ricocheted off the courthouse and the storefronts and filled the Oxford town square with a cacophony of impending bloodshed. "That was the awfulest sound I ever heard," B Company's Captain Bill Peters remembered. The crowd pulled back.

No sooner had the convoy started moving again than the MPs were intercepted by Mississippi Highway Patrol cars and deputy sheriffs who zoomed in to block and split up the caravan. The MPs repeatedly had to push Highway Patrolmen and various state sheriffs and deputies off the road with their trucks and sometimes their bare hands as they moved through Oxford.

When the MPs physically restrained Highway Patrolmen, the crowds of rioters were enraged, especially when black troops were involved. "Believe it or not," remembered black Specialist Fourth Class David Wharry, "we'd clear people away from the vehicle, and as we pulled away, they'd try to run up to the vehicle with bats, sticks, pieces of iron or steel and try to *behead* us. It's a good thing we had steel pots [helmets] on. There were sneak attacks while we were pulling away. It took us awhile to get to campus because every time we pulled away we'd get attacked."

An unidentified Oxford policeman appeared and led the MPs to the National Guard Armory. From there, Major Le Van established radio contact with Lieutenant Colonel Flanagan at the Lyceum at 4:00 A.M., and ordered First Lieutenant Joseph Cooke to reconnoiter the route to the university a mile away. Cooke grabbed the biggest MPs he could find as "volunteers" and raced off.

"The whole area was saturated with gas," Cooke remembered. As his Jeep neared the campus, rioters fired five-inch railroad spikes at the vehicle, using slingshots made by stretching bicycle inner tubes between trees. By the time the Jeep reached the Lyceum and sped back to rejoin the convoy, all its lights and all four tires were shot out, the windshield was shattered, and the radiator was punctured by bullets.

In a Jeep at the back of the convoy was James W. Kennedy, an Alabama-born first sergeant in B Company. The forty-year-old Kennedy was a career army man and a combat veteran of World War II and the Korean War. Off in the distance he could see some commotion happening at an intersection, so he ordered his driver to peel out of the convoy to investigate. It was still dark.

A black lady of about fifty was crouched down in a fetal position in the middle of the intersection. A gang of some twenty half-drunk white men was hiding in the dark and bombarding her with rocks and whiskey and beer bottles. She couldn't tell where the ambush was coming from, Kennedy later reported, so "she squatted down and was just hunkered down in the street."

"I told my driver to get between them and the lady," Kennedy recalled. "Beer bottles were busted all over the street. A bunch of drunks can't hit their butt with both hands." The lady explained to the MPs, "I'm trying to get to work."

Now that they were blocked from their target by the U.S. Army, one of the mob members mumbled something about throwing a rock at Sergeant Kennedy. Kennedy laid his hand down on his .45 pistol and announced, "You'd better change your mind, buddy. All of you'd better get out of here. Hit the street running now, or I'm going to knock a hole through you big enough to run a horse through."

Sergeant Kennedy concluded, "I'm going to count to ten, and I don't want to see nobody on this corner. If you don't start running, I'm going to start shooting." Kennedy supposed they took him at his word, he said, because "by the time I got to three, the intersection was cleared."

Sergeant Kennedy was amazed to see two Mississippi Highway Patrolmen on the corner leaned against their squad car, doing nothing. "They hadn't offered to help this woman at all," Kennedy reported. He recalled telling the two officers, "You're a pair of sons of bitches, and I oughta shoot you just on general principles."

The black woman decided to retreat back to the safety of her home, so the MPs kept watch over her until she was safely inside the house. Sergeant Kennedy and his driver then peeled off for the university to catch up with the convoy.

At 4:45 A.M., the sovereign state of Mississippi exercised its final dying vestige of states' rights, in the form of an announcement by a state Highway Patrolman in front of his squad car, facing down the incoming 503d Military Police Battalion convoy at the entrance to the university.

The state trooper placed his hand on his holster and announced, "I'm under orders by the governor of the state of Mississippi not to let anyone on campus." Major Ray Le Van replied, "I'm under orders by the president of the United States to proceed. Now stand aside!"

The convoy charged onto the campus, and another Highway Patrolman remarked to an MP in a passing Jeep, "Welcome to Ole Miss, motherfucker." The MP cheerfully retorted, "You keep your mother off the street, and everything will be OK!"

Sunlight was starting to break across the sky, and other army units were closing fast on the university. More than four hundred troops of the 716th Military Police Battalion from Fort Dix, New Jersey, had followed the 503d's convoy down from Memphis, and they were now approaching the campus, preparing to storm the grounds on foot with gas masks and unsheathed bayonets, a fearsome show of strength.

From the east, marching columns of the Mississippi National Guard's "Dixie Division," the 155th Infantry, were advancing along University Avenue. Their mission was to secure the school power plant.

The 503d MP caravan barreled up to the Lyceum, lined up all the way around the Circle and finally stopped. It was a ghostly, desolate scene. The heart of the campus seemed almost empty, as most of the other federal forces were completing their sweeps toward the edges of the campus. Smoldering cars littering the Circle were wailing unearthly death cries as their horns burned up. Civilian POWs, hands clasping their heads, were being moved across campus at rifle-point by GIs.

More than four hundred MPs in the 503d's convoy had been struck with flying objects or debris. Of the 161 vehicles in the caravan, 128 windshields were shattered, and 635 headlights were knocked out. Miraculously, though, none of the MPs were seriously injured.

Captain Bill Peters spotted a group of Ole Miss students approaching him with a Confederate battle flag. Peters, who was born in Albany, Georgia, and graduated from West Point, had two grandfathers who served in the Confederate army. To Peters, the Confederate flag was a symbol of respect for his ancestors, not a sign of anarchy and disorder. He ordered his MPs to take the flag away from the students. "Under those circumstances," Peters remembered, "Southern boys didn't mind taking those flags away. I didn't think the rioters were using the Confederate flag in a way Robert E. Lee would approve of. They would not have made Robert E. Lee proud."

Sergeant James Kennedy and his driver were negotiating down a hill inside the campus, still keyed up from the encounter with the drunks downtown. On top of which, Kennedy explained, on the way into campus, "I had just run a bunch of peckerheads out of a billet and taken a shotgun away from a guy." Now, a group of twenty-five civilians was charging toward his Jeep. "Uh-oh," he thought, "it's time to fight."

Then Kennedy noticed women and little children in the group running toward them, and he had to stop the Jeep, as it was surrounded by the crowd. The MPs were in the faculty housing area, and the civilians were university instructors and their families.

The civilians were jumping for joy at the sight of the gas-masked MPs, and their hands were reaching into the Jeep to hug the soldiers. "They just surrounded us," Kennedy remembered. "Women started hugging us; some old men were shaking our hand and patting our back, saying how really, really glad they were to see us. They ran out with coffee and cookies. They were frightened to death. Some of those women were standing there shaking like somebody with a palsy." The MPs told the civilians they were safe now; they would be protected.

In front of the Lyceum building, university chaplain Rev. Wofford Smith looked out at the flagpole and noticed that a banner hoisted by rioters as the battle began the night before was still flying. He went up to the flagpole and pulled down the Confederate flag.

On the now-secure, quiet Lyceum steps at 5:00 A.M., two exhausted federal officials sat down and chatted. "What'll we do in the morning?" asked Justice Department press spokesman Ed Guthman.

"Why," replied Deputy Attorney General Nicholas Katzenbach matter-of-factly, "We're going to register Mr. Meredith at eight o'clock."

The federal government had finally reestablished its sovereignty over the disputed territory of the University of Mississippi, and symbolically over the entire state.

But the insurrection was still not yet crushed. In its waning hours it was flickering in agony, and it soon flared up in broad daylight not far away.

CHAPTER FIFTEEN

After the Dawn

▦　▦　▦　▦

The wall is rent, the ruins yawn;
And, with to-morrow's earliest dawn,
O'er the disjointed mass shall vault
The foremost of the fierce assault.

—Lord Byron, "The Siege of Corinth"

THE GRAY LIGHT OF DAWN spread over Oxford.

As the sun rose, army troops were flushing insurgents out of bushes at bayonet point, and rioters were withdrawing from the campus en masse, drifting east into the city of Oxford.

Incredibly, the University of Mississippi was still standing. In fact, the actual physical damage to the school was so light that university and federal officials agreed to keep the school open, in hopes of a quick return to normality.

At 6:30 A.M., James Meredith woke up in his dormitory suite at Baxter Hall to the smell of tear gas and the sight of dozens of federal marshals and other officials swarming outside his door. Though he had been awakened by gunfire and commotion a few times, he had managed to sleep through much of the night. Meredith dressed in his businesslike gray suit and red tie and grabbed his beige attaché case. There would be no breakfast for him this morning. No one remembered to buy food for his kitchen.

Meredith looked out his window and saw troops marching across campus. He didn't have a full picture of what had happened until marshals told him about the injuries and fatalities. Meredith felt terrible about the abuse sustained by the marshals, whom he had grown close to in the past weeks.

At 7:55 A.M., James Meredith, with Chief U.S. Marshal James Mc-Shane and Assistant U.S. Attorney General John Doar by his side and flanked by a squad of marshals still wearing battle helmets, drove in a battered Border Patrol car to the Lyceum back door to register as a junior in the College of Liberal Arts as a transfer student.

Meredith strode through a blood-stained hallway choked with exhausted marshals, some sprawled asleep in contorted positions, still wearing their gas masks, others devouring C-rations. Prisoners were being shoved through the corridor with their hands behind their heads. Meredith rubbed his inflamed eyes with a handkerchief, prompting John Doar to chuckle, "Aw, you'll get used to it, like we did last night."

James Meredith looked lean and ice-cool as he stood in the Lyceum hall and patted at the tear gas lingering on his face, waiting for university registrar Robert B. Ellis to open up his office. Propelled by fierce, stubborn determination, James Howard Meredith had launched a one-man revolt against white supremacy, conducted a bruising, sixteen-month legal struggle, forced the federal courts and the president to his side, squared off against the political, legal, and police forces of an entire state, and triggered the greatest constitutional crisis since the Civil War, all to simply honor his rights as an American citizen.

Today, as he entered the Lyceum, James Meredith had the physical force of thousands of American combat troops traveling literally right behind him. And now it all came down to this moment, this small particle of time, filling out some routine forms in the spotlight of history.

Meredith was standing not far from the Lyceum's front door, the same door through which Union troops dragged their wounded almost a century earlier during the Union occupation of Oxford, when the Lyceum was used as a hospital. It was the same door that Reverend Clennon King knocked on and walked through in 1958 to try to register for classes, only to be seized by police and packed off to an insane asylum. And it was the door through which federal marshals dragged their injured brothers the night before.

When Registrar Ellis opened the door to his neat blue office, Meredith entered and sat down in front of Ellis's desk to face the bespectacled school official, who appeared stiff and, like most everybody else, in a state approaching shock at the historic spectacle unfolding around them. Meredith parked his slender attaché case on the desk, and a gaggle of federal men squeezed into the office: Nicholas Katzenbach, John Doar, Ed Guthman, Jim McShane, Deputy Marshal Cecil Miller and U.S. Border Patrol officer Charles Chamblee. The only Ole Miss representative other than Ellis was Assistant Registrar Freeman Gober.

James Meredith studied the face of Registrar Ellis and decided that on this dismal morning that he was "the only man on the scene with spirit—a spirit of defiance, even of contempt, if not hatred." For his part, Ellis felt no hostility toward James Meredith personally, but he felt, in his words, "shattered" at the scenes of destruction and military might he had just encountered as he drove onto the university grounds. Ellis betrayed no warmth to his newest student as he tried to go through the motions of a routine, though much delayed, registration. "I want to give you a late registration form," said Ellis. Although Meredith had tried to register on time, the university was two epochal weeks late in registering him. Meredith said, "Thank you." Ellis gave Meredith paperwork for his veteran's benefits through the G.I. Bill, and explained that the $230 in tuition charges could be paid in cash or check.

James Meredith filled out the forms and studied his schedule of classes, which featured required courses in Spanish, algebra, and English, and electives in politics and history. A news photographer was allowed in to snap a photo of the event, showing a relaxed Meredith with his forms as Registrar Ellis stood at attention.

The tables of Mississippi history were turning right-side up, and James Meredith was forcing the state government at gunpoint to do what it always should have done: treat him as an American citizen.

A few signatures and suddenly it was over. James Meredith was officially a student at the school he dreamed of attending since he was a boy.

Meredith was exiting through the front door of the Lyceum with his entourage when a proud black cleaning man got his attention by gently touching him with his broom handle. Meredith immediately understood the message. Every last one of the scores of Negro workmen, maids, janitors, and food-service workers on campus was now looking after him and his safety.

In the chaos of the day and night before, federal officials hadn't had time to choreograph Meredith's movements for today, so they decided to surround him with bodyguards and try to walk him through his school day.

Any hopes they might have had of James Meredith being treated remotely like a normal student were dashed as soon as he walked out of the Lyceum. Within moments, Meredith was being taunted by students, as he often would be for the rest of his stay at the university: "Nigger—black nigger!"; "Black bastard!"; "The blood is on your hands!"; "Was it worth two lives, nigger?" As photographers snapped away, various students jeered, "Smile, nigger, smile!"

A small crowd approached dangerously close to Meredith's entourage, and the battle-frazzled marshals popped a few rounds of tear gas to disperse it. Almost everyone on campus was reeling from the lingering gas. Chief Marshal McShane and Justice Department official Doar started wandering around in search of Meredith's first class, followed by a small phalanx of reporters and students, some curious and others hostile. The federal men blundered off on foot in one direction leading Meredith, then stopped.

They were lost. John Doar studied a map of the campus, but couldn't figure how to get to Peabody Hall. They couldn't find Meredith's first class, which had already started at 9:00 A.M.

"I think it's that building over there," said Doar.

"Let's start over," whispered Chief Marshal McShane, "in a car this time."

History professor Dr. Clare L. Marquette was teaching his American colonial history class in a classroom seasoned with eye-stinging tear-gas fumes. His topic today was "The Beginnings of English Colonization."

At 9:14 A.M., he answered a knock on his door. When he opened it, he was greeted by his department chairman, who introduced him to Meredith's federal escorts, flanked by a pair of helmeted marshals with nightsticks and a group of inquisitive students. After pointing out an empty seat to Meredith, Dr. Marquette asked the federal men if they could wait outside during the class. McShane agreed.

At first, no one looked at James Meredith, who went to his seat, his eyes tearing from the gas. A nearby girl was crying, too, but Meredith wasn't sure if it was because of the gas or his presence. A male student furtively said hello to Meredith.

Dr. Marquette shut the door, handed Meredith some paper, and pointed out to Meredith the place where the class had reached in the outline. "I then began the first known legally integrated class in the long history of the University of Mississippi," wrote Marquette. "Meredith never missed a meeting of the class the whole semester and complied to all requirements set up for the course."

As James Meredith absorbed his first lecture, U.S. Marshals peered into the classroom through a glass-pane door window, just as Melba Pattillo's bodyguard from the 101st Airborne had done at Little Rock's Central High School five years earlier.

Across Mississippi, citizens were waking up and reading the horrific news reports of the fighting at Oxford. For some white citizens, the impact of the riot was enough to shock them into entirely new ways of thinking.

In Jackson, a business executive named W. H. "Billy" Mounger woke up early, listened to the news on the radio, and was horrified. As president of the Lamar Life Insurance Company, Mounger was one of the state's top business leaders. He was furious at himself and other businessmen for allowing the disaster to happen.

Mounger sped over to the studios of segregationist WLBT-TV and WJDX radio, burst in unannounced, marched into the broadcast booth and demanded to be put on the air. The stunned technicians had no choice but to comply with Mounger's demand—his company owned both stations.

"As a citizen of Mississippi, I apologize for not having spoken out," Mounger announced on the air to the statewide audience. "We adult leaders have failed our children. We have allowed them to be incited to the point where they themselves have caused violence and resisted the United States of America. . . . We are part of the United States of America, and we must obey the laws of the United States of America."

Within hours, Mounger and a group of 150 leading state businessmen, half of them Citizens Council members, issued a call for law and order in Mississippi.

Early Monday morning, a man slowed down to make a turn at an intersection at Marks, Mississippi, west of Oxford. The man was Dr. J. C. Shirley, a dentist from Sunflower County who was one of the original founding members of the Mississippi Citizens Council. He was listening in horror to the radio reports from Oxford. He was going to try to get his daughter, an Ole Miss student, out of the campus war zone. The dignified Dr. Shirley was a quiet man, hardly a firebrand, not even an activist. Like many white Mississippians, he'd supported the Citizens Council until today, for one good reason—he thought he was doing the right thing.

As he made the turn toward Oxford, Dr. Shirley noticed a group of men having an animated conversation on the side of the road. He recognized them—they were Citizens Council leaders. He decided that on this tragic morning they must be up to no good.

Dr. Shirley pulled over to the side of the road, took his Citizens Council membership card out of his wallet, and tore it up into little pieces. From that moment on, he never had anything to do with the Citizens Council again.

At the same time James Meredith was beginning his walk into history this morning, the Battle of Oxford was flashing to life a few blocks away.

There were almost no television images of the daytime fighting and military invasion of Oxford this morning, and the newsreel and still photos were fleeting and fragmentary. For the soldiers and citizens who experienced what happened next, the reality of it was mind-boggling.

Despite U.S. Army and Mississippi Highway Patrol roadblocks, people were still streaming toward the city: outsiders, states'-rights activists, and self-styled patriotic citizens bearing license plates from Georgia, Texas, Alabama, and Louisiana, even the West Coast. A camper with California plates appeared with six men inside, and they announced they had "come to help Mississippi." "Louisiana is here," read the message on a car parked just off the town square. On the rear window it said: "We drove 400 miles and we ain't quit yet." Some civilian volunteers parked their vehicles, walked around the roadblocks, and marched in on foot.

Three college-age boys announced they were the advance party of a twenty-car caravan from Pascagoula, a Gulf Coast city more than three hundred miles to the south. Hearing General Walker's public plea on the radio for volunteers, they brought tents and skillets. Two thousand students from Mississippi State University at Starkville were rumored to be arriving soon, to join the hundreds of fellow students who were already inside Oxford. A hundred armed men from Jackson were reported to have left for Oxford. A chartered bus from Hattiesburg full of men armed and ready to fight was said to be already inside the city limits. There was no way for federal authorities to know which rumors were true and which were false.

Pockets of rioters were taking up positions at two rebel flashpoints: the Courthouse Square and the intersection of University Avenue and South Lamar Avenue, just south of the Square. Scores of young men and adults milled about, arming themselves with baseball bats, bricks, and bottles, looking for federal troops. Some carried small arms, and a few held rifles at their sides. Confederate flags were planted on utility poles.

At 6:30 A.M., the insurrectionists saw an irresistible target. As rioters streamed away from the campus, they were colliding with dozens of black civilians going the other way, many dutifully reporting this Monday morning to their service jobs at the university, the biggest employer of blacks in the city. The black citizens entered a gauntlet of violence.

Near the courthouse, a car carrying two blacks was bombarded with stones. The car careened into a gas station, where the two men jumped out of their car and ran inside for cover. Several Mississippi Highway Patrolmen looked on impassively and did nothing.

A black motorist stopped for a red light and was trapped. A pack of one hundred youths, some wearing emblazoned Mississippi State University jackets, surrounded his car, shouted curses, and showered his vehicle with bottles and bricks. Then they cut his back right tire. An empty case of Coke bottles was pitched at his windshield. The light turned green, the driver tried to speed away, but a Mississippi Highway Patrol car raced over and cut him off, forcing him to back up and drive through a gas station to escape. The policemen laughed. One shrugged his shoulders at a reporter and said, "We don't have any orders to stop it."

Isaiah Thompson, a black construction worker, slowed his car down at South Lamar and University and heard someone crying, "Look out—run, run, run!" Thompson didn't want to run the red light in view of the police, and he was quickly engulfed inside the pack of rioters. The same voice called, "Take off! Take off!" But it was too late. All but one of Thompson's windows were bashed in with bricks before he could escape.

Even the elderly were at risk. A black lady in her seventies was slowly navigating her car around the turn at the courthouse when a bottle was thrown toward her face. Another elderly black woman walked north on Lamar Avenue, toward the mob congealing on the south side of the courthouse. "Oh, no," thought eyewitness Bill Burk, "they can't hurt her. She's defenseless." Then with the impenetrable illogic of a mob, the crowd of rebels fell silent and did not touch her as she passed through them, her head held high.

Ted Lucas Smith from Batesville, Mississippi, recalled, "I can't wipe from my memory the look of terror in the eyes of the occupants of the cars as the missiles of bricks and concrete slammed into their windshield and side windows." As he watched the rampage, Memphis reporter Bill Burk thought, "I never knew human life could stoop so low." Another man, a gray-haired white Oxford restaurant owner, looked on and wept softly as he said, "These aren't our people. They are outsiders. My people wouldn't do that."

At the town square, bands of young men were parading around the courthouse waving Confederate flags. A boy in a Confederate uniform was directing traffic into the gauntlet of assaults. If they were white Southerners, he grandly took off his hat and bowed to them. If they were blacks or had Northern license plates, he waved them into a brick-and-bottle attack.

The mayor of Oxford, Richard Elliott, arrived on the Square and beseeched a Mississippi Highway Patrolman to stop the mayhem, but the lawman replied, "We have orders not to interfere." Another Highway Patrolman was leaning against his car, laughing at the scene, and when one rioter's bottle hit its target, he called out, "You really hit that one a good lick!"

Mayor Elliott reported, "There were a number of Highway Patrolmen standing there, just watching" the attacks. Then a group of hoodlums rushed past Mayor Elliott, carrying highway flares and Molotov cocktails, saying, "Hey, let's go burn the nigger churches!" Elliott realized in horror that they were running in the direction of Oxford's black neighborhood Freedman's Town, located just northeast of the university.

Mayor Elliott frantically called federal officials at the Lyceum to plead for troops to defend the churches, then rushed to the Oxford radio station to order all the stores in town to close down and warn civilians to stay home. Captain Murry "Chooky" Falkner collected a squad of his National Guardsmen from Oxford's Troop E and raced them over to Freedman's Town, and just as a band of rioters was scampering around one of the black churches preparing to start a fire, Falkner and his men chased them off.

Three blocks south of the Square at the corner of Lamar and University, rioters were ambushing passing National Guard military vehicles running the gauntlet between the National Guard Armory to the university. Mob leaders stationed lookouts toward the campus. They'd call down, "Here comes a Jeep!" The soldiers would pass, and the rioters would fall upon the vehicle. One rioter threw a double-bladed ax at the driver of a National Guard truck, scoring a direct hit on the center post of the windshield.

After passing through the gauntlet, a stunned Mississippi National Guardsman said, "These are our own people. They came at us with a big tractor chain. I don't understand it. I'm one of them. And they did this to us."

At 7:00 A.M., beside Highway 7 on the outskirts of Oxford, Second Lieutenant Charles Shockley was holding a tiny steel contraption in one hand and a can of Army C-Rations in the other.

Lieutenant Shockley and his one thousand fellow infantrymen of the Second Infantry Division's Second Battle Group, Twenty-third Infantry Regiment, who comprised Task Force Bravo of the Mississippi peacekeeping plan, were parked on the side of the road at the end of an eighteen-hour convoy from their base at Fort Benning, Georgia. They were originally supposed to rally at the Memphis naval air station, but as the riot exploded through the night their hundred-vehicle convoy was diverted directly to Oxford.

Shockley was bewildered. This was his first command as an officer and his first meal in the field, and he couldn't figure out how to open up his breakfast. The tall African-American officer was a former schoolteacher, a brand-new ROTC graduate, a former head of the NAACP chapter at all-black Virginia State College, but he had no clue how to work the little gizmo, called a P-38, into the can so he could liberate his chow.

Trying to hide his dilemma from his fellow officers, Shockley took the tiny device and discreetly tapped it, banged it, and scratched it on the can, to no avail. Finally he broke down and asked his first sergeant,

"How do you open this damn thing?" Chuckling, the sergeant took pity on him and showed him how.

Even this far out of town, the air was heavy with the sweet, sticky odor of tear gas spreading out from the university. The scene looked to Shockley like a strange circus procession: A solid wall of civilian cars was lined up on the side of the road, sporting Confederate flags, some decorated in housepaint with the slogan: "Alabama Volunteers." The civilians were being blocked from entering Oxford by a Mississippi Highway Patrol roadblock.

During a rest stop earlier in the morning, Shockley and his fellow officers had huddled up over aerial photos of the Oxford area as their troops donned bulletproof flak jackets. As a contingency, the army had been drilling the battle group in riot-control training for two weeks, in case the Mississippi crisis blew up. Now that it had, their training was about to be tested in action. The orders for B Company's three rifle platoons were to take the town square and seal it off.

At the same rest stop, a group of infantrymen had a candid, friendly exchange of opinions on the Meredith case over coffee. Their views seemed split down the middle. One side wondered, as a white soldier asked, "Why is he causing all this trouble? Why is he doing this? He has his own schools. This is unnecessary and uncalled for." The other half, which included all the black soldiers, agreed with Lieutenant Shockley, who argued, "He's an American citizen, he's a veteran, he's academically qualified. He should be allowed to attend."

At 8:00 A.M., Lt. Charles Shockley marched his thirty-six-man rifle platoon of B Company onto the town square of Oxford and secured one of the four corners, as A and C companies sealed off the other two. This left one corner open, and rioters, who had briefly retreated into the side streets, began flowing back into the Square, with nearly a hundred men taking up position in and around the courthouse building.

Seeing that almost a third of the infantrymen were black, the rioters taunted them with a frenzy of racial insults. The troops gritted their teeth and remained at parade rest. Lieutenant Shockley knew that his black troops had heard these epithets before, as civilians living in the South. He was more concerned at the shock that was registering on his white soldiers as civilians screamed that they were "nigger lovers." "They had not heard such language hurled at them before," Shockley explained. "It seemed the crowd focused particularly on the white soldiers as if they were traitors. We all had helmets to protect our heads and bulletproof vests to protect our bodies, but we had nothing to ward off the ugly words."

Now the rioters started firing bottles at Lieutenant Shockley and the men of the Second Infantry, sometimes at point-blank range. "They would look you right in the eye, rear back, and throw a bottle as hard as they could at your face," remembered Shockley. "I could see the veins in the neck and temples of some of these people. They had not only anger, but fear—fear of losing a system they'd enjoyed for all of their lives."

As a highly visible black officer, Lieutenant Shockley was taking an extra beating from the insurrectionists. As the bottles sailed toward his head, Shockley recalled, "I would grab my helmet on both sides and just bend into them, they would ricochet off the helmet and deflect into the plate-glass windows." "Within minutes hundreds of missiles were hurled at the soldiers," wrote eyewitness Jack Thompson, a reporter from Providence, Rhode Island. "Bottles bounced off their helmets, their arms and bodies. Although they flinched when they were hit, they did not advance."

Now the rioters expanded their field of fire to include columns of new army vehicles passing through the Square. "Almost every jeep and truck ran a gauntlet of bricks and bottles," Thompson reported. "Hardly a truck escaped without at least one smashed windshield. The soldiers—many of them in open vehicles—covered their heads with their arms. Wild throws sailed over the trucks and smashed against windows of stores and parked cars."

Eyewitnesses marveled at the gallantry and restraint of the black soldiers trapped by the mob. "The dignity of the Negro soldiers has been little short of inspiring," noted Scripps-Howard reporter Richard Starnes. "I never saw any men subject to such vile, obscene, sickening abuse." The troops, reported Starnes, were absorbing a shower of missiles "as if it had been nothing more than a gentle spring rain."

The attacks ebbed and flowed for an hour, then two, and civilian onlookers were dumbfounded at the restraint of the besieged soldiers. One girl wondered aloud, "When are they going to shoot back?"

On the town square, finally, after what reporter Richard Starnes described as "a magnificent display of poise in the face of repeated provocation," the infantrymen, now joined by an advance platoon of military policemen from the 716th Military Police Battalion from Fort

Dix, New Jersey, took the offensive. The GIs shuffled and stomped along the sidewalks, trying to clear the civilians from the square, but the rioters laughed and melted into stores and doorways when the troops passed. The soldiers had bayonets locked on the front of their rifles, but they were still sheathed to prevent an accidental stabbing.

After deserting the battle for the previous six hours, former general Edwin Walker reappeared in the midst of the smoldering insurrection, having slept off the last few hours at his Oxford hotel room. Wearing his fawn-colored Stetson, Walker took command of a sidewalk overlooking the square and yelled encouragement to the rioters: "Good going, boys!" They responded with hoorays for the celebrity general.

A squad of infantrymen approached Walker and flushed him out of his little command post at bayonet point. Walker wandered across the Square, flanked by a crowd of one hundred civilian admirers and onlookers. "Walker walked right through our line," Lieutenant Shockley remembered. "The crowd cheered him like a baseball hero after the home run that won the game, patting him on the back. They followed him out of the square like the Pied Piper."

A thirty-eight-year-old man from the Delta town of Clarksdale, Mississippi, stood on the sidewalk watching the infantrymen standing stoically as they withstood the attack. He was practically bursting with pride. Charles M. Bolen was a U.S. Army major and the operations officer of the Second Infantry's Second Battle Group, Twenty-third Infantry Regiment. These white and black soldiers standing shoulder to shoulder with bottles crashing into them were his own troops. For the last three weeks he had supervised their crash program of riot training.

Right now Major Bolen was the senior U.S. military officer on Oxford's Courthouse Square. He knew the town well. He briefly attended Ole Miss himself, entering the school in the fall semester of 1941 in hopes of getting a degree in education. But in a few months came Pearl Harbor, and Bolen became an army combat officer instead, fighting his way across Europe. Today, on the gray Monday morning of October 1, 1962, as Major Bolen watched civilians assaulting his men, he thought, "By God, these aren't Nazi soldiers, and these aren't Japanese soldiers. These are American people."

A call came in on Major Bolen's field radio.

It was from Infantry Lieutenant Robert Clark, who was supervis-

ing the army roadblock several blocks south of the Square on Highway
7. A line of cars was slowly passing through the military checkpoint as
the troops searched for armed rioters, and one of the GIs had spotted
former general Edwin Walker in an approaching sedan. Minutes earlier, Walker had openly walked through the Second Infantry's lines on
Courthouse Square because the troops had no specific orders or authority to stop him. The Justice Department was still trying to figure
out the legalities and logistics of capturing Walker. Now it looked like
the general was about to escape from Oxford.

"General Walker is about three cars back," Lieutenant Clark radioed to Major Bolen, "heading south, going down towards Water Valley on Highway Seven."

"Let me get on the horn right quick," replied Bolen, who then
called his superior and Task Force Bravo commander Colonel Lucien
Fairfax Keller, who was huddling up with General Billingslea at the
Lyceum.

"Sir," said Bolen, "it looks like we got General Walker trying to
head out of town."

"Oh, hell," said Keller.

The army officers now faced a very tricky dilemma. For the last
fourteen hours, civilian law enforcement in the area had completely
broken down. The Mississippi Highway Patrol had withdrawn from
the riot, refused to arrest a single one of the scores of civilians committing crimes of assault before their eyes, and, apart from manning
roadblocks, had taken no action. The tiny Oxford police force could
not handle a calamity of this scale. The U.S. Marshals were recovering
from their night of hell at the Lyceum, and U.S. Army troops were
providing the only semblance of law and order.

But the Posse Comitatus Act passed by Congress in 1878 forbade
U.S. military personnel from enforcing civilian criminal law on American soil. In the absence of a declaration of martial law, which federal
authorities had considered but so far avoided in Mississippi, troops
could not arrest civilians or serve warrants. However, the act exempted
any actions authorized by the Constitution or by statute, and President Kennedy had invoked a part of the U.S. Code (Chapter 15 of Title 10, Section 332) that expressly authorized him to use both state
militias and federal armed forces to enforce federal laws and suppress
rebellions.

Despite this loophole, federal authorities did not want to inflame the civilian population by testing these conflicting principles in the field and having soldiers perform civilian police duties. As a result, the standing instruction for the U.S. Army forces in Mississippi was to temporarily "detain" any troublemakers prior to being handed off to U.S. Marshals to be formally arrested.

With General Walker nearing the checkpoint, the soldiers weren't sure if they had authority to detain him, since they still didn't know if the U.S. Marshals had a warrant for his arrest.

The order was radioed to Major Bolen from his superiors: "Delay him." The brass had to stall for time as they awaited clear instructions from the Justice Department.

Then Major Bolen had a brainstorm. As far as he knew, there weren't any laws against either slowing down a checkpoint or against a soldier politely requesting a civilian to accompany him.

Bolen radioed Lieutenant Clark at the checkpoint and ordered, "Delay him."

"Sir?"

Bolen explained, "Take more time to investigate the cars in front of him. Go up to Walker and ask him very politely if he would accompany you to the Lyceum building. If he doesn't want to go, just do what you think you might be able to do to talk him into it without causing any problems.

"The checkpoint slowed down by fifteen or twenty minutes," Major Bolen recalled in 2000. When the car containing Walker and a few cronies came up, Bolen said, "The young Lieutenant was just as nice and courteous as could be."

Walker, looking a bit surprised, responded to the officer's invitation by saying, "I'll be glad to."

Lieutenant Clark climbed into a Jeep and led Walker's car to the Lyceum. Using a warrant that was finally drawn up by the Justice Department, Walker was placed under arrest by U.S. Marshals at 11:30 A.M.

At the White House, President Kennedy thought things in Mississippi were getting quiet when he went to bed at 5:30 A.M., Washington, D.C., time, Monday morning. But when he awoke a few hours later, reports were coming in of continued fighting in Oxford, so he resumed managing the crisis by remote control. Once again he called his nemesis and erstwhile negotiating partner Governor Ross Barnett.

When Barnett answered the call, he appeared to be worried about one thing above all else: that JFK might reveal their secret negotiations to the world. If Barnett's segregationist supporters found out about this, his political career could be ruined. Barnett began by asking the president not to "let the public know we talked so many times."

The president was in no mood. He ignored Barnett's plea and commanded, "Now, I want your help in getting these state police to continue to help during the day, because they're their own people. And we're going to have a lot of strange troops in there; we're going to have paratroopers in and all the rest. And I think that the state police should be the key. And that depends on you."

Barnett demurred: "Well, you'll have the whole force that we have, but our men are not equipped like yours."

"I understand that," insisted the president, "but during the daytime they can help keep order on these roads and keep a lot of people from coming in. And that doesn't change your position on the issue but at least it helps maintain order, which is what we've got to do today."

"All right, Mr. President," Barnett stated cordially, without clearly agreeing to the president's proposal. "I'll stay here now."

"Thank you, Governor, thank you very much," the president said, reminding the governor to "keep after your state police now."

As he hung up the phone, John Kennedy had no way of knowing how this crisis might end. Civilians were attacking U.S. soldiers in the street; outsiders were still moving in; and the fighting could intensify to a bloody climax of unknown proportions. Fearing the worst might happen, the president telephoned Archibald Cox, the solicitor general of the United States, and asked him to map out the legalities of arresting the governor of Mississippi.

Next, JFK called Secretary of the Army Cyrus Vance to check the invasion timetable. "I understood they're having some rioting downtown," Kennedy said, "throwing rocks at the troops—now how are we doing on our schedule?" Vance said, "Our schedule is still proceeding as I gave it to you." The president asked, "I talked to Secretary McNamara; he said you may be able to have 20,000 troops by midnight?"

The Secretary of the Army replied, "That's right, we're taking steps to get them in; the orders have been given. The only limiting factor is the weather, which is closing in, but we're developing alternates, so we can get them in one way or the other. Just a second. Bob is here."

Secretary of Defense Robert Strange McNamara came on the line, his voice as always barking with blowtorch self-confidence: "Mr. President, I think that with the priority the Air Force is giving this, and diverting all our mass aircraft and our troop-carrying aircraft, we can get them there by midnight."

Through the morning, the president continued his frenetic hands-on micromanagement of the crisis. A presidential order was flashed to the temporary mobile army control tower at the Oxford airport to deny landing clearance to any aircraft carrying Governor Ross Barnett. Army troops were rushed to reinforce the airport and to secure a small Champion Oil Company airfield eight miles south of Oxford. Their orders were to physically seize Barnett if he landed.

When a private plane began circling the Oxford airport, a federal marshal told Mississippi National Guard Major William Callicott, "We think the governor's on the plane. When the plane lands, we want you to take your troops, surround the plane, and put him under arrest."

"Mister," replied Callicott, "I don't know where you live. But I live forty miles up the road. I'm in the legislature and the governor's my boss. I don't think he's fool enough to come, and I'm sure not fool enough to arrest him. I'm not going to do it."

After a moment's pause, the marshal said, "I withdraw the request." Then Callicott said, "Good, 'cause I wasn't going to honor it." He was right—Barnett stayed away from Oxford.

The tiny Oxford airport had no permanent tower, no taxiways, and only a five-thousand-foot landing strip. But on this day it became the nation's busiest airport, handling even more air traffic, in the form of a multitude of U.S. Air Force transports, Army aircraft, and U.S. Marine Corps helicopters, than the previous record holder, Chicago's O'Hare Airport. No more than four aircraft at a time could land, and each incoming craft had to unload and take off immediately.

The president of the United States had pushed the button, and the military escalation of the invasion of Mississippi was exploding to troop levels that approached unreality. John Kennedy may have waited too long to send troops in, but today it looked like he was not going to stop pouring troops into Mississippi until the last molecule of the insurrection was obliterated.

A staggering number of army troops was cascading toward Oxford. All five task forces in the initial invasion plan had been activated. Task Force Echo, built around the 720th Military Police Battalion from Fort Hood, Texas, dropped two hundred fresh MPs into Oxford by helicopter, and they were in action as of 9:25 A.M., Monday morning. Three hundred more 720th MPs were speeding down by convoy from Memphis, due in that afternoon.

The First Battle Group of the National Guard's 155th Infantry was being rushed to the west of Oxford to blockade the junction of Highways 6 and 315 when a large number of armed civilians was reported to be moving in from the direction of Batesville. Thousands of incoming GIs were creating immense bottlenecks on the little country roads of the state. When it approached Oxford early this morning, Task Force Bravo's convoy alone stretched well over one hundred miles.

Almost ten thousand regular army troops and federalized National Guardsmen were in Oxford or the immediate vicinity by midday. Thousands more were coming in right behind them. Many years later, Johnny Arnold, a company commander at 108th Cavalry's Headquarters, said he thought that President Kennedy "must have seen a complete revolution coming; he must have been scared to death." Arnold, who landed on Utah Beach on D-Day-plus-one with the Army Signal Corps and was strafed by German machine gunners, looked back on October 1, 1962, and marveled, "We had enough men to capture the whole South."

The immense display of strength was being made not just to meet a potential worst-case military threat, but as a deterrent to scare off any more civilians and radical segregationists from moving on Oxford.

As a dramatic psychological coup de grâce, the president had even approved an incredible new deployment this morning. He was dispatching combat teams of paratroopers of the army's elite 82nd and 101st Airborne Divisions, the premiere attack forces of the army. The paratroopers were a highly mobile, elite shock force designed to be dropped in behind enemy lines and strike with lightning speed, using their own infantry. Airborne paratroopers were among the heroes of D-Day, the Battles of the Bulge and Bastogne, and had helped liberate

Normandy, Holland, Belgium, Sicily, Italy, and North Africa. Today the paratroopers of the 82nd Airborne and 101st Airborne were being ordered to restore order to Oxford.

Even with this fantastic degree of firepower, the president was still worried. Defense Secretary McNamara was already scrambling one hundred extra army helicopters this morning for emergency troop airlifts to Oxford, but Kennedy feared that even twenty thousand army troops might not be enough.

The president now wanted to know how fast the U.S. Marine Corps could be dropped into northern Mississippi. The marines did some emergency calculations and reported back to the White House. According to the Department of Defense's internal history of the incident, the marines reported: "One battalion (about 1,250 men) at Camp Lejeune [North Carolina] could depart on 12 hours' notice, plus the additional hour and a half required to reach Cherry Point [Virginia] where they could board their aircraft. Another battalion could leave Camp Pendleton [California] on 24 hours' notice, and the remainder of the Division/Wing Team located on either coast would be available for subsequent movement on short notice."

A Marine Division/Wing Team was an immense strike force capable of quickly conquering a medium-size country. In 1962 the U.S. Marines had three such units, composed of about forty thousand men and three hundred combat aircraft each. Each Division/Wing Team boasted a galaxy of ground and aerial weapons and equipment, with a strong emphasis on helicopter-delivered infantry and "vertical assault" operations.

With the stratospheric levels of force the president was contemplating, he seemed to be trapped in some kind of waking nightmare.

At 10:00 A.M. in Oxford, the rebellion was making its last stand, as some one hundred die-hard rioters in roving bands prowled the Courthouse Square, the intersection of South Lamar and University Avenue and the side streets and back alleys in-between, attacking military and civilian vehicles.

In a pincer movement planned by Colonel Martin, commander of the 108th Armored Cavalry, two forty-man formations of Mississippi National Guardsmen moved up to the intersection of South Lamar and University Avenue from two directions. As the first task force, which included men from Oxford's Troop E, dismounted its vehicles, the mob charged and fired bottles, bricks, spikes, and iron pipes at the troops so intensely that for a moment it looked like the soldiers would be overwhelmed. The Guardsmen stood fast, fired warning shots of live ammunition over the mob, and the rioters scattered into side streets and back alleys.

The second task force, commanded by Ole Miss alumnus Captain William Austin of the Third Squadron at Senatobia, advanced north up Lamar Avenue. Austin was proud to be taking part in this operation, and years later he explained, "I did not want to see my university burned down by a bunch of outsiders."

One of the Guardsmen spotted a formation of rioters running in the alley behind Blaylock's Drugstore, and shouted, "There they go!"

"Shoot over their heads!" ordered Captain Austin. At 10:15 A.M., the Guardsmen entered the alley, firing fifteen rounds over the heads of the trapped band of rioters, running and shooting at the same time.

"They were all hunters and excellent marksmen," reported Austin. "One old boy just cut loose with his carbine and clipped off some of the wood on the Mansion Restaurant roof. It was sort of like Road Runner and Coyote. You could almost see sparks coming out from under their heels. We took twenty-five to thirty POWs. It was like we'd hit the mother lode. We loaded the truck with prisoners and put a line of POWs behind the truck. We surrounded them in a walking semicircle and took them back to the Armory. None of them were from Mississippi."

On Courthouse Square, Lieutenant Chuck Shockley and the Second Infantry troops methodically donned their gas masks and pitched gas grenades toward the remaining rioters. The troops swept briskly around the courthouse in a V-shaped riot wedge formation, holding their rifles at high port.

Women were staggering out of stores, choking from tear gas as convoy loads of troops kept swarming through the square and ten military helicopters hovered overhead, sweeping the city and the surrounding countryside.

The infantrymen swept away the last remnants of the riot and lined up around the courthouse, bayonets pointed skyward. Their ammo was close by, but they had never loaded their guns. Towering above them was the statue of a Confederate soldier gripping his rifle, guarding the center of town.

Carloads of rioters were scattering and fleeing the town, in the words of one black Oxford resident, "like rabbits." The heart of Oxford was recaptured. All was quiet. The insurrection was crushed.

"My God," one local merchant exclaimed to Major Charles Bolen and his young GIs, "you guys have saved the town."

The curtains of drizzle fell away, and a brilliant sun broke over the city.

CHAPTER SIXTEEN

The New Age

▪ ▪ ▪ ▪

These people can be decent.

—Moses Meredith

A YOUNG MAN QUIETLY PACED around the Circle in front of the Lyceum building.

It was Charlie Berryhill, who returned in mourning to the place where his best friend Ray Gunter was killed the night before. All around him were scores of dead birds and squirrels littering the Circle, victims of the intense tear-gas barrages. The charred hulks of six incinerated vehicles were scattered around the park. "God, I can't believe this," Charlie Berryhill thought.

Not far away, a wreath of red, white, and blue wildflowers lay on the spot where the slain Paul Guihard was found.

As the sun burned over the university, vapors of tear gas rose up and choked students, marshals, and newsmen. The gas blended with the burning-paint fumes coming from a still-smoldering automobile.

U.S. Deputy Marshals were sprawled on patches of grass in total exhaustion. They looked like scattered toy soldiers. "Hell, this was close," said one. "We almost lost by minutes."

One marshal from Alabama, whose helmet was creased by a .22 bullet, declared, "There's nothing I hate more than seeing that nigger going to school here. But that was my job." A deputy from Georgia said, "There wasn't a man among us who had any stomach for what he was doing Sunday night. It made us sick. But, damn it, we're officers."

A riot edition of the campus newspaper *The Mississippian* was already being circulated. In the editorial, editor Sidna Brower blamed both students and outsiders for the violence: "When students hurled rocks, bottles and eggs, the federal marshals were forced to resort to tear gas to back off the crowds. When outsiders show their objections in the form of violence, they are seriously injuring the students in their attempt to continue their education. As a student, I beg you to return to your home. This is a battle between the State of Mississippi and the United States government; the University is caught in the middle."

In Jackson, Governor Barnett ordered all state flags flown at half-mast to mourn the invasion of his state. He then made a broadcast plea for peace: "We must have no violence. Law and order must prevail." He asked outsiders to leave, and asked Mississippians to stay home.

In Washington, Robert Kennedy was back on duty in his gigantic Justice Department office early this morning. "I think last night was the worst night I ever spent," he said to one reporter.

Oxford, Mississippi, endured its first day as an occupied American city. Within forty-eight hours, there would be twice as many soldiers in the immediate vicinity of Oxford—nearly fifteen thousand—as there were civilians, a superiority so overwhelming that it was unnecessary for the federal government to declare martial law.

A grand total of nearly 31,000 federal troops were mobilized in the invasion of northern Mississippi in the first week of October 1962, including 11,000 Mississippi National Guardsmen called into federal service and 20,000 regular army troops. Of the Guardsmen, 2,700 were deployed directly into the Oxford area, including the entire 108th Cavalry Regiment and two battle groups of the 155th Infantry Dixie Division. The remainder of the Mississippi National Guardsmen were held at their hometown armories, including Lieutenant Ross Barnett, Jr., in Jackson.

Of the regular army troops, fully twelve thousand made it into Oxford or the immediate vicinity, including three military police battalions; two infantry battle groups; ten airborne battle groups; various support elements such as signal corps, medical, engineering, quartermaster, and transportation units; and headquarters troops from the

Eighteenth Airborne Corps and the Second Infantry Division. The rest of the regular army troops were held at the two staging points: Millington Naval Air Station at Memphis and the U.S. Air Force base at Columbus, Mississippi.

The total of 31,000 troops mobilized in the Mississippi operation was more soldiers than the United States had in Korea, and the peak troop strength of nearly fifteen thousand in the Oxford vicinity was three times more American troops than were stationed in West Berlin. Within hours of the riot's end, fifty FBI agents were rushed into Oxford to interview witnesses and detainees and investigate the attacks on federal marshals. Twenty army intelligence agents were in position in Oxford by October 4, along with some two hundred Department of Justice personnel.

Almost three hundred journalists were in Oxford by October 1, some coming from as far away as Poland and Japan. The crisis was triggering banner headlines around the planet: in Tokyo, London, Rome, Vienna, Paris, Munich, Denmark, and Sweden. In Mexico City the headline was ONE NEGRO ROCKS UNCLE SAM; in Copenhagen, BRAVO, MEREDITH; and in Portugal: CIVIL WAR LOOMS, KENNEDY USES FORCE. Both Peiping radio and the *Singapore Straits Times* chimed in with editorials, and Soviet newspapers argued that the crisis was the "shame of America" and proved "the depravity of the American way of life."

Never in the twentieth century had an American city suffered such images of military conquest. Machine-gun nests and tripods bristled from the tops of buildings. Cars were stopped and searched at military roadblocks; foxholes sprouted along the roadside at two-hundred-yard intervals; GIs lunged and screamed, "Yaah-huh!" in bayonet drills in parking lots.

As he was being evacuated from Oxford, wounded U.S. Border Patrolman Dan Pursglove saw army machine-gun nests being set up along the roadside, and began to weep.

"My God," he thought, "this is America."

The heavy equipment of war roared into Oxford from all directions. Army medical trucks, communications trucks, troop carriers, and Jeeps choked the back roads as far as the eye could see. At the Oxford airport, mammoth C-124 Globemaster transport planes were landing and taking off nonstop, disgorging battle-ready paratroopers of the 82nd Airborne Division and the 101st Airborne Division's Screaming Eagles. Stepping onto the tarmac, a dazed captain of the

101st asked, "Are we in Cuba?" Replied a local National Guardsman, "No, you're in Oxford, Mississippi." The officer fell to his knees and kissed the ground.

Stunned Mississippians were treated to the sight of African-American combat troops with high-powered rifles in command of their streets. Nothing like it had been seen in the state since Reconstruction. On Courthouse Square, black infantry Second Lieutenant Chuck Shockley became a field judge, deciding which captured rioters should be detained and which should be set free.

On top of the all-white Oxford elementary school, a radio-equipped army observation post kept on the alert for trouble. Since most of the school's black support staff stayed home, paratroopers of Company C, First Battle Group of 101st Airborne Division, pitched in to prepare lunch for the kids. When soldiers camped on the school grounds in pup tents later in the week, children traded their fresh milk and chocolate milk for cans of awful-tasting C-rations. The kids thought it was the greatest deal in the world, because they wanted to be soldiers, too.

In scenes that evoked the Civil War daguerreotypes of Matthew Brady, army tent cities blossomed at the airport, at the university football stadium and practice fields, and on a nearby golf course and cow pasture.

Paratroopers in camouflage helmets and full combat gear patrolled the streets of the city, crouching, jumping over hedges, and probing the bushes for any lingering rioters with their bayonets. Local dogs trotted alongside the paratroopers, and when one tail-flapping puppy fraternized with a group of GIs, a man shouted, "You'd better get back over here, dog, if you intend to stay in Oxford!" Everyone laughed, including the soldiers.

Some local people voiced anger at James Meredith, blaming him for causing the mayhem. "That nigger's had it," a townsman sitting in a coffee shop told reporter Rick Tuttle of the *Miami Herald*. "He ought to be taken out and shot. I'd pull the trigger." The correspondent heard a woman on the street say, "Lord, that boy should be shot and I reckon he will 'fore long."

After the bedlam of the riot, however, many civilians welcomed the arrival of federal troops. "I like the troops here," one businessman explained. "I wish they had come sooner than Sunday night. They are needed here for the protection of property and the lives of our children. Governor Barnett stood us all up by making a lot of promises that he would keep the college segregated when he knew he couldn't. And that's what caused the riot."

A restaurant owner argued, "The marshals should have fired the gas sooner. They took too long." A woman dime-store clerk marveled, "My, aren't you glad to see those soldiers?" Another Oxford businessman said, "Thank God for the troops."

A total of 166 U.S. Marshals and forty-eight American soldiers were treated for injuries incurred in the Battle of Oxford. Two civilians, Paul Guihard and Ray Gunter, were killed. Thirty of the federal marshals sustained gunshot wounds. The soldiers were treated for lacerations, contusions, and cuts from thrown objects and flying glass. Additionally, three Mississippi Highway Patrolmen, twenty students, and eight other civilians were treated at the university infirmary.

Dr. L. G. Hopkins worked nonstop inside the Lyceum through the night without assistance and was too busy to keep a list of injuries. He estimated it could have been anywhere from fifty to one hundred or more, which included marshals, soldiers, and civilians. At least twelve civilians were treated at the Oxford hospital, and an unknown number of other people either weren't treated or were treated outside Oxford. The *New York Times* estimated the total number of people injured at Oxford at 375.

Some three hundred American citizens were taken prisoner by federal troops and marshals from September 30 to October 2, 1962. The prisoners ranged in age from fourteen to fifty-seven and came from coast to coast, from Georgia to California, with most coming from Mississippi, Tennessee, Alabama, and Louisiana. Some of the prisoners were captured in error, simply because they had firearms in their vehicles and the soldiers couldn't distinguish them from rioters. Many civilians in the region routinely carried shotguns and rifles in their cars and pickup trucks for hunting, especially in this first week of squirrel-hunting season.

A number of prisoners were held captive in the cramped basement of the Lyceum building through the evening of October 1. Some prisoners later complained of beatings and brutal treatment at the hands of federal marshals, charges that were repeated in a scathing report by a Mississippi state legislative committee the following year. Most of the stories appear to have been exaggerated, and at the time, no such complaints were made either to Deputy Attorney General

Katzenbach or to the Oxford chief of police. In 1998 Chooky Falkner, the Oxford National Guard commander, unequivocally dismissed reports of brutality. "I was there," he said. "It didn't happen."

By October 2 and 3, most of the prisoners were moved to a temporary army detention center at the Oxford airport and to a federal Department of Agriculture soil-project facility on the Ole Miss campus. Of the prisoners, only twenty-five were students at Ole Miss, and another fifteen were students from Mississippi State at Starkville. Eight of the University of Mississippi students were disciplined by a student judicial council, and none were expelled. The vast majority of all prisoners were released by October 3 for lack of evidence after being interviewed by FBI agents.

Hundreds of weapons of every possible description were seized by marshals and soldiers at roadblocks and in raids, including high-powered hunting rifles, squirrel guns, revolvers, sabers, knives, sawed-off shotguns, a Thompson submachine gun, and a Japanese pistol.

On October 1, army officials got a tip that a cache of weapons was located inside the Sigma Nu building, the fraternity presided over by Trent Lott.

The same day, according to the Pentagon's history of the incident, a squad of military policemen from the 716th MP Battalion conducted a surprise raid on the fraternity house with the concurrence of Chancellor Williams, and "turned up two rifles (a .22 and a .30 calibre), twenty-one shotguns, and a .22 Colt pistol, but no ammunition. These weapons were turned over to University officials." A total of twenty-four weapons were seized by the military policemen and removed from the Sigma Nu house.

In response to a Freedom of Information Act request during the research for this book, the Federal Bureau of Investigation in Washington, D.C., made approximately nine thousand pages of previously unseen FBI records on the Oxford crisis available to the author. Among the raw FBI files was a document numbered 157–401–371, an FBI agent's report that detailed the assortment of weapons confiscated by the army at the Sigma Nu fraternity house. It included a J.C. Higgins 12-gauge pump shotgun, a Remington .20 automatic shotgun, a Winchester 12-gauge pump, a Wesley-Richards 12-gauge double-barrel shotgun, a Gewek Fabrik 2.29 caliber double-barrel shotgun, and a Colt Woodsman .22 caliber automatic pistol.

The national Sigma Nu organization later awarded Trent Lott the

Achievement of the Year Award for his peacemaking efforts during the riot on campus. In 2000 U.S. senator from Mississippi and Republican leader Trent Lott's aide Guy Hovis declined to respond to repeated requests for Lott to be interviewed for this book.

On the morning of day two of the occupation, October 2, the city of Oxford was still paralyzed, with the town square sealed off by federal troops and the shops and banks shut down, although the university remained open as it had the day before. Early that morning, students were treated to the thunderous sound of hundreds of 101st Airborne paratroopers jogging in cadence in combat boots through the campus.

But by midday, Tuesday, October 2, it was clear that the insurrection was totally crushed, and federal authorities decided to lift their blockade of the Square and let the shops and restaurants reopen. One merchant told a friend, "I'm glad to see you are still alive!" Oxford city police joined the U.S. Army in conducting searches and guiding traffic. By Tuesday afternoon, the old men were back on their segregated green benches around the courthouse, basking in the sun, flanked by battle-ready paratroopers still ringing the Square. At Ole Miss, U.S. Marshals and MPs kept a tight guard on James Meredith as they walked him through his second day of classes.

There was good reason to continue bodyguarding James Meredith. The FBI was picking up alarming intelligence reports from informants that the Ku Klux Klan was not accepting defeat at the Battle of Oxford. At a United Klans of America council held at Bessemer, Alabama, on October 2, the Klan leadership reportedly decided that due to the overwhelming number of troops in Oxford, they would, the informant said, "lay low for awhile and then try to get Meredith and hang him from a gate on the campus when the situation permitted."

That same night, at a cafe in Columbus, Georgia, an FBI informant overheard a man identifying himself as a Ku Klux Klansman say that the Klan planned to drop explosives on federal troops in Oxford from small rental airplanes. He added that the Klan was considering aerial bombing of the naval air station at Memphis, too.

On day three of the military occupation of Oxford, U.S. Marine helicopters conducted an emergency airlift of twenty-seven hundred sleeping bags and air mattresses for the troops occupying the city. Hearing that Mississippi National Guardsmen were still eating canned C-rations, the citizens of Senatobia, Mississippi, organized a relief convoy of hundreds of pounds of fried chicken, potato salad, candy, and cigarettes for their troops. The National Guardsmen of Oxford's Troop E, bivouacked in a cow pasture south of town, were treated to ice cream, soda pop, and other delicacies by the town's businessmen.

Bill Mayes of the 503d Military Police Battalion reported that on the second and third days of the occupation of Oxford, there was so much fear lingering in the black Freedman's Town district that some residents were afraid to go into the street. In one area, Mayes reported, "We were looking for black people, and we couldn't find any. We finally found black families up in the hills, huddled together, camping. They had abandoned their homes and gone up to the forests with tents. We found them up there, and we gave them our rations and blankets. Ten to fifteen families had abandoned the town. We found them in the woods."

Of the multitude of surreal events that swirled through the Battle of Oxford, one episode was so unbelievable that it vanished from history almost as soon as it happened. At the center of the enigma was the spectacle of American combat troops being disgraced by their own government. In the first hours of the invasion of northern Mississippi, scores of incoming white army officers and enlisted men were stunned to learn that hundreds of black troops were being stripped from their ranks.

Back on September 27, Attorney General Bobby Kennedy had secretly approved the Pentagon's plan to segregate the army invasion force, according to the Department of Defense internal history of the incident. In 2000 former secretary of the army Cyrus Vance was too infirm to be interviewed on the subject. Although Pentagon records document Vance's superior, former secretary of defense Robert McNamara, discussing the segregation order with the president in the first week of the occupation, in 2000 McNamara said he had no memory of the order. Robert Kennedy was never publicly asked why he did it, but a logical assumption is that the purpose of segregating the troops was to avoid inflaming whites in the Deep South with the image of black combat troops in action.

Now the segregation order was being implemented in the field, but in a typically confused bureaucratic fashion. The policy was so politically sensitive that it was being communicated in writing only among the top brass and in most cases being relayed down through the ranks verbally, and sometimes haphazardly, with the result being widespread confusion and disbelief.

Some units, like the 716th Military Police Battalion from Fort Dix, New Jersey, were largely stripped of their black soldiers before reaching Oxford. Others, like the paratroopers of the 82nd and 101st Airborne Divisions, made it into Oxford with their black troops, where they were then segregated. As the first regular army troops to be dropped into Mississippi, the 503d Military Police Battalion was ordered by Eighteenth Airborne Corps headquarters to leave its black troops behind at Fort Bragg before flying to the Memphis staging point, but the order was discarded at Fort Bragg by Major Raymond Le Van, on the basis that the battalion couldn't function without its black troops.

On Monday morning, October 1, General Earle D. Wheeler, the new army chief of staff, sent a personally written order to be given to General Hamilton Howze, the new chief of army operations at Memphis: "Pass to Gen. Howze the instructions we gave Abrams & Billingslea forbidding use of Negro troopers on operational missions bringing them in contact with the public. . . . Keep Negro troops in base camps or administrative support duties."

The morning of October 1, Deputy Attorney General Nicholas Katzenbach got wind of the policy when he witnessed army formations in Oxford being pulled apart to implement the order. Mortified at the explosive public-relations risk and colossal stupidity of the move, he pleaded by telephone both to Bobby Kennedy and to Secretary of the Army Cyrus Vance, "This is just crazy! Don't do it!"

Katzenbach said that there were intermediate steps they could take, like having white troops take the lead in talking with the locals. But segregating the forces would be a disaster, he argued, because it would destroy the army's whole system of squads and patrols. Over Katzenbach's protests, the segregation policy continued.

Katzenbach was shocked. Recalling the incident in 2000, he marveled, "I didn't believe anybody could be so stupid."

On the morning the riot ended, rumors of lingering snipers in and around Oxford provided a cover story and excuse for the army brass to justify the segregation order to the troops.

When the 503d Military Police Battalion's commander Lt. Col. John Flanagan was ordered on the morning of October 1 to pull his black troops out of Jeep security patrols, he and Major Le Van raised hell about it with their superiors, insisting the battalion couldn't function on a segregated basis. Later in the week, black troops in the 503d learned that they were going to be pulled off security checkpoints, supposedly for their own safety to avoid snipers zeroing in on them.

In 2001, African-American Sergeant Russell Amos disclosed that when he and other black troops of the 503d's A Company learned they were going to be pulled off checkpoints and confined to their bivouac area, they, as a group, requested of the 503d's Major John Templeton that they instead be sent back to Fort Bragg rather than endure the outrage of being segregated.

"I took a very deep offense," Sergeant Amos remembered in disgust, "against the fact that after we got there and caught pure hell and got Meredith registered, we, the black soldiers, were told we were going to be taken off checkpoints.

"We felt very proud about participating in this mission," Amos explained, practically shouting in anger at the memory, so many years later. "Then you're going to pull us off of it? You're going to pull us off the front lines that we were fighting overseas on? What for? For our safety? They didn't pull my ass out of Vietnam! You think about all this. When I joined the military, I took an oath. Now you're asking me to violate the oath that I took! My oath didn't tell me I had to separate my duties because of who I am or who you are! That stuck in my craw real bad. Oh, man, this is deep!

"It just wasn't fair," Amos charged. "It wasn't fair under the army organization, and it wasn't fair under what the hell we were down there for. We requested to go back to North Carolina. They put us back out on checkpoints after we protested."

At the Oxford airport on October 1, Sergeant Martin Lentz, a white rifle-squad leader with the 82nd Airborne Division, received verbal orders to leave all the black members of his company at the airport and not take them into town. "We were told that this directive came from the Secretary of the Army, Cyrus Vance," Lentz reported. "The idea was that it would be inflammatory to have black soldiers attempting to control angry white Southerners."

The directive meant that his platoon sergeant and a number of other paratroopers had to be left behind. "Thus, ethnically cleansed," Lentz recalled decades later, "we moved into Oxford."

One black sergeant from the 82nd Airborne, after being ordered to separate his black paratroopers and keep them in hiding at the Oxford airport, relayed the order to his men with tears in his eyes. 82nd Airborne paratrooper William Johnson, another African-American sergeant, got the order from his company commander: "Tell all your black troops they won't be coming with us." He and his fellow black platoon sergeants and leaders were, in Johnson's words, "so bloody shocked and pissed off" that they collectively told the commander, "The hell with this—you tell them."

Jamie Brewer, a seventeen-year-old black private in the 82nd, couldn't believe it. "The men of the Airborne are considered the best troops in the world," Brewer thought. That's what they told him, and until now he had believed it. He saw with his own eyes the teamwork, the pride, and the morale of the paratroopers. He saw no racial problems at all in his outfit.

But now, while his brother white paratroopers were patrolling Oxford, Jamie Brewer and the other black soldiers were being forced to empty garbage cans at the Oxford airport. "I thought the military was integrated," the soldier remembered. "Here we were emptying garbage cans. We felt they had no faith in us."

Officers of the 82nd Airborne and 101st Airborne protested the segregation order in writing, according to Pentagon records. So did the commander of the 716th Military Police Battalion, who, when forced to leave his black troops behind before moving into Oxford, lost two company commanders and his communications sergeant, totally disrupting his unit's ability to function.

"How can we face our companies now after being taken out of the fight?" asked Howard Lomba, a black army sergeant from New Jersey. "We're professional soldiers and we're supposed to fight anywhere." A flabbergasted black army private named David Adams stood in embarrassment and disbelief as he watched the white troops move out to serve. He felt what he described "a voice in our collective souls" screaming, "This is my fight, too. This is my issue; the wrong, the hurt was done to James Meredith, my forefathers, my children and myself."

According to Lieutenant Charles Shockley, in one Second Infantry encampment, the black troops were held back from patrols and relegated to nonstop guard duty and KP duty, cleaning pots and pans and peeling potatoes while white troops got to relax. Shockley was confronted by a furious black platoon sergeant who declared, "This crap about only Negro troops doing KP and guard duty has got to stop! If it doesn't, there is going to be a major riot right here in this camp. I don't know what your position will be, but I am going to be with them!"

Lieutenant Shockley had learned during his NAACP organizing days that in a bureaucracy, you can get things done faster by appealing to someone's job security rather than their sense of morality. He told his superior officer of the brewing riot and noted, "The commanders will be very embarrassed if this riot erupts. With all the national press around, it would be difficult to keep it from them, and a story like this would embarrass and anger the president who sent us here. I'm sure heads would roll if we do not prevent this."

Early in the first week of the occupation of Oxford, Mississippi-born white captain William Parks of the 101st Airborne Division, commanding a four-hundred-man task force of paratroopers, got a call on the red phone patched into his tent command post on the campus of the University of Mississippi. Robert Kennedy was on the line, with an astonishing direct order.

Parks described what happened next: "The attorney general's order to me was to remove all black troops in my command from the campus. And I remonstrated. The thing that concerned me the most was that a very large percentage, something like 65 percent, of my key noncommissioned officers were black. So what I was having to do was pull out my leadership and send them to the rear. And I thought it was just about the stupidest thing I had ever heard or seen. But I did it. We had words about it. The point I made was, Don't just think you're taking troops away; you're taking my leadership away from me. What the hell do I do about leaders? I was in essence told that it was an order; he didn't call me up to discuss it with me. I thought it strange that he was giving an order. I felt I should have gotten it from General Abrams or my own chain of command."

One morning a few days later, Captain Parks saw something he couldn't believe. "I looked up and there was a garbage detail picking up trash at the football practice field [near James Meredith's dormitory, Baxter Hall]. They were all black soldiers, but they had no helmets on and no weapons. They were disarmed."

"What in the shit are they doing?" exclaimed Captain Parks, whose surprise turned to fury when he realized the soldiers-turned-garbage-men were men of his own 101st Airborne Division, the Screaming Eagles. "I thought I was going to have an apoplectic stroke," Parks re-called. The black paratroopers were being allowed back on the cam-pus, but only after being stripped of their guns, their helmets, and their dignity, while the white troops, according to Parks, remained "all decked out in full battle dress complete with weapons and steel hel-mets."

"I went through the roof," Parks said. "I was fairly well infuriated about it, and I knew damn well that James Meredith was going to see this and realize what's happening. I barreled off to get them in uni-form. 'You watch,' I thought. 'He'll have a press conference.' And that's exactly what happened."

In fact, James Meredith had already realized the troops were being segregated days earlier, and protested vigorously in private to federal officials, who assured him that the policy was being rescinded.

President Kennedy, who according to Defense Department records approved the continuation of the segregation policy with Pen-tagon brass as late as October 3, then abruptly canceled the order on day five of the occupation. That day, October 5, he ordered Secretary of Defense Robert McNamara to reintegrate black troops into normal army operations, except for individual sentinels or isolated missions. Since President Kennedy, like his brother, was never publicly asked about the policy, his reasons for approving and then revoking the seg-regation order are unknown.

But on Monday, October 8, at the start of his second week of classes, James Meredith was outraged to see that while black troops were back on duty, the ones he saw were disarmed and picking up garbage. Meredith called a news conference and blasted the army, charging, "This condition constitutes a dishonor and a disgrace to the hundreds of thousands of Negroes who wear the uniform of our mil-itary services."

Unless the segregation stopped, Meredith said he would leave the University of Mississippi. "My conscience," Meredith declared, "would not allow me to go on observing this situation without, at least, letting the Negro soldiers know that I did not like them being dishonored." The army issued a bland non-denial of the charge, and the story dis-appeared in a single news cycle. But all black troops were soon reinte-grated in all units, completing the presidential order of October 5. A number of the black troops sent letters to James Meredith to thank him for taking his stand.

James Meredith was swamped by letters from other well-wishers across the United States and around the world, offering him encouragement. For Mississippi blacks used to almost perpetual oppression and defeat, the symbolism of James Meredith's sudden, decisive victory was almost earth-shattering. Some could hardly believe it.

On a plantation in the Delta, an astonished black woman huddled over a cotton bag said quietly, "You mean a colored boy's done gone to the University of Mississippi and the Government is helping him out?" Said a seventy-eight-year-old man picking cotton, "Meredith is just like Moses to me. He's delivering us from Mississippi."

Roger Thompson, a retired black carpenter at Ole Miss, put down his saw, hitched up his overalls and pointed toward the university: "I'm so glad there's a black face over there," he said. "I'm proud of it and I hope there'll be more. I'm not afraid." A delighted old black man with white hair strolled along a street in the capital city of Jackson, and said, "He's really done it!" In Jackson, black lawyer R. Jeff Brown noticed that the city's sixty-five thousand blacks seemed "to walk a bit straighter because of Meredith."

In Oxford a black cab driver announced, "I sure would hate to see those troops leave, but I'll be prepared. Those soldiers taught me how to defend myself." Also in Oxford, a seventeen-year-old black girl named Cecelia Kimmons was overjoyed. "I think I'll go to Ole Miss in a few years," she predicted. "Boy, I'm glad this is happening!"

For his part, Nicholas Katzenbach thought James Meredith was a "strange man" who didn't have a very good sense of reality. Meredith would ask him, "Could you please remove all these troops? We don't need troops." And Katzenbach would reply, "James, you won't live very long if we do that." In fact, as the situation stabilized quickly in the weeks after the riot, the vast majority of army troops were withdrawn from the Oxford area.

Katzenbach thought that Meredith might even have welcomed being killed. "It could be precisely this lack of reality that made him so courageous," Katzenbach said, "but nobody can ever question his courage. He might have had more courage than judgment."

For the next eleven months James Howard Meredith was subjected to constant verbal harassment by a hard-core minority of students at the University of Mississippi and was guarded twenty-four hours a day by reserve teams of U.S. Deputy Marshals and Army troops. For safety reasons, Meredith's wife stayed in Jackson.

On Meredith's second night at the university, a black-faced effigy labeled with "Go back to Africa where you belong" was hung from a window facing his dorm and set ablaze.

On October 5, federal authorities decided to try to let Meredith cross the campus on foot for the first time, rather than by car. He was hissed and cursed at as he walked. A pretty coed said, "Why doesn't somebody kill him?"

Meredith ignored the taunts and jeers by walking sprightly, and softly smiling. Outside the university cafeteria, a crowd of thirty students jeered and cursed Meredith and his escorts as they hustled into a car.

The next day, as Meredith sat in the cafeteria eating a lunch of steak, green beans, mashed potatoes, and lemonade, a girl peered at Meredith through a bank of potted plants. "Why, they're just sitting as if he wasn't there," she said. Her friend advised, "That's the best way to treat him—just ignore him."

On the night of October 8, three hundred students gathered in front of the cafeteria, some yelling, "Get that nigger" and "Kennedy is a coon keeper." The demonstrators erupted in rebel yells, school chants, and a chorus of "Glory, Glory Segregation—the South Must Rise Again." Firecrackers started popping, and a rock crashed through the window next to Meredith, who ignored it and moved to another table. Two students walked over, and laughed. "Negro, why don't you just leave the school?" one of them said. "There was nothing unique about the time I spent at the University of Mississippi," Meredith later reflected. "What people can't seem to realize is that what happened to me is the usual treatment received by all Negroes every day in Mississippi."

Meredith reported that it was a full ten months before he could walk down the steps of his dormitory without hearing somebody call him a nigger. But he also discovered that he had more friends than he could handle throughout his stay at Ole Miss. Many students were congenial, visited him in his room, and chatted with him on the campus.

One day during his second week of classes, James Meredith was turning away from his mailbox in the Student Union when a young coed came up to him. "As hundreds of dumbfounded rednecks looked on," Meredith wrote in his 1966 book *Three Years in Mississippi*, "she introduced herself and said in a thick southern accent, 'I C-O-M-E from AR-KAN-SAS and I just wanted to tel-l y-o-u how proud we are to have you he-r-e.' "

A small riot broke out on the night of October 29, when nearly 150 students besieged the cafeteria as Meredith ate dinner, firing eggs and firecrackers at the military-police guards posted outside. Later that evening, students near Meredith's Baxter Hall dormitory used slingshots to launch firecrackers and cherry bombs at the troops, and a Molotov cocktail was ignited next to the dorm. Chancellor Williams expelled five of the students involved in the incident.

In November 1962, a shadowy, anonymous group calling itself the Rebel Resistance distributed an anti-Meredith pamphlet on campus, which proposed that Meredith be totally shunned. "Let no student speak to him," the handbill read, "and let his attempt to 'make friends' fall upon cold, unfriendly faces."

Meredith began noticing that fewer students and faculty acted friendly to him in public. When several students had dinner with Meredith, two of them found their dorm room torn apart, with the words "Nigger Lovers" scrawled on the wall in shoe polish.

By late fall, Meredith's studies were suffering badly with the pressures of celebrity and often intolerable academic conditions. He was spending up to ten hours a day giving interviews to journalists, posing for pictures, and huddling with government and school officials. At the same time, some students in Meredith's dorm were trying to sabotage his studying by bouncing basketballs and moving furniture around all night.

When a reporter asked how his grades were, Meredith replied, "That's not the most important thing. The right to fail is just as important as the right to succeed."

On Christmas Eve 1962, night riders in a speeding car blasted Meredith's family home in Kosciusko with a shotgun, barely missing his teenaged sister Willie Lou. A distressed Meredith asked for federal protection for his family, but it was denied. The Justice Department explained that the attack violated no federal law and would have to be handled by local authorities.

On January 7, 1963, Meredith threatened to leave Ole Miss unless conditions for his studying improved. Three days later, more than five hundred students followed him to the school library to harass him as he tried to prepare for exams. Campus police had to break up the demonstration.

On January 30 Meredith announced he would stay at the university. He somehow marshaled the strength to buckle down, improve his studies, and endure his ordeal.

A force of three hundred army troops and a small team of federal marshals guarded Meredith twenty-four hours a day through the spring of 1963. Additionally, an emergency-evacuation fleet of four army helicopters and one fixed-wing aircraft stood by on alert at the Oxford airport into mid-May, ready to pluck Meredith out of Mississippi.

It wasn't until April 1963 that James Meredith was able to have a black friend visit him on campus. When James Allen, a former classmate at Jackson State, joined Meredith for a meal at the cafeteria, he was amazed to see students cursing at them in front of women and faculty members: "Now we got two black sons of bitches!"

When one student yelled, "Niggers are not supposed to eat here," Meredith, who may have secretly felt relief that he finally had someone to share the abuse with, kidded Allen, "Your friends are talking to you!" Then Meredith shook his head sadly and told him, "I go through this every day."

On May 22, 1963, Lafayette County sheriff Joe Ford, who must have harbored bad feelings toward the army since being briefly detained in error by troops the night of the riot, was given a VIP tour of U.S. Army headquarters at Oxford. The troops treated him to a fancy dinner version of army chow, featuring roast chicken, "corn a la southern" and cake with butter-cream icing. Two days later, the sheriff, who until then had insisted that James Meredith's security was strictly a federal matter, announced that he would personally help guarantee the peace at the university if the army needed his assistance.

When a black applicant named Cleve McDowell journeyed to Oxford on July 5 to register for summer law classes backed by a court order, army forces in Oxford went on full alert and gave McDowell an aerial escort as he drove up from Jackson.

If Governor Ross Barnett tried to appear on campus, the army planned to snatch him away from his police escort, pack him off in a helicopter, and fly him back to Jackson. Barnett stayed away, and McDowell registered uneventfully as Ole Miss's second official black student. He became James Meredith's roommate.

On the day the riot ended, Governor Ross Barnett issued a statement in which he tried to explain his actions and defend against rumors that were already circulating that he had made some kind of "secret deal" with the Kennedys. "When it was made known to me," Barnett announced, "that they would forcibly put Meredith in the University either Sunday, September 30, or Monday, October 1, I realized that Oxford would be crowded Monday with thousands and thousands of people, not only from Mississippi but from many other states. I knew there would be many deadly weapons there on Monday and that hundreds of people would probably be killed. . . . I was compelled to admit that it would be better for them to place him on the campus by helicopter than to force him in with widespread bloodshed during the day of Monday."

Governor Barnett continued with his states' rights and segregationist rhetoric until his last day in office in 1964, but abandoned any attempts to resist school integration with physical force. While some segregationists admired his attempts to resist the federals during the Ole Miss crisis, many ordinary Mississippians viewed the episode as a disaster and a tragedy, and blamed Barnett for mismanaging the crisis. He remained popular through the end of his term, but began to be seen by many whites as a relic of a past they would rather put behind them.

The last U.S. Army troops quietly withdrew from Oxford on July 24, 1963, ending an almost ten-month occupation. Without any fanfare or announcement, twenty army trucks slipped away from town at noon, carrying dismantled equipment and communications gear, heading north toward Memphis. A few hours later, Company A of the 716th Military Police Battalion left for Millington by bus. A small reserve squad of federal marshals stayed on to see Meredith through graduation.

When he heard that the military occupation of Mississippi was over, the ever-enigmatic James Meredith said that the troops and marshals should have left a long time ago. "It was a lonely victory for James Meredith," wrote the makers of *Eyes on the Prize*, Henry Hampton's epic documentary film about the civil rights movement, "but it was a victory for him and the country. The Constitution had held and been affirmed in a major crisis. Thousands of black people felt the victory and saw James Meredith as an example to follow. A symbol, like the Little Rock Nine, of their power to move the nation."

On the beautiful summer afternoon of August 18, 1963, a small black boy jumped across the folding chairs in the Ole Miss Grove, and a little white boy nearby waved an American flag as the university prepared to honor its graduates.

Wearing black caps and gowns with tassels, James Howard Meredith and some four hundred white classmates gathered in the slanting sunlight near the school library. Meredith was wearing a sharp eighty-five-dollar suit his parents helped him pick out in a big department store.

At a signal, a black university employee rang the chimes of a bell tower, and the graduates walked into the Lyceum building, through what had been the epicenter of an American insurrection and the last battle of the Civil War, into the tall oaks of the Grove.

In the audience, Meredith could see his proud mother and father, his wife and his young son, and dozens of family members who had convoyed up from Kosciusko to join the celebration. Sixteen federal marshals hovered unobtrusively on the edge of the crowd.

At 5:12 P.M., campus police and officials surged close to the platform as Meredith walked up to Chancellor J. D. Williams, shook his hand, and walked down with his diploma bearing a bachelor of arts degree in political science. "At that moment," wrote *New Orleans Times-Picayune* reporter Bill Minor, "a slight electric feeling was felt throughout the audience, in the fading afternoon light."

As the graduates marched off to the organ strains of "Pomp and Circumstance," one white woman said to another, "Well, I'm glad he's gone." Her friend replied, "There'll be others." Then the first woman said, with Deep Southern understatement, "Well, let's hope it'll all be quieter." It was otherwise a peaceful day, with no hostile signs to be seen or heard.

Underneath his graduation robes, James Meredith had hidden an ornament he picked off the ground the year before, as dawn rose over the Battle of Oxford. It was a red-and-white cardboard badge reading, "Ross is Right!" Meredith was wearing it upside down.

The seventy-one-year-old Moses Meredith, a tall, distinguished son of a slave, said of his son's victory, "I'm proud just to see a man get an education. That's all he ever asked for."

Reflecting on the day's events, completely unthinkable just a year ago to probably anyone except these two men, Moses Meredith confided to his son, "These people can be decent."

The Greatest Suppertime of All

■ ■ ■ ■

It's all *now* you see. Yesterday wont be over until tomorrow and tomorrow began ten thousand years ago.

—William Faulkner

AMERICA HAS ALMOST COMPLETELY forgotten the Battle of Oxford, and the event dwells in a dark, distant landscape of lost national memory—a turning point in history that is also nearly invisible.

With a single stroke, James Meredith forced America to face the contradiction of second-class citizenship for multitudes of its black citizens, not with speeches, boycotts, or sit-ins, but on a battlefield. He conducted a military assault on the holiest temple of white supremacy in the nation, and won such an overwhelming victory that few could comprehend the full impact at the time.

"I wasn't there as a student—I was there as a soldier," Meredith explained years later. "I was a general. I was in command of everything."

The significance of James Meredith's achievement was impossible to absorb at the time because it came as suddenly as a bolt of lightning. At Ole Miss, Meredith crushed forever the Southern strategy of "massive resistance" to integration, and opened a doorway of American history through which all the epic civil rights events of the 1960s would follow.

On September 30, 1962, massive resistance, while defeated in several Southern states, still ruled much of the Deep South. Beyond the skirmish at Little Rock, the federal government had yet to confront the issue with physical force. That night, James Meredith forced an American president for the first time since Abraham Lincoln to send American troops into battle to guarantee the rights of citizenship for black Americans.

Before that night, segregationist strategists in Mississippi were convinced that integration could be blocked in the streets by a wall of flesh. If the federal government sent troops to try to force integration, they were convinced that a wide-scale popular insurrection and bloodshed would result, forcing the federal government to retreat indefinitely from the battlefield.

Indeed, as he sat with Ross Barnett inside the Mississippi Governor's Mansion listening to the first reports of combat coming from Oxford on the night of September 30, Citizens Council of America chief William Simmons was convinced that this was beginning to happen, and that history was now sure to turn in their favor.

But the vast majority of white Mississippians, when forced to choose between a full-scale revolt and obeying the law, chose law and order.

The messengers of peace were the eleven thousand National Guardsmen of Mississippi, several hundred of whom risked their lives to help keep the peace in a vicious, forgotten battle, along with the regular army troops who followed them. Years later, Simmons acknowledged admiringly of the Guard, "They really kept it from degenerating into a bloodbath."

The Mississippi segregationists gambled everything on the Battle of Oxford, and they lost. "We got run over," said Bill Simmons. The integration of the University of Mississippi "put an end to massive resistance," said former NAACP counsel and Meredith attorney Constance Baker Motley. "After that," she noted, "there was no further need for federal troops in the struggle."

The following year, fearful of an Oxford-style disaster, Governor George Wallace of Alabama went through the motions of "standing in the schoolhouse door" in a carefully choreographed charade, then capitulated peacefully to the integration of the University of Alabama.

Federal troops were standing nearby in reserve then and during the Selma crisis, but never after Ole Miss would a president have to deploy soldiers into battle in the struggle. That issue had been settled at Oxford. "By the time we got to Alabama," recalled then Deputy Attorney General Nicholas Katzenbach, who faced Wallace down in the televised Kabuki showdown at the schoolhouse door, "we knew what the hell we were doing."

As the Civil War was largely decided with the collapse of Pickett's Charge at Gettysburg, the ultimate outcome of the civil rights struggle was symbolically settled with the full-scale federal military invasion and recapture of Mississippi on October 1, 1962. Tremendous struggles remained ahead for the civil rights movement, but segregationists would never again doubt that the full sovereignty of federal law would be delivered with physical force, and from then on, all their efforts to delay integration were essentially rear-guard actions.

"It was the final battle," said former Mississippi State Sovereignty Commission member and Citizens Council supporter Horace Harned, Jr. "It was the last stand for sovereignty and states' rights in the big scale. Since then they've taken the balance of what sovereignty we had left."

Many factors combined to relegate the Battle of Oxford to the historical shadows.

The mayhem of the riot was so severe that many reporters fled the scene early in the fighting or couldn't get there until after the fighting ended. Since the crisis occurred in the days just before national TV networks began covering such events live, there were almost no TV images of the battle. There were exceedingly few newsreel or still images, either, since it was a nighttime battle and photographers on the scene were threatened and attacked by rioters. There do not appear to be any newsreel or video images of the daytime rioting in downtown Oxford on the morning of October 1, though a few still photos were made.

The very few photographic images that emerged from the riot were quickly and completely wiped off the national memory banks by the Cuban missile crisis, which occurred just three weeks later.

Many of the participants in and witnesses to the Battle of Oxford recoiled in shame or disgust and rarely spoke of it again. Virtually all of the army troops and Guardsmen involved were under orders not to speak to the press, and until now their eyewitness testimony was lost to history.

In the years that followed, the Battle of Oxford vanished into a strange historical vapor. It is an unknown event for most Americans, even in Mississippi, where most choose not to remember what some of the old-timers call "the Meredith Crisis," "the Oxford Rebellion," or simply "the Insurrection."

Although three hundred people were arrested and detained by federal officials during and after the riot, most of them were released for lack of evidence. Twelve people were formally charged with insurrection, seditious conspiracy and interfering with U.S. marshals, but they never went to trial.

Of the twenty-five University of Mississippi students detained, eight were disciplined by the student judicial council. None were expelled by the university. Not a single rioter was ever convicted or punished.

"Oxford was something everybody wanted to put behind them," noted Larry Williams, a former Second Infantry sergeant who was attacked with bricks as his army truck moved through the town square on October 1, 1962. "It was something that they wanted to hush up. Because it was a disgrace, the way the people acted." Sergeant James Kennedy of the 503d Military Police Battalion said the crisis "was one of the sorriest shows of leadership that I have ever seen in this country, on all sides."

In the immediate aftermath of the riot, many people in Mississippi blamed the violence on "trigger-happy" U.S. marshals who "jumped the gun" by firing tear gas too soon. This view was shared by the governor, the Highway Patrol, much of the state news media, and a majority of the state legislature. In response, on October 4, 1962, the local chapter of the American Association of University Professors, including sixty-five Ole Miss faculty and staff, issued a public statement declaring that attempts to blame the marshals were unfair and "almost completely false."

"Those marshals," said University of Mississippi chaplain Rev. Wofford Smith, "were the bravest men I ever saw."

For James Meredith, the Battle of Oxford was both a triumph and a curse.

After he graduated, Meredith largely vanished from the national radar screen and spent much of the rest of his career in relative obscurity. When he sporadically surfaced, his actions sometimes obscured his 1962 triumph. He is a true American hero, but a complex and controversial one.

Meredith went on from Ole Miss to earn a law degree from Columbia University law school in New York in 1967. He served briefly as a New York City landlord and spent two days in jail for allegedly harassing his tenants.

The notoriety Meredith won at Oxford helped transform him into a misunderstood, iconoclastic figure, considered by some to be eccentric. Meredith often startled audiences and reporters with his habit of making blunt, provocative statements, offering a highly idiosyncratic blend of folk wisdom, flashes of historical insight, and messianic mysticism. When he wasn't feuding with the traditional civil rights movement, he ignored it.

Reflecting on Meredith, University of Mississippi historian David Sansing observed, "He has never been in the mainstream of the civil rights movement. He was often critical of the leadership. He has always been a loner. He really does march to the sound of a different drummer."

When asked in late 1963 if he'd seen any improvement in race relations, Meredith replied, "I don't believe in 'improvement' in the area of human dignity. Either an individual has all the human rights or he does not." He added, "If a person in Mississippi has the right to kick me ten times a day, it is of no benefit that next week he kicks me only five times. Either he kicks me with impunity or he does not."

In 1966 Meredith published his autobiography, *Three Years in Mississippi*, a penetrating, comprehensive account of his life, his journey back to his homeland, and his own in-depth account of the Ole Miss crisis. The book received very positive reviews.

In 1966, armed with a Bible, a pith helmet, an ivory-tipped ebony walking stick, and hiking boots, James Meredith began a one-man, 213-mile "March Against Fear" from Memphis to Jackson to promote voting rights. On June 6, just one day into the march, two miles south of the town of Hernando on Highway 51, a sniper opened fire on Meredith from the bushes with an automatic 16-gauge shotgun.

Meredith absorbed nearly one hundred pellet wounds on his head, back, neck, shoulder, and legs. Aubrey James Norvell, a forty-year-old white unemployed hardware contractor from Memphis, was arrested and charged with the crime. Photos of a screaming Meredith hitting the pavement were flashed around the world, and civil rights leaders converged on Mississippi to finish the march.

During the resumed "Meredith March," tensions erupted between

younger, more militant black activists and mainstream leaders such as
the Reverend Martin Luther King, Jr. To King's dismay, young
marchers took up the clenched-fist chant of "Black Power!"—a cry
that marked both the symbolic birth of the Black Power movement
and the worsening of tactical and organizational disputes in the civil
rights movement.

Meredith recovered from his wounds and rejoined the march in
time to enter Jackson triumphantly and address a mass rally from the
steps of the Mississippi State Capitol building. Squabbling among the
organizers almost prevented Dr. King from speaking.

In 1967 Meredith announced a bid for the Harlem congressional
seat of black patriarch Adam Clayton Powell. At the time, Powell was
engulfed in an ethics scandal and many civil rights figures were trying
to protect him. After various powerbrokers pleaded with Meredith to
cancel his bid, Meredith announced he would withdraw.

Over the years Meredith engaged in a variety of business ventures,
including tree farming, investment banking, and the restaurant and
TV repair businesses. In 1984 he joined the faculty of the University of
Cincinnati as a visiting professor, but, reported *People* magazine,
"Within months he had enraged students and faculty alike with inac-
curate charges of racist enrollment, his grandiose self-visions ('God
sent me to Cincinnati,' he once boasted) and incorrect public claims
that he was a full professor."

In 1985, during a lecture to an Ohio Wesleyan University American history class, Meredith charged that integration was "the biggest
con job ever pulled on any people" and a "sham" perpetrated by vote-
hungry liberal whites and a handful of puppet "black bourgeoisie."

With typical flamboyantly brutal logic, Meredith asked, "Have you
ever heard of Irish, Poles, Germans, Italians and Jews being integrated?
They can go anywhere and just enjoy their rights. Why call it integration when black folks do the same thing? It's just a con job." Refusing
to play the role of a noble civil rights icon, Meredith reflected on his
Ole Miss experience by saying, "To me it was an insult to hear people
say this was a first for the black race, for me to enjoy my rights. It was
humiliating to hear people say I integrated a school."

Through the years, James Meredith maintained a ruthless, jarring
intellectual integrity and courage that considered the traditional discussion of civil rights as an insult to him as an American citizen, as in-

valid, even preposterous. "Why do you have to call it anything?" he asked in 1989. "My son comes in and all of a sudden the room is integrated? . . . If you put one ounce of emphasis [on black rights], what are you saying? That I am not entitled to these rights?"

In 1989 Meredith joined the U.S. Senate staff of ultra–right wing Republican senator Jesse Helms, long considered a bitter foe of the civil rights movement.

Meredith explained the move by citing his agreement with Helms's opposition to affirmative action, welfare, and busing, programs that Meredith argued made blacks dependent, second-class citizens. "I will be, in the future, the most important black leader in America and the world," he declared, displaying the messianic flourish that often perplexed his audiences. "I have a divine responsibility to lead the black race to its rightful destiny."

In 1989 Meredith was reported to have issued a statement on Senator Helms's letterhead which alleged that 60 percent of the delegates to the NAACP convention were involved in the drug culture, and 80 percent were engaged in illegal actions. In response, Benjamin Hooks, then executive director of the NAACP, lashed out at Meredith, calling him "an intellectual vagrant" who "has obviously lost touch with reality."

Decades after Ole Miss, James Meredith had yet to achieve his goal of becoming a leader in the traditional sense. "Believe me," he said in 1989, "I have yet to do anything that I consider worthy of recognition."

In 1990 Meredith created a brief media firestorm when he announced he was supporting former Klan leader David Duke's bid in the Republican governor's race in Louisiana. He cited Duke's efforts to reform the welfare system.

Meredith returned to Ole Miss in 1997 to donate his personal papers to the University of Mississippi archives. He was received with a standing ovation, and said, "After I walked across the stage in 1963 and received my graduation certificate, my father said, 'These people can be decent.' I want to report to my father today in Mississippi, 'These people are decent.' " He then announced he was running for mayor of Jackson, Mississippi, the latest in a string of quixotic attempts at public office designed mainly to provide him with a media platform.

In 1997 Meredith reflected on the hero's welcome he received from the University of Mississippi. "For 35 years they never said I existed. Then they said I was the most important graduate in the history of the school. That's the way it is with me. It's either all or nothing. There is no middle area for me."

University of Mississippi history professor David Sansing observed of Meredith, "He has become a loyal son of Ole Miss. Generally he is considered by both the black and white community as kind of a maverick, a guy that just does his own thing. He has never been given the credit he is due." Sansing concluded, "He remains one of the central figures in the civil rights movement in America, not through some big sustained campaign or movement, but through his personal individual action and his personal bravery." Duncan M. Gray, Jr. observed that "Meredith is obviously a man of tremendous courage. It took all the guts anybody could possibly have to do what he did in 1962." In 1989 longtime Mississippi NAACP leader Aaron Henry agreed, saying, "Most of us couldn't have withstood the pressures. If any of us has earned the right to be eccentric, Jim has."

Today, Meredith reported, he still carries at least eighty birdshot pellets in his head and body from the 1966 shooting. "They hurt twenty-four hours a day," he said in 2000, "every day."

James Meredith lives today in Jackson, Mississippi, with his wife, journalist Judy Alsobrooks. He has three grown sons by his late first wife, and a teenage daughter and stepson with Ms. Alsobrooks. One of his sons attended Harvard and is now a doctoral candidate at the University of Mississippi's business school. Meredith's stepson and niece attended Ole Miss on scholarships.

In 2000 James Meredith was asked if anyone ever apologized or expressed regret to him over what happened in 1962. He replied, "It happens on a regular basis, in the grocery store, anywhere." It started happening to him in 1971 when he returned to live semi-permanently in Mississippi. "It's been intensifying now," he said. "They are people mostly over fifty. They come up and tell me how they felt then and how they feel differently now. They'll even tell me that in front of their kids."

Then Meredith was asked what comment he hears most often today from these Mississippi white people about his entering the university in 1962. He reported that he hears one statement over and over: "It's the best thing that ever happened to Mississippi."

In his "Letter from a Birmingham Jail" dated April 16, 1963, the Reverend Martin Luther King, Jr., predicted, "One day the South will

recognize its real heroes. They will be the James Merediths, courageously and with a majestic sense of purpose, facing jeering and hostile mobs and the agonizing loneliness that characterizes the life of the
pioneer."

King's prediction has not yet come true, at least not on the scale
warranted by Meredith's contribution to history in 1962. Meredith
was like a time traveler, traveling both from the antediluvian soil of
Mississippi's prehistory and from the distant future Mississippi to
come, who landed in 1962, engineered a stunning historical coup, and
then vanished.

"I was creating images then," Meredith explained in 1999, "that
were designed for forty years in the future."

In Mississippi, the aftereffects of the Battle of Oxford were especially profound.

"It had a tremendous sobering effect on a number of people in the
state, and it changed the direction of the state," noted veteran Mississippi reporter Bill Minor. "It discredited the direction the state was being led by the Citizens Council and their ilk. It was a turning point.
From that day forward, the Council went into decline."

In the year after the riot, though, it looked like the Citizens Council might continue to dominate Mississippi. Council activists sponsored a purge of political, education, and church figures, and some
white moderates, such as University of Mississippi history professor
Jim Silver, soon left the state. In 1963 the dean of the Ole Miss law
school, Robert Farley, was hounded out of the state for having the au-
dacity to argue that James Meredith had the right to attend the university.

On September 24, 1963, the school's second black student, Cleve
McDowell, was suspended and expelled from the law school the day
after a fellow law student saw a pistol fall out of his pocket as he was
going to class. McDowell said the pistol was for self-defense, since all
the federal marshals were pulled out of Oxford the month before, and
he felt his life could be in danger. He later expressed relief that he was
expelled. Otherwise, McDowell speculated, "I probably would have
been killed."

With McDowell's expulsion, the university was briefly a nonblack
school again, but in 1964 another black student named Cleveland
Donald applied to the school, armed with a court order, and was en-

rolled. After that, the state college board abandoned its policy of blocking black students from registering at historically white schools.

The nation would be cursed with racial turmoil through the 1960s, and Mississippi, a place the Reverend Martin Luther King, Jr., once described as "a desert state sweltering with the heat of injustice and oppression," would often be the center of the storm. "It is no accident that Mississippi elicits such rage and passion and fidelity in its sons and daughters of both races," wrote native son Willie Morris in 1982, "or that Northerners have always been obsessed with what takes place here, for Mississippi has always been the crucible of the national guilt."

On the moonlit early morning of June 12, 1963, a fanatic Citizens Council member named Byron de la Beckwith crouched in a honeysuckle thicket in Jackson, Mississippi, holding a 1917 model Enfield rifle with a six-power Golden Hawk scope, and just before 12:30 A.M., squeezed the trigger. The bullet killed James Meredith's close friend and ally Medgar Evers, a man Meredith credited as being indispensable to his victory at Ole Miss.

During Byron de la Beckwith's first trial in 1964, former governor Ross Barnett strode into the courtroom and shook the accused assassin's hand. The next day, former general Edwin Walker did the same thing. Beckwith was not convicted of the crime until he was retried in 1994. He died in prison in 2001 at the age of eighty.

On January 21, 1964, Ross Barnett was succeeded by his lieutenant governor, Paul B. Johnson, Jr. Johnson's campaign ads featured photos of his confrontation with Chief U.S. Marshal McShane and James Meredith, trumpeting the slogan "Stand Tall With Paul." During the campaign, Paul Johnson had ridiculed the NAACP as "niggers, alligators, apes, coons and possums."

But in the instant that Paul B. Johnson, Jr. was sworn in as governor, he began turning the state away from its neo-Confederate immediate past and into the twentieth century. In his inaugural speech, Johnson declared, "You and I are part of this world whether we like it or not. . . . We are Americans as well as Mississippians. . . . Hate or prejudice or ignorance will not lead Mississippi while I sit in the Governor's chair.

"If we must fight," Johnson promised, "it will not be a rearguard defense of yesterday. It will be an all-out assault for our share of tomorrow." When his speech concluded, he looked up from his text and added a spontaneous ending to the address that was, in the context of this time and place, almost revolutionary: "God bless every one of you, all Mississippians, black and white. . . ."

Governor Johnson soon cut off state funding to the Citizens Council, oversaw the dismantling of barriers to black voting, and welcomed federal civil rights officials. In 1964 the business leaders of Jackson defied the Citizens Council and decided to comply with the Civil Rights Act and integrate public facilities in the city. Paul B. Johnson, Jr., served as governor from 1964 to 1968 and died in 1985 at the age of sixty-nine.

Some Mississippi whites were radicalized by the Battle of Oxford and the accelerating civil rights revolution. One of them, a man named E. L. McDaniel, decided within days of the federal invasion that he would resurrect the Ku Klux Klan in Mississippi, which had been dormant for decades. He soon launched a thriving Mississippi chapter of Robert Shelton's United Klans of America and became the state's Grand Dragon, or state commander.

By 1964 an extremely violent, secretive new Klan faction called the White Knights of the Ku Klux Klan was eclipsing the United Klans in Mississippi, attracting a membership of two thousand. The members included, the FBI estimated, some thirty sheriffs, local police, and Mississippi Highway Patrolmen before Governor Johnson and local officials purged them.

The White Knights launched a rampage of torture and mayhem across the state, conducting more than 180 cross-burnings, at least six murders, a wave of church-burnings, and uncounted shootings and beatings of black civilians.

During the Freedom Summer of 1964, the thought police of the state Sovereignty Commission, still in operation under Governor Johnson, distributed the license-plate numbers of out-of-state civil rights volunteers to local sheriffs, including a Ford used by civil rights workers James Chaney, Andrew Goodman, and Mickey Schwerner. Acting on the commission's intelligence, Neshoba County deputy sheriff Cecil Ray Price and a gang of Klansmen abducted and murdered the three on the night of June 21, 1964. In October 1967, a white jury found seven Klansmen, including Price and White Knights gang leader and Imperial Wizard Sam Bowers, guilty of conspiracy and sentenced them to federal prison.

By 1969, after crackdowns by state and federal law-enforcement agencies, the Mississippi Klan shriveled to fewer than one hundred members. State funding for the notorious Sovereignty Commission was cut off in 1973, and it officially closed down in 1977. The commission's files were sealed for the next twenty-one years, until 124,000 pages of documents were opened by a court order in March 1998. Some Mississippians, both white and black, were stunned to discover that their elderly fathers or dead uncles were secretly paid informants for or collaborators with the commission.

By 1970 black voter registration in Mississippi had increased to 67 percent, up from 6 percent in 1960. In the late 1990s, the state capital of Jackson had a black mayor, a black police chief, a black majority on the city council, and 25 percent of the seats in the state legislature were held by African-Americans. In the early 1970s, federal courts ordered blacks onto the state highway patrol, and by the mid-1990s, 27 percent of the force was black.

William Simmons continued as an activist in the Citizens Council and became president of the Southern Independent School Association. After a long decline, the council finally disappeared in 1989 with the closing of its office in Jackson. Simmons retired from politics.

In the 1980s, remnants of the Citizens Council in some states reformed into a new organization, the Council of Conservative Citizens, using membership lists from the original council dating from the 1960s. One man active in the new organization was Robert "Tut" Patterson of Mississippi, who had helped form the original Citizens Council in 1954.

Republican Senator Trent Lott of Mississippi addressed a national board meeting of the Council of Conservative Citizens in 1992 in Greenwood, Mississippi, declaring, "The people in this room stand for the right principles and the right philosophy." Lott also welcomed CCC leaders to his office on Capitol Hill. When press reports surfaced about the meetings, Lott claimed ignorance of the council's white-supremacist philosophy, which was featured prominently in its literature, and later disassociated himself from the CCC's racial views. He never apologized for addressing the group.

In one of the few public statements he has made about the 1962 riot, Trent Lott was quoted in *Time* magazine in 1997 as saying, "Yes, you could say that I favored segregation then. I don't now." He added, "The main thing was, I felt the federal government had no business sending in troops to tell the state what to do."

Although President John Kennedy lost control of the Oxford crisis and had to restore order to Mississippi with a full-scale invasion of the state, he escaped political fallout as the nation backed his performance and then quickly turned its attention to the Cuban missile crisis. While JFK's popularity in the South dropped off in the weeks after Oxford, from 65 percent job approval in September to 51 percent in late October, it rebounded quickly after the missile crisis and stayed strong into the next summer.

Both President John Kennedy and Attorney General Robert Kennedy escaped any political damage from their across-the-board segregation of thousands of black troops in the invasion and the early days of the Oxford occupation. Aside from some brief press coverage, the story quickly vanished. The troops never forgot, though, and a number of the black troops who were disgraced in this manner still remember what happened to them with outrage and disgust.

In November 1962, the Mississippi state senate passed a resolution calling for the impeachment of President Kennedy for inciting an insurrection at Ole Miss.

A few weeks after Ole Miss, in the fall 1962 congressional midterm elections, the Democrats won more black votes than ever before. Finally, on November 20, JFK signed the long-delayed executive order banning discrimination in federal housing, fulfilling a promise he had made two years earlier, but the order was watered down considerably, applying only to new construction.

In the same midterm elections a few weeks after the riot at Oxford, an epochal shift in American politics was triggered, a shift that would have reverberations into the next century: the rebirth of the Republican party in the South. "In the eleven states of the old Confederacy," wrote Richard Reeves in *President Kennedy: Profile of Power,* "the Republicans had not put up serious candidates since the Reconstruction period after the Civil War. But, in 1962, Republicans won four new house seats and 31% of the total House vote in the South, almost double their 1958 midterm total of 16%."

On June 11, 1963, prodded by the blossoming civil rights revolution, John F. Kennedy proposed new federal civil rights legislation in a TV address to the nation. "We are confronted primarily with a moral issue," Kennedy proclaimed. "It is as old as the Scriptures and is as clear as the American Constitution." That night Medgar Evers was killed, and days later, Kennedy sent Congress a sweeping civil rights bill that would fight discrimination in voting, public facilities, jobs, and education.

Kennedy spent much of the final months of his life trying to lay the groundwork to pass the legislation, but in November 1963 it looked like the bill, and much of his domestic program, was stalled indefinitely in Congress.

On April 10, 1963, a sniper shot at former general Edwin Walker through his living-room window in Dallas, missing his head by an inch. The sniper was later identified as Lee Harvey Oswald, who dubbed himself a "hunter of fascists" for the deed. Seven months later Oswald was charged with assassinating President Kennedy.

On November 22, 1963, University of Mississippi junior David Crawley was walking on the campus near the Student Union when the announcement was broadcast on the public-address system that the president had been killed in Dallas. According to Crawley, "A group of thirty or forty students gave a spontaneous cheer. I was stunned."

A week after Kennedy was killed, James Meredith called him "the only president to take the racial issue as a moral and personal one." Said Meredith, "He was the only president to recognize the Negro as a full American citizen."

Among the mourners at John Kennedy's funeral was Mississippi governor Ross Barnett, who paid his respects at the White House with his wife and son.

After President Kennedy's murder, Robert Kennedy continued briefly as attorney general under President Lyndon Johnson, then ran for and won a term as U.S. senator from New York. In 1966, just three years after James Meredith graduated, Senator Kennedy visited Oxford to address the University of Mississippi law school. Things were changing quickly in Mississippi, and many white citizens were impressed that the national celebrity would travel to the center of the lion's den, and they eagerly turned out to hear what he had to say.

At Oxford Robert F. Kennedy received close to a hero's welcome. He thoroughly charmed an overflow audience of forty-five hundred and regaled delighted students with a satiric rendition of his bizarre telephone negotiations with Governor Barnett. He was vigorously applauded when he declared that not "all the errors are on one side. We have tremendous problems in my own state of New York, so many problems that, in the future, I'd like to concentrate on those and forget some of these past differences."

In Jackson, an angry former governor Ross Barnett charged that RFK "twisted statements or willfully misrepresented the facts" in explaining Barnett's actions during the crisis, and called Kennedy "a hypocritical, left-wing beatnik without a beard."

Robert Kennedy was assassinated in Los Angeles in 1968 while campaigning for the White House.

In 1982 the John F. Kennedy Library began releasing JFK's secret White House tapes, including Dictabelt phone recordings of his conversations with Barnett and others during the crisis, and Cabinet Room and Oval Office reel-to-reel tape recordings of White House meetings on September 30–October 1, 1962. Among the dumbfounded people expressing total surprise that John Kennedy, like Richard Nixon, would tape them without their consent, were former members of Kennedy's own White House staff.

Former major general Edwin Walker was charged with insurrection and conspiracy to incite rebellion at Oxford, and on October 1, 1962, was hustled off to a psychiatric hospital by federal marshals for an examination. A federal grand jury failed to indict him, and the charges were dropped.

Walker sued the Associated Press and other news organizations for more than $35 million, charging he was libeled by their reports that he personally led charges of rioters against federal marshals the night of the riot. Despite testimony from several witnesses who said he did exactly that (including Ole Miss campus police chief Burns Tatum, who quoted Walker as shouting, "Charge!" to the rioters), a Fort Worth district court civil jury awarded Walker an $800,000 libel judgment against AP in June 1964.

In 1967 the U.S. Supreme Court dismissed the judgment, and held in a historic ruling that public personalities were equivalent to public officials, and the media should be protected if it made mistakes without malice.

On June 23, 1976, Walker was arrested and charged with public lewdness for allegedly fondling a plainclothes policeman in a public toilet in Dallas. He was arrested again on a similar charge a year later.

In 1982, the Department of the Army quietly reinstated Walker's pension, which had been cut off in 1961 when he resigned from the army, following charges that he indoctrinated his troops with right-wing propaganda. Calling him "a truly dedicated American soldier," the army awarded him a major general's pension of $45,120 a year. In his retirement, Walker raised prize chickens. He died of lung disease in 1993.

Reverend Duncan M. Gray, Jr., the rector of St. Peter's Episcopal Church in Oxford, who plunged into the Ole Miss riot and tried to stop it with his bare hands, later became, like his father, the Episcopal bishop of the Diocese of Mississippi.

Throughout his career, Duncan Gray was a forceful, daring, and relentless advocate of racial justice and reconciliation in the state. In 1991 he was elected chancellor of the University of the South. Gray retired as bishop in 1993 and lives in Jackson, Mississippi. His towering son Duncan Montgomery Gray III also was rector of St. Peter's Episcopal Church in Oxford, and serves today, as his father and grandfather did, as bishop of the Diocese of Mississippi.

Clyde Kennard, the black applicant who tried to enter Mississippi Southern College two years before James Meredith's attempt on Ole Miss but was packed off to a state prison, suffered a worsening of the intestinal cancer he contracted there, which was exacerbated by neglect and bad medical care. After a public outcry, Governor Barnett granted Kennard early release, but he died soon after, on July 4, 1963, when Meredith was still attending Ole Miss. As he was dying, former army paratrooper Kennard said he had no regrets about his attempt. "It was a matter," he explained, "of being a man."

Nicholas Katzenbach succeeded Robert Kennedy as attorney general under President Lyndon Johnson and helped write and enact the Civil Rights Act of 1964, which Lyndon Johnson hammered through Congress through sheer brute force. Katzenbach later became general counsel for IBM. He now serves as an international and domestic arbitrator.

Looking back on the Battle of Oxford in 1999, Nicholas Katzenbach said candidly, "I thought it was a failure. We should have been able to accomplish everything without sending in troops, and we didn't. I think the administration deserves criticism for too much dilly-dallying. But it was the first time, it was difficult, and we couldn't get a straight story out of Ross Barnett." He added, "We wanted to create a situation where the local people handled it themselves. We wanted a minimum show of force. That is why we failed."

John Doar went on to become president of the New York City school board. During the Watergate scandal, he served as chief counsel to the House Judiciary Committee that recommended the impeachment of President Richard Nixon. Today he continues to practice law.

Of James Meredith's NAACP attorneys, Constance Baker Motley is a federal judge in New York, and Jack Greenberg is a law professor at Columbia Law School.

The killers of Paul Guihard and Ray Gunter were never identified. No tangible leads of any kind were ever reported.

In the wake of extremely bitter feelings in the state right after the riot, Chief U.S. Marshal James McShane was indicted by a Lafayette County grand jury in November 1962 for supposedly starting the riot at Ole Miss. He surrendered to Sheriff Joe Ford in Oxford and was released the same day when the Justice Department obtained a writ of habeas corpus. The indictment was dismissed in 1964 by a federal judge, who found that McShane had reasonable cause to order the firing of tear gas. McShane died in 1968, despondent over the death of his good friend and mentor Bobby Kennedy.

For the American soldiers who served with untold courage, restraint, and professionalism in the Battle of Oxford and successfully conducted one of the greatest rescue operations in American history, there would be no parades, no medals, and almost no recognition of their service.

Despite recommendations by various army commanders, the Defense Department issued not a single commendation medal for the bravery of U.S. troops during the Battle of Oxford. After it was all over, remembered Joseph Cooke of the 503d Military Police Battalion, "the Eighteenth Airborne Corps commander put a lot of the officers of the 503d in for the Army Commendation Medal. But we were told that you do not get Commendation Medals for Americans fighting Americans. So the army gave us a certificate of appreciation, which to a young officer don't mean squat. That's like putting a dozen donuts on your desk. It doesn't even go into your personnel file."

All of the eleven thousand officers and enlisted men of the Mississippi National Guard put on their uniforms, reported for duty, and served their country during the Oxford crisis.

"It is my opinion," Oxford National Guard Captain Murry Falkner wrote in his after-action report, that if Troop E had not reached the Lyceum in time, "the marshals, as well as many others, would have been rushed and killed. Initially, the mob would have won! Many buildings would have been burned and destroyed. The University of

Mississippi may have failed to exist and probably part of Oxford and vicinity would have been destroyed."

The Second Infantry Division sent Falkner a plaque of commendation for his unit, which was the only official recognition Troop E ever received from the federal government. Falkner talked the City of Oxford and the Oxford Jaycees into issuing commendations for the unit.

One day in the second week of October 1962, Captain Falkner was summoned to 108th Cavalry field headquarters in the sprawling army tent city occupying Billy Ross Brown's cow pasture. "I knew for sure I'd fouled up somewhere," Falkner recalled. He was handed a telephone receiver and got the shock of his life. It was Attorney General Bobby Kennedy, calling to congratulate him on "a job well done." "Later I told the troop of my call and conversation," Falkner recalled. "Rather than the compliment being a morale booster, it had an adverse effect, making us more disgusted than ever."

Murry Falkner was later promoted to General and lives today in Oxford, Mississippi. Major William Callicott, the 108th Cavalry squadron commander from Senatobia who marched his men onto campus the night of the riot, was reelected to the state legislature a few weeks later without opposition. "The people here did not hold anything against you for carrying out your duties," he recalled. Troop G commander Hassel Franklin lives in Houston, Mississippi, and runs a major furniture company.

Billy Ross Brown still lives in Oxford, and keeps in his office the 2.5-inch metal hose-connection piece that was fired point-blank at his head so many years ago. Troop E's Harold "Happy" Antwine, the driver of the first army vehicle onto campus after the riot started, and who stood on the skirmish line in front of the Lyceum as the mob closed in, completed his pharmacy degree at Ole Miss and is a pharmacist in Jackson. He still has the steel helmet he wore the night of the riot, which has a large dent from a brick impact.

They and their fellow soldiers in the 108th Armored Cavalry Regiment and 155th Infantry Division went on with their lives and became the bank presidents, judges, dentists, teachers, salesmen, farmers, fathers, and grandfathers of Mississippi. They rarely, if ever, spoke publicly of the Oxford debacle. A few of them quit the Guard in disgust.

"You've got to understand," recalled Oxford National Guard

Sergeant Buford Babb, "that there were Guardsmen on one side and relatives and townspeople and people you knew on the other. It wasn't something that we asked to do. It just happened." Major Oscar "Gray" Megginson of Tupelo remembered that at the time, "none of us wanted to be thanked, because we didn't want to be there in the first place."

One former Guard officer reported that "we were looked on as traitors by some of our friends, several of us were attacked verbally, and a few got in fistfights."

"We were betrayed by the governor and the Mississippi Highway Patrol," Hassel Franklin recalled thirty-eight years later. "We were not proud of it and didn't like to talk about it. We were disgusted at the political demagoguery of the Kennedys and Barnett that put people's lives at risk. We were all of the opinion that we'd been deserted by the governor and the state. But we were not Mississippi National Guard anymore, we were federal troops, there to enforce and obey the law."

One former Mississippi National Guard officer, Vernon Bullock, explained the Guardsmen's perfect performance this way: "This area down here is the most patriotic part of the United States of America. Bar none."

As he stood guarding a roadblock during the rescue of Oxford, a young Mississippi private in the 155th Infantry Dixie Division had explained simply, "It's a matter of an oath I took."

Charles M. Bolen, the Mississippi-born Second Infantry Major who helped command the rescue of downtown Oxford, later went back to Ole Miss to complete the degree that was interrupted by World War II. In 1983 he was awarded a degree in education.

Charles Shockley, the Second Infantry officer who marched his rifle platoon onto Oxford's Courthouse Square, served as an army aviator in Vietnam, retired as a major, and went on to become the first black corporate-jet pilot for a Fortune 500 company.

Dr. L. G. Hopkins still practices medicine in Oxford.

Gene Same, the U.S. Deputy Marshal from Indiana who sustained a near-fatal gunshot wound to the throat during the riot, recovered from his wound, and from a 1982 stroke caused by complications from the injury. He still carries the slug in his lung today.

The white people of Oxford understandably tried to quickly forget the horrors of the riot, especially since most of them had nothing to do with the violence. Many of them believed that the city was unfairly tarnished by the disaster. "We just don't talk about that any more," a lady merchant on town square told a visiting journalist in 1964. "It was just a bad dream," an Oxford businessman added, "and it's all past now."

The city of Oxford looks much the same as it did in 1962. The white stucco courthouse is still guarded by the Confederate soldier holding his long gun, scanning the distant horizon. Blaylock's Drug Store—where General Walker briefly held court during the riot and behind which is the alleyway where the last shots of the American Civil War were fired on the morning of October 1, 1962—is now Square Books, a leading independent bookstore and a mecca for Ole Miss students and faculty and book lovers across the region.

In the tradition of Faulkner, Oxford has become an intellectual center of the South, and has been home to writers such as Willie Morris, Barry Hannah, Donna Tartt, Richard Ford, Larry Brown, and Ellen Douglas. Ole Miss law school graduate John Grisham today serves as publisher of the *Oxford American* literary magazine, based in the city. The city was recently named one of the top six college towns in the nation by *USA Today*.

A month after the riot, University of Mississippi chancellor J. D. Williams described the experience as a "night of horrors." "We must not forget it," he said, "lest it happen again." But Mississippi has spent much of the last four decades trying to forget the Battle of Oxford, and because the full story of the bravery of its National Guard troops was never told, the cost has been a portion of its own soul. The Guardsmen and their fellow army troops would probably reject the title of "American heroes," but few men are more qualified to wear that title.

In 1992 the U.S. Supreme Court ruled that the state of Mississippi still perpetuates segregation at its state universities and colleges and neglects its historically black institutions. The ruling was on a lawsuit first brought in 1975 dubbed the Ayers case, after plaintiff Jake Ayers, Sr. Since 1995 the state has spent $83 million to upgrade its three traditionally black schools, but in 2001 Mississippi governor Ronnie Musgrove estimated that "the complete settlement of the Ayers case will take 15 to 20 years to reach."

In some superficial ways, the University of Mississippi today resembles a shrine to the rebellion of 1861. The school band still plays "Dixie," the football team is still known as the Rebels, and campus streets are still named Confederate Drive and Rebel Drive. The Confederate statue still guards the entrance to the Circle. The school mascot is still a cartoon character with white whiskers named Colonel Rebel, who until the late 1990s dressed in the style of an Old South colonel. Today, his attire is styled to reflect the sport in season, although he still wears his planter's hat. In 1983 the university formally rejected the Confederate battle flag as an official school symbol, but students and fans proudly waved the banner at athletic events until 1997, when the student senate voted to ask students and fans to stop. Today, very few, if any, Confederate flags can be seen at Ole Miss games.

In many other ways, the university has traveled light-years since sustaining a near-deathblow to its reputation in 1962. Today the school boasts well-respected programs in law, writing, pharmacy, business, and accounting; ranks in the top ten American public universities in producing Rhodes scholars and is featured in both *The Student Guide to America's Best College Scholarships* and *The Student Guide to America's Best College Buys*. Additionally, the online magazine *Yahoo! Internet Life* ranks the University as number thirty-six among the nation's one hundred most wired colleges.

In the 1990s, Ole Miss nearly doubled the number of its black undergraduates to 12 percent, in a state whose population is about one-third black. "Visitors to the Ole Miss campus," reported Chancellor Robert Khayat in 1999, "find a vibrant, diverse, energetic and open community."

In February 2000, the University of Mississippi elected its first black student body president, Nic Lott. He was president of the statewide College Republicans. In the academic year 2000–2001, the student body president, newspaper editor, quarterback, and head basketball coach were all African-Americans.

Ross Robert Barnett was prohibited by law from running for a second term as Mississippi governor, and he returned to private law practice in Jackson in 1964. "No man ever went into public office as ignorant as he did," charged University of Mississippi history professor James Silver, "and no man ever stayed in office for four years and is coming out as ignorant as he is."

The historical forces that collided in Mississippi in September 1962 were so volatile that only a statesman of supreme vision and a leader of unparalleled courage could have navigated the state peacefully through the crisis. In Ross Barnett it had neither. But it would be wrong to blame him alone for what went wrong at Oxford, for in trying to block the integration of Mississippi's schools he was simply doing what the majority of white voters in the state expressly wanted him to do when they elected him governor. Barnett was channeling the feelings of a great many white Americans who at the time strongly believed that integration was a bad idea.

Once he was back in private law practice, Ross Barnett resumed his practice of tackling cases for poor black clients.

Governor Barnett and Lieutenant Governor Johnson were never penalized for their contempt of the federal courts. Weeks after the riot, the U.S. Fifth Circuit Court of Appeals ordered the Justice Department to launch criminal proceedings against Barnett and Johnson, on top of the court's $10,000-per-day civil contempt judgment against Barnett. But in 1965, the court found that there was by then "substantial compliance" with its orders, and both civil and criminal proceedings were dropped. Barnett was never compelled to pay the court's $100,000 civil contempt penalty. Fifth Circuit Judge Richard Rives noted, "You sentence a man to three years for stealing a car, and here's a man who almost destroyed a university."

Although Ross Barnett presided over the greatest industrial expansion in the state's history until then, he is remembered almost exclusively for the Ole Miss crisis. He ran again for governor in 1967, but dogged by rumors that he secretly negotiated with Bobby Kennedy to capitulate at Ole Miss, he lost. To Barnett's horror, he was endorsed by none other than James Meredith.

Unlike the former segregationist Alabama governor George Wallace, who late in his life repeatedly begged black audiences for forgiveness, there would be no transformation, no catharsis, and no apologies by Ross Barnett. "I didn't make any mistakes," he said two decades after the Oxford crisis. "I don't think of a thing I'd have done differently. I used the best judgment in everything I did and everything I said."

As late as the 1980s, Ross Barnett was still telling "nigger jokes" in public, although he eventually changed the punch lines to use "colored boy." "I admire a lot of the black people," he explained, "but there are a lot of them that aren't as trustworthy. They just get in trouble and go to the penitentiary as a rule."

In 1983 Ross Barnett was invited by Medgar Evers's brother Charles to the Medgar Evers homecoming parade, an event that honored the memory of the martyred civil rights prince. The elderly Barnett agreed to appear and rode in an open limousine as part of the parade. James Meredith also planned to appear, but was prevented from doing so by a last-minute scheduling conflict. Meredith saw Barnett from time to time around Jackson, but the two never had the occasion to speak to each other.

In a 1998 interview, James Meredith offered a startling salute to Barnett and his performance during the Oxford crisis. "Barnett managed it perfectly," argued Meredith. "There was not a single black hurt during the entire episode in the whole year. Not one. He is almost exclusively to be credited with that reality. He knew what he was doing. Things could have been a lot worse.

"There were plenty of people in Mississippi who wanted to see change," Meredith speculated, "and I'm sure he was one of them."

Ross Barnett retired from his law practice on April 1, 1984, and entered a nursing home nine days later. His empire had shrunk to a single room with an American flag painted on the door and his guitar placed alongside the bed.

One day the previous summer, Barnett put on his red-and-blue Ole Miss tie, took his guitar, and set off for the Neshoba County Fair. It was an annual pilgrimage he made ever since 1919, when he won an oratory contest and was awarded a silk shirt. Every year Barnett regaled the crowd with a homespun joke routine, then plucked his guitar while he warbled tunes like "Polly Wolly Doodle" under the scorching tin roof of Founders Square pavilion.

Like all the years before, Ross Barnett closed the show. The crowd stomped and cheered as he shuffled onto the stage and bellowed an old tune into the microphone, "Are you from Dixie? / I said from Dixie! / Where the fields of cotton beckon to me. / I'm glad to see you, / Tell me how be you? / 'Cause I'm from Dixie, too . . ."

Then the old man raised his head to the heavens as he recalled his happiest memory from childhood: his own mother's voice singing to him from the back steps of his old Leake County home. "I wish I could hear that voice once more," Barnett said as he searched the sky above and softly sang: "When all God's children will gather round the table. That's the greatest suppertime of all."

Ross Barnett died in 1987. His son Ross Barnett, Jr., practices law in Jackson, Mississippi. The two men never had occasion to talk about the younger Barnett's National Guard service during the Oxford crisis.

Ross Barnett's daughter Ouida Barnett Atkins teaches history at a predominantly black public school in Jackson.

In April 2001, Mississippi voters decided by a two-to-one margin to retain the Confederate emblem as part of the state flag. Oxford was one of the very few predominantly white voting districts to vote in favor of a new flag that would have eliminated the Confederate design. Mississippi is the last state to feature the design so prominently in its state flag.

Today Mississippi is still the poorest state in the Union. The state has more black elected officials than any other state.

Nine days after Ray Gunter was killed while watching the Battle of Oxford, his widow Virginia Gunter gave birth to a baby girl. Ray had chosen her name, Debra Jane. Virginia later remarried.

The grave of Ray Gunter lies on a hillside east of Oxford at the edge of a pine forest laced with red oak, sweet gum, and wild cherry trees. His mother still lives not far across the hollows.

Today, there are no monuments to James Meredith or to the men of the Mississippi National Guard on the campus of the University of Mississippi, no buildings or statues or scholarships bearing their name.

But if you look very closely, and if you know where to look, you can still see bullet marks in the great columns of the Lyceum, from guns fired almost forty years ago, by ghosts from the dead Confederate legions.

ACKNOWLEDGMENTS

One day in 1996, while working on an A&E television special on the history of presidential audio recordings, I heard something that startled and fascinated me so much that it directly triggered this book.

As my production partner and director Carol Fleisher got ready to videotape Kennedy aide Burke Marshall speaking about JFK's tapes of the Oxford crisis, Marshall said, "That was the night we had a little war." I soon discovered that this was the biggest domestic military crisis of the twentieth century, an event that *U.S. News & World Report* (October 15, 1962) reported "came close to being a small-scale civil war," a turning point in history that climaxed in the president of the United States ordering a lightning invasion on American soil by more than thirty thousand combat troops.

In the nearly five years since then, I have been helped by many hundreds of people in Mississippi and elsewhere, and I am most indebted to my family: Naomi, William, Marilou, Kate, and Joe.

My editor, Gerald Howard of Doubleday, and my agent, Mel Berger of William Morris, made this book happen, and they have my extreme gratitude for the countless hours and insights they have given to this book.

In the long list of Mississippi heroes I met while researching this book, three stand apart, both for the courageous roles they played in the Oxford crisis and for the help they have given me. Since I first met James H. Meredith in 1998, he has been a most valued source of insights, enthusiasm, and research advice, and he graciously granted me a series of interviews. I am most indebted to this remarkable American for his inspiration and for writing this incredible chapter in our history. General Murry C. Falkner, Mississippi National Guard (ret.) of Oxford, and his good friend Bishop Duncan M. Gray, Jr., of Jackson were also warriors for peace at the Battle of Oxford, and I have been honored for them to share their memories with me.

Hundreds of American soldiers told their stories of the Battle of

Oxford for the first time for this book, and their courage, restraint, and professionalism under fire, in my opinion, is one of the proudest untold chapters in our history. I am especially grateful to the veterans of the Mississippi Army National Guard, the 503d Military Police Battalion, the Second Infantry Division, the 716th and 720th Military Police Battalions, and the 82nd Airborne and 101st Airborne Divisions; especially Mack Mullins, John Flanagan, William Peters, Donnie Bowman, John Migliore, Fred Villella, Charles Shockley, George Baldwin, Joseph Cooke, William Mayes, William Newton, Hassell Franklin, Charles London, James Gore, John Hodges, Lannon Franklin, Billy Ross Brown, William Callicott, Loyd Gunter, Jim McNew, Harold Antwine, Robert Crowe, Ted Cowsert, Robert Hanania, James Kennedy, William Austin, Charles Bolen and William Parks.

A number of former deputy U.S. Marshals and U.S. Border Patrol officers who served at Oxford agreed to be interviewed for this book, and several deserve special thanks: Al Butler, Dan Pursglove, Richard Dick, Siebert Lockman, and Graham "Gene" Same, who was kind enough to share with me documents from his personal papers.

David Sansing, Professor Emeritus of History at the University of Mississippi, has been very helpful to me in my research, as has longtime Jackson journalist Bill Minor. Professor Sansing read the manuscript and offered many helpful suggestions. William Simmons, former Citizens Council leader, was most gracious in sharing his time and memories.

Former Justice Department officials Nicholas Katzenbach, H. M. Ray, and former FBI agent Robin Cotten were very helpful in sharing their memories of the Oxford crisis, as were scores of former University of Mississippi students, Mississippi Highway Patrolmen, Mississippi civil rights activists, and other Mississippi citizens.

I thank Colin Callender and Keri Putnam at HBO Films for supporting early research on what became this book. I am greatly indebted to Lany McDonald, Pat Clark, and their superb staff at the Time, Inc. Research Center, and to archivists of the Mississippi State Department of Archives and History, the J. D. Williams Library at the University of Mississippi, the Freedom of Information Act section at FBI headquarters in Washington, D.C., and the John F. Kennedy Library.

I also thank Judy Alsobrooks, Pedro Sanjuan, Donna Bagdasarian, Deborah Baker, Walter McPherson, Oland Little, William Lamb, Ellis

Nassour, Charlie Berryhill, Art Richardson, Will Campbell, Carol Fleisher, Bill Perkins, Augusto Failde, Ed Meek, Dick Wilson, Gray Jackson, Richard Reeves, Wayne Furman of the New York Public Library, Richard Howorth, Will Lewis, Jr., Ouida Barnett Atkins, Ross Barnett, Jr., Mrs. Raymond Le Van, Joseph and Deborah D'Agostino, Jennifer Ford, E. H. Pleasant, Vernon Bullock, Charles Eagles, Cartha DeLoach, John Leslie, Don Proehl, Chuck Allen, Don Elliott, Gerald Walton, Verner Holmes, Robert B. Ellis, JoAnne Prichard Morris, James Mayo, Georges Biannic, Duncan M. Gray III, Ruth Gray, Nathan Hodges, Deirdre Hare, Jay Crosby, Amelia Zalcman, Johnny Vaught, Anson Sheldon, Bill Geoghegan, Joe Dolan, Ed Guthman, Omar Craig, Dr. L. G. Hopkins, Felix Bolo, Sparky Reardon, Gloria Kellum, Doris Smith, Patricia Ford Reaves, and the family and friends of Ray Gunter.

SOURCE NOTES

This book is based on four years of research, including interviews with more than five hundred eyewitnesses to and participants in the Battle of Oxford, most of whom have not talked publicly about the crisis for more than thirty-five years, and in most cases never. Many of these witnesses responded to notices placed by the author in dozens of newspapers across Mississippi and the South and in veterans' newsletters.

Archival sources were consulted at the University of Mississippi Archives in Oxford, the Mississippi State Department of Archives and History in Jackson, and the John F. Kennedy Presidential Library in Boston, including Kennedy's White House audiotapes of the crisis.

Other key sources include the U.S. Army's official history of the event; Mississippi Highway Patrol files (made available to the author by a source not affiliated with the MHP); Mississippi State Sovereignty Commission files (first unsealed in 1998); books and news accounts covering the crisis and related subjects; and some nine thousand pages of FBI files accessed by the author through a Freedom of Information Act request, files that include FBI agent interviews in October/December 1962 with more than five hundred witnesses to and participants in the crisis.

Times indicated for events during the riot are estimates from the best available evidence, since the chaos of the riot resulted in sometimes widely differing chronologies from eyewitnesses. Job titles are as of September 1962.

ABBREVIATIONS USED IN NOTES

JCL	*Jackson* (Mississippi) *Clarion Ledger*
JDN	*Jackson* (Mississippi) *Daily News*
MCA	*Memphis Commercial Appeal*

MPS	*Memphis Press-Scimitar*
NYT	*New York Times*
NYHT	*New York Herald Tribune*
NYWT	*New York World Telegram*
NYJA	*New York Journal American*
NYP	*New York Post*
WP	*Washington Post*
WES	*Washington Evening Star*
LAT	*Los Angeles Times*
NOTP	*New Orleans Times-Picayune*
LCJ	*Louisville Courier-Journal*
WSJ	*Wall Street Journal*
CSM	*Christian Science Monitor*
USNWR	*U.S. News & World Report*
SEP	*Saturday Evening Post*
FBI	FBI file, FBI headquarters, Washington, D.C.
MDAH	Mississippi Department of Archives and History, Jackson, Mississippi
UMASC	University of Mississippi Department of Archives and Special Collections, Oxford, Mississippi
JFKL	John F. Kennedy Presidential Library, Boston, Massachusetts
SERS	Southern Educational Reporting Service microfilm clipping files
MHP	Mississippi Highway Patrol
Army History	Paul J. Scheips, "The Role of the Army in the Oxford, Mississippi, Incident 1962–1963" (Department of the Army, June 25, 1965)

Epigraphs

ix *"I was creating"*: Int. James Meredith, September 20, 1998.

ix *"This story"*: David Sansing interview of Verner Holmes and E. R. Jobe, Verner Holmes Collection, Box 6, p. 182, UMASC.

Prologue · The Past Is Never Dead

1 *"The past is never dead"*: William Faulkner, *Requiem for a Nun* (New York: Random House, 1951), p. 92.

1 scene and dialogue in Governor's Office, May 22, 1865: T. J. Wharton, "Charles Clark," *MCA,* December 29, 1895, Charles Clark Vertical File, MDAH; correspondence between General Osband and Governor Clark, May 20 and May 22, 1865, Charles Clark Vertical File, MDAH.

2 background on post-Civil War Mississippi: James W. Loewen and Charles Sallis, ed., *Mississippi: Conflict & Change* (New York: Pantheon Books, 1974), pp. 145–167.

3 lynchings 1882–1952: Ibid., p. 178.

3 *"Mississippi's official policy"*: David Sansing, *Making Haste Slowly: The Troubled History of Higher Education in Mississippi* (Jackson, Mississippi: University of Mississippi Press, 1990), p. 72.

3 no paved road until the 1930s: Paul B. Johnson, Jr., quoted in James Reston, "Oxford, Miss.: The Conflict of Memory and Ambition," *NYT,* March 5, 1965.

Chapter 1 · Whom Shall I Fear?

5 *"We could have another Civil War"*: Stephen E. Ambrose, *Eisenhower: The President* (New York: Simon & Schuster, 1984), p. 308.

5 Eckford's walk to Central High; Little Rock crisis details: Will Counts, *A Life Is More Than a Moment: The Desegregation of Little Rock's Central High* (Bloomington, IN: Indiana University Press, 1999), pp. 32–46; Daisy Bates, *The Long Shadow of Little Rock: A Memoir* (New York: David McKay Company, 1962), pp. 70–76; "Making a Crisis in Arkansas," *Time,* September 16, 1957, p. 23; "Quick, Hard and Decisive," *Time,* October 7, 1957, p. 24; September 8, 1962 editions of *Arkansas Gazette, NYHT* and *NYP.* Eckford's impressions are from Bates, *The Long Shadow,* pp. 73–76.

6 Eckford dwelled on Twenty-seventh Psalm: *NYHT,* September 8, 1957, p. 1.

7 *"Don't let them see you cry"*: Bates, *The Long Shadow,* p. 76.

7 *"Leave this child alone!"*: Ibid., p. 70.

7 *"She's just a little girl"*: Editor's note, *Life,* June 19, 1964, p. 6.

8 Little Rock Nine's entry; withdrawal from Central High on September 23: Robert Baker, "Mob Had Job and Leaders Saw It Done," *WP,* September 24, 1957, p. 1; Benjamin Fine, "Mob Compels 9 Negroes to Leave School," *NYT,* September 24, 1957, p. 1; Counts, *A Life Is More Than a Moment,* p. 17.

8 *"Run, nigger, run!"*: Counts, *A Life Is More Than a Moment,* p. 47.

8 *"Strangely, the vision"*: Ibid., p. 51.

8 *"They would have had to kill me"*: Ibid., p. 47.

8 *"I looked into"; "Don't kill him"*: Ibid., p. 54.

9 Eisenhower furious: Herbert Brownell with John P. Burke, *Advising Ike: The Memoirs of Attorney General Herbert Brownell* (1993: University Press of Kansas, Lawrence, Kansas), p. 105.

9 *"He double-crossed me"*: Herbert Brownell, Gettysburg College (Pennsylvania) forum on Eisenhower and Civil Rights, October 11, 1990, C-SPAN broadcast.

9 Grant, Lee on Oval Office wall: Virgil Pinkley with James F. Scheer, *Eisenhower Declassified* (Old Tappan, New Jersey, Fleming H. Revell Company, 1979), p. 275.

9 *"The immediate need"*: Ambrose, *Eisenhower,* pp. 419, 420.

9 Eisenhower feared insurrection: Taylor Branch, *Parting the Waters: America in the King Years, 1954–1963* (New York: Touchstone, 1989), p. 224.

10 *"I'm at sea"; "Not enough people"; "Unless you've lived there"; "We could have another Civil War"*: Ambrose, *Eisenhower,* p. 308.

10 *"When emotions"; "School segregation itself"*: letter from Eisenhower to Swede Hazlett, July 22, 1957, Ann Whitman Diary Series File, Dwight D. Eisenhower Presidential Library.

10 Ike met civil rights leaders once: Kenneth O'Reilly, *Nixon's Piano: Presidents and Racial Politics from Washington to Clinton* (New York: Free Press, 1995), p. 184.

10 *"Now, you people"*: Ibid., p. 165.

10 *"definitely not friendly"; "the President hardly knew"*: Ibid., p. 168.

10 Ike's "nigger jokes": Ibid., pp. 165, 166.

10–11 experience of Morrow: E. Frederic Morrow, *Black Man in the White House* (New York: Coward-McCann, Inc., 1963), passim.

11 *"Literally, out on my ear"*: Ibid., p. 185.

11 Ike's inaction on civil rights events: O'Reilly, *Nixon's Piano,* pp. 171–75.

12 Ike's inaction on Shivers actions: Ambrose, *Eisenhower,* p. 337.

12 Eisenhower disgusted by Democrats: Ibid., p. 179.

12 *"bitterly disappointing"*: Ibid., p. 411.

12 *"Troops"*: Notes on White House stationery, September 24, 1957, Ann Whitman Diary Series File, Dwight D. Eisenhower Presidential Library.

12 *"there must be respect"*: Letter from Eisenhower to Swede Hazlett, July 22, 1957, Ann Whitman Diary Series File, Dwight D. Eisenhower Presidential Library.

12 *"If you have to use force"*; activation of 101st Airborne: Brownell, *Advising Ike,* p. 106.

13 *"We hold it to be"*: "U.S. Troops Sent into Little Rock Five Years Ago," *NYT,* October 1, 1962, p. 6.

13 background on Walker: Homer Bigart, "U.S. Troops Enforce Peace in Little Rock", *NYT,* September 26, 1957, p. 16; Eric Pace, "Gen. Edwin Walker, 83, is Dead; Promoted Rightist Causes in '60's", *NYT,* November 2, 1993, p. 10.

13 Walker offered resignation: John Hanchette, "Walker's Life Touched by Oswald, JFK, Controversy," Gannett News Service, November 4, 1993.

13 Little Rock tactical plan: "The Battle of Little Rock," *Life,* October 7, 1957, pp. 42, 43.

13 Negro troops hidden: Army History, p. 57.

14 final entry of the Little Rock Nine: Jack Setters, "Negro Pupils Enter School," *Nashville Banner,* September 26, 1957, p. 1; "Negroes Reenter School Under Armed Escort," *Birmingham News,* September 25, 1957, p. 1; Benjamin Fine, "Students Accept Negroes Calmly," *NYT,* September 26, 1957, p. 1.

14 *"As an officer"*: "Text of General's Address at School," *NYT,* September 26, 1957, p. 12.

15 *"We began moving"*: Melba Pattillo Beals, *Warriors Don't Cry: A Searing Memoir of the Battle to Integrate Little Rock's Central High* (New York: Pocket Books, 1994), p. 132.

15 *"For the first time"*: Bates, *The Long Shadow,* p. 104.

15 *"We are now an occupied territory"*: Beals, *Warriors Don't Cry,* p. 127.

15 *"darkest day"; "The South is threatened"; "If I were Governor"*: "The Prick of the Bayonet," *Time,* October 7, 1957, p. 26.

15–16 Gallup Poll; *"no one can deplore"*: "Was Ike Right?" *Time,* October 14, 1957, p. 31.

16 *"My heart skipped a beat"*; soldier watching; *"Sunlight flooded"*: Beals, *Warriors Don't Cry,* p. 143.

16 *"Won't you join us?"; "Gee, thanks"*: *NYT,* September 26, 1957, p. 1.

Chapter 2 · The Warrior

17 *"I considered myself"*: James H. Meredith, *Me and My Kind: An Oral History by James H. Meredith* (Jackson: Meredith Publishing, 1995), p. 14.

17 Meredith enthralled by reports of Little Rock: Int. James Meredith, December 10, 2000.

18 *"If I know what a mystic is"*: William Thomas, "Meredith: I Came with a Plan to Destroy the System", *MCA,* September 1, 1982, p. 12.

18 *"a lonely, taciturn"*: Arthur M. Schlesinger, Jr., *Robert Kennedy and His Times* (Boston: Houghton Mifflin, 1978), p. 317.

18 Meredith's ancestors: James H. Meredith, *James Meredith vs. Ole Miss* (Jackson: Meredith Publishing, 1995), pp. 2, 5, 15, 19; int. James Meredith, December 10, 2000.

18 *"My great-grandfather"; "Campbell was"*: Int. James Meredith, November 26, 2000.

18–19 *"Everything I have ever done"*: Int. James Meredith, November 10, 1998.

19 background on Cap and Roxie Meredith: Nadine Cahonas, *The Band Played Dixie: Race and the Liberal Conscience at Ole Miss* (New York, The Free Press, 1997), p. 58; "Battler in Mississippi: James Howard Meredith," *NYT,* September 21, 1962, p. 13.

19 *"We were most isolated"*: Int. James H. Meredith, November 26, 2000.

19 Meredith caught grasshoppers and crickets: Int. James Meredith, November 26, 2000.

19 he dreamed of a city: James H. Meredith, "I'll Know Victory or Defeat," *SEP,* November 10, 1962, p. 14.

19 Meredith had boy's dream: "Not a Well-Adjusted Negro", *Evening Bulletin* (Providence, Rhode Island), September 20, 1962, p. 16.

19 *"The train wasn't"*: "Though the Heavens Fall: Race Riot at University of Mississippi," *Time,* October 12, 1962, p. 19.

19 Meredith thought military desegregation was epochal: *SEP,* November 10, 1962, p. 14.

20 *"I never felt as free"*: *Evening Bulletin* (Providence, RI), September 20, 1962, p. 16.

20 Meredith's stomach trouble: James H. Meredith, *Three Years in Mississippi* (Bloomington, IN: Indiana University Press, 1966), p. 129.

20 *"I don't ever want to think":* Evening Bulletin (Providence, R.I.), September 20, 1962, p. 16.

20 *"The outcome will depend":* SEP, November 10, 1962, p. 14.

20 Meredith's walk in Japan; encounter persuaded Meredith: Ibid; int. James H. Meredith, November 26, 2000.

20–21 *"I really thought":* Lois Romano, "The Long, Long Journey of James Meredith," WP, November 3, 1989, p. C 1.

21 *"Little Rock was":* Int. James Meredith, November 26, 2000.

21 Meredith's return to Jackson: Meredith, *Three Years,* pp. 20–49.

21 per capita income of $1,233: Thomas Buckley, "State's Interference and Poverty Hinder University of Mississippi," NYT, October 8, 1962, p. 22.

21–22 conditions for Mississippi blacks: James W. Silver, *Mississippi: The Closed Society* (New York: Harcourt, Brace & World, 1966), pp. 84, 85.

22 twenty-two thousand black voters to eight thousand: Ibid., p. 90.

22 Medgar Evers's background: "His Name on Death List Since 1955, Evers Refused to Abandon Civil Rights Fight," Jet, June 27, 1963, pp. 18, 19.

22 *"affidavits":* Mrs. Medgar Evers with William Peters, *For Us, the Living* (Garden City, New York: Doubleday, 1967), p. 205.

22 attacks on black civilians: Ibid., pp. 155–57, 169, 170, 204, 211–213, 377.

22 *"A map of Mississippi":* Ibid., p. 204.

23 Meredith at Jackson State: Meredith, *Three Years,* pp. 50, 51; int. James Meredith, November 26, 2000.

23 *"To me, a person is":* Meredith, *Me and My Kind,* p. 22.

23 *"Divine Responsibility":* Meredith, *Three Years,* pp. 21, 22.

24 Meredith consulting with Evers: Ibid, pp. 55, 56.

24 Evers applying: Evers, *For Us, the Living,* p. 155.

24 university admitted students of all colors except black: University of Mississippi 1961, 1962, and 1963 Yearbooks; UMASC. In most accounts, the school is incorrectly referred to as "all-white" prior to Meredith's registration. In fact, yearbooks for 1962 and earlier show dozens of students of Asian, Hispanic, and other ethnicities.

24 Oxford on ridge: David G. Sansing, *The University of Mississippi: A Sesquicentennial History* (Jackson: University Press of Mississippi, 1999), p. 23.

24 *"It's better than Harvard":* Walter Lord, *The Past That Would Not Die* (New York: Harper & Row, 1965), p. 95.

24 Ole Miss academic strengths: Joe David Brown, "Babes, Brutes and Ole Miss", *Sports Illustrated,* September 19, 1960, p. 117; William Chapman, "Ole Miss Hopes," WP, October 21, 1962, p. E 3.

25 *"William Nichols patterned":* Sansing, *The University of Mississippi,* pp. 168–69.

25 *"There are magnolias":* Sports Illustrated, September 19, 1960, p. 117.

25 *"Inspired by Ole Miss";* background on Vaught and Ole Miss football: "Coach Johnny Reb," Time, November 28, 1960, p. 34.

25 *"their dewy-eyed acceptance":* Sports Illustrated, September 19, 1960, p. 117.

26 John Leslie's Walgreen drugstore: Int. John Leslie, February 4, 2000.

26 Faulkner's writing habits: dispatch by "Carmichael," July 9, 1962, Oxford, Time Inc. archives.

26 *"he didn't exaggerate":* Rick Tuttle, "Mississippi's Roots Are Deep in Past," *Miami Herald,* October 2, 1962, p. 1.

26 *"In the beginning"*: William Faulkner, "Mississippi," *Holiday,* April 1954, p. 35.

26 Faulkner's walks, pipe-smoking: John Faulkner, *My Brother Bill: An Affectionate Reminiscence* (New York: Trident Press, 1963), pp. 250, 251, 254, 256, 265.

27 Faulkner took manuscripts to Gathright-Reed's: Ibid., p. 237.

27 Faulkner trained horses: Ibid., p. 250.

27 *"dead skunk"*: "Will Was Here," *NYT,* September 21, 1997, section 6, p. 31.

27 Murphy at Ole Miss: Art Sears, Jr., "White Pals Glad Negro Was Ole Miss Student," *Jet,* October 11, 1962, p. 18; Layhmond Robinson, "Negro Attended U. of Mississippi," *NYT,* September 25, 1962, p. 26.

27 Mayfield and Dubra experiences: Sansing, *The University of Mississippi,* p. 271.

27–28 post-Brown integration; massive resistance: Francis M. Wilhoit, *The Politics of Massive Resistance* (New York: G. Braziller, 1973), passim.

28 King's registration attempt; *"They are going to kill me!"*: Sansing, *The University of Mississippi,* p. 277.

29 Kennard registration attempt: Ibid, p. 280.

29 *"Anybody who thinks"*: Int. James Meredith, September 20, 1998.

29 Meredith's debates; *"You've got to understand"*; *"The objective was to put pressure"*: Int. James Meredith, November 26, 2000.

30 *"We are very pleased"*: Meredith, *Three Years,* p. 54.

30 *"I sincerely hope"*; *"With all of the changes"*: Meredith, *Three Years,* pp. 57, 58.

30 Meredith's college credits: Meredith, *Three Years,* pp. 144, 145. Technically, Meredith failed a European History course in 1959, but not for academic reasons: He failed to fill out a withdrawal slip when he was transferred by the air force. (James V. Mathis, "Meredith's Past Grades Cited," *NOTP,* January 24, 1963, Section 2, p. 7.)

30 *"It has been found necessary"*; *"It grieves me keenly"*: Sansing, *The University of Mississippi,* pp. 282, 283.

31 *"The objective"*: Nadine Cohodas, *The Band Played Dixie,* p. 63.

31 *"I am making this move"*: Meredith, *Three Years,* p. 56.

31 Marshall/Meredith phone call: Meredith, *Three Years,* p. 56.

31 crusade would have ended: Meredith, *Me and My Kind,* p. 17.

32 Marshall/Motley dialogue: Int. Constance Baker Motley, January 9, 1998.

32 *"Meredith was"*: Int. Jack Greenberg, September 20, 1998.

32 *"We never"*: Int. Constance Baker Motley, January 9, 1998.

32 *"He's got more guts"*: Ted Poston, "James Meredith: a Portrait in Courage", *NYP* Magazine, March 11, 1967, p. 2.

32 *"James Meredith is crazy"*: Int. Bill Minor, September 18, 1998.

32 *"I asked myself"*: Paul Vanderwood, "Meredith Says He's Getting No Outside Help," *MPS,* September 19, 1962, p. 3.

33 *"The change of tide"*: Evers, *For Us, the Living,* p. 235.

33 Freedom Riders: Branch, *Parting the Waters,* pp. 418–49.

34 *"Why did you"*: Constance Baker Motley, *Equal Justice Under Law: An Autobiography* (New York: Farrar, Straus and Giroux, 1998), p. 164.

34 *"I considered myself"*: Meredith, *Me and My Kind,* p. 14.

34 *"he was the important one"*: Int. James Meredith, November 26, 2000.

34 Meredith's legal struggle: Meredith, *Three Years,* pp. 105–66.

34–35 Meredith read Theodore Roosevelt quote: *SEP,* November 10, 1962, p. 14.

35 *"leads the Court"*: Meredith, *Three Years,* p. 143.

35 *"just about the type"*: Meredith, *Three Years,* p. 158.

35–36 background on Black; quote on Klan: "Justice Black, Champion of Civil Liberties, Dies at 85", *NYT,* September 26, 1971, p. 76.

Chapter 3 · The Incendiary Man

37 *"He was the greatest actor of our time"*: Hugh Sidey, "He Asked Me to Listen to the Debate," *Time,* November 14, 1983, p. 69.

37 *"the last year"*: Branch, *Parting the Waters,* p. 562.

37–38 *"an incendiary man"*: Gerald S. Strober and Deborah H. Strober, *Let Us Begin Anew: An Oral History of the Kennedy Presidency* (New York: HarperCollins, 1993), p. 156.

38 *"like the sun"*: Int. Pedro Sanjuan, September 14, 1997.

38 JFK popularity up after Bay of Pigs; thought it incredible: Richard Reeves, *President Kennedy: Profile of Power* (New York: Touchstone, 1993), p. 106.

38 *"this is a damned good job"*: Hugh Sidey, *John F. Kennedy, President* (New York: Antheneum, 1964), p. 69.

38 JFK personal energy: William Manchester, *Portrait of a President: John F. Kennedy in Profile* (Boston: Little, Brown & Company, 1962), p. 12.

38 *"The outline is slender"*: Gore Vidal, "A New Power in the White House," *The Sunday Telegraph* (London), April 9, 1961.

39 *"He had this extraordinary"*: Strober and Strober, *Let Us Begin Anew,* p. 148.

39 *"half his time"*: Michael R. Beschloss, *The Crisis Years: Kennedy and Khrushchev, 1960–1963* (New York: Edward Burlingame Books, 1991), p. 227.

39 JFK Oval Office detail: William Doyle, *Inside the Oval Office: The White House Tapes From FDR to Clinton* (New York: Kodansha America, 1999), p. 98.

39 ashtray on JFK's desk: Oval Office exhibit, JFKL.

39 Hoover's files on JFK: Reeves, *Profile of Power,* pp. 66–67, 288–93, 626–27

39 *"J. Edgar Hoover has Jack Kennedy"*: Reeves, *Profile of Power,* p. 288.

39 JFK's sex life: Reeves, *Profile of Power,* pp. 288–91, 679n, and 707n. In Seymour M. Hersh's 1997 *The Dark Side of Camelot* (Little, Brown), former Secret Servicemen provided details of JFK's frequent encounters with prostitutes, starlets, secretaries, and perfect strangers.

39 *"like God"*: Reeves, *Profile of Power,* p. 291.

39–40 JFK's illnesses: Reeves, *Profile of Power,* pp. 36, 42, 43.

40 Kennedy's injections by Jacobson: Reeves, *Profile of Power,* pp. 684n, 685n, 699n. At the JFKL, in the records of the U.S. Secret Service, White House Post and Gate Logs, Boxes 2–12, Reeves found records confirming that Jacobson entered the White House more than thirty times in 1961 and 1962.

40 *"adulterated drugs"*: Iver Peterson, "Jacobson Loses License," *NYT,* April 26, 1975, p. 1.

40 dangers of amphetamines; *"There were cauldrons"*: Boyce Rensberger, "Amphetamines Used by a Physician to Lift Moods of Famous Patients," *NYT,* December 4, 1972, p. 1.

40 toxic psychosis with hallucinations: *Encyclopaedia Britannica Online,* 2001.

40 Capote experience and quotes: Edward Klein, *All Too Human: The Love Story of Jack and Jackie Kennedy* (New York: Pocket Books, 1996), p. 256.

41 *"He took a syringe"*; Jacobson explained: "The Story of a 'Dr. Feelgood,' " *Newsweek,* December 18, 1972, p. 73.

41 RFK wanted shots tested: Reeves, *Profile of Power*, p. 699*n*.

41 *"I don't care"*: ibid.

41 fraction of 1 percent of black students: Arthur M. Schlesinger, Jr., *A Thousand Days: John F. Kennedy in the White House* (Boston: Houghton Mifflin Company, 1965), p. 927.

42 *"The next President"*: James Reston, "Kennedy's Strategy," *NYT,* October 2, 1962, p. 21.

42 *"No presidential candidate"*: Carl Brauer, *John F. Kennedy and the Second Reconstruction* (New York: Columbia University Press, 1977), p. 43.

42 *"a grace and a charm"*: Lewis J. Paper, *The Promise and the Performance: The Leadership of John F. Kennedy* (New York: Crown Publishers, 1975), p. 134.

42 1956, 1960 black vote margins: Reeves, *Profile of Power*, p. 62; and Branch, *Parting the Waters*, p. 374.

42–43 *"What disappointed me"*: Harris Wofford, *Of Kennedys and Kings: Making Sense of the Sixties* (New York: Farrar Straus Giroux, 1980), p. 124.

43 *"The President believed"*: Branch, *Parting the Waters*, p. 398.

43 *"There is no sense"*: December 1962 broadcast, Oval Office discussion with network TV reporters, JFKL.

43 *"Every president must endure"*: Theodore C. Sorensen, *Decision-Making in the White House: The Olive Branch or the Arrows* (New York: Columbia University Press, 1963), p. xii.

43 greeted by George Thomas: Reeves, *Profile of Power*, p. 314.

43 *"He had at this point"*: Schlesinger, *A Thousand Days*, p. 930.

44 JFK's Gallup scores: "Polls," *Time,* September 28, 1962, p. 9.

44 *"I'm afraid that the fact"*: Schlesinger, *Robert Kennedy and His Times*, p. 316.

44 "essentially cautious": Schlesinger, *A Thousand Days*, p. 939.

44 Sanjuan quotes: Int. Pedro Sanjuan, December 3, 2000.

45 *"a pain in the ass"*: Strober and Strober, *Let Us Begin Anew*, p. 294.

45 *"Tell them"*: Wofford, *Of Kennedys and Kings*, p. 153.

45 *"You're making my life"*: Reeves, *Profile of Power*, p. 357.

45 *"niggers"*; *"chimpanzees"*: "Judge in Rights Case: Judge William Harold Cox," *NYT,* February 26, 1965, p. 14.

46 *"God-damned civil rights"*: Reeves, *Profile of Power*, p. 53.

46 *"has the President's confidence"*: Anthony Lewis, "What Drives Bobby Kennedy," *NYT Magazine*, April 7, 1963, p. 34.

46 *"Management in Jack's"*: Richard Reeves, "The Lines of Control Have Been Cut," *American Heritage*, September 1993, p. 62.

46 early Kennedy administration's civil rights background: Branch, *Parting the Waters*, pp. 379–632; Schlesinger, *A Thousand Days*, pp. 931–39.

46 *"I wasn't lying awake"*: Anthony Lewis, "What Drives Bobby," *NYT Magazine*, April 7, 1963, p. 34.

46 *"Bobby was"*: Int. Pedro Sanjuan, December 3, 2000.

47 5 percent of blacks registered in Mississippi; Justice Department planned legal attack: Anthony Lewis, "U.S. Sues to Widen Mississippi Voting," *NYT,* August 29, 1962, p. 1.

47 background on Marshall: Branch, *Parting the Waters*, p. 388.

47 background on Doar: Ibid, pp. 331, 334, 335, 387, 410.

47–48 background on Katzenbach: Benjamin Welles, "Cool-Nerved Statesman," *NYT,* October 19, 1968, p. 11; " 'Great Big Guy' Leader for U.S. at University," *Mont-*

gomery Advertiser, June 12, 1963, p. 12; *Current Biography,* 1966; Edwin Guthman, *We Band of Brothers* (New York: Harper & Row, 1971), p. 100.

Chapter 4 · We Shall Be Invincible

49 Barnett background: Int. Ross Barnett, Jr., February 11, 2000; biographical notes on Barnett by Gene Wirth, *JCL,* January 17, 1960, Section E, p. 3.

50 *"as bitter a racist":* "Mississippi Mud," *Time,* September 7, 1959, p. 13.

50 Barnett's office details: John Hebers, "How Barnett Press Chat Would Look on Television," *JDN,* August 5, 1962.

50 *"as astonishing":* Ira B. Harkey, Jr., *The Smell of Burning Crosses: An Autobiography of a Mississippi Newspaperman* (Jacksonville, Illinois: Harris-Wolfe, 1967), p. 131.

51 Barnett's early jobs: Jo Ann Blissard, "Get-Up-and-Go-Policy Wins for Attorney Ross Barnett," *JDN,* August 3, 1947.

51–52 Barnett as Wearever salesman: Erle Johnston, Jr., *I Rolled with Ross: A Political Portrait,* (Baton Rouge, Louisiana: Moran Publishing Company, 1980), pp. 60, 61.

52 *"He was not":* David Sansing interview of Robert J. Farley, May 15, 1979, Verner Holmes Collection, Box 6, p. 24, UMASC.

52 Barnett's black clientele: Int. Bill Minor, November 15, 2000; int. Ross Barnett, Jr., February 11, 2000; int. Rev. Clifton Jackson, December 8, 1999.

52 *"What doctor do you want":* Int. Sue Turk (secretary for Governor Barnett), November 29, 1999.

52 Barnett referred to "niggers": "Mississippi's Barnett," *Time,* October 5, 1962, p. 17.

52 *"I believe that the Good Lord":* "The Voice of the South," speech by Ross Barnett to the Mississippi Citizens Council, Jackson, Mississippi, August 1959 (exact date not indicated) Ross Barnett Vertical File, MDAH, Jackson, Mississippi.

52 *"Mixing the races":* "Strength Through Unity!" speech by Barnett to Citizens Council rally in New Orleans, March 7, 1960, Citizens Council pamphlet, SERS.

52 *"The Negro is different":* Time, September 7, 1959, p. 13.

52 *"If a Negro";* funding of schools: "Governor Says State Won't Mix," *Dallas Morning News,* September 6, 1962, sec. 4, p. 1.

52–53 *"Nobody wants violence":* "The Voice of the South" speech, August 1959.

53 *"Ross Barnett will rot":* Wilhoit, *The Politics of Massive Resistance,* pp. 89, 90.

53 *"militantly stubborn,":* Silver, *Mississippi: The Closed Society,* p. 43.

53 *"Friends, I am a Mississippi":* Eyes on the Prize, PBS documentary, 1987, episode 2, "Fighting Back: 1957–1962," Blackside Inc., Steve Fayer, writer, Henry Hampton, executive producer.

53 industrial projects: Robert Nelson, "Mississippi's Challenge," *CSM,* September 11, 1962.

53 *"veneered savage":* "Mississippi Politics," dispatch from Dudley Morris, Atlanta, January 27, 1964, Time, Inc. archive.

53 *"lazy, lying":* Silver, *Mississippi: The Closed Society,* p. 19.

53 *"Why squander money":* Dudley Morris dispatch, January 27, 1964, Time, Inc. archive.

54 *"You know and I know":* Hodding Carter, " 'The Man' from Mississippi—Bilbo," *NYT Magazine,* June 30, 1946, p. 12.

54 *"damn few white men":* "Mississippi: A Vote for Reason," *Time,* August 27, 1965, p. 13.

54 *"pick out a nigger girl and a horse!"*: O'Reilly, *Nixon's Piano*, p. 207.

54 *"The south is armed for revolt"*; *"The trouble is the North"*: Russell Warren Howe, ed., "Talk with William Faulkner," *Reporter*, March 22, 1956, pp. 18–20.

54 William Faulkner's racial views: Marjorie Hunter, "Faulkner Sensed Impending Crisis," *NYT*, October 7, 1962, p. 61.

54–55 *"the Southerner already knew"*: William Faulkner, "Letter to the North," *Life*, March 5, 1956, pp. 51, 52.

55 Sovereignty Commission detail: "Sovereignty Commission Agency History," 1999 MDAH paper; John Cloud, "KGB of Mississippi," *Time*, March 30, 1998, p. 30; Paul Hendrickson, "Unsealing Mississippi's Past: In the Name of Segregation, the State Ran Its Own Spy Agency," *WP Magazine*, May 9, 1999, p. W8.

55 *"private Gestapo"*; *"public funds"*: James Graham Cook, *The Segregationists* (New York: Appleton-Century-Crofts, 1962), p. 89.

55 Green as collaborator: "Journalist's Efforts Aided Sovereignty Panel," *Baton Rouge Sunday Advocate*, June 7, 1998, p. 6B.

55 *"The tragic truth"*; *"neighbor informs"*: Claude Sitton, "Methods of Citizens Council Stir Up Attacks in Mississippi," *NYT Magazine*, March 30, 1961, p. 18.

56 Barnett taught Sunday school; *"He was nice"*; hosted schoolchildren: Int. Mrs. Ellsworth Howard (Barnett's personal secretary), September 29, 1998.

56 *"you wanna have potluck"*; worked past 9 o'clock; locked the Capitol doors: Int. with former assistant to Barnett.

56 *"My door is always open"*: Dan Davis, "Barnett's Unwavering Course," *JDN*, September 21, 1962, p. 7.

56 Barnett gave out twenty-dollar bills; tried to balance budget: Int. Sue Turk, November 29, 1999.

56 Barnett's difficulties as governor: James Saggus, "Barnett is Satisfied with Record in Office," *Baton Rouge State Times*, January 17, 1964, p. 6B.

56 Barnett's spending on mansion: "Mississippi's Barnett," *Time*, October 5, 1962, p. 17.

57 prominence of Simmons: Silver, *Mississippi: The Closed Society*, pp. 40–43.

57 birth of Citizens Council: Int. Robert Patterson, February 28, 2000.

57 background on council: Silver, *Mississippi: The Closed Society*, pp. 35–44.

57 council claimed 250,000 members: Wilhoit, *The Politics of Massive Resistance*, p. 111.

57 *"everybody in the South"*: Int. Robert Patterson, February 28, 2000.

58 Simmons biographical detail: Ints. William Simmons, September 21, 1998; March 5, 1999; October 15, 2000; Cook, *The Segregationists*, pp. 68–72; "Racists' Strategist: William James Simmons," *NYT*, September 28, 1962, p. 22.

58 thinking and strategy of Simmons: Ints. William Simmons, September 21, 1998; November 29, 1999; October 15, 2000.

58 *"The general aims"*: William J. Simmons, "A View from the South," *Yale Political Quarterly*, Summer 1963, p. 8.

58 *"the average Negro brain"*: Robert Massie, "What's Next in Mississippi?" *SEP*, November 10, 1962, p. 20.

58 *"In our section"*; *"Segregation is not perfect"*: "Why Segregation Is Right," William Simmons speech to Notre Dame University, March 7, 1963, SERS.

58 Jackson council members: Joseph M. Guilfoyle, "Mississippi Supports Barnett," *WSJ*, September 28, 1962, p. 1.

59 *"Council is infinitely"*: Hodding Carter III, "Citadel of the Citizens Council," *NYT Magazine*, November 12, 1961, p. 24.

59 Citizens Council's subversive organizations: Silver, *The Closed Society*, p. 90.

59 *"the blackout of TV news"*: Evers, *For Us, the Living*, p. 238.

59 *"The dissenter"*: NYT Magazine, November 12, 1961, p. 24.

59 *"Three men came to see me"*: SEP, November 10, 1962, p. 20.

59 *"What the niggers want"*: Ibid.

60 council tactics: James Desmond, "New Klan Rides in South, Its Whip: Economic Terror," *NYP*, November 22, 1955, pp. 2, 32.

60 *"wonderful cooperation"*: "White Supremacists Hire Woman to Teach Hate to School Children," *NYP*, April 25, 1958.

60 *"God wanted"; "Famous scientists say"; "We in the South do not intend"*: Silver, *Mississippi: The Closed Society*, pp. 68, 69.

60 *"The closed society"; "Based on antique"*: Ibid., p. 151.

61 *"line in the sand"*: Int. William Simmons, September 21, 1998.

61 *"One of Mississippi's great problems"*: Int. Bill Minor, September 18, 1998.

61 Barnett thought segregationists in Little Rock too divided; *"We're all standing together"*: "Governor Says State Won't Mix," *Dallas Morning News*, September 6, 1962, sec 4, p. 1.

62 *"Don't wait for your daughter"*: Wilhoit, *The Politics of Massive Resistance*, p. 187.

63 *"Through it all"*: NYT Magazine, November 12, 1961, p. 23.

63 Barnett and Simmons's electoral strategy: Bill Minor, "Barnett Also Played Presidential Politics," *JCL*, November 11, 1987, page G 3.

63 *"so horrible"*: Edward T. Folliard, "Segregation Fight Is Matter of Life and Death to Barnett," *WP*, September 27, 1962, p. 10.

64 *"Barnett just couldn't"*: Int. Bill Minor, September 18, 1998.

64 *"As a politician"; "It's the last man"*: Neil Maxwell, "Behind the Zeal of Ross Barnett," *WSJ*, October 1, 1962, p. 3.

64 *"Some politically astute"*: WSJ, September 28, 1962, p. 16.

64 *"was never about me"*: Int. James Meredith, September 20, 1998.

65–66 Barnett's September 13 speech: *The Citizen* (Citizens Council publication), September 1962, pp. 6–9. The most obvious legal reality that cancels the theory of "interposition" is the "Supremacy Clause" of the U.S. Constitution, Article VI, which reads in part that United States law "shall be the supreme Law of the Land . . . any Thing in the Constitution or Laws of any State to the Contrary notwithstanding."

Chapter 5 · Order of Battle

67 *"This could be"*: Int. Robert Shelton, September 18, 2000.

68 background on U.S. Marshals: "Federal Marshal, Basically Court Officer, Now Serves as 'Soldier' in Civil Rights Army," *WSJ*, October 1, 1962, p. 10; int. with former U.S. Marshals Service historian Ted Calhoun, February 6, 2001.

68 *"political hacks"*: Int. with former U.S. Border Patrol officer.

69 First Baptist siege: Branch, *Parting the Waters*, pp. 454–62.

69 Kennedys' lessons from siege: *Parting the Waters*, p. 469.

69 *"some of the details"*: Lord, *The Past That Would Not Die*, p. 143.

70 *"agreeable rogue"*: Edwin O. Guthman and Jeffrey Shulman, ed., *Robert Kennedy in His Own Words: The Unpublished Recollections of the Kennedy Years* (New York: Bantam Books, 1988), p. 159.

70 *"That will take about a year"*: Lord, *The Past That Would Not Die*, p. 143.

70 RFK/Barnett conversation on note-taking: Int. Angie Novello (then RFK's personal secretary at the Justice Department), December 23, 1999.

70 *"code of the Ivy League"; "reasonable men"*: Victor S. Navasky, *Kennedy Justice* (New York, Atheneum, 1971), p. 16.

70 *"Those who understand the swamp-fox"*: Bill Minor, "Behind-the-Scene Events in Ole Miss Crisis," *NOTP,* October 2, 1982.

70 *"every encouraging word"*: "Compilation—1962," Verner Holmes Collection, Box 4, Folder 7, p. 12, UMASC.

71 September 19 meeting: David Sansing, *Making Haste Slowly,* pp. 174, 175; David Sansing ints. with Thomas J. Tubb (p. 31), S. R. "Doc" Evans (pp. 25–27), and Tally Riddell (p. 41); Box 6, Verner Holmes Collection, UMASC.

72 *"My plan was"*: Int. James Meredith, November 23, 1998.

72 Meredith's movements on September 20: Larry Still, "Ex-GI Hopes His Actions Changed Course of Miss. History," *Jet,* October 4, 1962, pp. 16–20.

72–73 efforts to block Meredith: "Compilation—1962," Verner Holmes Collection, Box 4, Folder 7, p. 13, UMASC.

73 *"Hell, no!"*: "Integration Web Tangled," *MCA,* September 21, 1962, p. 40.

73 *"Do you think"*: Lord, *The Past That Would Not Die,* p. 155.

73 *"the most beautiful land"*: Larry Still, "Man Behind the Headlines," *Ebony,* December 1962, p. 32.

73 background on Oxford: McCandlish Phillips, "Quiet Town Plays a Role in History, *NYT,* October 1, 1962, p. 8.

73 watermelon, okra, sweet potatoes: Anthony H. Harrigan, "Conflict on Ole Miss Campus Hits Lull," *Charleston News and Courier,* September 30, 1962, p. 1.

73 *scene at drugstore:* John Faulkner, "How Much Hate There Is Now," *SEP,* November 10, 1962, p. 25.

74 *"We got some boys"; "I don't particularly"*: Dispatch from Oxford by "Carmichael," July 9, 1962, Time, Inc. archives.

74 *"Supposing Ole Miss"*: Judd Arnett, "Gov. Barnett 'Soft Touch' to Despair of His Staff," *NOTP,* December 20, 1963, p. 16.

75 September 20 confrontation: September 21, 1962 editions of *MCA, MPS, NYHT, NOTP, JCL, NYT.*

75 *"I'd heard the word"*: Int. James Meredith, December 10, 2000.

76 reminded Meredith of Heston: *SEP,* November 10, 1962, p. 16.

76 *"I'd make them"; "That's exactly how far"*: Sansing, *The University of Mississippi,* p. 293.

76–77 *"I hope you'll go to jail"; "Of course I know"*: *SEP,* November 10, 1962, p. 20.

77 *"I am prepared to be"*: Sansing, *Making Haste Slowly,* p. 179.

77 *"Despite humiliation"*: Reeves, *Profile of Power,* pp. 354–55.

77 plan to send LBJ: Guthman, *We Band of Brothers,* p. 188.

77 decoy plane: Int. Jack Greenberg, March 22, 2001.

78 Sheriffs Association requesting barricades; university response: Interview with former Mississippi law enforcement official.

78 *"The closed society"*: "Excerpts from Professor's Address Denouncing Mississippi," *NYT,* November 8, 1963, p. 23.

79 Shelton's thinking, office, scene at desk: Ints. Robert Shelton, March 5 and September 18, 2000. Detail on Shelton and the Klan: Claude Sitton, "Ku Klux Klan Is Riding Again," *NYT,* September 18, 1962, p. 6 E; "Dedicated Klansman," *NYT,* October 19, 1965; Jules Loh, "Klan Is Dead," *Salt Lake Tribune,* December 19, 1994, p.

1; "Ex-Leader Says Ku Klux Klan Is Dead," *Greensboro News & Record,* July 5, 1995, p. B6.

79 *"mind and soul":* Victor Reisel, "Shelton Runs Riot in Power Hunt," *New York Mirror,* May 29, 1961, p. 16.

79 Shelton concern on Southern womanhood: Claude Sitton, "Klansmen Stage Albany, GA Rally," *NYT,* September 4, 1962, p. 12.

79–80 *"I saw nigra American soldiers":* David Murray, "Imperial Wizard Shelton," *NYP Magazine,* April 4, 1965, p. 2.

81 Shelton alerted Klan: FBI #s 157–401–27, 157–401–487.

81 *"This could be":* Int. Robert Shelton, September 18, 2000.

81–83 September 25, 1962, showdown in Jackson: September 26 editions of *MCA, MPS, NOTP, NYT, NYHT, LAT, CSM, JCL, JDN, WP, London Times, Meridian Star* (Meridian, Mississippi), news footage on file at the MDAH in Jackson (MP 80.01, reel D-06). A transcript of much of the confrontation in the doorway is in FBI # 157–401–157.

83 Meredith saw blacks waving: Meredith, *Three Years,* p. 196.

84 *"to be summarily arrested":* Charles M. Hills, "Proclamation Asks Jailing of Federals," *JCL,* September 25, 1962, p. 1.

84 RFK/Barnett dialogue: Transcript, September 26, 1962, Burke Marshall Papers, JFKL. These files contain transcripts of several RFK/Barnett conversations during the crisis. They were created by RFK's secretary Angie Novello listening in on RFK's phone line with Barnett's knowledge, according to Ms. Novello in a December 23, 1999 int. with the author.

84 *"Why don't you"; "It's best"; "But he likes"; "It's going to be"; "I hope so":* Guthman, *We Band of Brothers,* pp. 191, 192.

85 Mrs. Barnett and telegrams: Bonita Appleton, "Messages of Support," *JDN,* September 27, 1962, p. 1.

85 *"The voice of the moderates"; "It's fear":* Joseph M. Guilfoyle, "Mississippi Supports Barnett," *WSJ,* September 28, 1962, p. 1.

86 *"The Governor was in rebellion":* The Secret White House Tapes, Investigative Reports special, A&E cable television network special, director, executive producer, and co-writer Carol Fleisher; co-producer and co-writer, William Doyle, March 1997.

86 background on Paul B. Johnson, Jr.: Int. with his son Paul B. Johnson III, October 16, 2000; "It's Paul's Time!" Johnson 1955 governor's campaign brochure, Time, Inc. archives.

87 Barnett trip detail, scene at Calhoun City: Int. Brad Dye, November 20, 2000. Dye, then a state legislator, was traveling with Barnett in the motorcade.

87 FBI informant's details of state plan: FBI # 157–401–120.

88–90 September 26, 1962, showdown at Oxford: September 27, 1962, editions of *MCA, MPS, NOTP, NYT, NYHT, LAT, CSM, JCL, JDN, WP, London Times, Manchester Guardian;* Guthman, *We Band of Brothers,* pp. 192, 193.

90 *"I am not willing to go to jail":* "Compilation—1962," Verner Holmes Collection, Box 4, Folder 7, p. 10, UMASC.

90 one state legislator: Int. Brad Dye, November 20, 2000.

90 *"explicit and need no other":* Robert Nelson, "Stage Set at 'Ole Miss,' " *CSM,* September 27, 1962, p. 1.

90 *"This is ridiculous":* Edward P. Moore, Jr., "Students Fret About Future as Daily Drama Unfolds," *MCA,* September 27, 1962, p. 1.

90–91 *"In order to prevail"; "My greatest fear":* Strober and Strober, *Let Us Begin Anew,* pp. 306, 307.

91 *"I question your sincerity":* James A. Wechsler, "Private Hours," *NYP,* October 1, 1962, p. 24.

91 *"We know what we're doing":* Stan Opotowsky, "Barnett Ordered to Federal Court," *NYP,* Sept 28, 1962, p. 3.

91–92 September 27 federal attempt to enter Oxford: Russell H. Barrett, *Integration at Ole Miss* (Chicago: Quadrangle Books, 1965), pp. 115–18; Guthman, *We Band of Brothers,* pp. 194, 195; Lord, *The Past That Would Not Die,* pp. 167–73; Meredith, *Three Years,* pp. 204–6; September 28 editions of *NYT, WP, JDN, JCL, MCA, MPS, NOTP, The New York Mirror, Manchester Guardian, London Times.* RFK/Barnett/Johnson dialogue is from transcripts in Burke Marshall Papers, JFKL.

92 it looked to Simmons: Int. William Simmons, March 5, 1999.

92 observers from UKA in Oxford: FBI # 157–401–1004 and # 157–401–265; int. Robert Shelton, September 18, 2000.

92 Klansmen from Louisiana in Oxford: FBI # 157–401–122.

92 *"many scary people":* Ints. William Goodman, November 18, 1998, April 20, 2001.

93 Batesville deserted: Meredith, *Three Years,* p. 206.

Chapter 6 · In the Lord's Hands

95 *"A holocaust is in the making":* "Mississippi Crisis," *LAT,* September 29, 1962, p. 10.

95 *"We'd better get going"; "Maybe we waited"; "I wouldn't have believed it":* Guthman, *We Band of Brothers,* p. 197.

96 Barnett terrified by personal fine: Int. William Simmons, September 21, 1998.

96 *"police state and Gestapo":* "Mississippi Crisis," *LAT,* September 29, 1962, p. 10.

96 crosses burned: FBI # 157–401–150.

96 Adams announcement: "Miss. Chief Quits National Party," *WP,* September 29, 1962, p. 7.

96 *"We'll bring our guns"; "Don't":* Int. with Barnett office assistant.

96 background on Walker: Eric Pace, "Gen. Edwin Walker, 83, is Dead," *NYT,* November 2, 1993, p. 10.

97 Simmons thought Walker a right-wing extremist: Int. William Simmons, September 21, 1998.

97 face twitched and froze; *"war in the Fourth Dimension":* Videotape MP86.01 reel 0030, MDAH, Jackson, Mississippi.

97 *"could rebel":* FBI # 157–401–702.

97 *"I came here to meet":* The Citizen, January 1962, pp. 8–25.

97 *"It is time to make a move":* FBI transcript from a tape of the broadcast, FBI # 157–401–637.

98 report of one hundred armed volunteers: FBI # 157–401–1141.

98 report of armed men in Laguna Mountains: FBI # 157–401–351.

98 report of First California Volunteers: FBI # 157–401–220.

98–99 *"You called for":* "If Troops Pile in, I'll Be There: Walker," *Meridian Star,* September 28, 1962.

99 pledges from Rainach, Hockett, Clark, Champion: "Barnett Besieged by Offers of Aid," *LAT,* October 1, 1962, p. 15.

99 six hundred Klansmen rumored in Jackson: FBI # 157–401–260.

99 ham-radio report: FBI # 157–401–112. *Minuteman* may not have referred to the Minuteman terrorist organization, but to Citizens Council "minuteman" groups, rapid-response groups the council hoped to mobilize against integration.

99 town meetings planned: FBI # 157–401–260.

99 source in Birmingham advised: FBI # 157–401–190.

99 NSRP wired Barnett: FBI # 157–401–487.

100 alerted 250 supervisors and game wardens: *JDN,* September 29, 1962.

100 Breakdown of Barnett's forces: FBI # 157–401–475.

100 Sovereignty Commission postcards and planes: Peter Kihss, "Group Denounces 'Warfare' by US," *NYT,* September 30, 1962.

100 report of P-51 fighter planes: FBI # 157–401–155. Like many similar reports and rumors, this appears to have vanished into thin air, and FBI files contain no further information.

100 *"There is more power in the presidency":* "Though the Heavens Fall," *Time,* October 12, 1962, p. 20.

101 *"The Kennedys thought":* Strober and Strober, *Let Us Begin Anew,* p. 302.

101 president's uses of troops: "Authority Believed Ample for Use of Federal Troops," *MCA,* October 1, 1962; Bennett Milton Rich, *The Presidents and Civil Disorder* (Washington, D.C.: The Brookings Institution, 1941), pp. 169–83.

101 attack on Bonus Army: D. Clayton James, "The Years of MacArthur, Vol. 1, 1880–1941" (Boston: Houghton Mifflin Co., 1970) pp. 397–402.

102 *"the most extreme form":* Gunnar Myrdal, *An American Dilemma: The Negro Problem and American Democracy* (New York: Harper & Row, 1944), p. 566.

102 twentieth-century race riots: Ibid., p. 567.

102 *"The breaking point":* Ibid., p. 569.

102 Tulsa massacre: Tom Kenworthy, "Oklahoma Starts to Face Up to 1921 Massacre," *USA Today,* February 18, 2000, p. 4A.

102 1940s riots: Terry Ann Knopf, *Rumors and Race and Riots* (New Brunswick, NJ: Transaction Books, 1975), pp. 29–58.

103 RFK's military experience: C. David Heymann, *RFK: A Candid Biography of Robert F. Kennedy* (New York: Dutton, 1998), pp. 36–37; Victor Lasky, *Robert F. Kennedy: The Myth and the Man* (New York: Trident Press, 1968) p. 60.

103 Military planning to September 29: Army History, pp. 10–28.

104 background on 503d: Ints. with 503d veterans.

104 *"If we weren't":* Int. William Mayes, October 14, 1998.

107 martial law pre-planning: Army History, p. 45.

107 RFK meeting army on segregating troops: Army History, p. 58.

108 503d officers on segregation: Int. George Baldwin, November 5, 2000; Int. Joseph Cooke, March 30, 2001.

109 *"just as impossible":* John G. Rogers, "Meredith Is Unyielding in Both Word and Deed," *NYHT,* September 30, 1962.

109 RFK/Barnett phone dialogue at 1:35 P.M.: Transcript, Burke Marshall Papers, JFKL.

109 *"What I was trying to avoid":* Guthman and Shulman, *Robert Kennedy in His Own Words,* p. 160.

110 Barnett visited JFK: White House photo, June 4, 1962, JFKL.

110 JFK's recording systems: Doyle, *Inside the Oval Office,* pp. 102–4, 365n, 366n.

110 *"And now":* Schlesinger, *A Thousand Days,* p. 944.

110 Barnett/JFK dialogue, September 29: Dictabelt recording of Oval Office telephone line, JFKL.

111 *"You've been fighting"*; *"He's a rogue"*: Reeves, *Profile of Power,* p. 359.

113 seemed stadium would collapse: Int. Hassel Franklin, November 18, 1999.

113 felt like earth was shattering: Int. Mary Lynn Hendricks Lawler, December 11, 1999.

113 *"You would have"*: Int. William Goodman, November 18, 1998.

113 *"like a big Nazi rally"*; *"it was just the way"*: Lord, *The Past That Would Not Die,* p. 191.

113 if Barnett gave word: Int. E. L. McDaniel, February 5, 2000.

113 Barnett speech at halftime: Hampton, *Eyes on the Prize.*

113 *"thousands of Confederate battle flags"*: Jack Bass and Walter De Vries, *The Transformation of Southern Politics: Social Change and Political Consequence Since 1945* (New York: Basic Books, 1976), p. 201.

113 *"That night"*: Lord, *The Past That Would Not Die,* p. 191.

113 *"Barnett didn't know"*: Int. H. M. Ray, August 14, 1999.

113 *"I can't do it"*: Int. former adviser to Barnett.

114 JFK ordered Echo to Memphis: Army History, p. 77.

114 Taylor calling National Guard commanders; one said it would trigger the biggest exodus of AWOL troops: FBI # 157–401–228.

114 JFK signing papers after midnight: George Leonard, T. George Harris, and Christopher S. Wren, "How a Secret Deal Prevented a Massacre at Ole Miss," *Look,* December 31, 1962, p. 24.

115 Cotten in a sea of rumors; background on Cotten; *"I need help!"*: Int. Robin Cotten, January 15, 2000.

116–17 Ross Barnett, Jr.'s, experience and dialogue on September 30; his memories: Int. Ross Barnett, Jr., October 28, 2000.

Chapter 7 · Though the Heavens Fall

118 *"If rebellion was the certain consequence"*: "Though the Heavens Fall," *Time,* October 12, 1962, p. 19.

118 Oxford atmosphere; dialogue of farmers and man in restaurant: Hoke Norris, "Last Gasp of the Confederacy," *Chicago Sun-Times,* October 1, 1962, p. 3.

119 background on Duncan M. Gray, Jr.: Ints. with Duncan M. Gray, Jr.: September 1, 1998, August 14, 2000; Will D. Campbell, *And Also With You: Duncan Gray and the American Dilemma* (Franklin Tennessee: Providence House Publishers, 1997), passim.

119 Gray sermon: Barrett, *Integration at Ole Miss,* pp. 134, 135.

120 *"When I told them"*: Bill Wuomett, "Ole Miss: A Campus Smothered with Smoke and Tears," *Raleigh News and Observer,* October 7, 1962, section 3, p. 2.

120 Gray's singing; *"Lo! the hosts of evil"*: Campbell, *And Also With You,* pp. 178, 179.

120 JFK and RFK's activities September 30, A.M.: Carroll Kilpatrick, "President in Talk to Nation Urges Law and Order," *WP,* October 1, 1962, p. 1.

120 Barnett/RFK conversation: Transcript, Burke Marshall Papers, JFKL.

121 *"The plan was riddled"*: Guthman, *We Band of Brothers,* p. 200.

122 thought twenty thousand in Oxford, hundreds shot dead: "Text of a Statement by Governor Barnett," *NYT,* October 2, 1962, p. 25.

123 JFK's telegram to Barnett: "Kennedy Wires Barnett to Question Intentions," Associated Press dispatch, October 1, 1962.

123 *"Hey, Nick"*: Branch, *Parting the Waters*, p. 661.

123 *"the Kennedy panache"*: Ibid.

123–24 nobody told Army or Abrams: Army History, pp. 79, 91.

124 *"Many people express"*: Larry Still, "Man Behind the Headlines," *Ebony*, December 1962, p. 32.

124 Guihard and Schulman going to Jackson: *Look*, December 31, 1962, p. 23.

124 Guihard background: Int. Felix Bolo, then New York bureau chief of Agence France–Presse and Guihard's boss, December 12, 1999; letter from Bolo to author, December 5, 1999; Bruce Rothwell, "The High Price," *Daily Sketch* (London), October 2, 1962, p. 10; "Reporter Killed In Riot Was Called Flash for His Drive," *MPS*, October 1, 1962, p. 4.

125 *"a born journalist"*: *Daily Sketch*, October 2, 1962, p. 10.

125 *"Hey, don't worry"*: "Mississippi: The Sound and the Fury," *Newsweek*, October 15, 1962, p. 24.

125 *"Oh, I know"*; *"These people"*: *Look*, December 31, 1962, p. 23.

125 Guihard thought scene like a carnival: "Kennedy Tells Shock at Death of Frenchman," *LAT*, October 2, 1962, p. 2.

125 Scenes at Governor's Mansion: October 1, 1962, editions of *NYT, JCL, MCA, WSJ, Dallas Morning News*.

126 detail of Citizens Council office: "Tax Money, Some from Negroes, Fund Citizens Councils," *LCJ*, October 14, 1962, section 4, p. 1; James Graham Cook, *The Segregationists*, pp. 66–68.

126 Anyone that nice; *"The crowd laughed and sang"*: *Look*, December 31, 1962, p. 24.

126 Simmons swelled with pride; cheerleaders; *"They won't give up"*: James K. Kilpatrick, "Logic and Lunacy Mingle at Ole Miss," *Richmond News Leader*, October 1, 1962, p. 1.

127 Simmons believed law, nature, justice on his side: "Racists' Strategist: William James Simmons," *NYT*, September 28, 1962, p. 22.

127 floodgates would open; Simmons saw turning point; *"We thought we were doing"*: Ints. with William Simmons, March 5, 1999; October 15, 2000.

127 *"It's in the Lord's hands"*: *Richmond News Leader*, October 1, 1962, p. 1.

127–28 Barnett meeting with officials; *"We thought we were going"*; Newman made out will; Yarbrough called patrol; Moore alerted sheriffs: *Look*, December 31, 1962, p. 23.

128 signs on cars: FBI # 151–401–1432.

128 Texan in council office: *Richmond News Leader*, October 1, 1962, p. 1.

128 Shelton and Klansmen took off by plane for Oxford: Int. Robert Shelton, March 5, 2000; FBI # 157–401–1141.

128 *"I volunteer"*; Bruce's weaponry: FBI # 157–401–791.

128 Chattanooga incident: FBI # 157–401–315.

129 caravan left Prichard: FBI # 157–401–424.

129 arrival of marshals at Oxford: Guthman, *We Band of Brothers*, pp. 200–01; Barrett, *Integration at Ole Miss*, pp. 136–37; *Look*, December 31, 1962, p. 24.

129 marshals told it was a dry run: Int. Deputy Marshal Al Butler, February 22, 2001.

129 lost equipment: Lord, *The Past That Would Not Die*, p. 198.

129 *"We were sent in unprepared"*: Int. Al Butler, April 19, 1998.

129–30 marshal practiced golf swing; McShane and Birdsong at Oxford Airport: local newsreel footage, MDAH.

130 *"You know you're going"*: Lord, *The Past That Would Not Die,* p. 201.

130 waving Confederate flag: *Newsweek,* October 15, 1962, p. 24.

130 state officials fly in; *"It's completely occupied," "Bobby and Jack": Look,* December 31, 1962, p. 24.

Chapter 8 · The Gates of Bedlam

131 *"All hell had to break"*: Silver, *The Closed Society,* p. 106.

131 Details and dialogue of the buildup to the riot and the riot itself in this and following chapters are from hundreds of eyewitness interviews by the FBI in late 1962 and by the author in 1997–2001; Army History, passim; feature coverage in *Time, Newsweek, USNWR, Look, Life,* and the *SEP;* and from September 30–October 5, 1962 editions of *NYT, NYWT, NYHT, NYP, NYJA, WP, MCA, MPS, JDN, JCL, WES, NOTP, CSM, LCJ, Chicago Sun-Times, Denver Post, San Francisco Examiner, Miami Herald, Shreveport Journal, Birmingham News, Dallas Morning News, Houston Post, Atlanta Journal, St. Louis Post-Dispatch, Providence Journal-Bulletin, Nashville Tennessean, Greensboro Daily News, London Times, Manchester Guardian;* from the Barrett, Lord, and Silver books and from the Ellen Douglas book, *A Long Night* (Jackson, Miss.: Nouveau Press, 1986), which is the extended statement of an unarmed rioter.

131 *"I'd like to dismount"; "It's all right"*: Edward F. Woods, "Meredith Move to Campus Was Barnett's Idea," *St. Louis Post-Dispatch,* October 1, 1962, p. 1.

131 Butler surveyed the scene: Int. Al Butler, April 19, 1998.

131 Katzenbach actions: Int. Nicholas Katzenbach, April 17, 2000.

132 appearance of marshals: Color slide photographs by graduate student Don Proehl in front of the Lyceum on the afternoon and early evening of September 30, 1962, courtesy Don Proehl.

133 campus would need fifteen hundred troops to seal off: "The University of Mississippi and the Meredith Case," report issued by Chancelor J. D. Williams, November 15, 1962, p. 20.

133 *"we didn't have enough planning"*: Int. Nicholas Katzenbach, April 17, 2000.

133 *"Get a line"; "We don't want to"; "We want to keep"*: Strober and Strober, *Let Us Begin Anew,* p. 304.

133 Walker appeared at the gate: Local newsreel footage, MDAH.

134 Shelton denied clearance: Int. Robert Shelton, March 5, 2000.

134 toddler: photo in *Birmingham News,* October 1, 1962, p. 5.

134 buildup of crowd from 4:00 P.M. to 8:00 P.M.: Affidavit of James P. McShane, June 6, 1963, *State v. McShane* file, papers of William Lamb, courtesy William Lamb.

134 WLBT dispatched wagon: Int. WJDX/WLBT producer and host Chuck Allen, February 26, 2000.

135 *"Most of us"*: Karen Hosler, "A Call to Order; Trent Lott's Passion for Control and His Talent for Taking Charge Have Made Him What He Is Today," *The Sun* (Baltimore), February 23, 1997, p. 1 J.

135 *"Is he here yet?"; "They're bringing him"; "Klan is waiting"*: Wayne King, "Students Gave Little Hint of Violence," *Greensboro Daily News* (NC), October 7, 1962, p. 1.

135 campus policemen deployed: Int. campus police officer Robert Jackson, December 16, 1999.

135 *"I am just a little fuck"*: FBI # 157–401–1433.

135 student with flag: Int. Don Proehl, January 10, 2000.

135 officials pleading for crowd to disperse: Barrett, *Integration at Ole Miss,* p. 147.

135 marshals smiled: Int. Al Butler, February 22, 2001.

136 Mississippi Highway Patrol's attitudes; activities and confused orders: Ints. in 1998–2001 with nine patrolmen who were at Oxford on September 30/October 1, and interviews with then-MHP public-information officer Art Richardson. Richardson conducted the only known MHP departmental review of the crisis for Colonel Birdsong, who ordered that no copies be made of the report.

136 *"We're cooperating":* Int. Charles Staten, January 3, 2000.

136 *"What are you going to do":* Int. John McCauley, September 25, 1999.

137 no one could control crowd: Affidavit of John W. Cameron (McShane's assistant), June 19, 1963, p. 4, in *State v. McShane* file; William Lamb papers, courtesy William Lamb.

137 *"When we asked them"; "Let the mob go ahead":* "Marshal Describes Attack by Students," *JDN,* October 10, 1962.

137 *"hell with you":* Lord, *The Past That Would Not Die,* p. 206.

137 *"Cutting the tread":* Int. Border Patrolman Dan Pursglove, August 25, 1999.

137 *"We haven't"; "The nigger's on his way":* Stan Opotowsky, "Rebellion at Ole Miss," *NYP,* October 1, 1962, p. 2.

137 *"If you come over here":* FBI # 157–401–866.

137 *"Go on home":* Int. AP reporter Van Savell, October 11, 1999.

137 eggs, gravel, coat hanger hurled: Cameron affidavit, pp. 3–4.

137 *"Hotty toddy, God A'mighty":* FBI # 157–401–1041.

138 *"a little donnybrook":* Int. Al Butler, April 19, 1998.

138 *"They stood there":* "Marshal Describes Attack by Students," *JDN,* October 10, 1962.

138 nobody told Abrams: Army History, p. 91.

138 marshals gripped clubs: FBI # 151–401–1307.

139 *"Heil Hitler!":* John D. Harris, "Our Man at Ole Miss," *NYJA,* October 1, 1962, p. 1.

139 *"I'm going back to the dormitory":* FBI # 151–401–1426.

139 driver clutched eyes; earning assaulter ovation: FBI # 151–401–1484.

139 *"Those things":* Lord, *The Past That Would Not Die,* p. 204.

139 *"Let it burn!";* eggs hit driver: *NYJA,* October 1, 1962, p. 1.

139 *"I had not gone 100 yards":* Tom Joyce, "Savagery and Hatred Engulfed Ole Miss Campus," *WES,* October 1, 1962, p. 5.

139 *"Hold it off for awhile":* *Look,* December 31, 1962, p. 29.

140 reporters exhorting crowd: These statements might be dismissed as false rumors, but interviews with several crowd members suggest that at least one of the photographers was interacting with the crowd, no doubt unwittingly, in a way that some perceived as insulting or inflammatory, which served as one of many sparks of the riot.

140 attack on Yoder and wife; rescue: Int. Gordon Yoder, December 11, 1998; int. John McCauley, September 25, 1999.

140 *"You nigger-loving"; "Lord":* SEP, November 10, 1962, p. 26.

140 *"If you value your life":* FBI # 151–401–1426.

140 McCoy attack; quotes: *Newsweek,* October 15, 1962, p. 25.

141 riot manual: *Deputy United States Marshals Training Manual: Riot Control,* June 1962, McShane papers, JFKL.

141 equipment needed: "Measures for Police Control of Riots," FBI Law Enforcement

Bulletin, October 1, 1962, in Mississippi Legislature's Investigative Committee report, p. 22.

142 Wilson's crowd plan: Int. Dick Wilson, December 14, 1999.
142 *"Let them kill the nigger"*: FBI # 157–401–866.
142 *"no way"*: Int. Gene Same, May 28, 1999.
142 7:10 order on the patrol radio: FBI # 157–401–866.
143 *"Don't get caught up"*: Int. John Ashcraft, November 5, 1999.
143 Hendricks: Int. Mary Lynn Hendricks Lawler, December 11, 1999.
143 *"Get out of here"*: Int. Charles Hargroder, December 13, 1999.
143 *"I would like to see blood"*: FBI # 151–401–1484.
143 7:25 MHP order: Lord, *The Past That Would Not Die,* p. 206.
144 *"You rubber-nosed"*: Int. Al Butler, April 19, 1998.
144 *"Your wife's at home"*: Int. Gene Same, May 28, 1999.
144 *"Your wife is sleeping"*: Int. O. L. Hampton, January 22, 2000.
144 meeting of Yarbrough, Katzenbach, Birdsong: *Look,* December 31, 1962, p. 29; int. Nicholas Katzenbach, April 17, 2000.
146 *"We'll have to live here"*: McShane affidavit, p. 4.
146 *"You don't need to"*: Int. Buddie Newman, February 4, 2000.
146 orders preparing gas: *NYP,* October 1, 1962, p. 2.
147 missiles fired at eyepieces: FBI # 157–401–866.
147 Yarbrough addressing crowd: *Look,* December 31, 1962, p. 29.
147 *"Let's get Meredith!"*: *NYJA,* October 1, 1962, p. 1.
147 *"Damnit to hell, Chief"*: Int. Al Butler, April 19, 1998.
147 FBI agents approaching: Int. Robin Cotten, January 15, 2000.
148 army intelligence agents: Army History, p. 92.
148 thoughts of James Parks: Int. James Parks, December 14, 1999.
148 marshals hit with missiles: Int. Al Butler, April 19, 1998.
148 McShane prayed: *Newsweek,* October 15, 1962, p. 24.
148 McShane on mob: McShane affadavit, p. 4.
148 Same on mob: Int. Gene Same, May 28, 1999.
148 *"Those goddamn Feds"*: FBI # 157–401–996.
148 *"This is it"*: FBI # 157–401–1112.
148 *"You're chicken"*: "JFK asks Peace, Walker-Led Mob Attacks Marshals," *Nashville Tennessean,* October 1, 1962, p. 1.
149 pipe hit marshal's head; knocked him down: *SEP,* November 10, 1962, p. 18.
149 Jacobson treating JFK before speech; *"This one is a ball-breaker"*: Reeves, *Profile of Power,* pp. 364, 716, quoting unpublished memoirs of Max Jacobson, JFK chapter, p. 34.
149 Marshals aimed at heads and belts: Int. Gene Same, May 28, 1999.
149 *"It seemed like one man fired"*: "Gas Fired, Then Riots," *NOTP,* October 6, 1962, p. 2.

Chapter 9 · Demons Out of the Earth

150 *"Turn your eyes"*: Allen Tate, *Collected Poems, 1919–1976* (New York: Farrar Straus Giroux, 1977), p. 24.
150 Katzenbach startled; thought they could calm it down: Int. Nicholas Katzenbach, April 17, 2000.

150 *"helmeted U.S. marshals"*: *NYJA*, October 1, 1962, p. 1.

150 *"the campus became"*: Richard Starnes, "Eyewitness Story: Bricks, Bottles, Gas," *NYHT*, October 1, 1962, p. 15.

150 Brunt injury: FBI # 157–401–487, transcript of October 2, 1962 news conference, WLBT-TV.

151 McCauley experience: Int. John McCauley, September 14, 1999.

151 Gammel experience: Int. Loy Gammel, December 12, 1999.

151 Staten experience: Int. Charles Staten, January 3, 2000.

151 *"God damn them marshals"*: Fred Powledge, "Barnett Blames Marshals: Here's Eyewitness Story," *Atlanta Journal,* October 2, 1962, p. 10.

151 Birdsong rumor and Yarbrough: *Look,* December 31, 1962, p. 30.

152 James Mathis quotes: Charles M. Hills, "Eyewitness Account of Ole Miss Riot," *JDN,* October 14, 1962, p. 2 B.

152 *"I tried to get away"*: Sterling Slappey, "I Saw It Happen in Oxford," *USNWR,* October 15, 1962, p. 44.

152 *"That's the dirtiest trick"*: FBI # 157–401–487, transcript of October 2, 1962, news conference, WLBT-TV.

152 *"Well, you have just started a riot"*: Memo from Gwin Cole, MHP assistant supervisor, Identification Division, to Dave Gayden, assistant commissioner and chief of patrol, October 9, 1962, p. 2.

152 *"This is the most cowardly"*; *"somebody jumped the gun"*: "File #1; Statements," handwritten notes taken by Mississippi state official, late 1962; *State v. McShane* file; William Lamb papers, courtesy William Lamb. Katzenbach's statement "somebody jumped the gun" (which in an interview with the author he confirmed making) was sometimes cited as evidence that the marshals fired gas too soon, but testimony from hundreds of eyewitnesses in the FBI files and in author interviews strongly suggest that the crowd's explosion to full-scale rioting would have happened in minutes anyway. Parts of the crowd were already rioting, with the attacks on journalists and marshals that began after 6:00 P.M. A smaller pattern of opinion, held by Highway Patrolmen, state officials, and some crowd members, was that the firing of tear gas was premature or unnecessary.

153 *"Bob, I'm very sorry"*; *"I think I should really"*: *Look,* December 31, 1962, p. 30.

154 MHP surging into gymnasium: FBI # 157–401–1041, FBI # 157–401–1433.

154 *"They began shooting"*: George Metz, "Eyewitness Tells of Mob Takeover," *Birmingham News,* October 1, 1962, p. 1.

154 *"Let's get them Feds"*; *"Let's take care"*: FBI # 157–401–1041.

154–55 *"We can whip them!"*; *"We sure can"*; *"Put your guns away"*: Int. former Highway Patrolman.

154 *"Boys, I'm going to call"*: FBI # 157–401–1041.

155 Walker in restaurant: Clark Porteous, "General Walker at Federal Hospital," *MPS,* October 2, 1962.

155 *"Two of the girls"*: "There Was No Rioting Until Federal Marshals Fired," *USNWR,* October 22, 1962, p. 40.

155 beat nightsticks: Silver, *Mississippi: The Closed Society,* p. 164.

155 *"The light from his camera"*: Ted Lucas Smith, "Has 30 Years Already Passed Since Ole Miss Riots?" *Drew-Ruleville Pilot Progress* (Mississippi), October 1, 1992, p. 3.

156 *"They've got machine guns"*; *"We killed six"*: Wayne King, "Students Gave Little Hint of Violence," *Greensboro Daily News* (North Carolina), October 7, 1962, p. 1.

156 *"They shot a coed!"*: Ellen Douglas, *A Long Night* (Jackson: Nouveau Press, 1986), p. 8.

156 girl identified as Gillespie: "Report of Coed's Demise Is Still Grossly Exaggerated," *MCA*, October 9, 1962.

156 *"Let's move in!"*: *NYWT*, October 1, 1962, p. 1.

156 thirty thousand bricks: October 11, 1999 int. with Oxford National Guard captain Murry C. "Chooky" Falkner.

156 *"Get your ammo here!"*: Douglas, *A Long Night*, p. 7.

156 *"get ready to run"*; *"He heaved"*: *NYP*, October 1, 1962, p. 2.

157 acid hit Butler: Int. Al Butler, April 19, 1998.

157 Lockman experience: Int. Seibert Lockman, November 30, 1999.

157 Pursglove experience: Int. Dan Pursglove, August 25, 1999.

157–58 *"If I'd a stood"*; *"Sometimes you just couldn't"*; *"They'd cut loose"*; *"If you've ever heard"*; *"I was more frightened"*: Stephen Isaacs, "Marshal Recalls a Bloody Sunday," *WP*, October 14, 1962, p. 9.

158 *"foxhunt yip"*; *"peculiar corkscrew"*: *The Civil War*, PBS series, Florentine Films, Inc; Ken Burns, director and executive producer; written by Geoffrey C. Ward, Ric Burns, and Ken Burns, 1990.

158 experience of Terre Haute prison guards: FBI # 157–401–1433.

158 experience of El Reno prison guards; *"We were led"*: FBI # 157–401–866.

159 patrol withdrawal: *Newsweek*, October 15, 1962, p. 27.

159 *"All right"*: Lord, *The Past That Would Not Die*, p. 215.

159 *"Where you going?"*; *"Give 'em hell, boys"*: Douglas, *A Long Night*, p. 7.

159 *"Your men"*; *"Your information"*: *Look*, December 31, 1962, p. 32.

159 *"We've come to hep"*: Leon Daniel, "Legacy of James Meredith," *The Record* (Bergen County, NJ), June 3, 1987, p. D 11.

159–60 Quarles comments: Int. Mildred Quarles, November 18, 1998.

160 *"I can't believe"*: Edmond Lebreton, "I Can't Believe It's Happening at Ole Miss," *The Birmingham News*, October 1, 1962.

160 Gray experience: Ints. Duncan Gray, Jr., September 28, 1998; June 8, 1999; and March 6, 2000.

160 *"He didn't see it as courage"*: Will D. Campbell, *And Also With You: Duncan Gray and the American Dilemma* (Franklin, Tennessee, Providence House Publishers, 1997), p. 136.

160 *"Give me your brick"*: Douglas, *A Long Night*, p. 10

161 *"Please go on back"*; *"Some of the students"*: Int. Duncan Gray, Jr., June 8, 1999.

161 Smith parley with crowd: *Look*, December 31, 1962, p. 32. Some accounts combine this event with Buck Randall's later talks with the mob around 10:15 P.M., but the Smith parley appears to have occurred closer to 9:00 P.M.

162 *"They just wouldn't listen"*: *WES*, October 1, 1962, p. 5.

162 *"I can't guarantee"*; Guihard nodded: Bill E. Burk, "Reporter's Death Still a Mystery," *Knoxville News-Sentinel*, October 16, 1962, p. 2.

163 *"I was in Cyprus"*: Int. Flip Schulke, November 2, 1998.

163 events surrounding Guihard's death: Details are from a series of eyewitness ints. in FBI files in the 157–401 series; from the Lafayette County grand jury report (reproduced in *NYT* November 15, 1962); and from eyewitness ints. in MHP Bureau of Investigation case reports dated October 24, 1962 and October 29, 1962. An investigator for the State Sovereignty Commission interviewed some ten witnesses

on October 15–17. His October 19, 1962, report is in the Sovereignty Commission files, #2–19–20, MDAH. Despite five investigations in the weeks after the riot—by the FBI, the MHP, the Lafayette County grand jury, the Mississippi Sovereignty Commission, and Sheriff Ford—no one reported seeing Paul Guihard shot or knowing anyone who did. None of the scores of people on campus that night who were interviewed by the author reported seeing Guihard shot, knowing anyone who did, or even hearing of anyone who did. Both Paul Guihard and Ray Gunter's killings are still unsolved, and any solid information on the identity of their shooters should be forwarded to the state attorney general's office in Jackson (phone: 601–359–3680).

164 Gray seeing Guihard: Int. Duncan Gray, Jr., August 14, 2000.

165 civilian in jeans shooting: FBI # 157–401–866.

Chapter 10 · The Silent Pillar

167 *"He stood a foe"*: Jerome J. McGann, *Lord Byron: The Complete Poetical Works, Volume III* (Oxford, England: University Press of Oxford, 1981), p. 325.

167 Walker arrived at 8:43: Van Savell (AP), "I Was in Charging Mob Walker Led," *Miami Herald,* October 5, 1962, p. 21.

167 actions and statements of Walker: FBI agent reports and eyewitness interviews in FBI files and dozens of author interviews with eyewitnesses. Walker was tailed on and off by at least six FBI agents from 9:00 P.M. to 10:30 A.M. the next morning. Their reports are in FBI # 157–401–502. Walker later claimed that he tried to stop the riot, and he successfully sued the AP for libeling him for reporting that he led charges against the marshals. But testimony from a wide range of eyewitnesses demonstrates that Walker, while sometimes incoherent and contraditory, repeatedly exhorted parts of the mob to attack the marshals. The chief of the campus police quoted him as yelling, "Charge!" ("Walker's Order to 'Charge' Told," *LCJ,* November 21, 1962, p. 12.) Walker gave some four impromptu addresses at the scene of the riot, the first around 9:00 P.M. to a small group at the edge of the Circle; the second to a group estimated at between 200 to nearly 1000 from the base of the Confederate monument; and two more at the monument to smaller groups, one at about 10:45 P.M. and one soon after midnight.

167 students greet Walker: Lord, *The Past That Would Not Die,* p. 213.

167 *"now we have a leader!"*: Int. Duncan M. Gray, Jr., August 14, 2000.

167 *"General, will you"*: *Miami Herald,* October 5, 1962, p. 21.

168 *"Keep it up all night"*: "AP Testimony Given in Trial," *NOTP,* June 18, 1964, p. 20.

168 Walker/Gray dialogue: Int. Duncan M. Gray, Jr., August 14, 2000.

168 *"When word of his identity"*: Tom Yarbrough, "Tear Gas is used to Break Up Demonstration in Oxford Square," *St. Louis Post-Dispatch,* October 1, 1962, p. 1.

169 *"They fell"*: McGann, *Lord Byron,* p. 334.

169 background on "The Siege of Corinth": Ibid., pp. 325, 480–82.

169 *"I want to compliment you"*: "Campus Rioting," *LAT,* October 1, 1962, p. 11.

169 *"Don't let up now"*: *Newsweek,* October 15, 1962, p. 25.

169 Gray on statue: Int. Duncan Gray, Jr., August 14, 2000; int. Professor William Willis and Mrs. William Willis, March 5, 2000.

169 *"There is an Episcopal"*: Int. Duncan M. Gray, Jr., August 14, 2000.

170 *"Let's kill the minister!":* FBI # 157–401–791.

170 *"Let's don't hurt the preacher"; "Let's kill the son-of-a-bitch":* Campbell, *And Also With You,* p. 20.

170 Willis's thoughts: Int. William Willis, March 5, 2000.

170 *"stopping point!":* Int. Duncan M. Gray, Jr., September 28, 1998.

171 *"Is this America?"; "Go home"; "They were in tears"; "all eight hundred or nine hundred people":* Int. Duncan M. Gray, Jr., June 8, 1999.

171 *"Get the fire truck!":* NYP, October 1, 1962, p. 2.

171 *"he might have been riding":* Douglas, *A Long Night,* p. 13.

171 *"Keep it up!":* Donald Tate, "Bricks, Snipers, Tear Gas, Hate: Suddenly, Campus Is Battlefield," *MPS,* October 1, 1962, p. 1.

171 Walker; Molotov cocktail: Int. Van Savell, October 11, 1999.

172 *"What if we find"; "Fine":* Newsweek, October 15, 1962, p. 25.

172 *"Couldn't the marshals just quit"; "I'm going to tell people":* John Rogers, "Ole Miss Rioters Found Rallying Point and Adviser in General Walker," *WP,* October 6, 1962, p. 6.

173 Townsend quotes: Int. Pascal Townsend, October 21, 2000.

173–74 quotes of freshman and sophomore from Greenwood: Int. with two sources.

173 marshal with shotgun: FBI # 157–401–866.

174 memories and quotes of Clooskey: Int. with confidential source. "Nathan Clooskey" is a fictitious name used to protect this person's identity, a former student at Itawamba Community College. This is the only fictitious name used in this book.

174 Confederate fight songs: audiotape of WJDX/WLBT remote radio broadcast from campus entrance, September 30, 1962, MDAH.

175 influence of *The Mind of the South* on Meredith: Int. James Meredith, December 10, 2000.

175 *"the sentimental cult"; "a striking tendency"; "every boy growing up":* W. J. Cash, *The Mind of the South* (New York, Alfred A. Knopf, 1941), pp. 50, 121.

176 University Greys at Gettysburg: Stewart, *Pickett's Charge,* pp. 43, 183, 225; Maud Morrow Brown, *The University Greys: Company A, Eleventh Mississippi Regiment, 1861–1865* (Richmond, VA: Garrett and Massie, 1940), passim; Richard Rollins, ed., *Pickett's Charge!: Eyewitness Accounts* (Redondo Beach, California: Rank and File, 1994), pp. 273–75, 362. Additional detail from interviews with David Sansing; with Stark Miller, who is writing a book on the Greys; and with Kathy Georg Harrison, historian at the Gettysburg National Military Park.

176 *"If we grant":* George R. Stewart, *Pickett's Charge: A Microhistory of the Final Attack at Gettysburg, July 3, 1863* (Boston, Houghton Mifflin Company, 1959), p. 121.

177 *"For every Southern boy":* William Faulkner, *Intruder in the Dust* (New York: Random House, 1948), p. 194.

177 groups entering Sorority Row: FBI # 157–401–1433.

177 marshals shooting fire hose: FBI # 157–401–1305.

177 marshals ripped out wires: FBI # 157–401–1041.

177 gas drifting into dorms; gassing of Falkner Hall: Mississippi Legislature's Investigative Committee report, p. 28.

177 *"Some boys":* Tupelo Herald, October 3, 1962, p. 2.

178 *"It was like looking":* Int. Mary Lynn Hendricks Lawler, December 11, 1999.

Chapter 11 · The Guns of Midnight

179 *"I have a rendezvous with Death"*: from "Rendezvous with Death," Alan Seeger, *The Poems of Alan Seeger* (New York: Charles Scribner's Sons, 1916), p. 144.

179 shooting, treatment, and thoughts of Gene Same: Details and dialogue from ints. with Gene Same, May 28, 1999; September 8, 1999; and October 28, 1999; October 18, 1962, statement of Gene Same: "Recounting the Incident at Oxford, Mississippi," personal papers of Gene Same, courtesy Gene Same.

180 *"The cacophony of battle"*: Ed Shook, Marsh Clark, Charles Moore, "With the Besieged Marshals as the Wild Mob Attacks," *Life*, November 1962, p. 22.

180 *"My God"; "We don't have"*: WES, October 1, 1962, p. 5.

180 *"This man has been shot"; "No, no, get me a goddamned first aid kit"*: FBI # 157–401–1364.

180 Dunn actions: October 19, 1962, memo from William R. Dunn, Border Patrol inspector, to Robert L. Jarrett, chief Border Patrol inspector, Chula Vista, CA, "First Aid Administered to Deputy U.S. Marshal SAME at Oxford, Mississippi, on 'Operation Freeway,' " ("Dunn Statement") courtesy Gene Same.

181 *"No, I won't give the order"; "Then you just come over here"*: FBI # 157–401–1364.

181 Vaught, Rebels in Miller: William W. Sorrels and Charles Cavagnaro, *Ole Miss Rebels: Mississippi Football* (Huntsville, Alabama: The Strode Publishers Inc., 1976), pp. 221, 222.

181 Randall's background, attitudes, quotations, and actions: Int. George "Buck" Randall, November 16, 2000. Other versions of Randall's actions were reported in the October 1 editions of the *NYP* and *WP*, and in Douglas, *A Long Night*, p. 19.

181–82 *"Are you fucking people"*: Int. Al Butler, February 22, 2001.

181 Richard Dick shouting at Randall: A portion of these quotes, attributed to an unnamed marshal in Ellen Douglas's *A Long Night* (p. 18) were identified by former Border Patrol inspector Richard Dick during a December 14, 1999 interview as being his quotes. He provided this full account of his dialogue for this book.

182 *"Look, you'd better"*: Int. George Randall, November 16, 2000.

183 *"Propaganda!"*: NYP, October 1, 1962, p. 2.

183 cadet pulled out firing pins: Int. 503d Military Police Battalion commander Lt. Col. John J. Flanagan, April 22, 1999.

183 Lott's actions: Karen Hosler, "A Call to Order: Trent Lott's Passion for Control and His Talent for Taking Charge Have Made Him What He Is Today": *The Sun* (Baltimore), February 23, 1997, 1J.

184 *"Send somebody"*: WES, October 1, 1962, p. 5.

184 *"I haven't got any pulse"; "Do it by the numbers"*: October 18, 1962 statement of Gene Same.

184 evacuation of Gene Same: October 18, 1962, statement of Gene Same; October 19, 1962, Dunn Statement, pp. 1, 2; Int. Border Patrol Inspector Richard Dick, December 14, 1999.

184 Molotov cocktail hit: Int. Richard Dick, December 14, 1999.

185 *"We've got to have more gas. . . . My men are getting slaughtered"*: FBI # 157–401–1364.

186 *"We were now alone"*: FBI # 151–401–1517.

186 *"We can't let you"*: Barrett, *Integration at Ole Miss*, p. 161.

186 *"Mr. Katzenbach"*: Look, December 31, 1962, p. 34.

186 Cotten saw dozens of armed civilians; worried about his son: Int. Robin Cotten, February 14, 2000.

187 Louisiana men; *"You niggers listen";* announced they brought machine guns: Campbell, *And Also With You,* p. 32.

187 Stennis quote: Int. Hardy Stennis, October 1, 2000.

187 sniper at pile of bricks: Int. Duncan M. Gray, Jr., June 8, 1999.

187 sniper with .22: FBI # 157–401–866.

187 crowd cheering shot light: FBI # 151–401–1307.

187 *"We come to help kill"; "Want a drink?":* Douglas, *A Long Night,* pp. 15, 16.

187 *"God damn, this is war!":* Int. Ed Meek, January 18, 2000.

188 *"They walked straight into":* Ted Lucas Smith, "Has 30 Years Already Passed Since Ole Miss Riots?" *Drew-Ruleville Pilot/Progress* (Mississippi), October 1, 1992, p. 3.

188 Crider experience: Int. Bill Crider, November 11, 1999.

188 prison guard hit with pellets: FBI # 157–401–1041.

189 *"Damnit, Dan":* Int. Dan Pursglove, August 25, 1999.

189 *"I was a gunners mate":* Nellie Kenyon, "Oxford Worse, War Vet Says," *Nashville Tennessean,* October 12, 1962, p. 12.

189 *"For God's sake":* Newsweek, October 15, 1962, p. 26.

189 JFK's recording systems: Doyle, *Inside the Oval Office,* pp. 102–4, 365, 366.

190 *"was torn between"; "a terrible evening":* Guthman and Shulman, *Robert Kennedy in His Own Words,* p. 161.

190 quotes in Cabinet Room: Cabinet Room tape recording, JFKL.

190 Alamo exchange: Guthman, *We Band of Brothers,* pp. 204, 205.

191 *"My job had been finished":* Int. James Meredith, September 20, 1998.

191 JFK confirmed to RFK: Guthman and Shulman, *Robert Kennedy in His Own Words,* p. 162.

192 Barnett's hands shaking: Int. Ouida Barnett Atkins (who was at her father's side this night), November 5, 2000.

192–93 *"People were calling"; "Who do we report to?":* Int. Charles Marx, November 6, 2000.

193 atmosphere inside Governor's Mansion: 1998–2000 ints. with three witnesses: William Simmons; Mrs. Ellsworth Howard (then Barnett's personal secretary), and Ouida Barnett Atkins.

193 *"Governor, everybody thinks":* Look, December 31, 1962, p. 29.

193 arguments of Barnett's advisers: Ibid., p. 32

193 Clark confronting Barnett: Int. Charles Clark, April 23, 2001.

194 JFK/Barnett conversations: Dictabelt phone recording of Oval Office phone line, JFKL.

195 *"He wants us to move him"; "I can't get him out":* Cabinet Room tape recording, JFKL.

197 *"This is a direct order":* Int. Justice Department official William Geoghegan, June 6, 2000. Geoghegan relayed JFK's order to the army.

Chapter 12 · History Will Not Forget You

198 *"Stand fast, Mississippi!":* National Guardsman, November 1962, p. 6.

198 action of Falkner and Troop E: Except where otherwise indicated, the actions of Captain Falkner and Troop E and Falkner's thoughts and quotes in this and fol-

lowing chapters are from ints. with Murry C. "Chooky" Falkner and from his after-action report, dated March 1963; courtesy Murry C. Falkner ("Falkner Statement"). While some accounts have the Oxford Guardsmen reaching the Lyceum
as late as 10:45 P.M., the timing in this book follows that in Falkner's report. Additional detail on the Mississippi National Guard's 108th Cavalry and 155th Infantry Regiments' action in the crisis is from Army History, passim; from "Oxford!
The Mississippi National Guard Stands Fast!" *The National Guardsman,* November 1962, pp. 4–9, 48 (National Guard Report); and from 1998–2001 ints. with
scores of Guard officers and enlisted men who served in the action.

200 gas mask incident; Antwine background; *"We were on the side of the students";*
"This is a court-martial offense": Int. Harold Antwine, November 22, 2000. Additional source for gas-mask incident: Army History, p. 92.

200–1 *"I just got the craziest"; "Better do it":* Lord, *The Past That Would Not Die,* p.
221.

201 *"I'll tell you":* Int. Loyd Gunter, October 12, 2000.

202 *"Men, follow yonder knight":* Sansing, *The University of Mississippi,* p. 107.

202 *"I clearly remember":* Drew-Ruleville *Pilot/Progress* (Mississippi), October 1, 1992,
p. 3.

202 *"They knocked both windshields":* Int. Harold Antwine, November 22, 2000.

203 *"It's hard to feel":* Lord, *The Past That Would Not Die,* p. 223.

203 *"When we crossed":* Int. Loyd Gunter, October 12, 2000.

203 *"Leave it to the marshals":* St. Louis *Post-Dispatch,* October 1, 1962, p. 1.

203 *"Hey, we're Mississippi National Guard!";* thoughts of Sergeants Franklin: Int. Lannon Franklin, December 12, 1999.

204 *"Don't throw it at us":* Int. Maryanne Gulley (then Maryanne Harris), April 13,
2000.

204 marshals cheered: Int. Al Butler, April 19, 1998.

205 *"I never thought":* Int. Loyd Gunter, October 12, 2000.

205 *"Get your gas here, boys!":* Douglas, *A Long Night,* p. 22.

206 *"They're bringing up tanks!";* mob sounded like hunting dogs: Ibid., p. 17.

206 *"We were getting our asses shot off":* Int. Ed Guthman, March 22, 2000.

206 *"Every time":* Int. Richard Dick, December 14, 1999.

206 scene inside Lyceum: *Newsweek,* October 15, 1962, p. 27.

207 Hopkins's thoughts, experience, and dialogue on September 30/October 1, 1962:
Int. Dr. L. G. Hopkins, September 16, 1999.

Chapter 13 · A New Civil War Has Begun

211 *"What is taking place":* Personal diary of Professor Gerald Walton, October 1,
1962, courtesy Gerald Walton.

211 background on Ray Gunter: Ints. with Ray Gunter's brother John T. Gunter and
Mrs. John T. Gunter, September 21, 1999; int. Charlie Berryhill, September 10,
2000; int. Ray Gunter's then-wife, Virginia, September 20, 1999. Also Leon Daniel,
"Craving for Thrill Cost Life in Riot," *JDN,* November 8, 1962, p. 4.

212 movements and dialogue of Gunter and Berryhill; Berryhill's thoughts: Int. Charlie Berryhill, September 10, 2000.

213 *"the student of history":* Carol Reardon, *Pickett's Charge in Myth and Memory*
(Chapel Hill, North Carolina: University of North Carolina Press, 1997), p. 10.

213 reappearance of truck: Int. Richard Dick, December 14, 1999.

214 Butler grabbed handrail: Int. Al Butler, February 15, 2001.

214 *"Shoot the tire!"*: FBI # 151–401–1307.

214 *"as the truck swung past"*: FBI # 151–401–1305.

214 Border Patrolman fired three rounds; saw marshal fire shots: FBI # 151–401–1307.

214 marshal from Charlotte fired twice: FBI # 157–401–1217.

214 fourteen shots fired: This is the minimum number of shots fired by marshals at the fire truck, based on marshals' testimony in the previously mentioned FBI reports. One marshal reported that the truck was one hundred yards east of the Lyceum when it was finally stopped. (FBI # 157–401–1041) Many accounts of the riot incorrectly state that the marshals did not open fire with their service revolvers, but FBI and author interviews with marshals demonstrate that they were forced to shoot at least three times: once early in the riot when several shot down at a fire hose lying on the grass to disable it; the second time at the speeding fire truck; and a third time around midnight, when two shot at a driverless 1953 Chevrolet that was sent toward them.

215 shots were fired eastward: For example, the five shots reported in FBI # 151–401–1305 (FBI int. with U.S. Deputy Marshal from Alabama) were west to east.

215 rioters running toward Ray and Charlie; marshals in pursuit: FBI # 157–401–866.

216 Buffaloe experience: Int. George Buffaloe, November 25, 1999.

216 FBI testing of marshals' weapons: "Tests Negative on 450 Riot Guns," *MCA*, November 16, 1962, p. 4.

216 marshal quit before gun could be checked: Int. Seibert Lockman, November 30, 1999.

216 warning shot: An unnamed Justice Department official said that at one time during the riot, the marshals fired "warning shots" in the air; quoted in Cecil Holland, "Beleaguered Marshals Use Tear Gas," *WES*, October 1, 1962, p. 6.

216 Gunter's wife startled: Int. Gunter's then-wife, Virginia, September 20, 1999.

216 *"Daddy"*; newsman called: *JDN*, November 8, 1962, p. 4.

216 Ray's brother told: Int. John T. Gunter, September 21, 1999.

217 Guardsmen at Lyceum: Int. Buford Babb, December 13, 1999; int. Harold Antwine, November 22, 2000.

217 *"Here comes"*: Int. Loyd Gunter, October 12, 2000.

219 Barnett thought: Int. Ross Barnett, Jr., November 11, 1998.

219 Johnson in patrol car: Int. William Davis, September 11, 2000. Davis was the Mississippi Highway Patrolman at the wheel of the patrol car.

219 Johnson worried about tomorrow: *Oxford USA,* Citizens Council film, 1963, MDAH.

219 dialogue between Johnson and farmer: Confidential-source int. with former Mississippi state official.

220 felt like he was back in South Pacific: Int. Paul B. Johnson III, October 16, 2000.

220 *"Governor, if you can do this"*: Mississippi Legislature's Investigative Committee report, p. 22.

220 MHP at Kiamie's deciding to attack marshals: 1999–2001 ints. with six eyewitnesses: five Mississippi Highway Patrolmen and Mississippi state representative James Mathis.

220 patrolman wouldn't mind if marshals got bullets in their heads: FBI # 157–401–1041.

221 *"Let's go"; "Load up!"; "We thought Brunt was dead"; "It had been decided"*: Int. Charles Staten, January 3, 2000.

222 Gayden summoning Johnson: Int. Art Richardson, April 5, 2000.

222 *"Don't go up there"; "We cannot fight"*: Int. James Mathis, September 10, 1999.

223 *"there wouldn't have been a marshal left"*: Oxford USA, Citizens Council film.

223 Franklin and Pontotoc Guardsmen deployed; thoughts and quotes of Hassel Franklin: Int. Hassel Franklin, October 26, 1999.

224 *"an uncontrollable, vicious mob"*: Army History, p. 104.

224 Brown background, experience during the riot: Int. Billy Ross Brown, December 1, 1999.

Chapter 14 · A Wall of Fire

228 *"Keep going!"*: Int. Donnie Bowman, October 5, 1998.

228 *"Wake up captain!"*: Int. Bill Peters, July 28, 2000.

228 details of Billingslea: "Combat-Tested General: Charles Billingslea," *NYT*, October 2, 1962.

229 sequence of orders to Billingslea from Vance and president: Army History, p. 102.

229 confused reporting structure: see Army History, pp. 75, 266.

229 couldn't write orders down: Ibid., pp. 75, 76.

229 details of Task Force Alpha: Ibid., p. 107.

230 scene inside helicopters: Int. Lieutenant Colonel John J. Flanagan, 503d Military Police Battalion, April 22, 1999.

230 Lambert's thoughts: Int. Melvin Lambert, November 6, 2000.

230 helicopter over campus: Army History, p. 109; *USNWR*, October 15, 1962, p. 46.

231 McShane, Katzenbach agreed: Lord, *The Past That Would Not Die*, p. 227.

231 *"Where's the Army?"*; Kennedy shouting at Vance: Reeves, *Profile of Power*, p. 362.

231 RFK never saw JFK so furious: Guthman and Shulman, *Robert Kennedy in His Own Words*, pp. 162, 168.

231 Vance reports to JFK: Reeves, *Profile of Power*, pp. 362, 363.

231 "Damn Army!": Cabinet Room tape recording, JFKL.

231 *"They always give you their bullshit"*: Reeves, *Profile of Power*, p. 363.

232 Lincoln in the telegraph office: David Homer Bates, *Lincoln in the Telegraph Office: Recollections of the United States Military Telegraph Corps During the Civil War* (The Century Company, 1907), pp. 40–42, 118–22, 142.

232 Billingslea outpacing Signal Corps: Army History, p. 107.

232 *"People are dying in Oxford"*: Schlesinger, *Robert Kennedy and His Times*, p. 354.

232 *"the evening would have been"*: Guthman and Shulman, *Robert Kennedy in His Own Words*, p. 167.

232 twenty minutes wasted: Int. John J. Flanagan, April 22, 1999.

233 Billingslea screamed at MPs: Army History, p. 109.

233 *"Go, go"; "Sir"*: Int. Donnie Bowman, November 6, 2000.

233 landing of MPs; details and timing of deployment onto campus: Army History, pp. 108–14; author 1998–2001 ints. with twenty-one officers and enlisted men of the 503d MP Battalion, including John J. Flanagan, then battalion commander, and Fred Villella, then captain of A Company; Thomas Buckley, "Army Unit Chief Re-creates Action at Oxford," *NYT*, October 5, 1962, p. 19.

233–34 Bowman carried proclamation, *"Lieutenant"*: Int. Donnie Bowman, November 6, 2000.

234 Flanagan feared MPs and Guardsmen could fight; *"lock and load!"*: Int. John Flanagan, April 22, 1999.

234 *"What are you doing down here, nigger?"*: Int. Donnie Bowman, November 6, 2000.

234 *"I guess y'all"; "There aren't any"*: Int. Robert Crowe, December 10, 1999.

234 Brown delighted to put on mask: Int. Melvin Brown, October 6, 1999.

235 *"We don't know what's up there"*: Int. Donnie Bowman, October 5, 1998.

235 thoughts of Migliore: Int. John Migliore, May 20, 2000.

236 University officials saw black troops; dialed their congressmen to protest: Memo regarding 2:00 A.M., October 1, 1962, meeting in George Street Collection, Box 17, UMASC.

236 *"Keep going!"*: Int. Donnie Bowman, October 5, 1998.

236 MPs entered fire; Villella's thoughts: Int. Fred Villella, April 30, 2000.

236 *"We saw two sheets of flame"*: Silver, *Mississippi: The Closed Society*, p. vii.

236 *"You could see the troops"*: Strober and Strober, *Let Us Begin Anew*, p. 305.

236 *"Molotov cocktails"*: Douglas, *A Long Night*, p. 22.

236 *"I saw one marching soldier"*: MPS, October 1, 1962, p. 1.

237 *"Sometimes when the fire hits"*: Douglas, *A Long Night*, p. 22.

237 *"kick ass and take names"*: Int. with confidential source who was in the crowd.

237 *"I could not believe what I saw"*: Int. John Migliore, May 20, 2000.

237 *"I can't believe this is America"*: Int. Donnie Bowman, October 5, 1998.

237 Flanagan's thoughts and quotes: Int. John Flanagan, April 22, 1999.

237 Mullins never heard so much applause: Int. Mack Mullins, December 2, 1999.

237 *"They're here!"*: WES, October 1, 1962, p. 5.

238 *"I want you to clear"*: Int. John Shook, October 5, 1999.

238 *"Katzenbach, take that battalion"; "I only have 117 men"*; Villella's judgment: Int. Fred Villella, December 15, 2000.

238 Abrams reported to JFK at 2:30 A.M.: Dictabelt recording of Oval Office telephone line, JFKL.

238 *"I want to be called"*: Reeves, *Profile of Power*, p. 364.

239 *"you got any tear gas"; "Come on with me"*: Int. Donnie Bowman, October 5, 1998.

239 rioters conducting war dance: *Time*, October 12, 1962, p. 21.

239 *"If I were Meredith, I'd be ashamed"*: *Life*, November 1962, p. 23.

239–40 Guardsmen's quotes: *McComb Enterprise Journal* (McComb, Mississippi), October 1, 1962.

240 scenes and quotes at Senatobia Armory, thoughts and quotes of Callicott: Int. William Callicott, August 30, 1999.

242 Griffin leading students into battle: Int. Bob Griffin, December 17, 1999.

242 approach of First Squadron; *"The situation was still"*: *National Guardsman*, November 1962, pp. 6, 7.

242 approach of First Squadron: Int. Guy Gravlee, October 13, 1999.

243 *"We literally had to fight our way"*: Int. Bob Griffin, January 12, 2000.

243 *"They were like me"*: Int. Guy Gravlee, October 13, 1999.

243 First Squadron hit with gas: Int. Bob Griffin, October 13, 1999.

244 *"Glad to see you"*: *National Guardsman*, November 1962, p. 7.

244 *"If y'all hadn't"*: Int. William Callicott, August 30, 1999.

244 *"You people fall in"*: Int. Buford Babb, December 13, 1999.

244 *"Soldiers, load and cock"*: Int. Seibert Lockman, November 30, 1999.

244 *"Let's go, Mississippi!"*: Int. Fred Villella, May 22, 2000.

245 rioter planted flag: Campbell, *And Also With You,* p. 29.

245 *"double-timed over"*: Int. Loyd Gunter, October 12, 2000.

245 Crowe's experiences and dialogue: Int. Robert Crowe, December 10, 1999.

246 Troop G's actions at the Sorority Row entrance: All details and quotes from int. Hassel Franklin, October 26, 1999.

247–48 journey of 503d MP convoy: 1998–2001 ints. with fifteen of the MPs in the convoy; Army History, pp. 118–120; *NYT,* October 5, 1962, p. 19.

248 *"As military police"*: Int. William Mayes, November 25, 1998.

248 confrontation between 503d MPs and MHP: Ints. with MPs George Baldwin (December 18, 1998), and Joseph Cooke (January 10, 1999). They were at Major Le Van's side.

250 *"Goddamn Yankees"; "Crash it and keep going"*: Int. William Peters, October 6, 1999.

250 MP convoy attacked at bridge: Army History, p. 119; int. William Mayes, April 7, 2001.

250 *"But above all, the courthouse"*: William Faulkner, *Requiem for a Nun* (New York: Random House, 1951), p. 40.

250 Parris's thoughts: Int. William Parris, November 6, 2000.

251 rioters tossing debris: Int. Lester Lewis, November 30, 1998.

251 attacks on MPs in Square: Army History, p. 120.

251 crowd closing in; *"Load shotguns!"; "That was the awfulest sound"*: Int. William Peters, October 6, 1999.

251 *"Believe it or not"*: Int. David Wharry, November 23, 1998.

251 Oxford policeman led MPs to the Armory; Cooke's reconnaissance to school: Army History, p. 119.

252 Cooke's drive to campus; *"The whole area was saturated"*: Int. Joseph Cooke, January 10, 1999.

252 James Kennedy with drunks and black woman: Int. James Kennedy, December 8, 2000.

253 *"I'm under orders"; "Welcome to Ole Miss, motherfucker"; "You keep your mother off the street"*: Int. former 503d MP who requested anonymity.

253 closing of 716th MPs and 155th Infantry: Army History, pp. 121, 122, 125.

254 *"Under those circumstances"*: Int. William Peters, October 6, 1999.

254 James Kennedy with civilians on campus: Int. James Kennedy, December 8, 2000.

254 Smith pulled down Confederate flag: W. F. Minor, "Troops Hold Rigid Control at Oxford," *NOTP,* October 2, 1962, p. 1.

254 *"What'll we do?"*: Lord, *The Past That Would Not Die,* p. 191.

Chapter 15 · After the Dawn

256 *"The wall is rent, the ruins yawn"*: McGann, *Lord Byron: The Complete Poetical Works,* pp. 328, 329.

256 Meredith waking up: *SEP,* November 10, 1962, p. 25.

257 scene inside Lyceum; Meredith registering; going to first class: Meredith, *Three Years*, pp. 212–13; Michael Dorman, *We Shall Overcome* (New York: Delacorte Press, 1964), p. 110; *NYP*, October 2, 1962, p. 2; *Time*, October 12, 1962, p. 19.

258 *"the only man on the scene"*: Meredith, *Three Years*, p. 213.

258 feelings of Ellis: Int. Robert Ellis, March 15, 2001.

258 cleaning man touched Meredith: Int. James Meredith in Cox Communications cable TV special: *James Meredith: Breaking Down the Barriers*, 1994.

259 Meredith's first moments in class: Meredith, *Three Years*, p. 214; Clare L. Marquette, "The 'Meredith Incident' at the University of Mississippi," *Milton Today*, May 1963, p. 11.

260 *"I then began"*: Clare L. Marquette, "The 'Meredith Incident' at the University of Mississippi," *Milton Today*, May 1963, p. 11.

260 Mounger's thoughts and actions on the morning of October 1: *SEP*, November 10, 1962, p. 26; David Sansing interview with W. H. Mounger, September 21, 1978, pp. 34–36, Verner Holmes Collection, Box 6, UMASC.

260 background on and October 1 experience of Dr. Shirley: Int. with his daughter JoAnne Prichard Morris, February 11, 2000.

261 people walking around roadblocks: Army History, p. 149.

261 *"come to help Mississippi"*: FBI # 157–401–1041.

261 *"Louisiana is here"*: "GIs man 'Fort Oxford,' Miss.," *CSM*, October 2, 1962.

261 boys announced: Robert E. Baker, "Marshals Use Tear Gas Against 2000 Attackers," *WP*, October 1, 1962, p. 1.

262 bus from Hattiesburg: Int. Bill E. Burk, November 20, 1998.

262 morning fighting in downtown Oxford: October 1–4, 1962 editions of *NYT, NYWT, NYHT, NYP, NYJA, MCA, MPS, JDN, JCL, NOTP, Miami Herald, Shreveport Journal, Birmingham News, St. Louis Post-Dispatch, Providence Journal-Bulletin, Nashville Tennessean, Louisville Courier Journal*; *National Guardsman*, November 1962, pp. 7–9; int. Bill E. Burk, November 20, 1998; int. Richard Starnes, June 6, 1999; int. Murry C. Falkner, September 24, 1998; int. Nathan Hodges, September 18, 1998; int. Charles Shockley, November 1, 1999; int. Charles M. Bolen, December 8, 2000.

262 *"We don't have any"*: Int. Bill E. Burk, November 20, 1998.

262 attack on Thompson: Int. Mrs. Isaiah Thompson, March 1, 2000.

263 *"Oh, no, they can't hurt her"*: Bill E. Burk, "Newsman Views a Sickening Spectacle," *MPS*, October 4, 1962, p. 1.

263 *"I can't wipe from my memory"*: *Drew-Ruleville Pilot/Progress* (Mississippi), October 1, 1992, p. 3.

263 *"I never knew human life"*: *MPS*, October 4, 1962, p. 1.

263 *"These aren't our people"*: Rick Tuttle, "It Was War—and Marshals Were Losing," *Miami Herald*, October 2, 1962.

263 boy in uniform directing assaults: FBI # 151–401–1484.

263 Elliott trying to stop riot: Int. Richard Elliott, September 7, 1999; Richard Elliott, "Mayor's Reasons for Calling Federal Aid Told in Interview," *JDN*, October 8, 1962, p. 11.

263 *"There were a number of Highway Patrolmen"*: Jack Thompson, "Oxford Mayor Asked Troops to Quell Riot," *Journal Bulletin* (Providence, RI), October 4, 1962, p. 1.

264 Guardsmen chased off arsonists: Int. Murry C. Falkner, September 24, 1998.

264 *"Here comes a Jeep!"*: Int. Bill E. Burk, November 20, 1998.

264 rioter threw ax: Int. William E. Callicott, August 30, 1999.

264 *"These are our own people"*: Int. WJDX-WLBT reporter Chuck Allen, November 23, 1999.

264–65 Shockley and troops at rest stop and Oxford limits; Shockley background; *"Why is he"*; Shockley and B Company marching onto square: Int. Charles Shockley, November 1, 1999.

265 *"They had not heard such language"*: Personal journal of Charles Shockley, courtesy Charles Shockley.

266 *"They would look you right in the eye"*; *"I would grab my helmet"*: Int. Charles Shockley, November 1, 1999.

266 *"Within minutes"*; *"Almost every jeep"*: Jack Thompson, "Soldiers Quell Morning Riot," *Journal Bulletin* (Providence, RI), October 2, 1962, p. 1.

266 *"The dignity of the Negro soldiers"*; *"When are they going to shoot back?"*: Richard Starnes, "Shame Is Mood of Oxford," *NYWT,* October 3, 1962.

267 *"Good going, boys!"*: Richard Starnes, "Yahoos on the Loose in Oxford," *NTWT,* October 2, 1962.

267 *"Walker walked"*: Int. Charles Shockley, November 1, 1999.

267 background on Charles Bolen; his thoughts; dialogue of Bolen and Robert Clark; dialogue of Bolen and Keller; detention of Walker: Int. Charles Bolen, December 8, 2000. Additional source for Second Infantry's actions: "Flashback to Integration at University of Mississippi," Associated Press Newswires, May 28, 2000.

268 Posse Comitatus Act: Thomas R. Lujan, "Legal Aspects of Domestic Employment of the Army", *Parameters* (U.S. Army War College publication), October 11, 1997, p. 82.

270–71 JFK/Barnett; JFK/Cox; JFK/Vance/McNamara: Dictabelt recordings of Oval Office phone line; JFKL.

271 JFK ordered tower; troops to airfields: Army History, pp. 131–32.

271 marshal/Callicott exchange: Int. William E. Callicott, August 30, 1999.

271 Oxford airport became nation's busiest: Hamilton H. Howze, *A Cavalryman's Story: Memoirs of a Twentieth-Century Army General* (Washington, DC: Smithsonian Institution Press, 1996), p. 227.

272 action of Echo; First Battle Group: Army History, pp. 126, 127.

272 Bravo convoy more than one hundred miles: Int. Charles Bolen, December 8, 2000.

272 *"must have seen"*; *"We had enough men"*: Int. Johnny Arnold, January 24, 2000.

272 JFK deploying 82nd and 101st: Army History, pp. 143, 144.

273 McNamara scrambling 100 helicopters: Army History, p. 144.

273 JFK queries marines, marine response: Army History, p. 146.

273 detail of 1962 marine Division/Wing Team: Int. Bob Aquilina, U.S. Marine Corps Historical Center, Washington, D.C., January 25, 2001.

273 final actions of Guard: Army History, pp. 129–32.

274 *"I did not want. . . . They were all hunters"*: Int. William Austin, December 14, 1999.

274 Women choking; helicopters hovering: Al Kuettner, "Bayonets Rule Campus," *NYWT,* October 1, 1962, pp. 1, 15.

275 *"like rabbits"*: Int. Arthur Herod, November 18, 1998.

275 sun broke over the city: Charles M. Hargroder, "Troops Restore Uneasy Calm," *NOTP,* October 2, 1962, p. 5.

Chapter 16 · The New Age

276 Berryhill's thoughts; *"God, I can't believe this"*: Int. Charlie Berryhill, September 10, 2000.

276 wreath: Charles Whaley, "Public Schools Close in Riot-Torn Oxford," *LCJ*, Oct 2, 1962, p. 1.

276 *"Hell, this was close"*: Simeon Booker, "Negro GIs, White Marshals," *Jet*, October 18, 1962, p. 22.

276–77 *"There's nothing I hate more"*: Bill Wuomett, "Ole Miss: A Campus Smothered with Smoke and Tears," *Raleigh News and Observer*, October 7, 1962, p. 3.

277 *"There wasn't a man"*: Jim G. Lucas, "A Marshal May Be Biased but His Badge Comes First," *NYWT*, October 3, 1962.

277 *"When students hurled rocks"*: Editorial by Sidna Brower, *The Mississippian* (student newspaper), October 1, 1962, p. 2.

277 *"We must have no violence"; "I think last night"*: "Barnett, Bob Kennedy Clash on Cause of 'Ole Miss' Riot," *WP*, October 2, 1962, p. 7.

277 martial law unnecessary: Army History, p. 148.

277 troop deployment details: Ibid., pp. 147, 148.

278 troop levels vs. Korea; West Berlin: *NYHT*, October 5, 1962.

278 fifty FBI agents rushed to Oxford: Int. Robin Cotten, January 15, 2000.

278 twenty army intelligence agents in Oxford: Army History, p. 162.

278 three hundred reporters from as far away as Japan and Poland: "Oxford's Shame," *LAT*, October 2, 1962, p. 2.

278 global headlines and editorials: "World Press Plays Up Oxford Story," *NYHT*, October 2, 1962.

278 machine guns and tripods: Rick Tuttle, "Occupation Troops Cast Grim Shadow," *Miami Herald*, October 2, 1962, p. 1.

278 *"Yaah-huh!"*: Kenneth L. Dixon, "Courthouse Square is Authentic Picture of Occupied Town," *Meridian Star*, October 2, 1962.

278 *"My God"*: Int. Dan Pursglove, August 25, 1999.

279 *"Are we in Cuba?"*; captain kissed the ground: Int. Ray Sartor, January 3, 2000.

279 Shockley as judge: Int. Charles Shockley, November 1, 1999.

279 observation post atop school: Louis Silver, "3,600 Soldiers Leave Oxford," *MCA*, October 3, 1962.

279 Company C prepared lunch for kids: Warren Rogers, Jr., "Company C Falls into Rebel Trap," *Birmingham News*, October 5, 1962, p. 1.

279 kids trading milk: Int. Steve Bramlett, November 3, 1999.

279 scenes evoked daguerreotypes of Brady: W. J. Weatherby, "Anger of Mississippi Finds an Outlet," *Manchester Guardian*, October 3, 1962, p. 1.

279 GIs patrolling: Miami Herald, October 2, 1962, p. 1.

279 *"You'd better get back"*: Tom Gregory, "Residents of Oxford Getting Accustomed to 'Rule by Military,' " *Meridian Star*, October 2, 1962, p. 1.

279 *"That nigger's had it"; "Lord, that boy"*: Rick Tuttle, "Meredith Effigy Hangs at Dormitory," *Miami Herald*, October 3, 1962, p. 10.

279–80 *"I like the troops"; "The marshals should have fired"; "Thank God for the troops"*: USNWR, October 15, 1962, p. 60.

280–81 no brutality complaints: Int. Nichols Katzenbach, November 15, 2000; Army History, p. 135.

281 *"I was there"*: Int. Murry C. Falkner, September 24, 1998.

281 raid on Sigma Nu; discovery of weapons: Army History, pp. 148, 149; FBI # 157–401–371.

281–82 Lott getting award: *Baltimore Sun,* February 23, 1997, 1 J.

282 *"I'm glad";* old men back on benches: Edward P. Moore, Jr., "Oxford Is Returning to Life as Traces of Rioting Fade," *MCA,* October 3, 1962, p. 12.

282 Klan meeting at Bessemer: FBI # 157–401–159.

282 FBI informant heard plan to bomb Oxford and naval air station: FBI # 157–401–504.

282–83 airlift sleeping bags; mattresses; relief convoy: Louis Silver, "Comfort Speeds by Helicopter," *MCA,* October 4, 1962, p. 32.

283 Troop E treated: *National Guardsman,* November 1962, p. 9.

283 *"We were looking":* Int. William Mayes, October 14, 1998.

283 racial segregation of troops as approved by President Kennedy and Attorney General Kennedy: Army History, pp. 58–59 and 163–69. Although on September 27 Robert Kennedy approved the stripping of black soldiers off the front lines before they entered Oxford (Army History, p. 58), some units did not implement the order. Mississippi senator John Stennis was instrumental in pressuring the Kennedys to pull the remaining black troops off the front lines (Army History, pp. 58, 164).

283 JFK, McNamara discuss segregation: Army History, p. 166.

283 McNamara had no memory of the order: Conversation with the author, October 11, 2000.

284 Katzenbach witnessed formations pulled apart; pleaded to RFK and Vance, *"This is just crazy!"; "I didn't believe":* Int. Nicholas Katzenbach, November 15, 2000.

285 Flanagan and Le Van protesting segregation order: Int. John Flanagan, April 22, 1999.

285 memories and comments of Russell Amos: Int. Russell Amos, January 14, 2001.

285 segregation order to Lentz; *"We were told"; "Thus, ethnically cleansed":* April 28, 1999, letter to author from Martin R. Lentz, then E-5 Sergeant, 82nd Airborne Division.

286 black sergeant in 82nd relayed order with tears in his eyes: June 2, 1999, e-mail to author from George Hall, then PFC, E Company, First Airborne Battle Group, 82nd Airborne.

286 *"Tell all"; "so bloody shocked"; "the hell with this":* Int. Sgt. William Johnson, 82nd Airborne, August 20, 1999.

286 thoughts of Jamie Brewer: Int. Jamie Brewer, August 24, 1999.

286 officers of the 82nd Airborne and 101st Airborne, 716th Military Police Battalion protested resegregation in writing: Army History, pp. 168, 169.

286 *"How can we face our companies"; "a voice in our collective souls":* "Pulled from Oxford, Negro GIs Say, 'It's our Fight, Too,' " *Jet,* October 18, 1962, p. 24, 25.

286 events and dialogue in Second Infantry camp on segregation of troops: Int. Charles Shockley, November 1, 1999; personal journal of Charles Shockley, courtesy Charles Shockley.

287 Parks quotes; memories: Int. William Parks, December 6, 2000.

288 Meredith protested in private: Army History, p. 165.

288 *"This condition"; "My conscience":* "Army Guardians Practice Bias," *Baltimore Sun,* October 10, 1962, p. 1.

289 *"You mean"*: Dorothy Gilliam, "Mississippi Negroes Happily Stunned by Meredith," *WP,* October 7, 1962, p. 1.

289 *"Meredith is just like Moses to me"*: Larry Still, "Negroes Proud of Meredith," *Jet,* October 18, 1962, p. 15.

289 *"I'm so glad there's a black face"*: Dorothy Gilliam, "Mississippi Mood: Hope and Fear," *WP,* October 14, 1962, E1.

289 *"He's really done it!"*: *WP,* October 7, 1962, p. 1.

289 *"to walk a bit"*: *WP,* October 7, 1962, p. 1.

289 *"I sure would hate to see"*; *"I think I'll go to Ole Miss"*: *Jet,* October 18, 1962, p. 18.

289 *"Could you please remove"*; *"James, you won't live"*; *"It could be precisely"*: Int. Nicholas Katzenbach, April 17, 2000.

290 Meredith walk on campus; *"Why doesn't somebody"*: "Meredith Eats First Meal in Cafeteria," *JDN,* October 5, 1962, p. 12.

290 *"Why, they're just sitting"*; *"That's the best way"*: Dickson Preston, "Struggle Goes on for Meredith," *Knoxville News-Sentinel,* October 7, 1962, pp. 4, 13.

290 October 8 disturbance: FBI # 157–401–866.

290 *"There was nothing unique"*: "Interview with James Meredith," *The Black Student,* Spring 1966, p. 32.

290 called nigger for ten months: Meredith, *Three Years,* p. 274.

290 Meredith had more friends: Ibid., p. 286.

290 *"As hundreds of dumbfounded"*: Meredith, *Three Years,* p. 286.

291 October 29 disturbance: Army History, p. 201; Cohodas, *And the Band Played Dixie,* pp. 93, 94.

291 *"Let no student speak to him"*: "Rebel Resistance" flyer, Verner Holmes Collection, UMASC, Box 4, folder 7.

291 *"Nigger Lovers"*: Cohodas, *And the Band Played Dixie,* p. 94.

291 *"that's not the most important thing"*; *"The right to fail"*: "Meredith Admits He's Having Trouble Trying to Study," *Baltimore Afro-American,* November 24, 1962, p. 14.

291 attack on Meredith's home: "Meredith's Home Blasted by Shotguns," *Knoxville News-Sentinel,* December 24, 1962, p. 16.

292 Meredith security arrangements: Army History, p. 162.

292 *"Now we got two"*; *"I go through this"*: "Ordeal of James Meredith Drags on at Ole Miss," *Jet,* April 25, 1963, p. 22.

292 Army tour for Ford: "Headquarters USAFOX: Sheriff Ford, Oxford, Miss."; printed menu dated May 22, 1963; papers of Sheriff Joe Ford, courtesy Patricia Ford Reaves.

292 Ford would help guarantee the peace: Army History, p. 244.

292 army plans for McDowell: Army History, pp. 233, 234.

293 withdrawal of last army troops: Army History, pp. 248–50.

293 Meredith said they should have left: Army History, p. 249.

293 *"It was a lonely victory"*: Hampton, *Eyes on the Prize.*

294 graduation day: Fred Powledge, "Meredith Receives Mississippi Degree," *NYT,* August 19, 1963; Bill Minor, "Meredith Gets U of M Degree," *NOTP,* August 19, 1963, p. 3; Saul Pett, "Meredith Gets Diploma," *JDN,* August 19, 1963, p. 3.

294 *"At that moment"*: *NOTP,* August 19, 1963, p. 3.

294 *"Well, I'm glad"*; *"I'm proud"*: *JDN,* August 19, 1963, p. 3.

294 "Ross Is Right" badge: Meredith, *Three Years,* p. 322.

294 *"These people can be decent"*: Mandy Jones, "First Black UM Grad Donates Official Papers," *The Daily Mississippian*, March 24, 1997, p. 1.

Epilogue · The Greatest Suppertime of All

295 *"It's all now"*: Faulkner, *Intruder in the Dust*, p. 194.
295 *"I wasn't there as a student"*; *"I was a general"*: Cox TV special: *James Meredith: Breaking Down the Barriers*.
295–96 segregationist strategy, Simmons convinced history was sure to turn; *"they really kept it"*; *"We got run over"*: Int. William Simmons, October 15, 2000.
296 *"put an end to massive resistance"*: Int. Constance Baker Motley, January 9, 1998.
297 *"By the time"*: Int. Nicholas Katzenbach, April 17, 2000.
297 *"It was the final battle"*: Int. Horace Harned, Jr., March 19, 2000.
298 *"Oxford was something"*: Int. Larry Williams, October 5, 1999.
298 *"one of the sorriest"*: Int. James Kennedy, December 8, 2000.
298 many in Mississippi blamed marshals, statement by faculty and staff: Sansing, *The University of Mississippi*, p. 303.
298 *"Those marshals were the bravest men I ever saw"*: *SEP*, November 10, 1962, p. 18.
299 *"He has never been in the mainstream"*: Int. David Sansing, September 10, 1998.
299 *"I don't believe in 'improvement' "*: James T. Kaull, "All-or-Nothing Stand Cited by Meredith," *Journal Bulletin* (Providence, RI), October 29, 1963.
299 shooting of Meredith: Roy Reed, "Meredith is Shot in Back on Walk in Miss.", NYT, June 7, 1966, p. 1.
300 *Meredith's bid for Powell's seat; Meredith's business ventures:* Lois Romano, "The Long, Long Journey of James Meredith," *WP*, November 3, 1989, p. C 1.
300 *"within months"*: Arturo Gonzalez, Sandra Salinas, "The Long, Lonely Road of Rights Hero James Meredith," *People*, October 16, 1989, p. 40.
300 *"the biggest con job"*; *"Have you ever heard"*; *"To me it was an insult"*: Juan Williams, "Integration Is a 'Con Job,' " *WP*, February 23, 1985, p. G 1.
301 *"Why do you have to call it"*: *WP*, November 3, 1989, p. C 1.
301 *"I will be"*; *"I have a divine responsibility"*: *People*, October 16, 1989, p. 40.
301 *"I have yet to do anything"*: *WP*, November 3, 1989, p. C 1.
301 *"After I walked across the stage"*: *The Daily Mississippian*, March 24, 1997, p. 1.
302 *"He has become"*: Int. David Sansing, September 10, 1998.
302 *"Meredith is obviously"*: Int. Duncan Gray, Jr., June 8, 1999.
302 *"Most of us couldn't"*: *People*, October 16, 1989, p. 40.
302 *"They hurt 24 hours a day"*; *"It happens on a regular basis"*; *"it's the best thing"*: Int. James Meredith, December 10, 2000.
303 *"I was creating images"*: Int. James Meredith, September 20, 1998.
303 *"It had a tremendous sobering effect"*: Int. Bill Minor, September 18, 1998.
303 Citizens Council purge: John Herbers, "Mississippi Purge Ousts Moderates," *NYT*, November 8, 1963, p. 11.
303 Farley left: "New Dean at Ole Miss," *Time*, July 18, 1969, p. 53.
303 Donald admitted; board abandoned policy: Cohodas, *The Band Played Dixie*, pp. 113–16. Additional postscript: After the riot, Coach Johnny Vaught's University of Mississippi Rebels football team experienced the greatest year in its history, ending the 1962 season undefeated and untied, winning the Southeastern Conference

and the Sugar Bowl. Their star fullback was Buck Randall, the student who on September 30, 1962, tried to stop the riot as bullets flew over his head.

304 *"A desert state sweltering":* Rev. Martin Luther King, Jr., address to March on Washington, August 28, 1963.

304 *"It is no accident":* Willie Morris, "At Ole Miss, Echoes of a Civil War's Last Battle," *Time,* October 4, 1982, p. 11.

304 *"You and I"; "niggers, alligators"; "we are Americans"; "God bless everyone":* Time, January 31, 1964, p. 22.

304 Paul B. Johnson, Jr.'s actions in office: "Mississippi: A Vote for Reason," *Time,* August 27, 1965, p. 13.

305 E. L. McDaniel resurrected Klan in Mississippi: Int. E. L. McDaniel, April 6, 2000.

305 Klan postscript: John Herbers, "The Klan: Its Growing Influence," *NYT,* April 20, 1965, p. 1.

306 Lott and CCC; *"Yes, you could say":* Kevin Merida, "Three Consonants and a Disavowal: The More You Ask Trent Lott About His Ties to the White Supremacist C.C.C., the Less He Has to Say," *WP,* March 29, 1999, p. C 1.

307 JFK's popularity ratings in South: Brauer, *John F. Kennedy and the Second Reconstruction,* p. 201.

307 Mississippi senate called for impeachment of JFK: Silver, *Mississippi: The Closed Society,* p. 47.

307 *"In the eleven states":* Reeves, *Profile of Power,* p. 431.

308 *"A group of thirty or forty students":* Int. David Crawley, October 16, 2000.

308 *"the only president":* "Meredith's Prediction," *Atlanta Daily World,* November 28, 1963, p. 7.

308–9 RFK visit to Oxford; *"all the errors"; "twisted statements"; "hypocritical":* Andrew J. Glass, "Ole Miss Applauds Kennedy," *NYHT,* March 19, 1966.

309 JFK staff dumbfounded: Doyle, *Inside the Oval Office,* pp. 105.

309 Walker arrests: "General Walker Faces Sex Charges," *NYT,* July 9, 1976, p, 28; "General Walker Free on Bond," *NYT,* March 18, 1977, p. 13.

309 postscript on Walker: Eric Pace, "Gen. Edwin Walker, 83 is Dead; Promoted Rightist Causes in '60's," *NYT,* November 2, 1993, p. 10.

311 *"the Eighteenth Airborne Corps";* Int. Joseph Cooke, September 11, 1998.

311 *"It is my opinion":* Falkner Statement, p. 13.

312 *"I knew for sure I'd fouled up":* Falkner Statement, p. 11.

312 *"The people here did not":* Int. William Callicott, August 30, 1999.

312–13 *"You've got to understand":* Int. Buford Babb, December 13, 1999.

313 *"none of us wanted":* Int. Oscar "Gray" Megginson, December 1, 1999.

313 *"we were looked on as traitors";* Int. former Mississippi National Guard officer.

313 *"We were betrayed":* Int. Hassel Franklin, November 18, 1999.

313 *"It's a matter": National Guardsman,* November 1962, p. 6.

313–14 *"We just don't talk"; "It was just a bad dream":* Robert Colby Nelson, "Better Days in Oxford, Miss.," *CSM,* March 28, 1964.

314 *"night of horrors"; "We must not forget":* J. D. Williams speech at Greenville, MS, *MCA,* November 1, 1962, p. 33.

315 Ole Miss postscript: Int. David Sansing, April 19, 2001.

315 University's academic successes: "Quality Points," University of Mississippi pamphlet, February 4, 2000.

315 *"Visitors to the Ole Miss campus": WP,* January 7, 1999, C 1.

315 *"No man ever went"*: John Herbers, "Barnett's Term Ending Tuesday," *NYT,* January 19, 1964, p. 51.

316 *"You sentence a man";* greatest industrial expansion: "Ex-Gov. Barnett Dies at 89," *JCL,* November 7, 1987, p. 1.

316 Meredith endorses Barnett: "Last Roll for Ross," *Time,* July 31, 1967, p. 23.

316 *"I didn't make any mistakes"*: Greg Kuhl, "Ross Barnett, 86, Decides to Retire," *JDN,* March 7, 1984, p. 1.

316 *"I admire a lot of the black people"*: Sidney Cearnal, "Barnett to End 70-year String of Neshoba Fair Appearances," *The Daily Journal* (Tupelo, Mississippi), July 26, 1984.

317 Meredith planned to appear; saw Barnett around Jackson: Int. James Meredith, November 26, 2000.

317 *"Barnett managed it perfectly"; "There were plenty of people"*: Int. James Meredith, November 10, 1998.

317 Barnett's room: Steve Guyton, "Guyton Writes on Barnett," *Oxford Eagle,* August 6, 1984.

317 Barnett's last performance at Neshoba County Fair: Sid Salter, "Fairgoers Are Intrigued with Ross Barnett," *Times Leader* (West Point, Mississippi), July 20, 1984; *The Daily Journal* (Tupelo, Mississippi), July 26, 1984.

317 Barnett singing suppertime song: *The Daily Journal* (Tupelo, Mississippi), July 26, 1984; *JDN,* March 7, 1984, p. 1.

318 no monuments, scholarships: There is a plaque dedicated to James Meredith on the inside of Baxter Hall, which was his dormitory in 1962–1963.

318 bullet marks in the Lyceum: In the October 3, 1962, *JDN,* (p. 7), W. C. Shoemaker wrote that the "columns at the front of the Lyceum were pockmarked with bullet holes." FBI agents recovered nine bullets imbedded in the main door frame of the Lyceum (FBI # 157–401–310). James Meredith wrote that he often looked at the bullet holes during his stay at Ole Miss *(Three Years,* p. 322). The author saw marks in the two northernmost columns of the Lyceum during the author's first visit to Oxford in September 1998. Paul Hill, the current University of Mississippi superintendent of construction and maintenance, told the author in a May 16, 2000 interview that he learned in 1980 that bullet marks in the columns "had been left there on purpose. We've never done anything about it." In a March 30, 2001, interview, Mr. Hill reported that after a recent major renovation of the Lyceum, the bullet marks were still left in the columns.

SELECT BIBLIOGRAPHY

Books

Ambrose, Stephen E. *Eisenhower: The President.* New York: Simon & Schuster, 1984.

Barrett, Russell H. *Integration at Ole Miss.* Chicago: Quadrangle Books, 1965.

Bass, Jack, and Walter De Vries. *The Transformation of Southern Politics: Social Change and Political Consequence Since 1945.* New York: Basic Books, 1976.

Beals, Melba Pattillo. *Warriors Don't Cry: A Searing Memoir of the Battle to Integrate Little Rock's Central High.* New York: Pocket Books, 1994.

Branch, Taylor. *Parting the Waters: America in the King Years, 1954–1963.* New York: Touchstone, 1989.

Brauer, Carl. *John F. Kennedy and the Second Reconstruction.* New York: Columbia University Press, 1977.

Brown, Maud Morrow. *The University Greys: Company A, Eleventh Mississippi Regiment, 1861–1865.* Richmond, Virginia: Garrett and Massie, 1940.

Brownell, Herbert, with John P. Burke. *Advising Ike: The Memoirs of Attorney General Herbert Brownell.* Lawrence: University Press of Kansas, 1993.

Campbell, Will D. *And Also With You: Duncan Gray and the American Dilemma.* Franklin, Tennessee: Providence House Publishers, 1997.

Cash, W. J. *The Mind of the South.* New York, Alfred A. Knopf, 1941.

Cohodas, Nadine. *The Band Played Dixie: Race and the Liberal Conscience at Ole Miss.* New York, The Free Press, 1997.

Cook, James Graham. *The Segregationists.* New York: Appleton-Century-Crofts, 1962.

Counts, Will. *A Life Is More Than a Moment: The Desegregation of Little Rock's Central High.* Bloomington: Indiana University Press, 1999.

Dorman, Michael. *We Shall Overcome.* New York: Delacorte Press, 1964.

Douglas, Ellen. *A Long Night.* Jackson, Mississippi: Nouveau Press, 1986.

Evers, Mrs. Medgar, with William Peters. *For Us, the Living.* Garden City, New York: Doubleday, 1967.

Faulkner, John. *My Brother Bill: An Affectionate Reminiscence.* New York, Trident Press, 1963.

Faulkner, William. *Intruder in the Dust.* New York: Random House, 1948.

———. *Requiem for a Nun.* New York: Random House, 1951.

Garner, James W. *Reconstruction in Mississippi.* New York: Macmillan, 1901.

Giglio, James N. *The Presidency of John F. Kennedy.* Lawrence: University Press of Kansas, 1991.

Greenberg, Jack. *Crusaders in the Courts: How a Dedicated Band of Lawyers Fought for the Civil Rights Revolution.* New York: Basic Books, 1994.

Guthman, Edwin O., and Jeffrey Shulman, eds. *Robert Kennedy in His Own Words.* New York: Bantam Books, 1988.

Harkey, Jr., Ira B. *The Smell of Burning Crosses: An Autobiography of a Mississippi Newspaperman.* Jacksonville, Illinois: Harris-Wolfe & Company, 1967.

Heymann, C. David. *RFK: A Candid Biography of Robert F. Kennedy.* New York: Dutton, 1998.

Howze, Hamilton H. *A Cavalryman's Story: Memoirs of a Twentieth-Century Army General.* Washington, D.C.: Smithsonian Institution Press, 1996.

Huckaby, Elizabeth. *Crisis at Central High: Little Rock, 1957–1958.* Baton Rouge, Louisiana: State University Press, 1980.

Johnston, Erle. *I Rolled With Ross: A Political Portrait.* Baton Rouge, Louisiana: Moran Publishing Company, 1980.

Knopf, Terry Ann. *Rumors and Race and Riots.* New Brunswick, New Jersey: Transaction Books, 1975.

Lasky, Victor. *Robert F. Kennedy: The Myth and the Man.* New York: Trident Press, 1968.

Levine, Edward. *All Too Human: The Love Story of Jack and Jackie Kennedy.* New York: Pocket Books, 1996.

Loewen, James W., and Charles Sallis, eds. *Mississippi: Conflict & Change.* New York: Pantheon Books, 1974.

Lord, Walter. *The Past That Would Not Die.* New York: Harper & Row, 1965.

Manchester, William. *Portrait of a President: John F. Kennedy in Profile.* Boston: Little, Brown & Company, 1962.

Martin, John Barlow. *The Deep South Says Never.* New York: Ballantine Books, 1957.

Meredith, James. *James Meredith vs. Ole Miss.* Jackson, Mississippi: Meredith Publishing, 1995.

———. *Me and My Kind: An Oral History by James H. Meredith.* Jackson, Mississippi: Meredith Publishing, 1995.

———. *Three Years in Mississippi.* Bloomington: Indiana University Press, 1966.

Morrow, E. Frederic. *Black Man in the White House: A Diary of the Eisenhower Years.* New York: Coward-McCann, Inc., 1963.

Motley, Constance Baker. *Equal Justice Under Law: An Autobiography.* New York: Farrar, Straus and Giroux, 1998.

Myrdal, Gunnar. *An American Dilemma: The Negro Problem and American Democracy.* New York: Harper & Row, 1944.

O'Reilly, Kenneth. *Nixon's Piano: Presidents and Racial Politics from Washington to Clinton.* New York: The Free Press, 1995.

Paper, Lewis J. *The Promise and the Performance: The Leadership of John F. Kennedy.* New York: Crown Publishers, 1975.

Navasky, Victor S. *Kennedy Justice.* New York: Atheneum, 1971.

Rather, Dan, with Mickey Herskowitz. *The Camera Never Blinks: Adventures of a TV Journalist.* New York: Ballantine Books, 1979.

Reeves, Richard. *President Kennedy: Profile of Power.* New York: Touchstone, 1993.

Reardon, Carol. *Pickett's Charge in Myth and Memory.* Chapel Hill: University of North Carolina Press, 1997.

Rich, Bennett Milton. *The Presidents and Civil Disorder.* Washington, D.C.: The Brookings Institution, 1941.

Rollins, Richard, ed. *Pickett's Charge! Eyewitness Accounts.* Redondo Beach, California: Rank and File, 1994.

Sansing, David G. *Making Haste Slowly: The Troubled History of Higher Education in Mississippi.* Jackson: University of Mississippi Press, 1990.

———. *The University of Mississippi: A Sesquicentennial History.* Jackson: University Press of Mississippi, 1999.

Schlesinger, Jr., Arthur M. *Robert Kennedy and His Times.* Boston: Houghton Mifflin, 1978.

———. *A Thousand Days: John F. Kennedy in the White House.* Boston: Houghton Mifflin Company, 1965.

Sidey, Hugh. *John F. Kennedy, President.* New York: Antheneum, 1964.

Silver, James W. *Mississippi: The Closed Society.* New York: Harcourt, Brace & World, 1966.

Sorensen, Theodore C., *Decision-Making in the White House: The Olive Branch or the Arrows.* New York: Columbia University Press, 1963.

———. *Kennedy.* New York: Harper & Row, 1965.

Sorrels, William W., and Charles Cavagnaro. *Ole Miss Rebels: Mississippi Football.* Huntsville, Alabama: The Strode Publishers Inc., 1976.

Stewart, George R. *Pickett's Charge: A Microhistory of the Final Attack at Gettysburg, July 3, 1863.* Boston, Houghton Mifflin Company, 1959.

Strober, Gerald S., and Deborah H. Strober. *Let Us Begin Anew: An Oral History of the Kennedy Presidency.* New York: HarperCollins, 1993.

Wilhoit, Francis M. *The Politics of Massive Resistance.* New York: G. Braziller, 1973.

Wofford, Harris. *Of Kennedys and Kings: Making Sense of the Sixties.* New York, Farrar Straus Giroux, 1980.

Archives and Official Documents

John F. Kennedy Presidential Library

Robert F. Kennedy Papers
Burke Marshall Papers
James McShane Papers
James Meredith vertical file

Federal Bureau of Investigation

James Meredith file series, 1961–1963

Mississippi State Department of Archives and History

Ross Barnett Papers
University of Mississippi vertical file
James Meredith vertical file
Governor Charles Clark vertical file

Paul B. Johnson, Jr. vertical file

Mississippi State Sovereignty Commission files: James Meredith, Medgar Evers, University of Mississippi, Clyde Kennard, Ross Barnett, James McShane, William Simmons

University of Mississippi J. D. Williams Library,
Department of Archives and Special Collections

Verner Smith Holmes Papers
Russell Barrett Papers
James Meredith Papers
George Street Papers

University of Southern Mississippi

Civil Rights Oral History Collection

Paul J. Scheips, "The Role of the Army in the Oxford Mississippi Incident 1962–1963." Washington, D.C.: Histories Division, Office of the Chief of Military History, Department of the Army, June 25, 1965.

"In the United States Court of Appeals for the Fifth Circuit, Court Opinion, *James H. Meredith vs. Charles D. Fair, President of the Board of Trustees of the State Institutions of Higher Learning,* June 25, 1962, Judge John Minor Wisdom."

"The University of Mississippi and the Meredith Case," university report released November 15, 1962, commissioned by Chancellor J. D. Williams.

"The Board of Trustees of State Institutions of Higher Learning and the Meredith Case," undated paper issued by Mississippi Board of Trustees of State Institutions of Higher Learning, ca. 1963.

"A Report by the General Legislative Investigative Committee to the Mississippi State Legislature Concerning the Occupation of the Campus of the University of Mississippi, September 30, 1962 by the Department of Justice of the United States," 1963.

Mississippi Highway Patrol files, 1962

Publications and Articles

September 14–October 6, 1962 editions of: *Jackson Daily News, Jackson Clarion Ledger, Memphis Commercial Appeal, Memphis Press-Scimitar, New Orleans Times-Picayune, New York Times, New York Herald Tribune, New York Mirror, New York Post, New York World-Telegram, Washington Post, Christian Science Monitor, The Evening Star* (Washington, D.C.), *Denver Post, Los Angeles Times, Chicago Sun-*

Times, The Register (Mobile, Alabama), *Courier-Journal* (Louisville, KY), *The Tennesseean* (Nashville, Tenn.), *The Gazette* (Little Rock, Arkansas), *Post-Dispatch* (St. Louis, Missouri), *Birmingham News, Dallas Morning News, Houston Post, Montgomery Advertiser, Atlanta Journal-Constitution, Miami Herald, Charlotte Observer, Raleigh News and Observer, Richmond News Leader, Daily Mail* (London), *Daily Sketch* (London), *Manchester Guardian, The Times* (London).

"Battle of Words on Who Is to Blame: Accounts by Top Federal and State Officials." *U.S. News & World Report,* October 15, 1962.

Carter, Hodding III. "Citadel of the Citizens Council." *New York Times Magazine,* November 12, 1961.

Facts on Film, Southern Education Reporting Service, Nashville, Tennessee, (microfilm clipping collection of civil rights movement, national and local papers and magazines).

Faulkner, William. "Mississippi." *Holiday,* April 1954.

Gonzalez, Arturo, and Sandra Salinas. "The Long, Lonely Road of Rights Hero James Meredith." *People,* October 16, 1989.

Leonard, George, T. George Harris, and Christopher S. Wren. "How a Secret Deal Prevented a Massacre at Ole Miss." *Look,* December 31, 1962.

Marquette, Clare L. "The 'Meredith Incident' at the University of Mississippi." *Milton Today,* May 1963.

Massie, Robert. "What Next in Mississippi?" *Saturday Evening Post,* November 10, 1962.

Meredith, James. "I'll Know Victory or Defeat." *Saturday Evening Post,* November 10, 1962.

Meredith, James. "I Can't Fight Alone." *Look,* April 9, 1963.

Mitchell, Jason P. "The Role of St. Peter's Episcopal Church, Oxford, in the Integration Crisis at the University of Oxford." Paper published on the worldwide Web, 1999.

"Mississippi: The Sound and the Fury." *Newsweek,* October 15, 1962.

"Mississippi Tragedy: What It All Means, with Account by Sterling Slappey." *U.S. News & World Report,* October 15, 1962.

"Oxford! The Mississippi National Guard Stands Fast!" *The National Guardsman,* November 1962.

Still, Larry. "Ex-GI Hopes His Actions Changed Course of Miss. History." *Jet,* October 4, 1962.

Still, Larry. "Man Behind the Headlines." *Ebony,* December 1962.

"Though the Heavens Fall: Race Riot at University of Mississippi." *Time,* October 12, 1962.

Audiovisual Materials

Eyes on the Prize. PBS documentary, 1987, Blackside Films, Inc.; written by Steve Fayer; executive producer, Henry Hampton.

The Civil War. PBS documentary, 1990, Florentine Films, Inc.; Ken Burns, director and executive producer; written by Geoffrey C. Ward, Ric Burns, and Ken Burns.

James Meredith: Breaking Down the Barriers. Cox Communications cable TV special, 1994.

John F. Kennedy White House recordings, September 28–October 1, 1962, John F. Kennedy Library.

Oxford USA. 1963 Citizens Council film, Mississippi State Department of Archives and History.

Audiotape of WJDX/WLBT remote radio broadcast from University of Mississippi campus, September 30, 1962, Mississippi State Department of Archives and History.

ABOUT THE AUTHOR

William Doyle's last book, *Inside the Oval Office: The White House Tapes from FDR to Clinton*, was a *New York Times* Notable Book of 1999. In 1998 he won the Writers Guild of America Award for Best TV Documentary for the A&E special *The Secret White House Tapes*, which he co-wrote and co-produced. His e-mail address is bill-doyleusa@yahoo.com. He lives in New York City.